STUDIES IN HISTORY, ECONOMICS AND
PUBLIC LAW

Edited by the
FACULTY OF POLITICAL SCIENCE
OF COLUMBIA UNIVERSITY

———

NUMBER 549

CHURCH AND STATE IN GUATEMALA

BY

MARY P. HOLLERAN

CHURCH AND STATE IN GUATEMALA

BY

MARY P. HOLLERAN, Ph.D.

Associate Professor of History
St. Joseph College
West Hartford, Connecticut

NEW YORK
COLUMBIA UNIVERSITY PRESS
1949

To Professor Frank Tannenbaum

of Columbia University

who has so thoroughly understood the problems

connected with making this study

ACKNOWLEDGEMENTS

In this country I am deeply indebted to the Most Reverend Henry J. O'Brien, D.D., Bishop of Hartford, who furnished me with gracious introductions to the hierarchy of Guatemala, to Senator Raymond E. Baldwin, who in 1946 was Governor of Connecticut, and who appointed me to represent in Central America the Inter-American Division of the State Development Commission, and to Mr. Fred Grimley, the Inter-American Director of the Commission. Sister M. Rosa McDonough, Ph.D., Dean of Saint Joseph College, West Hartford, Connecticut, gave continuous and patient encouragement to the undertaking. Sister M. Irene O'Connor, Ph.D., Assistant Professor of Romance Languages at the College, greatly facilitated the work of translation. In addition, three other Faculty members, Sister M. Consilia Hannon, Ph.D., Sister Marie Benigna Johnson, Ph.D., and Sister Maria Clare Markham, M.S., contributed much time and effort to all phases of the photographic problems involved. The Librarian, Sister Marie Celine O'Connor, M.S., and her assistant, Miss Frances Carey, M.A., were most cooperative in supplying necessary reference materials.

This manuscript was read by Professors Frank Tannenbaum, Carleton J. H. Hayes, Garrett Mattingly and Salo W. Baron, all of the Department of History of Columbia University. Professor Mattingly, in particular, made many helpful suggestions.

Last, but not by any means least, I must make mention of the untiring interest with which my mother, Mrs. P. C. Holleran, and my sister, Mrs. Ruth H. Lawrence, followed me into distant places and the patience with which they have borne with me under what must have been often the most trying circumstances.

In Guatemala, special thanks are due to His Excellency Mariano Rossell y Arellano, Archbishop of Guatemala, who displayed a keen interest in the study and opened to me every possible avenue of information, to the Reverend Bishop Jorge García y Caballeros, Bishop of Los Altos, the Reverend Bishop Raymundo M. Martin, O.P., Bishop of la Verapaz, to the Maryknoll Missionaries, most particularly the Rev. Edmund McClear of Salamá, and to all the Catholic clergy whom I interviewed in their village parishes. Without exception all of the Protestant missionaries were courteous and anxious to furnish any requested information. Because there were no adequate facilities for my work in the National Archives, the distinguished Director, Dr. Joaquín Pardo, furnished me with a room in his adjoining dwelling place, where I worked for three months. Don Antonio Goubaud, Director of the Indigenous Institute, was always available for consultation and suggestions. Don Manuel Ramírez, the schoolmaster at Cobán, was the exemplification of grave and dignified courtesy, as was the shoemaker of Momostenango, whose name I do not know, but who guided me through darkness, rain and mud to the Mayan rites of the New Year. Personal friends turned over to me much material from their own libraries. Among these I must specifically mention Dr. Luis Beltranena S., a former Dean of the University of San Carlos, Guatemala City, and don Rafael Piñol of the Finca Las Charcas. Señor Arnoldo Hayter of the Maya Trails and his wife, doña María Luisa Hayter, arranged many of the details of my travels and señor Carlos Aparicio for three months drove me as far as the limited road facilities allowed. Doña María de Matheu, an American married to a Guatemalan, don Julio Matheu, accompanied me on several trips which had to be made by means of more primitive media than the car. Miss Maude Oakes, a well-known American lady sojourning in the Cuchumatanes village of Todos Santos, furnished information and hospitality which was appreciated. Don Roberto Alvarez, a distinguished photographer in Gautemala City, worked almost daily with me on details connected with photographing unedited documents in the National Archives and in the Archbishop's Palace.

MARY P. HOLLERAN

WEST HARTFORD, CONNECTICUT

PREFACE

No one can understand any country or people in Latin America unless he is familiar with the story of the Church, and yet, because it is complicated and difficult of interpretation, the whole subject has been generally ignored or evaded, especially since the Independence movements of the nineteenth century. The matter is a delicate one — some attempts to explain or discuss various phases and angles of church-state problems have resulted in explosions of ill-feeling, charges and counter-charges of prejudice, hostility or persecution.

Various articles written by well meaning members of the Catholic Church have aided the historical or academic angle very little because they have deteriorated into emotional apologiae.

Another group has brought a fine array of hostile prejudices to the task—they run the whole gamut, beginning with a general condemnation of everything Spanish and ending with an indictment of the Church as being responsible for " backwardness " (which for me becomes increasingly difficult to define), illiteracy, poor health, inadequate transportation and communication, dirt, reaction, poverty, and a general " lack of social consciousness."

This work is not intended to be pretentious or definitive. Its purpose is to set forth as clearly as possible, on a documentary basis, the main patterns and themes of church-state relationships in one specific Latin American area.

To do this it seems necessary to set the historical account into a broad background which, in this case, necessitates an examination of the formula for basic church-state relations in Spain, the Mother Country. This formula comes down to us in the present day as the " *patronato real* ".

TABLE OF CONTENTS

PART ONE

CHAPTER I
THE PATRONATO REAL

ALTHOUGH the purpose of this study is to consider the general phases of the relations of Church and State in Gautemala, it will soon become evident that much of the story will emerge in terms of the historical conflict which has been going on for centuries between the two. Sometimes the difficulties have been relatively latent, but on occasion they have rapidly risen to the surface. The battle lines have been sharply drawn when the energies of society at any given time have been inadequate for large scale organization and neither institution could gain much headway except at the expense of the other.

During the Middle Ages there were many drives conducted by secular rulers to bring the Church under their power. The reactions of the clergy were natural and usually took two directions, namely they sought to become independent of secular rule, and they in turn attempted to impose ecclesiastical controls on the machinery of the State.

When the Roman Empire was declining, barbarian kings often tried to usurp the rights of the Roman Empire over the Church; the Church in turn conceded or protested. With the rise of feudalism, the clergy, because they were disorganized or in need of protection, often surrendered control. As feudalism waxed strong, the secular rulers began to nominate and appoint clergymen to various church posts. Pope Gregory VII did not mince words when he identified lay investiture with simony, but such investiture was the means that civil rulers thought necessary in order to revive imperial power and to restore order to the State. Nevertheless, the opposition of the Popes to their tactics finally defeated the effort. The Empire was reduced to a shadow and the Medieval Church emerged supreme.

With the rise of the modern national governments the Papacy found that doctrinal unity could only be preserved at a price. That price had to be reckoned in terms of loss of some ancient privileges, liberties, or revenues. Otherwise, schisms were threatened. King Henry VIII of England actually seceded. King Francis I of France did indeed make a concordat with the Vatican, but he received in turn the power to make appointments and the right to a certain share in the church revenues. The Church weapons of interdict and excommunication were no longer effective.

The Spanish Kingdom of Castile was ultra-Catholic in medieval times. The monarchs, who traced some of their privileges to Visigothic origins, were protectors of the Shrine of St. James, were patrons and protectors of the Archbishop of Toledo, they were the champions of the Church against the infidel Moors. In turn they came to regard it as proper that they should be given a tremendous degree of jurisdiction over ecclesiastical affairs. This pattern of " lay patronage " became known as the *Patronato Real.*

It developed into a fixed policy which was the chief means by which the Spanish sovereigns, most particularly Ferdinand and Isabella, built their version of an absolute monarchy. Their great crusades against the Moors were useful in extending their power over both clergy and laity.

Emphasis must be placed on the fact that the Popes were not enthusiastic about making concessions. They surely felt the steady and insistent pressure exercised upon them. They were grateful because the Moors were eventually expelled from the Iberian Peninsula. They were cognizant of the signal virtues, piety and devotion of their Catholic Majesties. Surely no one had dreamed of a more Utopian Church State (*res publica Christiana*) than Isabella; her test of allegiance was orthodoxy; her objective in governing, the advancement of religion. Her sincerity has never been seriously challenged.

Before Isabella's death in 1504 she had set an enduring pattern for the official institutional psychology of Castile. That pattern was to be continued by her grandson and his Hapsburg descendants. There came to be vested in the Crown an absolutism as complete in the control of Church organization as the accepted doctrines of the Catholic Church were to be absolute in controlling the beliefs of the Spanish people.

On the one hand, Emperor Charles V was an unbending champion of orthodoxy throughout Europe and, on the other, he was a jealous guardian of his ecclesiastical privileges.

The Most Catholic King Philip II, who struggled stubbornly against Protestantism in Holland, was seldom considerate of the Bishops, and he did not for a moment hesitate to put meddlesome clergy in prison, even though their credentials came directly from Rome.

It may be truly stated that the Spanish Leviathan had two arms, of which the Church, the right limb, was by far the stronger and more responsive to the royal will than the left, the cumbersome semi-feudal machinery of several separate kingdoms.

It may be argued, however, that the ecclesiastical prerogatives of the Crown in the Iberian Peninsula rested on doubtful traditions, bold usurpations and grudging equivocal concessions, but it can never be denied that their vast power in the Indies rested securely, legally, incontestably and explicitly on a series of Papal Bulls.

The first of these documents, the famous Bull *Inter Cetera*, March 4, 1493, conferred on the Kings of Castile the exclusive right to propagate Christianity in the lands beyond the line of demarcation, and solemnly commanded them to see to it that the inhabitants of the new territories were instructed in the Catholic faith.[1]

It is apparent from this Bull that the conquest and government of the New World could not be separated from the preaching of the Gospel. The temporal power was establishing dominions in America on pontifical concessions. The Church

---

1 For the English translation *cf.* Davenport, F. G., ed., *European Treaties Bearing on the History of the United States and its Dependencies to 1648*, p. 75 ff., cited by Commager, Henry S., *Documents of American History*, New York, Crofts, 1944, pp. 2, 3.

could introduce the Cross only with the assistance of Spanish soldiers. Nor did it have any temples other than those erected by the Conquistadores.

This Bull may properly be said to have laid the foundation of the system of royal patronage for the New World. From then on the Spanish monarchs considered themselves as Apostolic Vicars empowered with the temporal and spiritual government of the Church.

A second Apostolic Bull, commencing *Eximiae devotionis,* dated November 15, 1501,[2] from the hand of the same Pope Alexander VI, conceded to the Spanish Kings all the prerogatives, faculties, exemptions and privileges previously granted by Apostolic Indults to the Kings of Portugal for their conquests in the East Indies, among which was the right of patronage, according to the Bull of Pope Calixtus III (1456).[3] The monarchs were granted the use of tithes in America,[4] and, in return, they were to defray from the Royal Treasury all expenses incidental to the propagation and maintenance of the faith.[5]

After the last voyage of Columbus (1504), the Catholic Kings, in order to consecrate their dominion over the new lands, were principally interested in organizing the Church, and therefore obtained from His Holiness Pope Julius II in 1508, for the increase of their honor and glory and all that would redound to them in wealth and security from the dominions of their kingdom, the exercise of the *Patronato* over all the churches of the Indies " for having raised the

2 Hernáez, Francisco Xavier, *Colecciones de Bulas, Brevas y otros documentos relativos a la Iglesia de América y Filipinas,* Brussels, Alfred Vromant, 1879, I, 12-14.

3 Frasso, Pedro, *De Regio Patronatu Indiarum,* Madrid, Blasii Roman, 1775, Chap. XIX.

4 Muriel, Domingo, *Fasti Novi Orbis et ordinationum apostolicarum,* Venice, Antonio Zatta, 1776, p. 74.

5 Ribadeneyra, Antonio Joaquín de, *Manual Compendio de el Regio Patronato Indiano,* Madrid, Antonio Marin, 1755, p. 60.

standard of the Cross over unknown lands." In other words, there were granted to the Catholic Kings, as if by an Apostolic privilege, those rights which they claimed in Europe as their own.[6]

It was really this Bull of Pope Julius II, *Universalis Ecclesiae*, dated July 28, 1508, which in very explicit form granted the *Patronato Real* of the Indies, even though it might be presumed, though not very definitely, nor at length, from the Bulls of Pope Alexander VI.[7]

The Bull of Pope Clement VII for the erection of the Church of Mexico, September 9, 1534, *De Erectione ipsius Ecclesiae*, folio VI, reiterated the concession of this right of patronage to the Kings of Spain.[8]

On December 18th of that same year, the Bull of Pope Paul III, erecting the See of Guatemala, *Illius Suffulti Praesidio*, likewise specifically conceded this right of *patronato real*.[9]

Pope Benedict XIV, in his first Bull of the Concordat with Spain on January 11, 1753, approved the continuance of the rights of the Spanish monarchs over the Indies, " there not having been any controversy over the nomination of the Catholic Kings to the archbishoprics, bishoprics and benefices which are vacant in the kingdoms of Granada and of the Indies."

In his second Bull, *Quam Semper,* dated June 9, 1753, Pope Benedict XIV stated:

> In adhering to the aforesaid agreement, we do not propose to establish anything new ... nor likewise in regard to the other Ecclesiastical Benefices of whatever nature or name which exist in the kingdoms and dominions of Granada and

6 Vélez Sarsfield, Dalmacio, *Relaciones del Estado con la Iglesia*, Buenos Aires, Librería La Facultad, 1919, p. 52.

7 Ayarragaray, Lucas, *La Iglesia en América y la Dominación Española,* Buenos Aires, J. Lajouane & Co., 1920, p. 164; Frasso, *op. cit.*, p. 3.

8 Ribadeneyra, *op. cit.*, p. 65.

9 Hernáez, *op. cit.*, II, 92.

of the Indies ... which have been and still are up to the
present time, without any contradiction whatsoever, under the
patronage of the said Catholic Kings by foundation or endowment, by privileges, letters or other legitimate title; rather do
we wish and decree that the aforesaid Churches or Monasteries and other Consistorial Benefices, as well as all Ecclesiastical Benefices existing in the said Kingdoms of Granada
and of the Indies and the others mentioned, be conferred or
provided for by the nomination and presentation of the said
Catholic Kings, as heretofore, whenever they become vacant
or lack pastors.[10]

These two Bulls of Pope Benedict XIV were ordered observed
by a third, *Postquam controversiae*, September 10, 1753, and
led to a new title in favor of the Spanish Kings, not only to
the Universal *Patronato Real* of the Indies, in the manner
in which they had enjoyed it by authority of the Apostolic
See, which declared it free and exempt from all controversy,
but also to the titles of endowment, foundation, privileges and
Apostolic Bulls.[11]

The Kings of Spain also mentioned this right in various
laws and decrees. The *Recopilación de Leyes de los Reynos
de las Indias*, Book I, Article VI, Law I, made the following
reference: . . . "the patronage having been granted to us
by Bulls of the Supreme Pontiffs of their own accord"; a
decree of June 1, 1574, referring to this right as belonging
to the Catholic Kings, used almost the same words: ". . .
since it was granted to us by Bulls of the Supreme Pontiffs
of their own accord. . ."; [12] and another, dated June 22,
1591: "therefore there belonging to me, as it belongs to me
by right and by Apostolic Bull as King of Castile and Leon,
the Patronage over all the Indies of the West." [13] In the
Instructions to the Viceroys of the Indies, after having en-

10 Ribadeneyra, *op. cit.*, p. 67.

11 *Ibid.*, p. 378.

12 *Cédulas reales*, I, 83.

13 *Ibid.*, p. 167.

trusted to the latter the preservation and safe-guarding of this right of royal patronage, the king added: ". . .as it has been conceded to the Kings of Spain by the Holy Apostolic See." [14] A royal decree of March 28, 1620 declared: ". . . since there can not be permitted abuses in defiance of our patronage, and such cannot be called custom, but rather corruption, evil innovations and sin." [15]

To the King belonged the power of erecting all the church buildings in the Indies, whether they were cathedrals, parish churches, monasteries, hospitals, chapels, or any other, in conformity with the law which read, "No church, nor pious place, may be erected without the permission of the King." [16] This, likewise, is in accord with the passage in the Bull of Patronage of Pope Julius II which prohibited the building in the Indies of any churches, monasteries, or pious places, without the consent of the King.[17]

The pattern of the royal patronage as developed in Guatemala was similar to its application in other areas of the Indies. The records show the Spanish King, as patron, approving the project of constructing the Cathedral of Guatemala and assigning additional incomes on several occasions.[18] Likewise from time to time His Majesty approved the foundation and endowment of various institutions, e.g. on April 17, 1553, the *Colegio de Doncellas de Nuestra Señora de la Presentación* in Guatemala.[19]

Also for the rebuilding, enlarging or moving of a monastery it was necessary to obtain the King's permission.[20] On

14 Ribadeneyra, *op. cit,* p. 62; Frasso, *op. cit.,* p. 5.

15 *Recopilación de Leyes de los Reynos de las Indias,* Madrid, Antonio Balbas, 1756, 2nd edition, Bk. I, Title VI, p. 26.

16 *Ibid.,* Bk. I, Title VI, Ley II.

17 *Universalis Ecclesiae,* July 28, 1508.

18 Pardo, J. Joaquín, *Efemérides para escribir la Historia de la muy noble y muy leal Ciudad de Santiago de los Caballeros del Reino de Guatemala,* Guatemala, Tipografía Nacional, 1944, pp. 11, 12.

19 *Ibid.,* p. 13.

20 *Recopilacion de Leyes de los Reynos de las Indias,* Bk. I, Title III, Ley II.

March 31, 1585 the Municipal Government of Guatemala wrote to His Majesty asking that he authorize the moving of the Convent of the Nuns of the Concepción to the house containing the Royal Hospital of Santiago, and the use of the building of the former for the hospital.[21] On June 3, 1718 the Bishop of Guatemala, Alvarez de Toledo, consulted His Majesty on the repairing of the Church of San Sebastian after the earthquake of September, 1717.[22] Again, after the earthquake of 1773, in the plans drawn up for the removal and rebuilding of the capital, the King was petitioned in the name of his *patronato real,* in the case of the Convent of the Presentation and that of the Poor Clares.[23]

There are many references to the privilege of the *patronato real* in documents of the Indies. After Bishop Marroquín was consecrated as the first Bishop of Guatemala by Bishop Zumarraga in Mexico City in 1537, he drew up a document in which he inserted two letters of the reigning Pontiff, Pope Paul III, in the first of which the parish church of Guatemala was declared raised to the rank of cathedral and the *patronato* over it given to the Kings of Castile and Leon, and in the second of which Francisco Marroquín was named first bishop. According to the latter, Marroquín was to establish five dignities: dean, archdeacon, *chantre, maestrescuela* and treasurer. He was to divide the tithes into four parts, of which one should be applied to the bishop and another to the chapter by virtue of the concession to the Kings of Castile. The other two parts were to be divided into nine portions (*novenos*), two of them applicable to the royal treasury in recognition of the *patronato,* four destined for the parish priests, and the last three to be divided into halves, one for the corporate body

21 Pardo, *op. cit.,* p. 28.

22 *Ibid.,* p. 150.

23 Carrillo, Agustín Gómez, *Compendio de historia de la América Central,* Guatemala, Tipografía Nacional, 1905, V, 162, 165.

administering the temporal goods of the church, and the other for the hospitals.[24]

The Council of the Indies proposed Bartolomé de las Casas for the bishopric of the province of Chiapas when it became vacant, and the Emperor Charles V, using the right of patronage, sent the decree naming him to the bishopric November 20, 1542.[25] In 1545 Bishop de las Casas and Fray Antonio de Valdivieso wrote to the Prince, don Philip, "Consider, Your Highness, that the Kings of Castile have these lands, conceded by the Holy Apostolic See, for the foundation in them of a new church and the Christian religion and for the salvation of these souls." [26]

There was no detail of the church administration that the King did not make his business. On May 22, 1553, he requested the bishop to inform him of the presence of priests and religious who were giving scandal or who were refugees from other dioceses now living in Guatemala. He asked Bishop Marroquín to treat the good friars better, to correct the bad ones, expel those known to be vicious and those who had deserted their monasteries elsewhere.[27]

Under the *patronato real* the King administered the Bull of Crusade, extended to the Indies by papal brief of 1578 and in force throughout the Spanish régime. The revenues were considerable and were in the hands of royal collectors who obtained a percentage of the revenues.[28]

The Bishops of the Indies, before they were handed the decrees of their appointment, had to take an oath that they would never oppose the *patronato real* and that they would

24 Remesal, Antonio de, *Historia General de las Indias Occidentales y particular de la gobernación de las provincias de Chiapas y Guatemala*, Guatemala, Tipografía Nacional, 1932, II, 288; Baluffi, Gaetano, *L'America en tempo spagnuolo riguardata sotto l'aspetto religioso*, Ancona, Gustavo Cherubini, 1845, II, 41.

25 Milla y Vidaurre, José, *Historia de la América Central*, Guatemala, Tipografía El Progreso, 1879, II, 288.

26 Ayarragaray, *op. cit.*, p. 19.

27 Milla, *op. cit.*, p. 111.

28 *Recopilación de leyes de Indias*, Book I, Title XX, Ley I.

preserve it and comply in every way with its ordinances, fully and without any exception—and this before a Notary Public and witnesses.[29]

At the beginning of the Conquest the catechizing of the Indians was left to any priest who could be found. These priests ministered to the Spaniards and Indians without obtaining nor even asking permission from the bishops, because in the early days there were none, and all was governed and directly administered and regulated by the King or by those appointed by him, " in virtue of the commission or delegation in this matter which he had received from the Apostolic See." [30] Bishop Bernardino Villapando, who succeeded Marroquín as head of the diocese of Guatemala, was reprimanded on November 3, 1567 by the King for having named clergymen to serve on mission stations without previous presentation to the Vice *Patron Real,* who was President of the *Audiencia.*[31] Because of his irregular procedure, the Bishop was ordered to make the presentation of the pastors to the Governor, who, in the name of the King, would choose those whom he considered as the most worthy. The Bishop refused to comply and heaped abuse upon the head of the Governor, who further complained that the Bishop had held a Synod without the consent of the King. King Philip II referred the matter to Pope Pius V, who sent two letters, dated March 24th and April 17th, 1567, to the Bishop ordering him to observe carefully the duties of his state, forbidding him to give parishes to priests without first presenting them to the Vice *Patron Real.*[32]

The King designated the boundaries of the bishoprics and regulated them according to political divisions, without any

29 *Ibid.,* Book I, Title III, Ley XIII.

30 Solorzano y Pereyra, Juan de, *Política Indiana,* Madrid, 1776, II, 122.

31 Pardo, *op. cit.,* p. 19.

32 Milla, *op. cit.,* pp. 153-5.

announcement or notice whatsoever from the Pope.[33] A royal decree on the establishment of the patriarchates of the Indies constituted a fundamental statute of the organization of the Church in the Indies. The King scrupulously gave instructions on the most minute details—officials, edifices, charges, appointments of the churches, provisions, candles, wax, bread, wine, vessels, hours of services, salaries, feasts and tithes.[34]

The King named a bishop and presented his name to the Pope. As patron, the King was obliged to present the most worthy subjects as bishops,[35] and the most talented.[36] But, in the meantime, he ordered the civil heads to hand over to the nominee the government of the diocese. An example of this procedure is the case of Bishop Juan de Santo Matía Saenz Manozca y Murillo, who took possession of the See of Guatemala on June 13, 1668, while the Bulls declaring him bishop did not arrive until June 11, 1669.[37] Another case is that of Bishop Ramón Casáus y Torres, who was nominated for the archbishopric of Guatemala by the Spanish Regency on March 30, 1811 and assumed office shortly after, in July, 1811, although the papal Bull confirming the nomination was not issued until 1815.[38]

All disputes between bishops, pastors, canons and other dignitaries concerning benefices or the canonical capacity for obtaining them, could be decided only by the sovereign of the Indies, even though these were considered spiritual matters, and among persons subject to ecclesiastical law.[39]

33 Muriel, *op. cit.*, p. 151.

34 Ayarragaray, *op. cit.*, p. 85.

35 *Recopilación de Leyes de Indias*, Book I, Title VI, Ley XXIV.

36 *Ibid.*, Ley XXVIII.

37 Pardo, *op. cit.*, p. 79.

38 Mecham, J. Lloyd, *Church and State in Latin America*, Chapel Hill, University of North Carolina Press, 1934, p. 370.

39 Ribadeneyra, *op. cit.*, p. 112; Vélez Sarsfield, *op. cit.*, p. 61.

The predominating tendency of the King was to make the religious who were embarking for the Indies very dependent on his authority or that of the State, and naturally, the tendency of the Holy See was to give them more liberty for their missionary work and keep them more closely bound to the Church, avoiding conflicts and infractions of canon law and of ecclesiastical immunity, especially of the religious orders.[40]

The great missionary orders of Franciscans and Dominicans sent ordinarily groups of thirty to fifty of their members to preach the Christian Doctrine in the Indies, always, of course, with the permission of the King, For example, in 1801, the King authorized the formation of a company of sixty-six Franciscans requested for Guatemala. The royal treasury was to pay the expenses of the voyage and, once arrived at their destination, their support would be assumed by the Franciscan Province of Guatemala.[41]

It was customary for these missionary groups to name a Superior from among their number to act during the time the ship delayed in Lisbon or Cadiz, and specially during the long voyage—and also to distribute the members of the group among the missions if their destination had not been arranged beforehand. The King, however, claimed that the choice of this Superior, or Commissary, was not the right of the Order, but his and the Council's.

Prelates were obliged to inform the King concerning the worthy subjects of their dioceses in conformity with the law which commanded that archbishops and bishops, at the same time that they sent reports of the dignities and prebendaries which were vacant in their sees, should inform the King about worthy, outstanding priests of their districts.[42] In 1559 the King nominated Fray Pedro de Angulo as the first Bishop of

40 Ayarragaray, *op. cit.*, p. 58.

41 Desdevises du Dézert, G., "L'Eglise Espagnole des Indes à la fin du XVIIIe siècle," *Revue Hispanique*, XXXIX, 1917, 268.

42 Fernández, Alonzo, *Historia Eclesiástica de Nuestros Tiempos*, Toledo, Pedro Rodríguez, 1611, p. 143.

Vera Paz, persuaded thereto by the report of Las Casas as to his sanctity, intelligence and zeal.[43]

The archbishops and bishops could not use nor permit the use in any form of Briefs or Bulls issued by His Holiness or the Nuncio Apostolic which had not first passed through the Royal Council of the Indies.[44]

The following notes from the *Biografía de don Fr. Juan de Zumarraga,* by Joaquín García Icazbalcete, might be taken as a summary of the pattern of the *patronato real* of the Indies:

a) No churches, monasteries nor hospitals could be built without the king's permission.

b) No bishoprics nor parishes could be organized, except by royal decree.

c) All clerics and religious going to the Indies had to have the express permission of the King.

d) The King named bishops who immediately took possession of their dioceses without awaiting the papal confirmation of the appointment.

e) The King set the boundaries of the bishoprics and changed them at will.

f) The King had the right of presentation to all benefices or employments connected with the churches.

g) The King might reprimand, recall to Spain or exile any bishop who disobeyed the orders of the government.

h) The King administered and collected the tithes, determining those who must pay such tithes and how, without referring to Bulls or exemptions of the Church.

i) The King fixed and regulated the incomes of the benefices at his good pleasure.

j) The King judged many ecclesiastical cases and impeded with his reversals of decisions the work of the ecclesiastical courts.

k) No disposition of the Pope could be carried out without the previous approval of the King.

43 *Ibid.,* p. 144.

44 *Recopilación de Leyes de Indias,* Book I, Title VII, Law V.

1) The problems of the bishops were presented to the King, rather than directly to the Pope.[45]

So much for the general pattern of the *patronato,* which set many precedents which evolved into thorny problems when the authority of the Spanish monarchs waned and was ultimately lost to republican governments. From a chart in the appendix, which demonstrates how the pattern of the *patronato real* was specifically applied in Guatemala some very interesting facts emerge. At first, almost entirely through the sixteenth century and over into the seventeenth, the King personally issued the decrees connected with church affairs, but gradually, it may be noted, the King's deputies, or the crown officials of the municipal governments, began to assume some of these powers in the King's name. This might properly be called a transitional period which made it as natural as breathing for these same practices to be continued without a break by officials of the republican governments.

It remains for us now to examine the nature of the *patronato real* of the Indies, and for this consideration we have, as is almost always the same in regard to any subject, two schools of thought. They might be called the " regalists " and the " canonists ". Briefly, the " regalists " believed that the royal patronage of the Indies was laical in origin and therefore inherent in temporal sovereignty. Solorzano affirmed it to be laical because the churches were endowed from royal possessions and thought that, although the right had somewhat of a mixed nature through having been granted by Apostolic privilege, still the laical quality predominated.[46]

The "canonists" contended that the patronage was not laical but spiritual, and was founded wholly on pontifical concessions which were rescindable and non-transferable.[47]

45 *Cf.* Mecham, *op. cit.,* p. 43.

46 *Fasti Novi Orbis*, p. 630.

47 Mecham, " The Origins of the *Real Patronato de Indias* ", *Catholic Historical Review*, Washington, D. C., April, 1928, VIII, No. 1, 205.

It will soon be noticed that the theoretical differences in interpretation came to have some bearing on reality when the Spanish Indies broke with the Mother Country. The new republics wanted desperately to be considered the natural and legal heirs of the *patronato* and loudly seconded the " regalists' " point of view. The Church, which now thought the time proper for asserting its independence, followed the "canonists' " view and contended that the *patronato* was passed down only to the monarchs and to their successors who were monarchs, i.e. the succession was personal and ended with the monarchical story. The Vatican has, quite naturally it seems, almost always followed the latter view and has maintained that the *patronato* was not inherent in sovereignty and so it could not be inherited by the new governments.[48]

During the war for independence in the colonies there was a diplomatic struggle of the rebelling governments to obtain the recognition of the nations of Europe, but above all to have the moral approbation of the Holy See, without which the new régime would lack its principle of authority, in view of the traditional prestige which Spain had granted the Holy See in the constitution of its dominions. Very soon the revolutionists realized the tremendous handicaps under which they labored so long as the Kings of Spain maintained their historical authority and governing ascendancy in the *patronato*, above all, the right of presentation for the vacant bishoprics in America. The prelates thus named were natural agents of the King, venerated nuclei around which radiated the forces

48 A notable exception is the concession made by Pope Pius IX to President Carrera of Guatemala in the Concordat drawn up between the Vatican and the republic of Guatemala on Oct. 7, 1852. Article VII declares: " In view of the aforementioned commitments of the government, the Holy See concedes to the President of the Republic of Guatemala and to his successors in this office the *patronato* or the privilege of presentation for any vacant benefices of Metropolitan churches or episcopal churches, canonically erected, of worthy and outstanding ecclesiastics, having all the qualities required by canon law, and the Supreme Pontiff, in conformity with the laws of the Church, will give those presented canonical institution in the usual form...." (*National Archives of Guatemala*).

of reaction, ideas of loyalty toward the Mother Country, and which in their turn sustained the native classes and the traditionalists, who either through prejudice or interest resisted the Revolution, considering it the result of irreverent or subversive ideas. When the emancipation of the colonies was virtually an established fact, Spain was still struggling to preserve the privileges of the *patronato,* considering them as the last symbol of her secular power in the Indies. As late as July, 1820, Ferdinand VII, clinging to his right as patron in the filling of an ecclesiastical vacancy, wrote to the Captain-General of Guatemala as follows:

Don Fernando VII, by the grace of God, and by the Constitution of the Spanish Monarchy, King of all Spain. The parish of Asunción Izalco having become vacant by the death of don Manuel Rivera who had held it; and edicts having been posted for its provision, in accordance with the regulations of the Holy Council of Trent and the laws of my royal patronage, several members of the secular clergy were examined in open competition by the Synodal Examiners, after having submitted the necessary credentials as to their competency for the administering to souls. The Very Reverend Archbishop of the Holy Metropolitan Church of the Capital of Guatemala, on the thiry-first of July wrote to my Captain-General, Chief Executive and *Vice Patron Real* of that Province, proposing three subjects from whom there might be chosen and presented in My Royal Name the one whom the *Vice Patron Real* wished, and naming in the first place don Tomás Saldaña. And by a decree which he issued on the first of this month, he approved of the latter and ordered the title forwarded at once, after having assured himself that the said subject possessed the necessary qualifications and merits for the exercise of the ministry; that he was of legitimate birth and of pure Spanish blood. He studied Latin and Philosophy, in the latter of which he took the degree of Bachelor, and attended classes of Theology with notable success. He was ordained priest in September last, and, after having become a priest as well as before, has manifested the most blameless conduct and sentiments most worthy of the sacerdotal

character. And in order that the above may have the necessary effects, in agreement with my Captain-General, the Chief
Executive, I issue this present, by which I choose, present and
name the aforementioned don Tomás Saldaña for the service
and the administration of the parish of the Asunción de
Izalco, in order that this nomination may be presented to my
Very Reverend Archbishop so that he may give it canonical
status and install the said cleric in the aforementioned parish,
from which he may not be removed.[49]

The *patronato* was an essential part of the character of
Spanish sovereignty in her possessions overseas, and in the
struggle to retain such privilege Spain not only adhered to
the most elementary principles of her imperialistic policy, but
also, by preserving this link with her dominions, maintained
its power morally, and her hopes for future revindications.[50]

For twenty years Spain with fierce tenacity tried to safeguard this foundation of her historic rights in the hope that
by some whim of fortune she might be able to restore the
empire. In her moment of downfall Spain turned to the spiritual cooperation of the Church and the mystical authority of
the Pope, both of which elements had served her in conquering and organizing the Indies. When Spain had become
convinced of the impotence of her arms in subduing the rebellion, it was logical for her to fall back on the *patronato*
in order to retain, at least in that realm, her power in America. For the same reasons, but with opposite ends in view,
revolutionary America struggled at the same time for the exclusive exercise of the *patronato* privileges.[51]

Their governments tried to negotiate and manoeuver
against the strong diplomatic influence of Spain in Rome.
The dramatic and painful quarrel began to organize in 1820

49 Vilanova Meléndez, Ricardo, *Apuntamientos de Historia Eclesiástica
Patria*, San Salvador, Imprenta La Luz, 1911, p. 150.

50 Ayarragaray, *op. cit.*, p. 173.

51 *Ibid.*, p. 176.

and each contending party exercised its ingenuity with untiring constancy around the Pope in order to divert to itself the most powerful moral support then existing in the world. When the Mexican government sent Francisco Vázquez to Rome in 1825 to appeal to the Pope for the restoration of ecclesiastical relations, the Guatemalan government entrusted to him the presentation of certain of its problems to the Pontiff at the same time.[52] The Holy See tried to avoid as long as possible any definite decisions or responsibilities. In the initial period of the struggle, the Pope frequently formulated declarations and, at times, assumed attitudes favoring Spain and the traditional principles of the *patronato* of the King. Among the decrees issued by Ferdinand VII on his release by Napoleon in 1812 was one enjoining the Archbishop in Central America and his bishops to see that their subordinates did their duty faithfully, and entertained only wholesome opinions. No associations were to be tolerated which might lead to a disturbance of the public peace. The Pope lent his support to this measure with an encyclical letter dated Aug. 15, 1814 against freemasonry and other secret societies.[53] Again, in 1815, the Court of Spain sought the intercession of the Pope in order that the latter might issue a Brief exhorting the rebels in America to obedience, through the medium of the prelates residing there.[54] Pope Pius VII did not oppose the request of the King and, on January 30, 1816, he sent a Brief to the Bishops of America exhorting them to obey the King.[55]

Inevitably, however, there rose before the Papacy a dramatic dilemma and crisis of conscience. How to abandon Spain, covered with venerable titles, in favor of America with its

---

52 Vilanova Meléndez, *op. cit.*, p. 81.

53 Bancroft, Hubert Howard, *History of Central America*, San Francisco, History Company, 1887, III, 22.

54 Ayarragaray, *op. cit.*, p. 182.

55 Leturia, Pedro, S.J., *El Ocaso del Patronato Real en la América Española, Madrid,* Imprenta Razón y Fé, 1925, pp. 281-2.

disorders, at a time when there prevailed the ultraconservative tendencies of the Holy Alliance and the quietism of the absolute monarchies? [56]

When America undertook its wars for independence there were very few learned and professional leaders. Hence, it was the clergy for the most part which composed the enlightened or intellectual group. This explains why the clergy played such an important role in the new governments and congresses. As time passed a patriotic clergy was established which, with the lawyers, undertook the civil and diplomatic functions in the period of the revolution and in the subsequent period. The ecclesiastic who was a native of America became " one of the prime movers in the secession of the Colonies," according to a declaration made to the King by the Council of Castile.[57]

This explains why the majority of the diplomats sent to Rome by the insurgent governments were priests; they were preferred to the seculars also because it was presumed that their ecclesiastical character would facilitate their mission to the Vatican. They could allege that their efforts were concerned with matters of conscience and spiritual needs. They were not having recourse to Caesar, but to the Vicar of Christ.[58] But—these representatives had to match wits with the astute, erudite and trained diplomats of both the Papal and the Spanish Courts.[59]

The exercise of the *patronato real,* especially through the right of presentation, implied always for Spain and, after the secession of the colonies, for the governments of America, an *instrumentum regni,* and it was principally for such reasons of state that both Spain and America disputed over it, as a basis for their integral authority.[60]

56 *Ibid.,* p. 284.

57 Ayarragaray, *op. cit.,* p. 204.

58 Ayarragaray, *op. cit.,* p. 208.

59 *Ibid.,* p. 180.

60 *Ibid.,* p. 181.

The early colonies claimed for themselves as heirs of the Mother Country all the political faculties inherent in and necessary to the organizing of the new sovereignties, and foremost among these were the privileges of *patronato*.

Beginning with Fray Pedro Luis Pachecho, a Franciscan from Buenos Aires, in 1821, a rapid succession of representatives from the new American republics descended on Rome to obtain from the Pope recognition of their independence and the transfer of the *patronato real*. In every case the Pope insisted that the presentation of bishops had to be made by the King of Spain.[61]

Although the Pope received these delegates as individuals he would never entertain a word about temporal or political matters.

Coinciding with these events, the head of the mission from Mexico, Fr. Vázquez, wrote from Paris initiating negotiations to enter Rome. The Court of Madrid and the Spanish Embassy at Rome intervened. The Cardinal Secretary declared that the Pontiff was disposed to receive the Mexican delegation in his character as head of the Church, but that he was likewise strongly resolved not to recognize politically any delegation from a country which was rebelling against His Majesty. However, the objections of Madrid were so strong against the Pope receiving the group at all that the Vatican refused them entry.[62]

In the meantime the revolutionary governments of America hastened to recognize as the State religion the Holy Roman Apostolic religion which was so well suited to a people whose education had been developed under the direction of Spain. The different Constitutions of the States of America proclaimed insistently the *patronato* as an indispensable basis of the American Church and necessary complement of the new sovereignties.[63]

61 *Ibid.*, p. 231.

62 *Ibid.*, p. 232.

63 *Ibid.*, p. 233.

The National Constitutional Assembly of the Republic of Central America, meeting at Guatemala on July 8, 1823 and believing itself "the lawful successor of the King of Spain in the patronage which he held over these Churches," drew up a law (Chapter II, Article 3) declaring that, since the nation had the right of proposing and presenting for bishoprics, dignities, prebendaries and benefices of the Church whose incomes it determined and sustained, it would undertake to regulate these matters in accord with the Holy See.[64]

At the time of the separation of the province of Chiapas from Guatemala (1824-1825) the Mexican government tried to induce His Holiness to declare the See of Chiapas annexed to the archepiscopal See of Mexico instead of that of Guatemala, and to extend the patronage over it as a right of the Mexican nation.[65]

Contained in the proclamation of the government of Guatemala during the Interdict of the Holy See in 1827 over the naming of a Bishop of San Salvador are the following words:

> The *Patronato* over these Churches, with all the faculties and actions which correspond to it, is intimately connected with and inherent in the sovereignty, and arises not only from the apostolic or pontifical benefactions, but also from custom, from the conquest of territory, grants of councils, and, briefly, from the dominion itself in possession; these are the reasons alleged by Spain for keeping and defending it from any attempt of Rome, and with these same principles and political views, America claims it and attempts to exercise it as inseparable from sovereignty.
>
> Thus we we must declare and thus we must defend it from any attempt of Rome or of the Holy Alliance which has such influence in that Curia. As a consequence, it is necessary to live prepared . . . in order that, under cover of religion,

---

64 Vilanova Meléndez, *op. cit.*, pp. 77-78.

65 *El Indicador* of Guatemala, April 18, 1825, cited by Marure, Alejandro, *Bosquejo histórico de las Revoluciones de la América Central*, Guatemala, El Progreso, 1877, I, 87.

they do not succeed in overthrowing, not only the bishopric, but also the State and independence itself.[66]

The policy of the Pope in regard to the Church in America and its Spanish patron was one of arbitration and vacillation until the year 1827. Among the means to which the Holy See had recourse to avoid conflict was the consideration of the dioceses of America as " mission lands " under the authority of the Congregation for the Propagation of the Faith.[67] Likewise, the Pontiff used to designate for the vacant Sees of America Vicars Apostolic, that is to say, simple administrators, bishops *in partibus infidelium,* or titular bishops, without jurisdiction.[68] At first both Spain and the rebelling governments tolerated this plan, as can be seen in the case of Guatemala. Among the ecclesiastics designated titular bishops were Francisco de Paula Peláez, administrator of the archbishopric during the exile of Archbishop Casáus y Torres and his successor, who had been named Bishop of Bostra; the marquis don José Aycinena, Bishop of Trajanopolis; José María Barrutia y Croquer, Bishop of Camaco; Tomás Saldaña y Pineda, Bishop of Antigona; and Mariano Ortiz as Bishop of Teya, all assigned to titular Sees " in infidel countries." [69] In the midst of these uncertainties the Spanish Embassy in Rome had drawn up a secret plan which it proposed to the Holy See, strange enough in view of the laws of *patronato* and canon law, but tending to facilitate the political plans of His Majesty in America. The King would send under his signature and seal and in absolute secrecy, without previous consultation with his legal advisors, a list of nominees for candidacies, from among whom the Pope, just as if he were proceeding of

66 Ayarragaray, *op. cit.,* p. 235.

67 *Ibid.,* p. 255.

68 Juarros, Fr. Domingo, *Compendio de la Historia de la Ciudad de Guatemala,* Guatemala, Tipografía Nacional, 1937, II, 11, 12.

69 *Gaceta de Nicaragua,* Feb. 16, 1867; June 14, 1873; Vilanova Meléndez, *op. cit.,* p. 155.

his own accord, would choose whom he pleased to recognize as Bishops. The attempt was halted, however, due to the keen watchfulness of the American ministers in Rome.

Slowly the pontifical court's attitude changed, and the Spanish Embassy complained that the American diplomats were gaining easy access to the Court of Rome to present their petitions under cover of " spiritual necessities and cases of conscience." [70]

As it became evident that there would be a definite emancipation of the provinces of the New World, Pope Leo XII decided, with his habitual reserve, to revoke the venerable Statute of *Patronato,* which for long centuries had regulated the relations between the Papacy and the Spanish monarchy. Before taking such a grave step he consulted the Ambassador of Austria, in order that the latter might inform the courts of the Holy Alliance. In May, 1827, in a celebrated consistory, he named bishops for the vacant sees of Columbia, omitting the *patronato real.*[71] Pope Leo XII died March 31, 1829 and was succeeded by Pope Pius VIII who refused to recognize the national *patronato*. Only death saved him from the radical action of confirming proprietary bishops having full jurisdiction for America. The new Pope, Gregory XVI, theologian and orientalist, was capable of solving without direct conflict with Spain the difficulties arising from the application of the *patronato* in America, and of recogniziing one by one the new republics, making use of an opportunist's policy adapted to reality and to facts.[72]

The Spanish ambassador was quick to see that with Gregory XVI there would be an end to the uncertainty which had dominated the relations between Spain and the Papacy for so long.[73]

70 Ayarragaray, *op. cit.*, p. 257.

71 *Ibid.*, p. 258.

72 *Ibid.*, p. 302.

73 *Ibid.*, p. 304.

First of all Pope Gregory XVI established as a norm for the filling of vacant Sees a reserve so impenetrable that he chose the bishops and gave their names to the Cardinal Secretary only a few hours before entering the Consistory, thus avoiding the habitual observations or protests of the Spanish Ambassador.[74]

The latent tendencies of the new policy became apparent, however, in another direction, when the Pope, on August 5, 1831, issued the Bull *"Sollicitudo Ecclesiarum"*, naming candidates for the vacant Sees of Portugal, whose ruler claimed the right of *patronato* previously held by the Spanish king. The principles upon which this Bull rested applied clearly also to the American situation. The document tended to free canonical acts of the Pontiff from all political character and connection, denying that they could signify temporal intervention, or even implicit recognition of the powers disputing, when he was filling vacant Sees in those lands. Nor did it, in the slightest degree, add any authority to those powers.

The Holy See was, therefore, disposed to exercise freely its spiritual rights and functions with no regard to political affairs. The Bull went on to declare that the Holy See was ready to establish relations with any government when it offered proof of stability. With such declarations, at long last there was virtually set down the position from which the Vatican has not often deviated.[75]

In 1832 Pope Gregory XVI named bishops for Mexico, as well as for Chile and Argentina. From then on the Pope began to develop his apostolic policy, and in reply to the protest of the Spanish ambassador at his naming the bishops without

74 *Ibid.*, p. 305.
75 *Ibid.*, pp. 306 ff.

the presentation of the King of Spain, declared, " The King would not wish me to abandon so many souls of whom God will ask me an account some day." [76]

In 1833 the Spanish ambassador, who had lost all heart in pleading for the privileges of the King over the bishoprics, convinced of the futility of " sustaining any longer the rights of His Majesty to present bishops in countries where for many years His royal authority had no longer been recognized," openly and frankly counseled the King to realize and admit that it was no longer possible to preserve " a shadow of the *patronato*."

When the Pope named a bishop to the vacant See of Quito, he announced the fact to the Spanish ambassador only a few minutes before the opening of the Consistory. This was one of those acts deliberately undertaken, no doubt, to make the King Patron realize that his secular prerogatives had ceased in the New World.[77] Probably to " save face ", the Spanish ambassador stated that the sharp dispute over investitures had been terminated by a " manoeuvre of the Pope." [78]

The death of Ferdinand VII and the turbulent civil war precipitated the end of the conflict. It was while Spain was engaged in the Carlist Wars that Pope Gregory XVI recognized the first republic in America, that of New Granada.[79]

Thus ended one phase of a great quarrel which arose out of the struggles for independence in the New World and in which Spain had exerted all her historic strength to maintain the *Patronato*, " mystical pillar of the Empire." [80]

76 *Ibid.*, p. 308.

77 *Ibid.*, p. 315.

78 *Ibid.*, p. 316.

79 November 26, 1835. *Cf.* Zubieta, Pedro A., *Apuntamientos sobre las Primeras Misiones Diplomáticas de Colombia*, Bogotá, Imprenta Nacional, 1924, pp. 597-598.

80 Ayarragaray, *op. cit.*, p. 315.

Spain, convinced of the inefficacy of so long a struggle, decided to retire from it in silence and, without any express renunciation of the *Patronato,* left it suspended.[81]

The tremendous and far-reaching concessions which the Vatican gave the Spanish monarchs had some interesting results, not the least of which was reflected in attitudes. In the New World, from the beginning, the Church was not free, and yet, because the early Spaniards had a deep devotion to the Church, it grew strong and prosperous, exercising a tremendous influence on all kinds of individuals and institutions.

The civil government of Spain for a long time had its hands full with the task of conquest and administration. It did not look with covetous eye on expropriating the educational program, the dispensing of charity, the care of the sick and the poor. This was to come about after the establishment of the independent republican régimes. The Kings exercised a constant and vigilant supervision over practically every detail connected with the Church. It would do violence to historical evidence, however, to believe that the fact that these monarchs were Catholic was sufficient to warrant a harmonious relationship between Church and State. Over and over again the churchmen had protested about encroachments—and the monarchs usually executed their royal policies. Nor did these patterns and attitudes end when republican government superseded the royal. They were to be projected likewise into the ensuing Church-State relations.

I have dwelt at considerable length and in some detail on this section because I am convinced that this account of the *Patronato* forms a good portion of the framework into which the whole general picture of the later Church-State story fits.

It was comparatively easy for Pope Gregory XVI to cut the Gordian knot which linked the Kings of Spain to the Church in America. He could not quite so simply prevent the new republics from arguing that the privileges now be-

81 *Ibid.,* p. 317.

came naturally transferred to them. It was not enough for the Vatican to state that now the Church would be free. One phase of the conflict, in truth, was ended, but it was to be renewed again, with only the names and the men changing— the issues remaining always the same.

CHAPTER II

THE CHURCH ON THE EVE OF THE REVOLUTION

Its Possessions

IN treating of the system of the *patronato real* the emphasis is placed on the concessions given to the civil government by the Church. In discussing the possessions of the Church it will be noted that it often acquired them by getting huge grants from the King for various purposes or in return for certain services, that various Church authorities bought properties, and that to them were often bequeathed land, houses, jewels, etc.

One of the most complete pictures of the Church in Guatemala in the seventeenth century was given by Thomas Gage, who visited the area in 1629. He wrote of sugar plantations, corn and wheat farms, flour mills, of cattle ranches, of even a silver mine—all owned by religious. Here is reproduced a sample of his report:

> The Churches (in Guatemala la Vieja) though they be not so fair and rich as those of Mexico, yet they are for that place wealthy enough. There is but one parish church and a cathedral which standeth in the market-place. All the other churches belong to cloisters, which are of Dominicans, Franciscans, Mercenarians [sic], Augustines, and Jesuits, and two of nuns, called the Concepción and St. Catherine. The Dominicans', Franciscans' and Mercenarians' are stately cloisters, containing nearly a hundred friars apiece; but above all is the cloister where I lived, of the Dominicans, to which is joined in a great walk before the church the University of the city. The yearly revenues which come into this Cloister, what from a water-mill, what from a farm for corn, what from an estancia, or farm for horses and mules, what from an ingenio, or farm of sugar, what from a mine of silver given unto it the year 1633 are judged to be (excepting all charges) at

least thirty thousand ducats; wherewith those fat friars feast themselves, and have to spare to build, and enrich their churches and altars. Besides much treasure belonging to it, there are two things in it which the Spaniards in merriment would often tell me the English nation did much enquire after when they took any ship of theirs at sea, and that they feared that I was come to spy them, which were a lamp of silver hanging before the high altar, so big as required the strength of three men to hale it up with a rope; but the other is of more value, which is a picture of the Virgin Mary of pure silver, and of the stature of a reasonable tall woman, which standeth in a tabernacle made on purpose in a Chapel of the Rosary with at least a dozen lamps of silver also burning before it. A hundred thousand ducats might soon be made up of the treasure belonging to that church and cloister. Within the walls of the cloister there is nothing wanting which may further pleasure and recreation. In the lower cloister there is a spacious garden, in the midst whereof is a fountain casting up the water, and spouting it out of at least a dozen pipes, which fill two ponds full of fishes, and with this their constant running giveth music to the whole cloister, and encouragement to many waterfowls and ducks to bathe themselves therein. Yet further within the cloister, there are other two gardens for fruits and herbage, and in the one a pond of a quarter of a mile long, all paved at the bottom, and a low stone wall about, where is a boat for the friars' recreation, who often go thither to fish, and do sometimes upon a sudden want or occasion take out from thence as much fish as will give to the whole cloister a dinner.[1]

Outside Guatemala City in the valley of Mixco, the Spaniards had a rich sodality, and the "blackamoors" or negroes, another. The hermitage of Our Lady of Carmel served the area and to that hermitage, according to Gage (who was not above a bit of exaggeration) were attached forty or fifty

1 Gage, Thomas D., *A New Study of the West-Indies*, London, E. Cotes, 1655, p. 127.

Spanish farms, and in the houses of these some three hundred slaves, men and women, blackamoors and mulattoes.[2]

In the various Indian towns, a governor was chosen from the principal family, but he was subordinate to the City of Guatemala and the Chancery. Although this governor had many privileges and attendants, he in turn waited on the friar of the town, doing nothing which the friar did not countenance. This churchman lived in as stately a manner (any one who reads Gage is impressed by his love of the word *stately*) as any Bishop, with servants for his house and his own private fishermen.[3]

Gage's own accounting for Mixco and Pinola is here set forth:

> 2 crowns for a Mass—every week—from the sodalities of the souls in Purgatory.
> 2 crowns every month from the Sodality of the Rosary.
> 2 crowns each every month from the Sodality of the Rosary of the Virgin Marta belonging to the Spaniards, the Indians and the blackamoors.
> 40 crowns—Christmas offering.
> 200 crowns—Thursday and Friday of Holy Week.
> 1 real—from each communicant—minimum of 1,000 reales.
> 1,000 reales—Confessions in Lent.
> 2 reales—every christening.
> 2 crowns—every marriage.
> 2 crowns—every death.
> 10-12 crowns—individual offering for Masses for the dead—2,000 crowns.
> Offering of eggs, honey, cacao, fowl and fruits.[4]

In another section Gage treats of the servants allowed by the Spaniards for the priest's service:

2 *Ibid.*, p. 132.

3 *Ibid.*, p. 133.

4 *Ibid.*, p. 161. The *real* in colonial times was worth approximately 12½ cents, with the *peso* equalling eight *reales* or about $1.00.

To the Church there do belong according as the town is in bigness, so many singers, and trumpeters, and waits, over whom the priest hath one officer, who is called fiscal; he goeth with a white staff with a little silver cross on top to represent the church and show that he is the priest's clerk and officer. When any case is brought to be examined by the priest, this fiscal or clerk executeth justice by the priest's order. He must be one can read and write, and is commonly the master of the music. He is bound upon the Lord's Day and other saints' days, to gather to the church before and after service all the young youths, and maids, and to teach them the prayers, sacraments, commandments, and other points of catechism allowed by the Church of Rome. In the morning he and the other musicians, at the sound of the bell, are bound to come to church to sing and officiate at the Mass, which in many towns they perform with organs and other musical instruments (as hath been observed before) as well as Spaniards. So likewise at evening at five of the clock they are again to resort to the church, when the bell calleth, to sing prayers, which they call completas, or completory, with the Salve Regina, a prayer to the Virgin Mary. This fiscal is a great man in the town, and bears more sway than the mayors, jurats, and other officers of justice, and when the priest is pleased, giveth attendance to him, goeth about his errands, appointeth such as are to wait on him when he rideth out of town. Both he and all that doth belong unto the Church are exempted from the common weekly service of the Spaniards, and from giving attendance to travellers, and from other officers of the law. But they are to attend with their waits and their trumpets, and music, upon any great man or priest that cometh to their town, and to make arches with boughs and flowers in the streets for their entertainment.

Besides these, "those also that do belong unto the service of the priest's house are privileged from the Spaniard's service." The priest has a change of servants by the week, who take their turns so that they may have a week or two to spare to do their own work:

3 cooks (if it be a large town; if small, but 2)—a week turn about, unless for a feast, when all come.

3 butlers (if a large town; otherwise, 2)—to preserve and distribute the provisions, take care of linen and dishes, set and wait on table.

3 or 4 boys (in large towns, a half dozen)—to do errands, wait on table, sleep in the house (and eat there, along with the rest). ...

6 young maids who " near the priest's house do meet to make him and his family tortillas or cakes of maize, which the boys bring hot to the table half a dozen at the time."

Some old women—to oversee the aforementioned maids in turn.

2 or 3 gardeners.

6 Indians for his stable—to bring morning and night *sacate* or grass for his mules or horses.

3 or 4 grooms of the stable—who come in turn—thrice a day.

2 or 3 sacristans for his church.

2 or 3 mayordomos for each cofradia or sodality—to gather alms for the sodality and eggs for the priest.

3, 4 or sometimes 6 fishermen to seek him fish, if any fishing place be near.[5]

Considerable revenue also accrued to the clergy on saints' days, because then the owner of the saint (meaning here, of course, a statue) made a great feast in the town, " and presenteth unto the priest sometimes three or four or five crowns for his Mass and sermon, besides a turkey and three or four fowls, with as much cacao as would serve to make him chocolate for all the whole octave or eight days following. So that in the churches, where there are at least forty of these saints' statues and images, they bring unto the priest at least forty pounds a year." [6]

After Mass, the priest and the mayordomos took and swept away from a saint's image whatever had been offered—so

5 *Ibid.*, p. 146.

6 *Ibid.*, p. 147.

that sometimes in a great town the priest might have in money twelve or twenty *reales* and fifty or a hundred candles which were worth between twenty or thirty shillings.[7]

Especially during Lent the Indians, when going to Confession, offered all kinds of gifts—honey, eggs, fowls, fish, cacao, money—and were expected to bring at least one *real* when receiving Communion. Special offerings were also made during Holy Week, All Souls' Day, and on other occasions.[8]

The town officials, the alcaldes and regidores, made monthly allowances to the priest (Gage received in some places twenty crowns, in others, fifteen). At the end of every year the books recording this income were examined by an officer from Guatemala City.

The church treasures at this time were already impressive. In the town of Petapa there were many sodalities of Our Lady and other saints, known as *cofradias,* which were (and still are to this day) enriched with crowns, chains and bracelets, besides the lamp censers, and silver candle sticks belonging to the altars.[9]

There are references to " goodly and sumptuous " cloisters. It was reported that at Amatitlán the Dominicans had 8,000 ducats (and surely the number had since increased) laid up in a chest with three locks, for the common expenses of the cloister.[10]

Interspersed throughout all this running commentary are what might be termed Gage's " asides "—when he finds friars running a mill, " What would they not do to satisfy their covetous minds—even dusty millers they will become to get wealth," [11] and again, " The churches of St. James, San Pedro, San Juan and San Domingo Senaco are exceedingly

7 *Ibid.,* p. 149.

8 *Ibid.,* p. 151.

9 *Ibid.,* p. 113.

10 *Ibid.,* p. 134.

11 *Ibid.,* p. 118.

rich; in the town of Santiago (St. James) there was living one Indian, who for only vainglory had bestowed the worth of 6,000 ducats upon that church and yet afterwards, this wretch was found to be a wizard and an idolator."[12]

I followed, over three hundred years later, much the same route as that taken by Gage. It is truly amazing to consider the distances he covered, in view of the transportation difficulties (they are still far from good). He referred to the dangers of going down the craggy and rocky mountain of Rabinal to get to Vera Paz (traveling in the rainy season, there is still danger) and finding in the valley of St. Nicholas an *estancia* which belonged to the Dominicans of Cobán and which was famous for the breeding of mules. Also in that valley was the farm of San Hierome, conducted by the Dominicans of Guatemala, where the very best horses, desired by all the gentry "who loved to prance about the street", were bred.[13]

The town of Zojabah, or Sacapula, was the largest and fairest of all the towns belonging to a Priory, and here the Indians " made their cottonwool into mantles, and had plenty of honey, and great flocks of goats and kids . . ."[14]

At this time (1629) most of the revenue of the bishops seemed to come from the great Indian towns. The bishop was accustomed to visit the area to confirm. A clergyman was appointed to hold the basin into which the required offerings were dropped. The Bishop of Chiapas on one of these journeys was reported to have received 1,600 ducats, besides the fees due him for visiting the several *cofradias*.[15]

There is considerable reference during this period to the fact that towns belonged to certain friars, e.g. "Chiantla . . . to the Mercenarian [sic] Fryers who doubtless would not

12 *Ibid.*, p. 137.
13 *Ibid.*, p. 137.
14 *Ibid.*, p. 116.
15 *Ibid.*, p. 102.

be able to subsist in so poor a place, had they not invented that loadstone of their picture of Mary and cried it up for miraculous, to draw people far and near, and all travellers from the Rode to pray unto it, and to leave their gifts and almes unto them for their prayers and masses." [16]

So much for a glimpse of what had been pretty well set up as the pattern in the 17th century, the activities engaged in by the religious orders, the sources of revenue, and the various allowances made to the ecclesiastics.

In the year 1791 in the archbishopric of Guatemala there were 108 parishes, 23 missions conducted by religious, 424 churches and 539,765 faithful.

The second bishopric of the Metropolitan, León, in the territory now known as Nicaragua, had 39 parishes, 3 reductions of Indians, 88 churches and 131,932 faithful.

The third bishopric, Ciudad Real, had 38 parishes, 102 churches, 69,253 faithful; and the fourth, Comayagua, 35 parishes, 1 reduction of Indians, 145 churches and 93,501 faithful.[17]

Twenty-seven years later, in 1818, it is possible to sketch a fairly comprehensive picture. In the archbishopric of Guatemala in the year 1818 there were:

Vicariates	Parishes	Churches	Confraternities	Faithful
17	131	424	1720	540,508

Missions

Valles	Haciendas	Trapiches
85	914	910

Religious Houses of Men in the City of Guatemala
1) Santo Domingo, established 1535, Dominicans
2) Franciscans, 1540; house of studies and colegio for young men who showed talent in sciences.

16 Ibid., p. 113.
17 Jaurros, op. cit., p. 14.

3) *Nuestra Señora de la Merced*, 1537, with house of studies and many mission convents.

4) San Lucas, *colegio* of the Jesuits (Expelled from the Spanish dominions, they left their possessions in charge of the Dean of the Cathedral)

5) the Augustinians, established 1610.

6) Convent of *Nuestra Señora de Belén*, founded by Hermano Pedro, a Guatemalan.

7) *Colegio de Cristo Crucificado* of the Apostolic Missionaries of the Propagation of the Faith, who worked among the Indians and gave missions in the parishes.

8) Oratory of the Order of St. Philip Neri.

Religious Houses of Women in Guatemala
Convents

1) Convent of the Order of the *Inmaculada Concepción*, cloistered, no longer having externs as in the past.

2) Convent of *Santa María Catalina Mártir*, founded from the overcrowding of the above in 1606.

3) Convent of the Discalced Carmelites, 1677.

4) Convent of the Poor Clares (The king was patron of this foundation and provided four burses or dowries for the daughters of the Ministers of the Royal *Audiencia*).

5) Convent of the Capuchin Nuns, *Nuestra Señora del Pilar*.

Beaterios or Houses of Pious Instruction.

1) *Beaterio de Nuestra Señora del Rosario*, established for the protection and instruction of Indian girls in womanly arts. In 1771 the inmates began to wear the habit and take vows in the order of St. Dominic. The King, displeased, ordered the *beaterio* to return to its primitive state as a simple house of protection for Indian girls from 7 to 12 years of age until 20 or 22 years.

2) *Beaterio de Santa Rosa de Lima*, for daughters of the highest nobility of the city. In 1818 the *beatas* were cloistered, had sufficient income, a splendid church, convent and school where daughters of the first families learned to sew, cook, read and embroider.

3) *Beaterio de Betlén.* Hermano Pedro had forbidden women in his hospitals, but some pious widows opened a little house for women next to his hospital, and soon there were 13 beatas who acted as nurses for the women. In 1781 they opened a school for girls, a public school where they taught reading and cooking.

Schools

1) *Colegio de la Presentación de Nuestra Señora,* first asylum founded in Guatemala for poor girls, who had neither dowry nor the inclination for married life. In 1635 this was turned into an asylum for the correction of women of evil life and gradually a shelter for penitents. Again, in the 18th century, it reverted to its original use and, besides girls sheltered, there were day students who learned Christian doctrine, reading, writing, cooking and other womanly duties.

2) *Colegio de la Visitación de Nuestra Señora,* founded in 1796 for girls.

Hospitals in Guatemala (under the care of the Church)

1) *Hospital de Santiago,* 1553, founded by Bishop Marroquín, caring for Spaniards and mulattoes, conducted by the Religious of San Juan de Dios.

2) *Hospital de San Alexis,* founded by the Dominicans, for the care of the Indians, with a yearly grant of 600 *pesos* by the King.

3) *Hospital of San Pedro,* caring for ecclesiastics.

On the outskirts of the city there were two other hospitals, *La Misericordia,* and that of *San Lázaro* for lepers.[18]

Associations

Third Orders

1) of the *Inmaculada Conceptión,* founded by the Municipal Government in 1527.

2) of Santa Vera Cruz, founded by the Municipal Government of Almolonga—church had been destroyed.

18 Juarros, *op. cit.,* pp. 72-140.

    3) of *Nuestra Señora de la Merced,* founded in 1583, had dis-
integrated by 1800, but the zeal of members restored it
again among the leading families.

    4) of the Holy Scapular—had the privilege of distributing
the scapular.

    5) of San Pedro—most respectable of all; head usually was
the archbishop, and the members either ecclesiastics or
those of the highest rank.

    6) of the *Santísimo Sacramento*—archconfraternity *par ex-
cellence*—whose members enjoyed the privilege of walk-
ing in Corpus Christi procession among the secular clergy.

    7) of the *Escuela de Cristo.*

    8) *Nuestra Señora del Socorro.*

    9) of *Las Animas.*[19]

As has been stated, the wealth of the Church increased
through gifts and bequests, even though the Crown controlled
the tithes. The Church was compelled to accept many of these
gifts in the form of liens on undivided landed estates, and,
since it invested a large part of its other funds in mortgages,
it gradually acquired an interest in agricultural properties
as well as in city real estate.[20] The Crown made half-hearted
efforts to check this process but with little result and, after
the Independence had been declared, the wealth of the Church
became a burning political issue[21] and a source of danger
to the Church itself. As early as June 14, 1822, the new government, in view of the grave condition of the public treasury,
ordered the Provincials of the Franciscans and La Merced
to turn over to the treasury of the nation all the funds collected for the redemption of captives in the Holy Land, under
the *Bula de Cruzada,* then existing in the capital, and to

19 Salazar, Ramón A., *Historia de Veintiún Años: la Independencia de
Guatemala,* Guatemala, Tipografía Nacional, 1928, p. 59.

20 Munro, Dana, *Latin American Republics,* New York, Appleton-Century,
1942, pp. 96-97.

21 Díaz, Victor Miguel, *Guatemala Independente, Recopilación de Documentos históricos,* Guatemala, Tipografía Nacional, 1932, p. 60.

order sent to the treasury as soon as possible all the funds stored for that purpose throughout the provinces.

There seems to be fairly general agreement that the churches and the possessions in Guatemala, even in the colonial period, did not compare in taste, riches or decorations with those of Mexico, and the edifices in both countries today lend weight to this opinion. Some of the gold and silver vessels and some of the images still extant (almost every town had an image of its patron saint) are fairly remarkable. Among others is the Virgin of Chiantla in silver (mentioned above by Gage) which is still in the village church, now in charge of an American Maryknoll missionary. The present appearance of the statue is somewhat ludicrous because the Indians have overlaid the silver work with all kinds of colored paper chains and artificial flowers. There are some good paintings and wood carvings, e.g. the famous carving of San Sebastian in the Cathedral of Guatemala City, but on the whole there is now relatively not much of great value.

Thomas Gage, as has been noted, mentioned the considerable revenue he observed accruing to the clergy of Guatemala in the early part of the seventeenth century. In view of this, it is interesting to find in the financial report of Mariano Herrarte, Treasurer of Guatemala on the eve of the revolution, dated September 29, 1821, an item indicating payments to the pastors of 5,812.6¼ *pesos,* out of a total salary expenditure of 77,967.9 *pesos.* If one notes further that the militia received 50,919.7¼ *pesos* and the judicial officials 12,302.6¼ *pesos* for the same period, there seems to have been no abuse in favor of the clergy.[22] However, it should be remarked at the same time that there were some wealthy churchmen for, when the Crown asked for contributions to help wage war against Napoleon's forces, the highest single subscription

22 Vela, Manuel, "Estado de la Tesoreria General del Exército y Real Hacienda de Guatemala Por el Mes de Septre. Hasta el 29 para la Entrega y Posesión del Tesorero D. Mariano Herrarte", *Anales de la Sociedad de Geografía e Historia*, vol. XII, No. 1, Sept. 1935, p. 23.

towards the $43,538 collected was that of Archbishop Penalver
y Cardenas, who gave $21,451.1⅝ to the cause.[23]

The religious orders still maintained many large estates,
as has been noted, and in 1821 when a decree was passed giving the negro slaves their freedom, a number who belonged
to the Dominicans on the plantation of San Jerónimo voluntarily continued to reside there.[24] The estate covered 473
caballerias, (each caballeria being approximately 33½ acres).
Besides San Jerónimo, the Dominicans possessed Cerro Redondo, having 150 caballerias, Palencia with 97, Cacabal y
Tuluché with 182, El Rosario with 83, La Compañía with 31,
San José with 25, Chacara de las Animas with 15, Chiroyo
with 14 and Pacayita with 17, besides many smaller properties.[25]

The Dominicans were generally conceded to have been the
richest order at the end of the colonial period.[26] Batres
Jáuregui asserts that more than 1,000,000 pesos of gold were
produced by the Hacienda de San Jerónimo and the income
from the parishes they held between 1775 and 1808.[27] They
had even founded five towns on the shores of Lake Amatitlán,
on land granted to them by royal decree of Charles V and, as
early as 1545, one Fr. Diego Martínez with much difficulty
had stocked the lake with fish which provided not only food,
but also a means of livelihood for those living in the area. In
1832 the Indians of that region complained that they had
been deprived unjustly of their lands, establishing their claim

23 Bancroft, op. cit., p. 17; Salazar, op. cit., p. 114.

24 Batres Jáuregui, Antonio, La América Central ante la Historia,
Guatemala, Sánchez & de Guise, 1920, II, 201.

25 Castellanos, J. Humbert, La Metrópoli Colonial Centro-Americana,
Antigua, Tipografía Azmitia, 1936, p. 208.

26 Thompson, George A., Narrative of an Official Visit to Guatemala,
London, John Murray, 1829, p. 249; Dunn, Henry, Guatimala, or the United
Provinces of Central America in 1827-8, New York, G. & C. Carvill,
1828, p. 69; Batres Jáuregui, op. cit., p. 201.

27 Ibid., op. cit., p. 592.

on the fact that the Dominicans had ceded them the territory as *ejidos* or common property.[28]

The Church of the Franciscans in Guatemala City was one of the handsomest buildings in the town, and the monks, not exceeding fifty in number, were considered to be rich, outdoing all other ecclesiastical establishments in the grandeur of their processions, the interior decorations of their temple, especially the pictures.[29]

The Augustinians in their monastery at Sonsonate, on the other hand, were said to have numbered not more than half a dozen.[30]

Canon Castillo furnished Thompson, the English traveler, who was making an official visit to Guatemala about this time, with a report on the state of the Church in Central America, which ran somewhat as follows:

> Parishes—about 300—most of which contained two, three or four settlements.
>
> Pastor's salary—$1,500 (£300) annually.
>
> Cathedral—Guatemala City—with bishops and canons.
>
> Suffragan Churches—
> León in Nicaragua—cathedral, bishop and canons
> Comayagua   "   "   "
> Ciudad Real   "   "   "
> (agitation for two other suffragan churches — at San Salvador and Costa Rica)
>
> Religious Orders—
> St. Francis
> St. Dominic (very rich)
> St. Austin
> St. Philip Neri
> Belén (with a hospital)
> Our Lady of Mercy and of the Reforma

28 *Recopilación de Leyes de Guatemala*, III, 18.

29 Thompson, *op. cit.*, p. 207.

30 *Ibid.*, p. 71.

St. Peter of Alcantara
Total Members of religious orders—about 300 in the
republic.
Schools—gratuitous in each convent.[31]

Although Antigua, the old capital, had had between fifty
and sixty edifices of public worship before the earthquake of
1773, there were no more than seven or eight in use in 1825.[32]

The Constituent Assembly in December, 1823, suppressed
any incomes arising from Papal Bulls and, although this action
might have given a decided impulse to national industry, it
left the treasury in an impoverished state. The federal government received little pecuniary aid from the several states
of which it was composed, and what it did receive was solely
from Guatemala and Honduras. The duty of 7% on the clear
value of all ecclesiastical revenues was inconsiderable.[33]

Before the expulsion of the Archbishop and the religious
in July, 1829, the Executive power of the State published a
circular order which contained the following article:

> The Reverend Clergy, in case of an invasion by the
> enemy, will take the means most opportune and efficacious
> for placing in security the possessions of their respective
> charges, and, if, through their carelessness, these things fall
> into the hands of the enemy, they must replace them at their
> own cost; and the political officials, alcaldes, municipal gov-
> ernments of the towns are to safeguard the treasures and
> silver of the churches; they will endeavor to transfer them
> to a safe place at the earliest opportunity, without or within
> their own departments, or at least hide them safely; they shall
> put in safe-keeping also the other goods and possessions of
> the Church; and let all this be done harmoniously by the
> ecclesiastical and civil authorities.[34]

31 *Ibid.*, pp. 207, 140.

32 *Ibid.*, p. 249.

33 *Ibid.*, p. 471.

34 Montúfar y Rivera, Lorenzo, *Reseña Histórica de Centro-América*,
Guatemala, Tipografía La Union, 1887, I, 83.

When the government asked the Church authorities to submit an inventory of all the church possessions and a list of the clergymen and their location, the Archbishop complied, but insisted that there was no such thing available as a complete record.[35]

Montúfar y Coronado comments on the property of the religious after the expulsion as follows:

> After the expulsion of the religious the convents remained deserted because the civil authorities did not intervene in the first steps, which were entrusted to the armed forces; the first care and responsibility of the latter were the persons of the expelled; thus, it is not strange that the government took no precautions for the guarding of the property of the convents. A periodical of Guatemala, *La Antorcha*, spoke of the sacking of them by the crowds; other periodicals contradicted this, and it is not to be believed that the military forces would have permitted it. It is possible that at first some trifling things were taken, but this does not merit the name of sacking. A decree of the Assembly adjudged to the state the possessions of the religious; the sacred vessels and articles were taken and handed over to the heads of the armed forces; there are rumors of the quantity of silver taken by other officials, now in lieu of salary, now for other reasons. . . . What is certain is that the religious possessed within their churches and convents and on their properties in the city and out in the country, and in capital stored away, riches of which the public has never seen an itemized description, nor any account of their disposal. In the convents of Guatemala there was more wealth than was calculated; and since the religious kept it during the troubles when the government was defending the city and their very convents, they have deserved to lose it. Many cargoes of wrought silver, such as is used in the service of the altar were taken out of the country to the British settlement of Belice by employees and individuals entrusted with this task; to Chiapas also there were sent at this time to a cer-

35 *National Archives of Guatemala*, Document No. 25502, June 19, 1829; No. 24769, Dec. 30, 1828.

tain functionary church silver and other effects belonging to the booty of Guatemala and the confiscations made on its inhabitants. These goods and temporalities, administered by a government capable of maintaining itself aloof from its own temptations and the greed of others could have sufficed to repair the losses of the state, substituting in place of the convents, establishments for education of the public, houses of correction, loans for the development of agriculture, commerce and highways; but the disorders of the first days and the confusion of the first measures taken impaired everything, and finally only a small number of individuals profited by it.[36]

But a still clearer view of the matter of the possessions of the religious and their disposal can be obtained from the lists of auctions of this property in the years following the banishment of the religious and the expropriation of their possessions. Montúfar y Rivera cites the following:

Date of Sale	Property Sold	Belonging to	Price
Aug. 8, 1831	Hacienda of San José	Dominicans	$5,226
Sept. 25, 1831	Plantation Cerro-Redondo with land and mills	Dominicans	12,416
Dec. 31, 1831	"Los Ojitos" in la Antigua	Order of La Merced	7,000
Jan. 14, 1832	House known as "La Rueta"	Order of La Merced	1,400
Jan. 16, 1832	Farm of San Francisco with provisional church of Third Order	Franciscans	
Feb. 11, 1832	Ranch	Order of La Merced	4,010
Feb. 18, 1832	House of Camposeco	Order of La Merced	1,900
Mar. 21, 1832	House of Fr. Granados-Calle Incienso	Order of La Merced	
May 24, 1832	Houses and orchard	Order of La Merced	
June 16, 1832	House of Fr. Casado	Order of La Merced	5,020
Sept. 29, 1832	Ranch of Borges	Franciscans	2,005
Nov. 2, 1832	House and gardens of Borges	Franciscans	3,300
Nov. 17, 1832	Park of La Merced	Order of La Merced	865/2r.
Dec. 17, 1832	Ranch of Santo Domingo	Dominicans	10,500
Dec. 27, 1832	Plantation of La Merced	Order of La Merced	6,100
Jan. 23, 1833	La Pena	Chaplaincy	400
Mar. 15, 1833	Plantation of Cacabal and Tuluché with 182 caballerias, houses and sown fields; with other plots in Tecpán, and the plantation of Choacorral		

36 Montúfar y Coronado, Manuel, *Memorias para la Historia de la Revolución de Centro-América*, Guatemala, Tipografía Sánchez & de Guise, 1934, pp. 203-204.

Date of Sale	Property Sold	Belonging to	Price
May 1, 1833	Mill	Order of La Merced	9,470
Oct. 5, 1833	Lot Number 4	Order of La Merced	1,397/6r.
Nov. 11, 1833	Plantations of Chicozo	Dominicans	86/7½r.
Nov. 18, 1833	Estate of Palencia with 96-¾ caballerias	Dominicans	28,075
Dec. 9, 1834	Lot Number 5	Order of La Merced	1,323/7r.
Mar. 27, 1835	Hacienda and Mill of San Jerónimo with products, furnishings, buildings, etc.	Dominicans	253,528 4¼r.
Apr. 15, 1835	Old Convent, site and new mill	Dominicans	18,256
July 2, 1835	Hacienda of Pacayita	Dominicans	1,012 4r.
Sept. 22, 1835	Mill of La Compañía	Dominicans	3,160
Dec. 18, 1835	Hacienda of San Andrés	Order of La Merced	400
Feb. 10, 1836	Buildings, Convent and farm, approx. 89,694 sq. ft.	Order of Recollect	4,000
June 1, 1836	House of doña Ignacia López	Order of La Merced	2,250
Jan. 21, 1837	Lot Number 3	Order of La Merced	1,106
Sept. 27, 1837	Colegio de Niñas—house of chaplain	Order of La Merced	5,473 3r.[37]

This property, originally owned by the Church and the religious orders, has changed hands many times during the last century. Expropriated during the liberal control of the early days of the republic, most of it was restored to the original owners, or, at least, for religious purposes, during Carrera's régime. Seized again when Granados and Barrios came into power, many of the former buildings of the church and the orders were converted into educational institutions such as normal, primary and secondary schools for the public school system, military academies and schools of manual arts for the less gifted. Others became mental asylums, prisons or reformatories. Still others served more utilitarian purposes —government offices, customs houses, barracks. Many were left to deteriorate and now form interesting ruins, e.g. the archway of the Convent of Santa Catarina Mártir in Antigua.

Among the churches still used for religious purposes, though the property of the state, are the cathedral, recently restored after the earthquake of 1917, the church of the Convent of *Nuestra Señora de la Merced,* and the partly restored church

37 Montúfar y Rivera, *op. cit.,* pp. 242-245. The symbol $ used by the author represents the one-ounce peso, today theoretically equivalent to about one dollar.

of the Convent of the *Recolección*. The Dominican church, destroyed during the aforementioned earthquake, was restored on a smaller scale. Its famous silver Virgin of the Rosary was crowned "Queen of Guatemala" on January 28, 1933, but the ceremony was a far cry from the elaborate crowning in 1541, in which civil and ecclesiastical authorities joined.

The vast Dominican Convent is now the site of private homes and government buildings. The old Church of the Carmelites is now a museum in a public park called "*El Carmen*", while the former Church of *El Calvario* is a national museum containing examples of the arts and crafts of colonial times, historical relics, rare books and incunabula. Only a small portion of the Church and Convent of the Capuchin nuns remains.

Among the buildings still used for religious purposes is the *Colegio de Infantes*, opened in 1781 as a training school for choristers, and now a boys' school conducted by the Marist Brothers.

Thus the vast possessions of the Church and the religious orders, one of the greatest points of contention between the Church and the State, have in time become practically non-existent. With the loss of possessions the Church suffered one of those setbacks of which there were to be so many in the battle waged with the State.

Its Status

Because of the close relationship between the Church and the colonial government of Guatemala, it was natural that the former should be involved in the movement for independence, with its clergy active on both sides, not entirely for religious, but also for political, social or economic reasons. Even before the first symptoms of a desire for independence were outwardly shown when Napoleon invaded Spain, the Governor of Guatemala and the Municipal Council, at the death of Archbishop de la Vera in 1808, had asked the

Regency to name as his successor a member of the Ecclesiastical Chapter of Guatemala, and not a Spaniard. Until then, Juan Bautista Alvárez de Toledo (1713-1723) had been the only native of America to become Bishop of Guatemala.[38] The resentment felt in Guatemala by the *criollos*, or those born in America, toward the *peninsulares* or Spanish born, who usually thought themselves superior, was reflected in other areas. The captains-general, governors, members of the *Audiencia* and royal officials, bishops and ecclesiastical dignitaries, officials of the military forces—all were Spaniards rewarded by royal favor. And outside of minor offices— parishes, university chairs, and employments of secondary nature—to which the *criollos* could aspire, all the rest remained in the hands of the Spaniards.[39] Even Napoleon, recognizing the influence of the Church in America and scattering agents to try to arouse the colonies against the mother country, had instructed them to gain the aid of the lower clergy, all of whom were American born.[40] In 1811 and in 1812, after the National Assembly held in Cadiz to which Guatemala sent as delegate the ecclesiastic don Antonio Larrazábal who so strongly defended the rights of the Americans that he was denounced and imprisoned by Ferdinand VII on the latter's return to Spain in 1814,[41] there were more positive movements in favor of independence, in which members of the clergy took part. On Sept. 25, 1812 the Constitution drawn up by that Assembly and representing a step toward popular government was sworn to by the clergy in the presence of the Archbishop of Guatemala.[42]

38 Salazar, *op. cit.*, pp. 131-2.

39 Valladares, Manuel, *Próceres de la Independencia*, Guatemala, Aguïrre Velásquez & Co., 1911, p. 6.

40 *Ibid.*, p. 121.

41 Bancroft, *op. cit.*, III, 8.

42 Salazar, *op. cit.*, p. 160.

One of the prime movers in disseminating ideas of independence in Guatemala was Canon Dr. José María Castilla, strangely enough a native of Spain and member of the nobility, who used to gather at his home a group of Guatemalans called the "*Tertulia patriótica*", composed of those working for the independence of Guatemala. This group, influenced by many of the ideas of the 18th century French philosophers and political theorists, which had spread through Guatemala in spite of the vigilance of the Tribunal of the Holy Office, published the *Editor Constitucional,* a periodical defending the rights of Americans and criticizing the abuses of the old administration. Under the editorship of Dr. Molina, who had become very popular, this circulated through the provinces of the Captaincy-General, awakening the sleeping minds of the future patriots of the struggle for independence. As time went on the government became aware of the influence of the group and its publication, and appointed don José Cecilio del Valle to organize a party to oppose it. The party of Molina, called "*fiebres*" ("The Hot Heads") because of their ardor and enthusiasm, was supported by some of the families called noble and the lower classes. The party of Valle, called "*españolistas*", or "*gasistas*" because of their supposed pompousness and affectation, was popular with the authorities of the time, with those adverse to innovations and with the artisans and weavers who were alarmed at the thought that independence might bring a free trade which would ruin them.[43]

The government of Spain had recognized very early these rebellious tendencies and had tried both by mild means and by force to repress them. On March 14, 1811 they sent General José Bustamante y Guerra to be Captain General of Guatemala. After studying conditions there he sent a report to the King, dated May 18, 1814, declaring:

43 *Ibid.*, pp. 95-111; 204-210.

There are three sources influencing the people: public opinion, religion and the law. Opinion, after being granted freedom of the press, has no other curb than that of censorship, which is in the hands of the enemy; the priests, natives of the country, are actuated by the same desire; the lawyers are members of their flock; and all are in favor of the ideas that are disturbing the public tranquility.[44]

Bustamante's zeal against any move toward independence and his rigor suppressed open attempts at emancipation, but did not extinguish them, and revolutionaries worked in secret and instigated movements and revolts in provinces most distant from his vigilance.[45] However, one conspiracy was organized in the Convent of Belén in the very capital itself, where secret meetings to discuss emancipation were presided over by the Sub Prior, Fray Juan Nepomuceno de la Concepción, and attended by outstanding laymen and ecclesiastics, who were severely punished when the plot became known.[46] Indeed, the Sub Prior, Fray Victor Castrillo, and Fray Manuel de San José were condemned to death for their participation in the movement, and Fray Benito Miguelena, to ten years in the chain-gang in Africa and perpetual banishment from Guatemala, but these sentences were revoked by the King in a decree dated July 28, 1817, on the petition of many distinguished persons of Guatemala.[47] In the provinces of San Salvador, Nicaragua and Honduras, where the spirit of independence was more universal and the action of Bustamante less directly felt, they did not limit themselves to plans, but openly revolted, with ecclesiastics outstanding in the movement.

44 Batres Jáuregui, *op. cit.*, p. 607.

45 Vilanova Meléndez, *op. cit.*, p. 40.

46 Aguirre Cinta, Rafael, *Historia General de Guatemala*, Guatemala, Tipografía Nacional, 1899, p. 72.

47 Marure, Alejandro, *Bosquejo histórico de las revoluciones de Centro-América*, Guatemala, Tipografía El Progreso, 1877; Salazar, *op. cit.*, p. 180.

San Salvador desired, not only its independence from Spain, but also complete separation from Guatemala, seat of the colonial government, with which there had always been rivalry and resentment, the origin of which, according to Arce, one would find " in the continuous presumption of the capital over the provinces and in the bitter complaints of the latter concerning the former, always ignored by the Spanish government." [48] Salvador had long resented, not only the political and economic, but also the ecclesiastical domination of Guatemala. Inspired, it is said, by Father José Matías Delgado, leader of the Independence movement and aspirant to the bishopric which the people of Salvador wished to have set up separate from that of Guatemala,[49] the Salvadoreans believed that ecclesiastical independence would follow civil independence.[50] Thus political affairs influenced the religious question and the latter aided, in its turn, in the attaining of the ends of the former.[51] The problem was long standing. In the first years of the conquest there were formed the bishoprics of Guatemala, Chiapas, Nicaragua, Honduras and Vera Paz, which were subordinate to different metropolitan churches in Spain and in the two Americas; but when the archbishopric of Guatemala was established in 1742, these dioceses became suffragan bishoprics of the Metropolitan See of Guatemala, with the exception of Vera Paz, where the episcopal See was suppressed and added to that of Guatemala. Salvador was then a part of the diocese of Guatemala. However, since the limits of each diocese were usually those of the respective states, it was quite probable that in time Salvador would have an episcopal See.[52] As early as 1778 the Archbishop of Guate-

---

48 Arce, Manuel José, *Memoria de la Conducta Pública y Administrativa de . . .*, Mexico, Imprenta Galvan, 1830, p. 5.

49 *Cf.* Marure, *op. cit.*, p. 129; Montúfar y Rivera, *op. cit.*, II, 16; Montúfar y Coronado, *op. cit.*, p. 75.

50 Vilanova Meléndez, *op. cit.*, p. 45.

51 Valladares, *op. cit.*, p. 33.

52 Montúfar y Coronado, *op. cit.*, p. 19.

mala, Dr. don Pedro Cortes y Lárraz, had informed the king, Charles III of the need of dividing the diocese and setting up a suffragan bishop in San Salvador.[53] On July 3, 1812 the Crown of Spain, in deference to a request of Salvador, issued a decree ordering the drawing up of the necessary documents and information for this purpose. But either because it was inopportune to transmit such a decree when the uprising of 1811 had not yet calmed down, or because he believed it unwise during the prevailing ill-will of the government of Guatemala towards Salvador, the Captain-General, Bustamante y Guerra, laid it aside and its existence remained hidden even from the Archbishop, as he himself showed later in a report of December 19, 1820. On December 8, 1818 the Court of Spain undertook the issuing of another decree urging the forwarding of the documents for the requested bishopric. It would seem from the foregoing that the erection of San Salvador into an episcopal See would come about naturally. However, Delgado convinced that the Court of Spain would not present him for the bishopric because of his adherence to the Independence movement and that the Holy See would not name him, resolved to obtain by civil authority and political means what was impossible to acquire from the authority of the Church and canonical means. He caused the government set up in San Salvador, of which he had become President, to issue on March 30, 1822 a decree erecting Salvador into an episcopal See and naming himself as its first bishop, an action declared null and void by both the Federal Government of Central America and the Holy See. It was not until Oct. 4, 1842 that the question was finally settled, and Salvador erected into a diocese by decree of Gregory XVI.[54]

Meanwhile Dr. Delgado promoted a conspiracy which broke out in favor of independence in San Salvador in November, 1811. About him had gathered, not only disting-

[53] Valladares, *op. cit.*, p. 31.

[54] Vilanova Meléndez, *op. cit.*, pp. 54-70; Montúfar y Rivera, *op. cit.*, pp. 13-15.

uished seculars including the future president, don Manuel
José Arce, but also many high ecclesiastics, among others
Fr. Nicolás Aguilar and his two brothers, also priests, don
Manuel and don Vicente, as well as don Mariano de Lara y
Aguilar and Dr. Simeon Cañas. The Vicars General of the
Provinces of San Vicente, don Manuel Antonio Molina y
Cañas, of San Miguel, Dr. don Miguel Barrueta, and of
Santa Ana, Dr. don Miguel Ignacio Cárcamo, had worked
ardently with him for independence, but had withdrawn when
a schism over the episcopate seemed inseparable from the
movement. According to Vilanova Meléndez, their with-
drawal, accompanied by that of a powerful part of the clergy
and people for the same reason, aided in the speedy suppression of the revolt.[55] On November 11, 1811 Col. don José
de Aycinena, don José Peinado, leading statesman, and Fray
José Vidaurre, Guardian of the Recollets, were sent to combat the insurrection in Salvador, the first by threats of arms,
the second by political overtures, and the last by exhortation.[56]

As Bustamante had in Archbishop Casáus y Torres a
strong arm to enforce his will, he asked the latter to order
the clergy to influence their faithful to contribute to the subscription for the campaign against Salvador. The Archbishop
issued a Pastoral urging the faithful " to do their share in
obtaining the common well-being, peace, tranquility and good
order by aiding the President in his vigilance and energetic
attempts to avoid the shedding of blood," begging them for
the sake of Jesus Christ, to be generous in contributing to
maintain the political body of which they all made a part.[57]

In the meantime the growing disaffection toward the
mother country had become more and more evident, and
meetings were held at which plans were laid down for de-

55 Vilanova Meléndez, op. cit., p. 46.

56 Valladares, op. cit., p. 34.

57 Salazar, op. cit., p. 157.

claring the independence of Guatemala. Excitement was running high when there arrived one Gavino Gainza, appointed by the National Assembly of Spain as governor of Guatemala. Destined to be the last representative of the colonial government, he favored the movement for independence in Guatemala, especially after Iturbide had proclaimed the Plan of Iguala on February 24, 1821.[58]

To counteract the increasing propaganda in favor of independence, on September 8, 1821, from the pulpit of the Cathedral, Archbishop Casáus y Torres, with the greatest vehemence protested against the injustice of a revolution. This only infuriated the insurgents, who proceeded to criticize him and to circulate handbills among the populace.[59]

On the 15th of September, 1821, the government, at the instigation of several of the provinces, formed a conference of all the existing authorities to deliberate on measures to be adopted. Gainza, as president, explained the purpose of the meeting, and certain documents drawn up by the Independence party in Mexico were read.[60] One of the communications suggested that each one present should manifest his sentiments in regard to independence. Thereupon Archbishop Casáus y Torres took the floor, declaring that it was not necessary to decide the question then and there—that it would be better to wait word from Spain, etc.—but he was peremptorily cut off and silenced.

The deputies to the meeting, including many ecclesiastics, with the provisional captain-general, remained in session with doors open, there joining them five members of the Municipal Government of Guatemala. Suddenly there entered about two hundred citizens prepared beforehand, it is suspected, with their speeches and petitions, taking for granted the separation

58 Aguirre Cinta, op. cit., p. 73.

59 Vela, Manuel, "Guatemala hace ciento catorce años," Anales de la Sociedad de Geografía e Historia de Guatemala, XII (1935) 11 ff.

60 Marure, op. cit., p. 21.

from Spain.[61] Canon Dr. José María Castilla voted first and most determinedly,[62] in opposition to his spiritual chief and friend, the Archbishop Casáus y Torres. Immediately after the declaration, Gainza took the oath of independence, offering to shed his blood to defend it—and finally, when all had followed his example, they passed to the Cathedral to sing a solemn *Te Deum*.[63] On adjourning, some of those who had spoken against independence were insulted, and most notably the archbishop, whom they seized by his robes, tearing his rochet and even stopping his coach on the street, without any consideration of his dignity.[64]

Evidence of the strong support given the revolutionary cause by ecclesiastics is found in the thirteen signatures of clergymen to the Declaration of Independence out of a total of twenty-nine. Among those signing, in the very presence of their monarchist archbishop, were the Dean of the Ecclesiastical Chapter of Guatemala, Dr. Antonio García Redondo, Canon José María de Castilla, the Penitentiary Dr. Antonio Larrazábal, Canon Manuel Antonio de Molina y Cañas, Dr. Simeon Cañas y Villacorta, Dr. Angel María Candina, the Rev. Marquis Juan José de Aycinena, Dr. José Matía Delgado, the Provincial of the Franciscans, don José Antonio Taboada, and the Superior of the Recollets, Fr. Mariano Pérez.[65]

The proclamation of September 15th was followed by a second manifesto to the provinces inviting them to elect representatives in the proportion of one for every 15,000 inhabitants, not excluding the colored population from the rights of citizenship, rights which had been strongly advocated by the ecclesiastic, Dr. Simeon Cañas, for those whom he called " our brothers, the slaves." [66] At the same time the prov-

61 Vela, *op. cit.*, p. 14.

62 Montúfar y Coronado, *op. cit.*, p. 76.

63 Vela, *op. cit.*, p. 14.

64 *Ibid.*, p. 11.

65 Valladares, *op. cit.*, p. 21.

66 Aguirre Cinta, *op. cit.*, p. 94.

inces were assured that, until this congress should meet on
March 1, 1822 in Guatemala to commence working on a constitution, no change should take place in authorities, and that
it should be a fundamental principle of the new government
to keep the Catholic religion unchanged, and to preserve that
pious spirit for which Guatemala had always been distinguished.[67] To these articles were added others signifying the
intention to coin a medal in commemoration of the independence and to hold a Solemn Mass to celebrate it.[68] Still
another article contained a plea to the heads of religious
orders to cooperate in the peaceful establishment of the independence and to urge their subjects to help bring about peace
and concord by their example and exhortation.[69] Article XIV
demanded that the oath of independence and fidelity to the
government be sworn to by the Archbishop, the Superiors
of the various religious orders, as well as their subjects, at
the same time as it was requesting the oath from the
Provisional Congress, the municipal governments, the court,
political and military officials, as well as from government
employees of all kinds, and the members of the military
forces.[70]

On December 27, 1821 Iturbide sent forces under Filísola
to protect, as he declared, the captaincy-general of Guatemala,
but really to force any unwilling sections of that province into
the union with Mexico. On Jan. 5, 1822 a decree of the
Provisional Congress, under Filísola as President, declared
in favor of the union of all the provinces of Guatemala with
Mexico. This union, however, soon ended with the downfall
of Iturbide. On June 24, 1823 forty-one representatives who
had gathered in Guatemala swore fidelity to the new Central

67 García, Miguel Angel, *Diccionario-enciclopédico de el Salvador*, San
Salvador, Imprenta La Salvadorena, 1829, I, 62.

68 *Ibid.*, p. 63.

69 *Ibid.*, p. 62.

70 *Ibid.*, p. 63.

American Confederation in the Cathedral; from there they passed to the University where Fr. José Matías Delgado, as President of the Assembly, pronounced the formula of installation.[71] On July 2, 1823 the Congress, in Article II of its decree of that date, declared solemnly that " the religion of the United Provinces is the Roman, Catholic, Apostolic, to the exclusion of all others ", and it added:

> ... therefore it shall be manifested as soon as possible to the Holy Apostolic See, by a special messenger or whatever other manner is most fitting, that our separation from Spain in no way hinders nor will weaken our union with the Holy See, in all that appertains to the holy religion of Jesus Christ.

Such was the sentiment expressed on the very eve of the Revolution. If it were as easy for the Guatemalans to put this sentiment into execution in the realm of everyday affairs as it was for them to make a statement apparently so simple, I would not have found it necessary to write so many subsequent pages for this study.

71 Marure, *op. cit.*, p. 61.

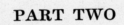

PART TWO

CHAPTER I

THE TRIUMPH OF THE LIBERALS

AFTER the establishment of the Confederation of Central American States in 1823, Manuel José Arce, candidate of the Liberals, attained the Presidency, but he soon deserted his party to join the Conservatives, composed largely of the aristocrats and the clergy.

It became apparent that a common resort of both parties in Guatemala when reduced to extremities was prolific of evil consequences. It was, namely, the practice of allying themselves by bribery or otherwise with the most successful military commanders who were willing to become their tools. The power thus acquired was often turned by the military despot against both parties.[1]

A seemingly fair description of Arce runs to the effect that he was a man of little character and no great ability, who was nominally a liberal and primarily a selfish politician.[2] After he had trampled over José del Valle, his rival for the presidency, he surrendered to the *Serviles* or Conservatives.[3] In the terminology of our present day, we might say that Arce was seeking security, and in his endeavor to obtain it, he tried to please both political factions and, in the end, offended his original supporters.[4]

Discords between many rival forces plagued the Central American Confederation, e.g. differences between Liberals and Conservatives, between the Federal and the Provincial authorities, between Salvadoreans and the Archbishop of

1 Crowe, Frederick, *The Gospel in Central America*, London, Charles Gilpin, 1850, p. 127.

2 Williams, Mary W., " The Ecclesiastical Policy of Francisco Morazán and the other Central American Liberals ", *Hispanic American Historical Review*, III, No. 2 (May, 1920), 120.

3 Crowe, *op. cit.*, p. 127.

4 Williams, *op. cit.*, p. 124.

Guatemala (under whose jurisdiction Salvador was, although the Salvadoreans, as we have seen, refused to recognize this when they elevated Dr. Delgado to the bishopric of Salvador).[5] As seems always to be true when examining the patterns of history, fear, suspicion, intrigue and warfare weakened the whole fabric and left scars on the structure of both Church and State.

In order the better to trace the relationship between the Church and State during this period, I include documents which throw some light on the course of events. Many of these show a clear imprint of friendly relations, of what indeed became a routine pattern of almost daily correspondence between civil and ecclesiastical authorities. Others definitely reflect an increasingly unfriendly tension and a determination on the part of state officials to regulate and to restrain church affairs.

On March 29, 1823, Vicente Filísola, President of the Provisional Congress, issued a governmental decree, Article 10 of which ran as follows:

The decisions of this Congress will be maintained by the present government of this capital and provinces and by the troops under its authority; until the assembly be held there will be guaranteed the security and property of all the inhabitants; order will be maintained, the Congress itself upheld, and there will be no innovation whatsoever in the government. When the Congress has convened, the Army will request it to guarantee the continuation of the employment of those now holding civil, military and *ecclesiastical* offices, in case that these provinces should be separated from the government of Mexico.[6]

There is a great deal of documentary proof of what was referred to above as the almost routine type of communication

5 Vilanova Meléndez, *op. cit.*, p. 58; Arce, *op. cit.*, p. 5.

6 Filísola, Vicente, *La Independencia de Guatemala*, Mexico, Imprenta Váldes, 1823, p. 3.

between ecclesiastical and state officials. The government would request the celebration of Masses and Te Deums, as in the following decree, interesting because it was issued by Iturbide while Guatemala was still in the Mexican Empire:[7]

> Agustín, by Divine Providence and by the Congress of the Nation, first Constitutional Emperor of Mexico, to all to whom it may concern, Be it known that, convinced as I am of the necessity of having recourse to God in order that the Almighty may grant me the help and enlightenment which I so much need and desire in order to govern well the people whom His Providence has deigned to confide to my care, I have resolved that in all the churches of the Empire, both secular and those belonging to religious orders, there be held for three days public prayers, there being forbidden during that period all amusements and especially public spectacles...

At other times the government would send copies of various decrees passed by the Assembly, particularly ones which affected church affairs. The archbishop, in turn, was acknowledging almost every day the communications of the government somewhat as in this note dated July 29, 1823:

> I have received fifty printed copies of the decree of the 2nd of this month, which prescribes the form of oath which must be sworn to by the authorities. I have examined it carefully and shall circulate it among the clergy of this archdiocese. God grant you many years. Palace of the Archbishop of Guatemala, July 29, 1823. Fr. Ramón, Archbishop of Guatemala. To the Chief Executive, don Tomás O'Horan.[8]

Other letters of the Archbishop to the civil authorities, like the following, indicated his compliance with various requests:[9]

7 Díaz, Victor Miguel, *Guatemala Independente: Recopilación de documentos históricos*, Guatemala, Tipografía Nacional, 1932, p. 258.

8 *National Archives of Guatemala*, No. 24708, July 29, 1823.

9 *Ibid.*, No. 24718, August 3, 1823.

August 3, 1823.

When, by decree of the Cortes of Spain, it was ordered that the books of the now extinct Inquisition be handed over, the Supreme Government commissioned Your Excellency, Judge Palomo and my Vicar General to take charge of them. A special room was set aside here in the Episcopal Palace for those which were left; here they have remained until now, except those which were claimed by their respective owners and handed over to them.

I have taken none except three or four through the Acting Vicar General, don José María Castilla. At the same time the Government ordered that no packages of books were to be sent through the Customs House without a permit from the Vicar General, and through this disposition some few have been acquired which have been placed with the others.

I hope that there may soon be designated the place and time of the delivery of these books which is referred to in the decree which you communicated to me in your letter of the first of this month.

May God grant you many years. Fr. Ramón, Archbishop of Guatemala. To the Chief Executive, don Tomás O'Horan.

August 4, 1823.

Kindly find attached two attested copies of the certification of the oaths sworn by the religious of Santa Teresa and the Capuchin Nuns in my presence; and by the religious of Santa Catalina, la Concepción and Santa Rosa, in the presence of the Vicar General, don Antonio Croquer. Please submit these to the Supreme Executive Power. May God grant you many years. August 4, 1823. To the Secretary General of the State of Guatemala.[10]

He even informed the government about his plans to make a visitation of his diocese in a letter dated November 29, 1823 and closed with the form ordered by the government to replace that of the Spanish régime:

10 *Ibid.*, No. 24719. *Cf.* also *National Archives*, No. 24721, No. 24722, No. 24723, No. 24725, No. 24726, No. 24731, No. 24735, No. 24740, No. 24742, No. 24743, No. 24746, No. 24749, No. 24751, all acknowledgements of decrees and laws.

I have decided to leave on December 6th next for the canonical visitation of the parishes of the province, delegating in charge of the ecclesiastical government during my absence my Vicar General, Dr. Bernardo Dighero. I hereby inform you for your convenience.

God, Union, Liberty.

Guatemala, November 29, 1823. Fr. Ramón, Archbishop of Guatemala. To the Citizen Chief Executive of Guatemala.[11]

Gradually the tone of the communications changed. The government began to complain about the refusal of various religious to take the oath of allegiance to the Republic. The following correspondence reveals one recalcitrant quickly brought to terms:

February 18, 1824.

The Citizen Secretary of State, Religious Matters and Ecclesiastical Affairs has communicated to me as of yesterday the order of the National Assembly of the 16th of this month by which there was declared revoked the decree of expulsion against Fr. don León Marroquín, of August 22nd last, but without permitting the reassuming of the rights of citizenship until he has proved his adhesion to the system by conclusive action; and that the Chief Executive, on decreeing the above, ordered that the said ecclesiastic should take the oath of recognition and obedience to the constituted authorities in the form specified. God, Union, Liberty. Palace of the Archbishop of Guatemala, Pedro de Bustamante. To the Chief Executive of this Province.[12]

February 20, 1824.

Father León Marroquín, having been notified of the order which you communicated to me in your letter of the 18th of this month, has appeared today to take the oath to which you referred, and I hereby notify you thereof and enclose the certification.

11 *National Archives of Guatemala*, No. 24744, Nov. 29, 1823.

12 *Ibid.*, No. 24813, Feb. 18, 1824.

God, Union, Liberty.   Palace of the Archbishop of Guatemala.   Pedro de Bustamante.   To the Chief
Executive of this Province.[13]

February 28, 1824.

Ecclesiastical Government

I have been informed that the National Assembly has
granted to Father don León Marroquín the rights of citizenship in these states, and that you have communicated this to
the aforesaid priest, as you advise me in your letter of today,
which I hereby acknowledge.

God, Union, Liberty.

Guatemala, February 28, 1824.   Pedro de Bustamante,
To the Citizen Chief Executive of Guatemala.[14]

A Dominican, Fr. Antonio Herrera, was ordered to leave the
Provinces of Central America for refusal to take the oath, and
his Superior indicated to the authorities that he was complying in every way with the directions given for the departure
of the religious:

In accordance with the orders of the Chief Executive of
the 9th of this month, because of the refusal of Fr. Antonio
Herrera to take the oath recognizing the National Assembly,
as you communicated to me on the 10th of this month, I
have ordered the aforementioned religious to prepare to leave
the territory of the United Provinces of Central America within one week, in conformity with the regulations.   For this
purpose he is preparing to present himself today at your office
with the permission which I gave him on the 10th of the
month, in order to obtain the necessary passport.

God, Union, Liberty.

Convent of Santo Domingo of Guatemala, August 18, 1823.
To the Chief Executive.[15]

---

13 *Ibid.*, No. 24815, Feb. 20, 1824.

14 *Ibid.*, No. 24816, Feb. 28, 1824.

15 *Ibid.*, No. 25350, August 18, 1823 (Dominican B83.4).

Again, when a Franciscan, Pedro Contreras, was reported by the civil authorities to have been spreading subversive propaganda, his superior's cooperation with the government in regard to his transferral from Sonsonate to Guatemala was most exemplary and makes interesting reading:

August 7, 1823.

I have received your communication of the 5th of this month in which you send me the order of the Supreme Executive Power that Father Pedro Contreras be transferred from the Convent of Sonsonate to that of Guatemala because he has disseminated in that town false notions and opinions against the liberty of the country.

I was not aware of the activities of this priest; but on receipt of, and in compliance with the order of the government, I have sent notice today to the Guardian of that Convent to inform him of the disposition, and my obedience to it, and have given orders that Contreras is to leave immediately for Guatemala, all of which will, no doubt, be carried out exactly by the Guardian, to whom I also sent the order you enclosed for the local executive in order that he may use it in case of resistance, which I consider quite improbable. On his arrival I shall give a suitable reprimand, and shall watch his conduct in the future.

God grant you many years. Convent of St. Francis, August 7, 1823. Fr. Pedro José Acuerdo. To the Chief Executive of Guatemala, don Tomás O'Horan.[16]

On February 24, 1824 Archbishop Ramón Casáus y Torres wrote a long letter to the Secretary of State in which he registered his protest against what he considered to be an unfair attitude of the Government, which seemed to be suspicious of the Church without the slightest provocation:[17]

16 *Ibid.*, No. 25369, Aug. 7, 1823 (Franciscans B83.5).
17 *Ibid.*, No. 24754, Feb. 24, 1824.

February 24, 1824.

My Vicar General, as an official in charge of the Ecclesiastical government, having received the communication dated the 22nd of this month, a copy of which I enclose (No. 1), answered it on the same date, no decree relative to the taking of the oath to the Constitution of the Republic having been received by the Ecclesiastical Chapter. But on the following day, the 23rd, he received a copy of the Constitution, with Decree No. 120 of the National Constituent Assembly and No. 29 of the Congress of this State; and at the end of the latter the communication of which I enclose a copy (No. 2). In view of this fact, I communicated that same afternoon with the Ecclesiastical Chapter, forwarding the aforementioned copy of the Constitution and the decree, and requesting the Chapter to meet today to take the required oath in the Cathedral in conformity with Article XV of Decree No. 29. I enclose their answer herewith (No. 3) together with my communication to them (No. 4).

Neither this Ecclesiastical Government nor its Chapter has ever given the slightest cause to suspect its submission and obedience to the Government; nor, likewise, the least provocation for its being treated in the manner and with the precipitation manifested by the communications of the Chief Executive.

Nor is it likewise at fault because of the omission resulting from the delay on the part of the Ministry in forwarding to it the Federal Constitution and the decrees which refer to the taking of the oath.

Besides, the Ecclesiastical Government has not been informed of the delegation of the ordinary and extraordinary faculties with which the Chief Executive claims to be endowed, nor of the derogation, in this case, of the decrees of the National Constituent Assembly of November 6 and 23rd, and of the Congress of this State, No. 6 and No. 12, which, arranging for the means by which the laws, decrees and orders were to be communicated, make the Tribunals, heads of governments, superiors and other functionaries responsible for their being carried out by others not expressly mentioned in the decrees themselves.

All this I refer to you in order that you may call it to the attention of the Executive of the State, hoping that he will have me informed for my guidance and for the peace of mind of my clergy, just which are the ordinary and extra-ordinary faculties with which he claims to be invested; and also, in view of the present state of my health, that, when-ever it may be possible, correspondence be carried on with my Vicar General, entrusted with the government of the Church.

God, Union, Liberty, Palace of the Arch-bishop of Guatemala, February 24, 1825. Fr. Ramón, Arch-bishop of Guatemala, to the Citizen Secretary General of this State.

On the other hand, from reading the answer of the Secretary General to the Archbishop,[18] it is made very clear that the authorities had discovered that certain religious were oppos-ing the oath of allegiance, and that they would not tolerate such procedure:

Because it was discovered that the superiors of the religious orders of this *corte* (meaning the political district) were opposing the taking of the oath to the Constitution, and because the authorities would not tolerate any neglect in this matter, it was necessary to delegate to the political government the ordinary and extraordinary faculties apper-taining to the Government for the exact adherence to all that relates to the said oath, in order that the decree of the Na-tional Assembly of November 20th last, and that of November 29th of the Assembly of this State be carried out.

A *providencia* (government order) was sent in order to avoid delay in the carrying out of this matter and to facilitate the changes which the circumstances might demand.

The clergy should not be disturbed by the delegation of those faculties which have been similar to others concerning the oath, and it is not expected that they resist the taking of the oath, since they have given so many proofs of sub-mission to authority.

18 *National Archives of Guatemala*, No. 24754, Feb. 26, 1825.

It is not to be wondered at that the Chief Executive should demand so insistently the certification of the oath, in view of his zeal; in order that the fundamental charter of the Republic of Central America be sworn to, he has not permitted himself to fear lest his scrupulosity be judged contrary to the duties of his office. Neither is there any matter for surprise in the note that the Vicar General would carry on the correspondence in the future because of the indisposition of the archbishop, since he has already done so in official replies directed to this Ministry.

Without it being in any way evident that the Chief Executive has violated the laws concerning the manner of transmitting communications, it has already been decreed that all communications to the Archbishop as well as to the Ecclesiastical Chapter should be made discreetly through this Secretariat.

The Government has the utmost respect and veneration for the clergy and its prelate; it has given proofs and will continue to give proofs that it maintains and will maintain the consideration due to them, and for the same reason, will instruct the public authorities and officials to treat them with the respect due to members of the ecclesiastical state; but, at the same time, the government itself expects that the Archbishop will see to it that the Chapter takes the oath on the day appointed, fully, and without any opposition whatsoever, removing any difficulty which might arise, and remitting the certificates required to the Government.

By order of the Executive Power I communicate the above to the Archbishop, in reply to his documented letter of the 24th of this month. God, Union, Liberty, Guatemala, Feb. 26, 1825. To the Archbishop of the Metropolitan Church of Guatemala.

The battle line was now being drawn up. The historian Marure indicated that in 1825 a peaceful interlude was enjoyed in Guatemala, " all the authorities functioning in the free exercise of their powers and the public order undisturbed except for the slight tumult caused by the religious orders in the capital." [19]

This comment was evoked by an incident which occurred while the religious communities were still in some cases refusing to take the oath to uphold the Constitution. On the 19th of February, 1824, as the Fathers of the Propagation of the Faith were about to open their mission, the officials interfered and ordered their superior to take the oath before he began the mission. When the populace rose up in protest, the National Executive Committee urged the Chief Executive to revoke his order stopping the mission, and demanded that the superior promise that his subjects would take the oath. The latter complied and the mission opened at nine o'clock that night. The Liberals and the civil authorities angrily resented the uprising. The government of the State brought pressure to bear on the religious to take the oath.[20]

Another device was at hand to strengthen the Liberals and the Government—a periodical, " El Melitón ", which began in May, 1825, to ridicule the noble families, the religious and the metropolitan prelate. All the "Serviles" or Conservatives were portrayed to their disadvantage, but the skill of its writers was so striking that even the victims admired the style.[21]

In the elections of April 21, 1825, because the code of the Republic of Central America ruled that only one of the senators from each state in the federation could be an ecclesiastic, Father José María Castilla, one of the nominees for President of Guatemala, was barred. In the local elections three priests were barred: Father José Antonio Alvarado of Sacatepéquez, Father Pedro Solís of Colutea and Father Francisco Márquez of Juticalpa.[22]

19 Marure, *op. cit.*, I, 120.

20 *Ibid.*, p. 121.

21 *Ibid.*, p. 123.

22 García, *op. cit.*, II, 225.

Both parties, Liberals and Conservatives, precipitated a crisis, the Liberals, by their heedless attacks on the clergy, restricting the Archbishop's powers and placing him to some extent under civil authority, suppressing traditional subsidies to parishes and abolishing certain privileges the clergy had till then enjoyed; reducing the tithes, forbidding persons under twenty-five years of age to take monastic vows,[23] and especially ridiculing the members of the clergy. The Conservatives brought on the crisis by fanning, jointly with the clericals, ill feeling among the lower classes whom it was easy to persuade that the Liberal party aimed at the destruction of their religion.[24]

During the latter months of the year 1825, the government began to interfere very actively in the appointment and regulation of the clergy. On October 17th there was issued a decree stating that the ecclesiastic, Fr. José León Taboada, was not to assume the pastorship of Huehuetenango without the consent of the government.[25] An official letter of the government declared that it had taken under its protection in conformity with the laws the Dominican monk Ignacio Barnoya who, emigrating from Chiapas because of the persecution due to his efforts in behalf of absolute independence in Central America, now wished to become secularized in Guatemala. A decree contained in the letter reads:

> The President of the Republic of Central America, bearing in mind the constant fidelity shown to our system of independence and absolute liberty by Fr. Ignacio Barnoya, Dominican, the persecutions and vexations which he has endured for this reason from the authorities of *Ciudad Real*, the strong sentiments of patriotism which he has shown, and finally, the advantages promised by his talents and circumstances when they are dedicated to the cause in this Republic, as he plans, has

23 Marure, *op. cit.*, I, 244.

24 Bancroft, *op. cit.*, III, 628.

25 *National Archives of Guatemala*, No. 24766, October 17, 1825.

resolved to grant his request, declaring that the taking of the oath which must be sworn by this religious and the other necessary details concerning his formal admission are entrusted to the Chief Executive of the respective State, to whom this decree will be forwarded. The Secretary of State will circulate it and make the necessary plans for its fulfillment. National Palace of Guatemala—August 5, 1825—Arce —To the Citizen Juan Francisco de Sosa.[26]

At the very end of the year 1825, the Archbishop was directed to report the number of parishes and priests under his jurisdiction, as well as the income. He complied with this order, especially difficult of execution because of the lack of statistics, on December 30th:[27]

December 30, 1825.
To the Citizen Secretary of the Government of this State.

I remit to you a list of the parishes of the State, their pastors and the incomes which were collected in the year 1815, according as could be calculated from the reports in my office. From then on, the change of circumstances and other events lowered generally the income of the parishes to a third less, which has obliged me to diminish in proportion the pensions upon them, one of which has supported the Colegio Tridentino.

There is no information in the Ecclesiastical government of a statistical nature, nor is it possible to report on population, in accord with your note of the 2nd of this month, to which I hereby reply.

God, Union, Liberty,
Palace of the Archbishop of Guatemala,
December 30, 1825.
Fr. Ramón, Archbishop of Guatemala.

In order better to assure the outcome of their machinations, the "*Serviles*" or Conservatives tried in 1826 to discredit the Liberals among the working classes, making them

26 *Ibid.*, No. 24835, August 5, 1825.
27 *Ibid.*, No. 24769, December 30, 1825.

believe that the preparations being made in the state to maintain its position in the conflict over the federation had as their principal object the destruction of the Catholic faith and the corruption of morals. The conduct of the Liberals at this time did, as a matter of fact, give support to these alarming accusations. They lost no occasion to ridicule the clergy as well as objects and customs regarded as sacred by the people; and, as has been previously noted, in periodicals as well as in private conversations and gatherings, one heard only diatribes against fanaticism and religious intolerance; the religious were mocked in public and there were divulged a thousand injurious anecdotes about them, painting them always as destructive elements which were undermining the social order. Not only did individuals act in such fashion, but the authorities of Guatemala adopted the same methods, and in the first two legislatures laws were passed which reflected the efforts of the Liberals to abolish the privileges of the clergy and make them dependent on civil power.[28] Among these were the law declaring that, in the provision of benefices, the Archbishop should always obtain first the approbation of the Chief Executive of the State,[29] that which ordered suppressed the service and incomes of the parishes,[30] that which abolished the exemption of churches and monasteries from paying duty on merchandise,[31] that which reduced the tithes by one-half,[32] that which determined that natural children were to inherit freely, including those of clerics and religious,[33] that which prohibited, under pain of expulsion, any religious superior performing any act of obedience to, or communicating

28 Marure, *op. cit.*, I, 160.

29 Mecham, *op. cit.*, p. 363.

30 *La Tertulia Patriótica*, No. 4.

31 Order of the Government, Nov. 8, 1824.

32 Decree of June 9, 1826, published in *El Liberal*, No. 36.

33 Decree of June 9, 1826.

with religious superiors in Spain,[34] that which abolished the institute of Carmelites of the Strict Observance, created in the old Convent of Santa Teresa without the approbation of the civil powers, and finally, the decrees of June 10th and July 20th, 1826, forbidding in all convents throughout the territory the entrance of subjects under twenty-three years of age, and their profession before the age of twenty-five years, and declaring that the unprofessed religious, living at that time in the convents of both sexes, could not be professed before the required age.[35]

The law on pastorals was dictated in this same antagonistic spirit—the provisions ran as follows:

1—No pastorals, edicts nor any other notices of the Ecclesiastical government may be published nor circulated without first obtaining the permission of the Chief Executive; the latter is to grant it or refuse it under the same conditions as, according to the law, the said permission was granted or refused to the pontifical Bulls.

2—Before granting or refusing the permission, the Chief Executive will consult the Council of Representatives; or, until the latter has been installed, that of the Congress.[36]

These laws, dictated in general against the clergy, but, as has been seen, sometimes against the Archbishop, irritated the Conservatives beyond measure, and must be considered as one of the causes of the revolt in September, 1826.

There was much agitation to change the opinions of the authors of the aforementioned laws, and some superiors of convents, while they were, on the one hand, appealing to the Assembly for the suspension of the laws, on the other hand, were stirring up the people against the authorities and were referring to them as "heretics" and "enemies of

34 Decree of Sept. 1, 1826.

35 Pineda de Mont, *Recopilación de Leyes de la República de Guatemala,* Guatemala, III, 262.

36 *Ibid.,* III, 250.

monastic institutions." A circular of the Provincial Prior of the Dominicans, dated Feb. 9, 1825, reflects some of the reaction to the laws:

> Miguel José Aycinena, Candidate in Sacred Theology, Provincial Prior of the Order of Preachers of Guatemala, to the Reverend Priors, Masters, Candidates, Preachers, Generals, Readers, Pastors, Administrators and other Religious, health and benediction.
>
> Whereas for an entire year we have endured and are enduring repeated attacks on the sacred rights of our immunity and property, on the part of those very authorities who should protect and preserve them by wise and just laws, as is well known ... I command you, Reverend Fathers, under pain of immediate suspension from duty, not to recognize, obey nor fulfill any decree issued by civil or ecclesiastical order which is not circulated according to our rule, bearing one of the seals of our office and authorized by our secretary, whether it be oaths, secularization of parishes, removal of pastors, suppression or alteration of confraternities, changes in fees, taxation of ecclesiastical possessions harmful to our property, or real estate, or upon any other point which, overlooking spiritual authority, could compromise your consciences and, consequently, ours, and in order that this our resolution have its desired effect and fulfillment, let each religious sign it after he has received it. Convent of St. Dominic of Guatemala, Feb. 9, 1825, F. Miguel José de Aycinena—Prior Provincial—By order of our Reverend Prior—Fr. Anselmo Ortiz, Candidate and Coadjutor.[37]

The editors of *El Indicador,* in spite of the fact that they were supposedly neutral on the question, took up the defense of the religious and wrote against many of the legislative dispositions.[38]

The alarm sown among the populace of the capital by the fanatical language of the partisans of the religious, the dis-

---

[37] *National Archives of Guatemala,* No. 25355, Feb. 9, 1825.

[38] Marure, *op. cit.,* p. 161.

content aroused in the villages by the exaction of unaccus-
tomed taxes, the violence which always accompanied forced
enlistments—all these factors were climaxed in a bitter feeling
against the State.[39] The property of the Conservatives was
almost exclusively affected by the constant demands of Morazán for money to support his forces. Their holdings, as well
as those of the Church, were taxed severely. Cayetano de la
Cerda, collector of taxes, acted without restriction.[40]

In October, 1826, the Lieutenant-General of the State,
Cirilo Flores, who had withdrawn to Quezaltenango when
friction arose between the state and federal governments in
Guatemala City, was received with enthusiasm upon his arrival. However, a tax imposed upon the convent of Quezaltenango aroused the populace against him.[41] The Franciscans,
offended, had the imprudence to say in public that, if the
town permitted them to be insulted, they would retire to their
convent in Guatemala City. At the same time a foreigner
named Pierzon, who had enlisted in the army and risen to
the rank of Lieutenant Colonel of Cavalry, had made a
requisition of horses in the town and had resorted to violence
to procure them. The resentment so evoked played into the
hands of the Franciscans.[42] Before the house where Flores
was stopping a crowd gathered shouting, " Death to the
heretic! " Flores went to the convent to calm the people, but
they clamored for his head. He sought refuge in the church,
where some fanatical women threw themselves upon him and
with great ferocity beat him. The pastor was able to climb
into the pulpit only with great difficulty in an attempt to
subdue the mob, but two Franciscans named Carranza and
Ballesteros murmured among the crowd that they were listen-

39 *Ibid.*, p. 161.

40 Bancroft, *op. cit.*, III, 153.

41 La Renaudière, Philippe F., *Mexique et Guatemala*, Paris, Firmin Didot
Frères, 1843, p. 296.

42 Montúfar y Coronado, *op. cit.*, p. 95.

ing to lies and empty promises.[43] The details of the affair differ somewhat in the various accounts. One version has it that Flores had climbed into the pulpit with a religious who promised that the Lieutenant-Governor Flores would be exiled, but that, at this point, one don Antonio Corzo, with a handful of militia, charged the crowd and this irritated them rather than intimidated them. The women seized Flores and killed him barbarously; they then turned upon the militia and disarmed it; finally, they hunted down the deputies, wounding one and sacking the houses of the others.[44] Many members of the Assembly and the Council were threatened with death, and had to flee for their lives.[45] The townspeople then armed themselves and went to meet Pierzon's troops outside the town. The latter subdued them and entered Quezaltenango on October 19, 1826.[46] The Franciscans were in the end blamed for the uprising. There is no doubt that much of what they had said had been of an inflammatory nature. Their threat to leave Quezaltenango had especially alarmed the natives.

During the years 1827 and 1828, when the Conservatives were in the ascendancy, the documents exchanged continually between the government and church officials bear evidence of more friendly relations. On March 16, 1827 the government urged the ecclesiastical authorities to be more solicitous for the exact collection and administration of the tithes, and to use every means at their disposal for the increase and preservation of them.[47] On March 27, 1827, the ecclesiastical authorities, in reply to a request of the government that pastors exert their influence in the enlisting of troops for the

43 García, *op. cit.*, II, 237.

44 Montúfar y Coronado, *op. cit.*, p. 95.

45 Marure, *Efemérides de los hechos notables acaecidos en la República de Centro América desde el año 1821 hasta él de 1842*, Guatemala, Imprenta de la Paz, 1844, p. 17.

46 Montúfar y Coronado, *op. cit.*, p. 95.

47 *Gaceta del Gobierno del Estado*, No. 7, March 16, 1827.

war against Salvador, declared that " the Ecclesiastical government, so interested in the outcome of the war which has so gloriously commenced, is aiding with all its powers for this result. And for this end, it has urged the pastors to co-operate with the government." [48] In reply to a brief command of the government on November 27, 1827 that the Metropolitan prelate order public prayers for the successful outcome of the efforts of the expeditionary forces, Archbishop Casáus y Torres replied the following day:" The necessary orders have already been given for the holding of public prayers in all the churches for the happy ending of the present war, as the Government has requested." [49] Finally, in order to uphold ecclesiastical censures against certain books, President Aycinena issued the decree of Dec. 6, 1828 which aroused such discontent against his administration, and which contained the following articles :

1—The Archbishop is requested and commissioned to proceed, according to canon law, against all those who, in violation of the edicts already published, introduce or keep in their possession the books or printed matter prohibited therein.

2—The civil and military authorities, whenever requested to do so by the ecclesiastical authorities, will seize such books and printed matter found in the possession of their respective subjects.

3—Without further evidence, there is to be applied to the holders of said books and printed matter the fine of ten *pesos* for the first offense, twenty-five for the second, and fifty for the third; and in default of payment, a corresponding number of days' imprisonment.

4—The proceeds of these fines is to be used for the benefit of the military hospital; and the books and printed matter are to be burned in the presence of the officials of both authorities.

48 *National Archives of Guatemala*, No. 25633, March 27, 1827.

49 *Ibid.*, No. 24776, Nov. 27, 1827; Nov. 28, 1827.

5—The Chief of Police is entrusted with the execution of this decree and will order it printed, published and circulated.[50]

A period of reaction followed Morazán's conquest of Guatemala, reaction to the Conservative Party which had held undisputed control over public affairs.[51] Then on June 22, 1829, the Federal Congress which had been dismissed in October, 1826 assembled, and José Francisco Barrundia became President of the State.

The expulsion of Archbishop Casáus y Torres and of many religious on the midnight between July 10 and 11, 1829, dramatically climaxed the conflict between Church and State which had been building up for a long time.

The years just preceding the first expulsion of an Archbishop during the Republican period were marked by the visits of two Protestant Englishmen to Guatemala. Mr. George Alexander Thompson wrote in 1825 an account of his official visit to Guatemala, and Henry Dunn, an Anglican clergyman, wrote of his experiences there in 1827 and 1828. It is to be noted that both works were published in 1829, although Thompson's visit pre-dated that of Dunn. Thompson's judgments in Church matters were much more tolerant than those of his fellow countryman. In fact, Dunn's purpose in keeping a diary was to show "the true character of the rigid Catholics." [52] And in almost no instance is the picture he drew of the so-called 'rigid' Catholics an edifying one. One must remember that both Dunn and Thompson considered Guatemala from a European point of view. Their observations were not too profound nor reflective of a knowledge of the complexities of the social, political and religious backgrounds.

In regard to the Archbishop, Dunn made no comment, but Thompson found him to be "a man of engaging manners

50 Marure, *Bosquejo histórico*, p. 88.

51 Crowe, Frederick, *The Gospel in Central America*, London, Charles Gilpin, 1850, p. 130.

52 Dunn, *op. cit.*, p. 128.

and vigorous with respect to years and intellect," [53] who invited the Englishman to live at his palace during his sojourn. However, Thompson's letters of introduction had a Mexican source and, since they were from " some of the most respectable of the old Spanish families in Mexico " of whose loyalty to the new government Thompson was dubious, he declined.[54]

Also, be it noted that the Archbishop stated that he had thought it his duty, in the first instance, to oppose the measures of the Independence party as being subversive of the principles of government which he was bound to uphold and by which his authority was protected, but that, as the march of events and public opinion gained ground and as he found it was absolutely the wish of the people at large to have an independent government, he was induced to relax his position and, afterwards, to prevent bloodshed which must naturally have taken place, pending a conflict of such domestic nature, to give his firm and decided support to the newly established government.[55]

The Archbishop, though formerly a friar, became the representative of the secular clergy and his opinions carried weight and influence with the most able ecclesiastics.[56]

Thompson observed that not three-tenths of the population had any political opinions or any notion of that type of temporal authority which causes men to feel an interest in their government.[57] But the other seven-tenths were favorable to independence only because personally they felt its benefits in remission of taxes and the abolition of slavery.[58] It is certainly true today, little more than a century after Thompson's visit, that there are not anywhere near seven tenths of the

53 Thompson, *op. cit.*, p. 142.

54 *Ibid.*, p. 140.

55 *Ibid.*, p. 142.

56 *Ibid.*, p. 143.

57 *Ibid.*, p. 228.

58 *Ibid.*, p. 229.

population of Guatemala who are politically minded. It was also true that the humble portion of the population was so far separated from the seat of government that it was ignorant of formal political organizations, yet they did know their respective parish priest, who was their foremost practical authority and whose example and advice they would follow.

This picture painted by Thompson is of great importance because he was of the opinion that, because most of the village priests were of American birth rather than old Spanish, they were favorable to the new constitutions. One of the main reasons for this attitude was the fact that under the colonial system all the highest clerical appointments were given to the Spaniards.[59] This matter comes up again and again, even to the present day when one can still observe the remnants of cleavage between the Spanish clergy and the native born. It is also a point relevant to the general charges eventually made by various Republican officials that seemed to imply that the clergy as a whole were disloyal to the government.

In contrast with Thompson, the Anglican clergyman was much concerned with the ignorance and superstition of the " lower orders " of the population, and their condition he attributed to the practices of the Church of Rome.[60] He deplored the lack of copies of the Bible [61] and other books, and was of the opinion that the clergy were reactionary and, in some instances, actually hopeful of the retention of power by the Spaniards.[62] Although some of the priests encountered were intelligent,[63] many were " sottish " [64] and " dissipated " (they actually played cards on Sunday and did not think it un-

59 *Ibid.*, p. 230.

60 Dunn, *op. cit.*, p. 85.

61 *Ibid.*, pp. 51, 123, 128.

62 *Ibid.*, p. 117.

63 *Ibid.*, pp. 128, 302.

64 *Ibid.*, p. 51.

suitable employment of the day).[65] He concluded that it was a general but suppressed feeling among the clergy that printing and education should be forbidden to the Indians, for the use of these two media of enlightenment would result in their being ungovernable.[66] This attitude may be somewhat better understood in view of the fact that, during the era of discovery and conquest, a very heated and lengthy discussion had gone on, settled in the affirmative by Brief of Pope Paul III on June 10, 1537, as to whether the Indians should be considered as human beings or not.[67] The influence of remnants of this attitude are still apparent in Guatemala today. It is not unusual to hear in casual conversation the point made over and over again that the Indians live like animals, breed like them and that, at the present time, they are becoming ungovernable because of "Communistic" agitation in their midst.

It may be recalled that, as of the law of Oct. 11, 1825, the religion of the State was "Catholic, Apostolic and Roman, to the exclusion of the public exercise of any other whatsoever."[68] In regard to this, the Archbishop observed that there was no objection to the private worship of Protestant denominations and that the Guatemalan constitution was as liberal as possible under the circumstances, in contrast to the Mexican, which prohibited the existence of any other religion except the Catholic.[69]

Although this attitude was undoubtedly shared by the hierarchy, Thompson very much doubted that any one professing a faith other than the established one would suffer any slight or any difficulty unless he directly violated the re-

65 *Ibid.*, pp. 123-140.

66 *Ibid.*, p. 135.

67 Herrera y Tordesillas, Antonio de, *Historia general de los hechos de los castellanos en las islas i tierra firme del Mar*, Madrid, 1601, p. 141.

68 Pineda de Mont, *Recopilación de Leyes de la República de Guatemala*, III, 251, Book IX, Title I, Law 6.

69 Mecham, *Church and State in Latin America*, p. 401.

ligious feelings of the people.[70] (In recent times the religious feelings of the natives have been offended particularly when tourists from the United States have invaded the churches to take pictures of the worshippers. The Indians have been known to become very excited and to object. Now, in the majority of the churches, multi-lingual signs forbid such activity on the part of visitors. I was never molested, however, and took pictures inside the churches with the consent of the Archbishop and certain parish priests whenever I wished). Thompson's conclusion was that the clergy of Guatemala were no unimportant part of the political establishment, and that the relationship between Church and State was that of friendly understanding.[71]

Both Thompson and Dunn treated in some detail the different difficulties which arose when the people of Salvador appointed Dr. Delgado a Bishop without the consent of Archbishop Casáus y Torres, who very naturally was not pleased, and refused to confirm the appointment.[72] The Archbishop's reply to the request of the President of the Republic, sent through the Chief Executive of the State of Guatemala, urging him to withdraw his opposition, was definite and final and ran as follows:

To the Citizen Secretary of the Government of the State:

With your letter of the 7th of this month, I have received a copy of that addressed to the Chief Executive of this State by the President of the Republic, who, following the advice of the Senate, has ordered that I be persuaded to suspend my action in regard to the erection of a bishopric in San Salvador, the election of a bishop and the taking possession by the one chosen. I regret deeply not being able to comply with the request of the Supreme Executive Power in this matter. I am Archbishop, and must act as such, nor can I abandon

70 Thompson, *op. cit.*, p. 148.

71 *Ibid.*

72 *Cf. supra*, pp. 64, 65.

the flock which God has placed in my care and under my pastoral jurisdiction. It is not within my power to break this bond, nor make this sacrifice in favor of anyone. I am strictly bound and am responsible to God and the Church in upholding the rights of my episcopal and metropolitan dignity. No one can be ignorant of what my conscience has obliged me to answer repeated times, that what has been done in San Salvador in this matter is a violation and abuse of the divine power in the governing of the Church. The peace and security of consciences, the purity of religion, the validity and lawful administration of the sacraments on which depends the eternal salvation of the souls which God has placed under my responsibility are all concerned in this matter. How, then, can a Bishop prescind from its results? How can he tolerate the authorization directly or indirectly of any intrusion in the spiritual government of souls, or the naming by a civil power of pastors, or the granting by that power of the faculties for hearing confessions or administering the other sacraments? Silence and dissimulation in regard to such errors once placed in execution would be the most scandalous prevarication. My conduct in this particular has been evident to all ... I have used all the legal means available; I have regretted their in-efficacy, hoping for an outcome which might spare me the pain of using the spiritual arms of religion against subjects who have been members of my clergy and over whose salvation and obstinacy I grieve.

Far from arousing and urging the pastors to leave their parishes, as has been calumniously imputed to me, I have expressly ordered them not to abandon them, until violence should drive them from the said parishes. Conditions have reached such a state that the towns no longer have pastors; there have been substituted for them men without morals, jurisdiction or religion. If the people refuse to endure this evil, the greatest which could befall them, if they come to realize that those whom they chose to bring about their well-being are oppressing them in regard to their dearest and most sacred interests ... if they themselves undertake to maintain their religion and its rights, and there takes place in Salvador what has happened in every country oppressed by tyrants,

I am not guilty of those lamentable results. Those are and will be considered guilty who have caused them, and the authority, constituted to maintain order, peace and religion, if its measures are not directed to that object.

The noblest and most sacred possession of this Catholic nation is that of the religion which it professes, and the free exercise of it, with the protection of its legitimate ministers. To persecute them is to bring about anarchy and schism, civil and religious wars. The innovators in matters concerning the authority of bishops and their canonical mission have no care for the consequences of their ambitious temerity... I have said before and I repeat it now, I am disposed and ready to adopt all the religious and political means of conciliation within my power and in conformity with the laws of the Church... but to abandon my soul, my honor and authority to serve the ambition of certain ecclesiastics, to withdraw my opposition, indispensable to my responsibility, to what has been done in that State and recognize and approve directly or indirectly any infractions of canon law and of the general ecclesiastical discipline... this is not within my power; nor to give the slightest indication of recognition of such a mitre erected in my diocese, or of considering as bishop a pastor who has appropriated to himself that jurisdiction... any more than it is in the power of the President of the Republic to permit San Salvador to change the political constitution which it has sworn to maintain... I fear no unjust threats, I forget and forgive offenses and injuries. Kindly present to the Government this reply, with the protestation of my respect and consideration. God, Union, Liberty. Palace of the Archbishop of Guatemala, January 18, 1826.[73]

Dunn was of the opinion that the whole affair and other disputes would strike a fatal blow at the influence of the Church, because of the rising tide of infidelity among the middle class of Guatemala. This disaffection was perceived by some of the clergy who were apprehensive about " the prevailing spirit among the people to penetrate into mysteries, and both in

[73] Vilanova Meléndez, *op. cit.*, pp. 63-65.

public and private to ridicule the dogmas of religion "—and the contagion was spreading far and wide.[74]

Thus did two English Protestants view the scene practically on the eve of the expulsion of the archbishop and the religious orders. It is interesting to note that, if one can blow away the bigotry that beclouds Dunn's commentaries in connection with " Popish " customs, his observations were often keen and quite remarkable. Thompson, on the other hand, while more objective, was certainly over-optimistic about the friendliness and understanding that he thought existed between Church and State.

As is to be expected in a situation so highly controversial as this one, historians have given differing impressions of the actual expulsion. The government insisted that Archbishop Casáus y Torres had been from the beginning an enemy of the Republic, who with various religious had been plotting subversively.

It is certainly easy to prove that Archbishop Casáus y Torres, as well as other clergymen, had opposed the separation from Spain, from his pastoral letters, edicts, sermons and even from an indulgence of eighty days which he had granted, as early as the Mexican revolt against Spain, to Guatemalans who refrained from participation in that revolutionary movement.[75] There can be no doubt that a number hoped for the restoration of Spanish power and their traditional privileges, but actually it seems to be extremely doubtful as to whether, at the time of the arrests and expulsion of the ecclesiastics, there had been any definite conspiracy. It is impossible to find documentary proof to this effect, although there is no dearth of source material about the situation immediately after the incidents. Certainly it would seem that

74 Dunn, *op. cit.*, p. 119.

75 *Cf. supra*, p. 67; Marure, *Bosquejo histórico de las Revoluciones de Centro-América*, I, 7; Montúfar y Rivera, *op. cit.*, V, 12; Salazar, *op. cit.*, p. 180.

any writer like Lorenzo Montúfar y Rivera, who had access to the Archives through his official position as compiler of the Constitutions under Barrios and who took great pains to justify the government, would have made the most of publicizing actual proofs of specific conspiracy. The charge may have been published by the government, as has been suggested, simply with a view to furnish a cause for its contemplated action in the eyes of the nation—especially since the officials who were arrested as fellow conspirators were released quietly, shortly after the accused clergy had been taken from the city. Finally, although the primary reason for the expulsion of the religious from Guatemala was the belief that they were a menace to the government, subsequent events showed that the political leaders of the time were not indifferent to the possessions of the religious which might help to replenish a sorely depleted treasury and maintain the army which was keeping them in power.[76]

As has been noted, there is not much material available which is concerned with the preliminaries of the expulsion. However, there are some documents of the time which seem to foreshadow the drastic measures to come. In a letter dated Jan. 5, 1829, the Chief Executive requested the Vicar General of the archdiocese to remit to him inventories of the treasures of the churches in the city of Guatemala.[77] The following day the Vicar General replied that he would send the inventories demanded.[78] On January 12th the government issued a decree declaring that the possessions of the churches would be turned over to the National Treasury.[79] On May 11th the government, impatient at the delay of the

76 William, Mary W., " Ecclesiastical Policy of Francisco Morazán and the Other Central Americaan Liberals ", *Hispanic American Historical Review*, III, No. 2 (1920), 132.

77 *National Archives of Guatemala*, No. 24846, Jan. 5, 1829.

78 *Ibid.*, No. 24847, Jan. 6, 1829.

79 *Ibid.*, No. 24848, Jan. 12, 1829.

church authorities in handing over the treasures, sent a sharp reminder reading as follows:

May 11, 1829.

To the Vicar General of this Archdiocese:

On February 23rd last I informed you on the part of the Government that it wished to hasten the turning over of the jewels and silver of the churches for the benefit of the National Treasury and urged you at that time to assist in smoothing over any difficulties which might arise in the matter, and co-operate in the prompt fulfilling of that order.

There has been no response to date. The National Treasury, deprived of the income it might have acquired from these articles, becomes daily more exhausted because of the increased demands occasioned by the war.

Therefore, since the jewels and silver will never be needed for public worship; since, even if they were, the Church should hand them over for the public welfare and, finally, because, if the Church refused to give them to the State, they might be taken by the enemy—the Government orders you to remit the jewels and silver without delay for the prosecution of the war and so that they may be used in the important object of our defense, especially since, in addition to the reasons repeatedly proposed by the Government, there has been and should be the one that the said property is a powerful incentive to the greed of the enemy, and might, if in their possession, aid them in capturing the capital.

The Government is confident that you will conclude this matter as soon as possible. I reiterate my protestations of consideration. God, Union, Liberty, May 11, 1829.[80]

This brought a reply the next day in the form of a list of the treasures which the Vicar General declared he was hand-ing over to the Government.[81] In this expropriation, which included possessions from the churches of the religious orders in the capital, can be seen a step toward the nationalization of all the goods of the religious orders.

80 *Ibid.*, No. 24849, May 11, 1829.
81 *Ibid.*, No. 24850, May 12, 1829.

Documentary evidence was found, likewise, of a ground-work laid for facilitating the expulsion of the religious orders. A letter of Morazán dated May 11, 1829 opened the way:

Federal Republic of Central America.

May 11, 1829.

To the Citizen Minister General of the Supreme Government of this State:

Ever since I took possession of this city, I have sought to overcome the influence exerted by certain priests in public affairs, bringing pressure to bear on the people and obliging them to aid the enemies of the State.

For this reason I spoke to the Reverend Archbishop and manifested to him the necessity of removing those pastors and putting in their places others who had given proof of adhesion to our cause, proposing to him for that purpose those whom I have included on the list which I sent you. The Archbishop agreed to all and has already sent out his orders.

So that these may be effective and so that the pastors who have been removed may not prevent the taking over of the parishes by those named thereto, I hope that your government will issue orders to the various officials in order that they may smooth the way for the coming of the new pastors and report to the Ministry any who do not appear, or any who fail to show respect to the Archbishop or to the other priests.

As those removed must go to Antigua to remain there for the present, they will dwell in private homes, or in their convents, or in some place indicated for them by the government of the said city, and as those who, in the opinion of the government, have no means of subsistence are to receive a monthly pension from the government treasury, it has seemed well for me to inform them through you.

I take advantage of this opportunity to manifest to you my deep appreciation.

God, Union, Liberty.

F. Morazán.[82]

82 *Ibid.*, No. 25502, May 11, 1829.

On May 18th the Supreme Government of Guatemala, in compliance with Morazán's request, sent to all the town officials
a list of the pastors to be removed and those who would replace them, asking the officials to cooperate in sending all
religious back to their motherhouses within twenty days.[83]
There followed a whole series of communications from officials of the different departments announcing their compliance
with the order, claiming some special exemptions for the religious of their parishes, or declaring that the religious must
wait the arrival of the newly appointed secular pastor. On
May 24th the Vicar General sent to the government a list
of the parishes filled up to that date by ecclesiastics proposed
by General Morazán and the government of the State.[84] The
Archbishop, as Morazán declared in his letter, had already
sent orders to the clergy on April 25th, as is evident from a
letter of the Superior of the Dominicans, dated April 27,
1829, announcing that they would comply at once.[85] On June
12th a circular was sent to the officials of all departments
urging prompt obedience to the order to send the religious
without delay to their motherhouse:

Circular

June 12, 1829.

To the Chief of the Department of ――――――.

The Chief Executive of Guatemala declares that in complying with his order to send all religious to their motherhouses
you are to take particular care that they do not delay en route.
Make sure, likewise, that none depart or travel without a passport. God, Liberty. Guatemala, June 12/29.[86]

A letter from the Vicar General of the archdiocese to the
government dated, June 16, 1829, protested against one of

83 *Ibid.*, No. 25502, May 18, 1829.
84 *Ibid.*, No. 25502, May 24, 1829.
85 *Ibid.*, No. 25502, May 27, 1829.
86 *Ibid.*, No. 25502, June 12, 1829.

the temporary appointments of Morazán, regretting that " the ecclesiastical government, which should at all times show itself in harmony with the government of the State, cannot, in this instance, defer entirely to the desires of the Supreme Government." [87] On June 19th, the Vicar General sent a list showing the parishes of the archdiocese whose pastors had not been changed (they were evidently sympathetic toward the régime), and those whose pastors had been removed. These latter were replaced by pastors chosen by Morazán and the government of the State. Out of 43 parishes listed, 18 had new pastors.[88] On July 4, 1829, just previous to the expulsion, in conformity with a decree granting amnesty to those who had taken part against the Liberals from 1826 on, but excluding those who " showed sympathy for or aided the cause of the usurpers ", condemning them to expulsion, certain ecclesiastics were imprisoned in the Convent of Belén to await sentence, among them don Antonio Croquer, Canon of the Cathedral of Guatemala, don Mariano Rodríguez, Treasurer of the Archdiocese, Dr. don Angel María Candina, pastor of the Church of Calvario in Guatemala.[89] On July 9th the Chief Executive of the State requested and received from the National Assembly extraordinary faculties which might be delegated to a trustworthy person in order to combat a conspiracy discovered by Morazán. The decree reads as follows :

> The Legislative Assembly of the State of Guatemala, considering that it is absolutely necessary to dictate the most prompt and energetic measures to preserve order and prosecute its disturbers, has determined to decree and hereby decrees: first—that there be granted extraordinary faculties to the Government for the period considered necessary for the restoration of order, to act in all cases necessary to secure it.

87 *Ibid.*, No. 25502, June 16, 1829.

88 *Ibid.*, No. 25502, June 19, 1829.

89 Arce, *op. cit.*, p. 113.

Second—The government may delegate these faculties for the time considered necessary to a person in its confidence.

Given at Guatemala, July 9, 1829.[90]

These are the faculties which Morazán later claimed to have used in the expulsion of the archbishop and the religious. Lorenzo Montúfar's comment on this matter makes interesting reading:

> It is evident that it was a case of granting the Government the faculties to enable it to proceed to the expulsion of those seized, and that the person in its confidence to whom it might delegate these faculties was General Morazán.
>
> The Government with these faculties proceeded to carry out on a small scale some of the secret measures adopted on a large scale by the Council of Castile to prepare for the decree which Charles II dictated against the Jesuits. At midnight of the 10th and 11th of July the Archbishop in his Palace and the monks of St. Dominic, St. Francis and the Recollets in their respective convents were taken and conducted to Gualan . . . [91]

In view of the preceding documents there is no cause for wonder at the events of July 10th and 11th.

There is a great deal of information descriptive of the actual expulsion and subsequent events related to it. One account mentions that there was unusual military activity in the barracks and in the main square all day on July 10, 1829, and that, at twilight, small groups of soldiers were sent to the Dominican, Franciscan and Recollet convents to prevent the escape of any religious.[92] Between nine and ten o'clock that evening the superiors received word from Morazán that they were to assemble their communities by 10:30 P. M. to

90 Montúfar y Rivera, *op. cit.*, I, 155.

91 *Ibid.*, p. 156.

92 "Apuntamientos para la Historia de la Revolución de Centro-América," San Cristóbal de Chiapas, 1829 (Anonymous work copied by F. D. L. and found in the Archives of Guatemala), p. 142.

meet with government officials, whereupon an investigation would be held to determine whether or not the Orders were actually concealing guns, cannons, munitions and other war materials preparatory to conspiring against the government. The representatives of the government did not appear at the appointed hour, and the religious retired, only to be summoned again at midnight.

It will be recalled that the government had earlier in the year 1829 ordered inventories of Church possessions,[93] and the compilation of lists of priests and pastors.[94] At the time the Church authorities complied, it would seem that there was no realization on their part of what actually motivated the request. However, when, on July 6, 1829, the Superiors of of the Dominicans, Franciscans and the Order of Recollets were requested to submit such lists, as documents in their respective Archives prove, there could have been little doubt left.[95] On the eve of the expulsion the officers commanded by Morazán read the names from the lists and ordered the individuals to leave immediately without manifesting to them any causes or crime for which they were being exiled.[96]

Manuel Montúfar y Coronado, who was of the opinion that Morazán dominated Archbishop Casáus y Torres, ventured to state that when the former saw he could not make further use of the Archbishop, he had the churchman expelled from his palace. All the servants were first locked in one room; the unprepared Archbishop was ordered to leave his bed and conducted out of the city without being given time to get his papers or any money. The Archbishop and the religious who accompanied him were taken to the port of Omoa,

93 *Cf. supra*, p. 100.

94 *Cf. supra*, p. 85.

95 *National Archives of Guatemala*, No. 25360, July 8, 1829; No. 25361, July 10, 1829 (Dominican B83.4); No. 25387, July 6, 1829 (Franciscan B83.5); No. 25412, July 6, 1829 (Recollets B83.6).

96 "Apuntamientos para la Historia de la Revolución de Centro-América", p. 143.

whence they embarked for Havana, while others went to New Orleans.[97] There are stories to the effect that they were treated with scant courtesy, and that the Archbishop was ridiculed.[98] The more reasonable view seems to be that in those days the very length of time required for such trips (sixteen days to Havana, fifty-two to New Orleans), the rough and limited quarters, the coarse food, bad water—all these factors made for great discomforts, especially for the aged. The fact that some of the religious died was made much of by the opposition.[99]

The documents dated July 11, 1829 and immediately after the expulsion are of interest for various reasons. The expulsion, having been carried out at midnight between the 10th and 11th of July, the government showed considerable care about explanatory details after the military powers had taken the action of exiling the Archbishop. As soon as the latter and the religious had gone, the President of the Republic, José Francisco Barrundia, sent a message to the Federal Congress in which he declared that, because of the necessity for secrecy, he had not communicated the project of the expulsion to the legislative power. However, the State government was ready to acquiesce to the desires of the national representation and, as the Archbishop and religious were still within the territory of the State, they would be brought back if that august body so desired. The Federal Congress approved the action of the State government and thanked the Executive authority for his efforts.[100]

The day following the expulsion must have been an extremely busy one for the government. First of all, it distributed a circular which contained the following announcement:

97 Montúfar y Coronado, *op. cit.*, p. 199.

98 "Apuntamientos para la Historia de la Revolución de Centro-América", p. 143.

99 Montúfar y Coronado, *op. cit.*, p. 199.

100 Montúfar, Rafael, *El General Francisco Morazán*, Guatemala, Tipografía Americana, 1896, p. 147.

The General in Chief of the Armed Forces, Francisco Morazán, to whom the Supreme Government of the State has delegated the extraordinary faculties invested in it by the Constitution and by the express consent of the Assembly, proceeded, in accord with the Government and the President of the Republic, to banish last night from the Republic the members of religious orders, leaving in each convent one who would care for the spiritual needs and safeguard the goods and temporalities.[101]

Then the Vicar-General was requested to deliver to the Archbishop a letter from the Government which urged him to delegate his faculties to the Vicar-General so that the latter might attend to the spiritual needs of the inhabitants of the diocese.[102] The nature of this particular letter from the Chief Executive to the Archbishop seems to be strangely contradictory because it stated flatly, on the one hand, that General Morazán was determined to remove the Archbishop from the exercise of his functions and, on the other hand, proceeded to comment on the love and zeal with which the churchman had always worked for the welfare of his flock, without permitting the slightest deviation from duty in circumstances so grave and difficult. This amazing epistle closed with a reiteration of sentiments of deepest respect and consideration from the Chief Executive![103] The Archbishop, already on his way to exile, complied,[104] and the Government of the State issued a decree announcing the delegation of powers, to the Vicar General, to the President of the Republic and to the Legislative Assembly.[105] In another document dated July 11, 1829 there is a report of the Committee appointed to determine pensions for the Archbishop and religious who have

101 *National Archives of Guatemala*, No. 25481, July 11, 1829.

102 *Ibid.*, No. 25465, July 11, 1829.

103 *Ibid.*, No. 25462, July 11, 1829.

104 *Ibid.*, No. 25466, July 12, 1829.

105 *Ibid.*, No. 25466, July 13, 1829.

been expelled;[106] and a decree based on this report was issued the same day,[107] granting to the religious a life pension based on the value of their goods sequestered by the government.[108] Still another document dated July 11, 1829 contained an order to the Vicar General of the Archdiocese to make an inventory of the possessions and furnishings of the Archbishop's palace.[109] The next day, July 12th, Archbishop Casáus y Torres acknowledged receipt of the pension offer and designated his secretary, Fr. don José Mariano Herrarte as his agent to collect the payments from the government and to make certain claims before the government in behalf of his superior.[110] On the 12th, the Vicar General was ordered to prepare a list of any religious still living in the convents of the Dominicans, Franciscans or Recollets, and to regulate the discipline of those houses for those lawfully left behind to guard the property.[111] On the same day the Commandant General was ordered to relax the imprisonment of some of the religious held in the Convent of Belén, because of feebleness and ill-health.[112] On July 13, 1829, the Chief Executive sent to the Commander in Chief of the Armed Forces, Francisco Morazán, a decree ordering an inventory of the possessions of all the religious houses of the State and the taking into custody with the "most inviolable secrecy and precaution" of all religious not yet expelled.[113] On July 14th there was issued a decree secularizing the choristers and lay brothers of the communities of St. Dominic, St. Francis and the Recollets.

106 *Ibid.*, No. 25461, July 11, 1829.
107 *Ibid.*
108 *Ibid.*, No. 25460, July 11, 1829.
109 *Ibid.*, No. 25459, July 11, 1829.
110 *Ibid.*, No. 24466, July 12, 1829.
111 *Ibid.*, No. 25506 (Secularization B83.13) July 12, 1829.
112 *Ibid.*, No. 25463 (Expulsion B83.12) July 12, 1829.
113 *Ibid.*, No. 25458 (Expulsion B83.12) July 13, 1829.

Most interesting in this connection are the documents referring to providing the religious with secular clothing:

July 20, 1829

The Government orders me to request you to have made as many complete outfits of secular clothing as there are lay brothers being secularized, the list of whom you may obtain from the Vicar General.

July 20. To Citizen Damaso Angulo.[114]

July 20, 1829

To Citizen Damaso Angulo:

Just as I told you on the eighteenth of this month, you will proceed to make the clerical clothes for the † s.[115]

August 17, 1829

To the Citizen Secretary General of the Government of the State:

I have learned from your note of the 13th of this month of the order given to Citizen Damasao Angulo by the Supreme Government for the provision of secular clothing and clerical outfits which are necessary for the poor religious just secularized, and hereby acknowledge it.

God, Union, Liberty.

Guatemala, Aug. 17, 1829.   J. Antonio Alcayaga.[116]

On July 15th, the Vicar General was asked to draw up a list of choristers, religious and lay brothers living in the capital, with their names, nationality, residence and rank.[117] All these events culminated in a decree which seemed to harmonize with the general agreement among the Liberal leaders in the province that the Church in all its branches should be placed beyond the possibility of harming the Liberal cause. The Legislative Assembly of Guatemala suppressed monastic estab-

114 *Ibid.*, No. 25515 (Secularization B83.13) July 20, 1829.

115 *Ibid.*

116 *Ibid.*, No. 25564, Aug. 17, 1829.

117 *Ibid.*, No. 25510 (Secularization B83.13) July 15, 1829.

lishments of men throughout the province, as inconsistent with republican freedom and equality, and on account of the hostility of the majority of their members against the new institutions.[118] An exception was made in the case of the Bethlemite Hospitallers who were engaged in teaching and caring for the sick, and had escaped suspicion. They were permitted to remain as secular priests.[119] In response to Article 4 of the decree of suppression, which permitted any of the religious to ask for secularization, there was a host of petitions as is evident from documents in the National Archives of Guatemala, under the title " Secularization B83.13." By June 18, 1830 there had been 86 petitions, some including the names of several individuals.

All the property of the suppressed establishments was confiscated by the State. Their buildings were put to various secular uses, generally in order to carry out the progressive plans of the Liberals.

The most valuable possessions confiscated were the landed properties, but the government had difficulty selling them, and the estates for the most part had to be leased. Both as regards the amount of treasure found in the convents and the ultimate disposal of it, commentators of the time differ. Haefkens was of the opinion that it did not come up to the expectations of the Liberals, while Manuel Montúfar y Coronado says it exceeded them. Arce seems to agree with the latter. According to Montúfar, the government ordered some of the sacred vessels and other articles of value and fine workmanship transferred to the cathedral, some distributed among the poorer parishes, and the remainder of the gold and silver melted down and coined into money.[120]

The Act suppressing religious orders was approved by the Federal Congress on September 7, 1829 and it was declared

118 Williams, *op. cit.*, p. 137.

119 Marure, *Efemérides*, p. 25.

120 Williams, *op. cit.*, p. 136.

that religious orders would no longer be received or recognized in the land; and the various provinces of the Confederation of Central America quickly ratified the declaration.[121] The messages from the various states are strikingly similar in tone, namely condemning the Archbishop and the religious for having taken an active part in the Revolution and for embracing the cause of the enemy. The heroism of the Guatemalan authorities was praised. Nothing but good could result from having the unhappy inhabitants of the country freed of the weight of supporting groups of selfish men who had long since forgotten their duties and obligations and who by their evil machinations were a constant threat to republican institutions!

In view of the fact that many years had elapsed between the Revolution in 1821 and the expulsion in 1829, it seems strange that the authorities waited so long to act against these " enemies." Likewise it is astonishing that the Archbishop was immediately granted a life pension of two-thirds of his income by the very authorities which expelled him. Not until almost a year later, June 13, 1830, was he officially declared to be a traitor. And that decree might reasonably be called a piece of retro-active legislation.

At the very time of all this anti-clerical legislation, as Lorenzo Montúfar y Rivera notes, the custom of combining religious acts with political, and vice-versa, was so strong that, according to a decree dated August 22, 1829, the ceremony for taking possession of an office under the Legislative Assembly of the State of Guatemala was to be the same as had always been in use: the oath taken in the presence of the President of the Assembly, a *Te Deum* in the Cathedral with the attendance of the Ecclesiastical Chapter and all the pastors of the city, and the ringing of bells and salvos of artillery. Furthermore, the Federal Congress, restored on September 1, 1829, ordered that throughout the republic

121 *National Archives of Guatemala*, No. 25458 (Expulsion B83.12); No. 25458, September 3, 1829.

there should be solemnly celebrated the inauguration of the pontificate of Pius VIII! [122]

Early in 1830 the government of Guatemala sent a diplomatic mission to the Holy See to assure the Holy Father of the desires of the authorities and citizens of the State of Guatemala to remain united to the head of the Church and to have legitimate pastors, to explain the expulsion of the Archbishop and religious with the causes motivating it, to request His Holiness to name a new Archbishop from a list to be drawn up by the government with information from the Ecclesiastical Chapter and suggestions of the Representative Council, while communicating temporary faculties to the Ecclesiastical Chapter of Guatemala and, finally, to authorize the secularization of certain religious who had been permitted to remain in Guatemala on the presumption that they would receive such papal authorization.[123]

Meanwhile the government was occupied with the exiled Archbishop himself. Measures were dictated on February 23, 1830 to learn whether the prelate had left Havana for Spain, according to rumor.[124] On April 1st the Vicar General Alcayaga forwarded to the government a note from the Archbishop withdrawing from him the faculties conferred before the latter's departure for Havana.[125] The Vicar General declared that he feared the note might cause disturbances in El Salvador if its contents were known because he had just named Dr. José Matías Delgado as Vicar of Salvador, declaring him to be "the most worthy and fitting ecclesiastic, not only to be Vicar General, but also Bishop of the State of Salvador." The exiled Archbishop cancelled the nomination and substituted that of Fr. José Ignacio Avila.[126] In view of

122 Montúfar y Rivera, op. cit., p. 175.
123 National Archives of Guatemala, No. 24789, Feb. 22, 1830.
124 Ibid., No. 24787, Feb. 23, 1830.
125 Ibid., No. 25466, April 1, 1830.
126 Valladares, op. cit., p. 45.

the old opposition of Archbishop Casáus y Torres to Dr.
Delgado, as well as the fact that he had been forced by Morazán to name Dr. Alcayaga as Vicar General of the Archdiocese,[127] and, on his expulsion, to grant the latter his faculties,[128] the action of the Archbishop is easily understood. In
view of the conflict between Guatemala and El Salvador ever
since 1811 over the bishopric question so closely connected
with Dr. Delgado, the fears of the Vicar General are equally
comprehensible.

Immediately on receipt of the note forwarded by the Vicar
General, the Supreme Government sent copies of it to the Legislative Assembly,[129] together with copies of a private letter
addressed from Havana in which the government believed
there was clearly indicated the existence of plots against independence.[130] The result was Order No. 78, dated April 6,
1830, commanding a search for evidence of political intrigue
carried on by Archbishop Casáus y Torres.[131]

Meanwhile the Vicar General Alcayaga wrote to the Supreme Government declaring that, as he had been named
Deputy to the Federal Congress from Sacatepéquez and
found his new duties incompatible with that of governing the
archdiocese, he was resigning his office in favor of don Diego
Batres, second alternative appointed by Archbishop Casáus
y Torres on his expulsion, the first alternative, don Pedro
Bustamante, being absent.[132]

On June 13, 1830 the Legislative Assembly of the State
of Guatemala decreed the perpetual banishment from the territory of the State of Archbishop Casáus y Torres, declared

127 Montúfar y Coronado, op. cit., p. 170.

128 National Archives of Guatemala, No. 25462, July 11, 1829.

129 Ibid., No. 25466, April 1, 1830.

130 Ibid., No. 25466, Jan. 30, 1830.

131 Ibid., No. 25466, April 6, 1830.

132 Ibid., No. 24874, April 31, 1830.

him a traitor and his See vacant.[133] On July 20, 1830 the Archbishop was notified of the action taken by the government of Guatemala in the following curt message, over a year after the actual expulsion!

> To the Illustrious and Most Reverend don Ramón Casáus y Torres:
>
> The Legislative Assembly of the State of Guatemala has issued a decree declaring Your Excellency incompetent for the governing of this Church; and by order of the President of the State I hereby communicate it to Your Excellency to whom I have the honor of offering my deepest consideration and profound respect.
>
> God, Union, Liberty,
> Guatemala, July 20, 1830.[134]

The decree of June 13th was communicated to the Ecclesiastical Chapter in order that it might comply with Article 5, calling for the naming of a Vicar. Only four members of the Chapter were present at the sessions and they differed in opinion as to their right to name a Vicar in the given circumstances. According to the laws of the Church, when there is a vacant See, the jurisdiction of the Bishop falls on the Chapter, which names a Vicar General to exercise the power. But some members of the Chapter said that Fray Ramón had not died, and that a decree of the Legislative Power could not dissolve what they called the bond between the See and its Bishop; hence, the See was not vacant. Fr. Martínez said, however, that the jurisdiction of the Bishop expired not only by death, but also by transfer, renunciation, exchange and deposition, and, at times, civil death. Fr. Larrazábal was of the opinion that either the person who now held the office should continue in it, or that the Chapter should elect another in the manner dictated by the Council of Trent. Fr. Valdes and Canon Castilla declared that when the Bishop was expelled by

133 *Ibid.*, No. 25466, June 13, 1830.
134 *Ibid.*, No. 24789, July 20, 1830.

political jurisdiction his Vicar General should govern, but that they could not name a Vicar General since the one named by the Archbishop was still in office.[135] On July 31, the Government, exasperated over their delay, ordered them to comply with the command within twenty-four hours:

> To the Vicar General and the Ecclesiastical Chapter:
>
> The delay on the part of the Ecclesiastical Chapter in complying with Article V of the law of June 13th, which declares this archepiscopal See vacant, being already scandalous, and the Chief Executive considering that this delay deceives the public which desires the fulfilling of the laws, and that it may have its origin in principles quite unfavorable to the tranquility of the public or in some deference toward the expelled Archbishop, departing dangerously from the required obedience to the law, the Supreme Government orders me to request the Chapter to comply with the aforesaid matter within the prescribed period of twenty-four hours, naming the Vicar General of the Chapter as is there expressed, and within forty-eight hours remit to this office a certified copy of all the acts agreed upon in this matter.
>
> Guatemala, July 31, 1830.[136]

After several scrutinies don Pedro Ruíz de Bustamante was elected, but the Assistant Chief Executive Rivera Cabezas refused in the name of the government to approve the choice. A second election was held and the vote fell upon don Diego Batres, the very Vicar named by Archbishop Casáus y Torres. This time the government approved. The election of the Chapter did not change the person, but it changed the source of the jurisdiction. The Archbishop in exile was angered by this move, and sent letters and pastorals from Havana, declaring null and void all that Father Batres would do as Vicar General, and naming Vicars who worked secretly carrying out orders sent from Havana.[137]

---

135 Marure, *Bosquejo histórico*, XX.

136 *National Archives of Guatemala*, No. 25466, July 31, 1830.

137 Marure, *Bosquejo histórico*, Chap. XX.

In the decade following the expulsion of Archbishop Casáus y Torres (1829-1839) the Church lost ground at every turn. In instance after instance the Church resisted, the government insisted. For example, the government insisted on the establishment of a Commission of Public Worship and Welfare in spite of protests by the Vicar General. On July 15, 1832 the National Assembly decreed the setting up of this new department. On November 8th the Executive wrote to the Vicar General requesting promptness in the forming of the Commission and in arranging for the collection of tithes by that organization.[138] On November 24th, the Ecclesiastical Chapter informed the Government that it did not consider it advisable to erect such a department to administer the incomes of the Church,[139] while the Vicar General wrote, on November 28th, that the administration of the tithes of an archdiocese was not in the province of a Commission on Public Worship and Welfare.[140] However, very reluctantly, on December 4, 1832, the Ecclesiastical Chapter finally informed the Government that the Commission had been installed.[141] The government put an end to the matter in a letter of Dec. 31st, insisting on the administration of the income from tithes by the newly erected Commission.[142]

The property confiscated by the government from the religious orders at their expulsion was gradually being allocated. On December 5, 1829 a decree of the government of Guatemala had transferred to the University of San Carlos the buildings of the former Convent of St. Dominic,[143] with the exception of the church, which, together with those of the Franciscans and the Order of La Merced, was erected, on December 6, 1829, by order of the Legislature, into a parish

138 *National Archives of Guatemala*, No. 25023, November 8, 1832.

139 *Ibid.*, No. 25301, November 24, 1832.

140 *Ibid.*, No. 25029, November 28, 1832.

141 *Ibid.*, No. 25302, December 4, 1832.

142 *Ibid.*, No. 25031, December 31, 1832.

143 Montúfar y Rivera, *op. cit.*, I, 238.

to which was assigned a fixed salary for the priests who administered it, to be deducted from the sale of the goods of the respective convents.[144] When the pastors of the six remaining parishes in Guatemala City manifested to the government that they lacked funds for subsistence, the latter issued a decree, on March 10, 1831, ordering the Treasury of the State to pay them 1,800 *pesos* annually.[145] For a number of years after the expropriation most auction transactions included property which had belonged to the religious orders and the Church.[146]

With the assumption of the leadership of the government by Antonio Rivera Cabezas on March 9, 1830, the State of Guatemala had begun to taste for a while the blessings of peace. While Rivera Cabezas accomplished many reforms, he did much harm to the Conservative cause by his pen as editor of " *El Melitón* " mentioned above.[147]

The removal of the seat of the federal government to San Salvador in March, 1831, which freed Guatemala from the constant conflict between state and federal authorities, aided the Conservatives because many of the officials who moved away were their Liberal enemies. The Conservatives were also favored during the short term of the Assistant Chief Executive Gregorio Márquez, who had as his secretary general a talented ecclesiastic, Fr. Antonio Colóm.[148]

A decree of March 1, 1831 informed the Vicar General that all ecclesiastical employees, as well as civil, must be such as could be trusted absolutely by the government. Hence he was not to place secularized religious in parishes formerly held by their communities, nor to appoint any pastor without the previous approbation of the government.[149]

144 *Ibid.,* p. 277.

145 *Ibid.*

146 *Supra,* p. 58.

147 *Supra,* p. 83.

148 Bancroft, *op. cit.,* III, 156.

149 *National Archives of Guatemala,* No. 24901, March 1, 1831.

In August, 1831 Mariano Gálvez became Chief Executive
of the State of Guatemala and governed until Feb. 2, 1838
when he was forced to resign. At first he tried to conciliate
both Liberals and Conservatives, but was not successful.
Many measures were passed which were unfavorable to the
Church, and under him some considerable degree of separation of Church and State was achieved, e.g. toleration of all
religions was allowed.[150]

On August 3, 1831 a decree of the Federal Congress declared that all Bulls, Briefs, Rescripts, etc. from the Holy See
had to be approved by the government before being circulated
in Guatemala.[151] This was a natural outcome of its decision
in the previous month that the *Patronato* belonged to the
Nation, and its exercise to the President of the Republic in
the same manner as it had been exercised by the monarchs
of Spain.[152]

The government showed great vigilance over the appointment of ecclesiastics,[153] and brought complaints to the Vicar
General of subversive tendencies in sermons, worded generally
like the following:

> To the Vicar General,
>   The Chief Executive has been informed that in Antigua, on
> the occasion of the feast of Our Lady of Mt. Carmel, Fr.
> Ventura Quiróz preached a subversive and critical sermon
> against our present system of government. The Chief Execu-
> tive, wishing to see the original, has requested me to ask you
> to give the necessary orders so that the sermon may be in my
> Ministry as soon as possible.
> God, Union, Liberty,
Guatemala, July 25, 1831.[154]

150 Montúfar y Rivera, *op. cit.*, II, 346-7.

151 *Recopilación de Leyes de Guatemala*, III, 276, Book IX, Title II, Law 4.

152 Batres Jáuregui, *op. cit.*, II, 344.

153 *National Archives of Guatemala*, Nos. 24922, 24923, 24924, 24925, 24926,
24927, 24928, 24929, 24933, 24938, 24939, 24942, 24943, 24944, 24947.

154 *Ibid.*, No. 24952, July 25, 1831.

This type of protest is made over and over again even down to the present day.

The civil authorities appropriated at need not only the goods of the religious orders, but also funds existing in the ecclesiastical treasury:[155]

> To the Vicar General,
>
> The Chief Executive, considering that the present exigencies demand prompt and active attention to the clothing and feeding of the forces of the State, has disposed that all funds existing in the ecclesiastical treasury for distribution to the needy are to be placed in the general treasury for the extraordinary expenses of the present time, as well as the urgent ordinary ones, with the understanding that the Government will use them conscientiously for the purpose indicated.
>
> I offer you, Citizen Vicar General, the sentiments of my deep respect. God, Union, Liberty, Guatemala, October 14, 1831.

On May 2, 1832 the Federal Congress declared that all the inhabitants of the Republic were free to adore God according to their belief, and that the national government would protect the exercise of this liberty. This decree was accepted by the legislatures of the various states of the confederation and prompt execution ordered.[156] It was declared, moreover, that the appointment to church dignities belonged to the nation and should be made by the Chief Executive.[157]

Many of Gálvez' reform measures were effected by the use of the expropriated goods of the religious. A decree of March 1, 1832 had transformed a convent into a Lancaster system normal school and the old schools founded by Archbishop Francos Monroy and the Order of Belén were converted into modern primary schools. The Dominican Convent in Guatemala was destined to be a model prison like those in the United

155 *Ibid.*, No. 24979, October 14, 1831.

156 Marure, *Efemérides*, p. 31.

157 Montúfar y Rivera, *op. cit.*, I, 292.

States.[158] Just in passing it might be noted that over 150 years later I found no supposedly model prison in Guatemala. Another convent became a hospital and several were converted into military barracks.[159]

On September 15, 1832 the University of San Carlos was suppressed, and in its place there was established an Academy of Sciences, Law and Pre-Medical Studies,[160] veering sharply away from the ecclesiastical preparation which had always been stressed, from the earliest days of the university.

Among other measures directed against the power of the Church was the declaration by the Assembly of the State of Guatemala that the *días de hacienda,* or working days, would be all those of the year except Sundays, Thursday and Friday of Holy week, Corpus Christi, September 15 (Independence Day), November 1, December 8 and 25th.[161] This measure was resented by the people, who continued in their old customs and practices, even after the publication of a Bull of His Holiness Gregory XVI, in July, 1840, suppressing or transferring to the nearest Sunday many feasts which had formerly been of precept.[162] There were also prohibited religious processions on the streets, one of the most deeply rooted of Guatemalan traditions.[163]

On February 27, 1834, the Legislative Assembly passed a decree in regard to convents of nuns whose constitutions were considered too severe. The decree declared:

158 Crowe, *op. cit.,* p. 136; Pineda de Mont, *Recopilación de Leyes de Guatemala,* III, 18, Book VIII, Title I, Law 7.

159 Crowe, *op. cit.,* p. 136.

160 Marure, *Efemérides,* p. 32.

161 *Ibid.,* p. 35; Montúfar y Rivera, *op. cit.,* II, 76; Dunlop, Robert Glasgow, *Travels in Central America,* London, Longman, Brown, Green, Longmans, 1847, p. 190.

162 Marure, *Efemérides,* p. 35.

163 Montúfar y Rivera, *op. cit.,* I, 307-319; II, 76.

1—The authorities of the State will retain no nun who wishes to leave the convent to which she belongs by profession; rather, on the contrary, if she is refused permission to return to the world, the Supreme Government of the State will intervene in her regard.

2—Those nuns who of their own will leave their convents have a right to the dowry which they brought with them, in proportion to the present state of the funds of the convent.[164]

Another decree of the Legislature of Guatemala, dated April 16, 1834, declared the secularized religious eligible to inherit, and to enjoy all the rights of citizenship.[165]

Still another decree, that of August 25, 1835, dealt with the religious orders, stating that each year, at least four times, the President and Treasurer of the Court, together with the Vicar General, would inspect the convents of nuns to ascertain whether imprisonment or corporal punishments were resorted to in these establishments. They would inquire privately of each nun whether she wished to leave, and in case of an affirmative answer, they were to expedite the matter. They were to guarantee that each nun might speak or write without the censorship of the superior or other person, and that she might ask for medical attention when she was ill.[166]

On March 5, 1836 there reached Guatemala at last the approval by the Holy See of the faculties granted to don Diego Batres as Vicar General of the archdiocese.[167]

Even the cemeteries were to come under the power of the government, and the latter, in answer to protests of those who wanted their dead buried in holy places, replied that the priests could bless the cemeteries. To cover the cost of cemeteries, it was decided that the funds of the *fábrica,* or those

164 Pineda de Mont, *Recopilación de Leyes de Guatemala,* III, 261, Book IX, Title I, Law 16.

165 *Ibid.,* p. 292, Book IX, Title III, Law I.

166 *Ibid.,* p. 261, Book IX, Title I, Law 17.

167 Montúfar y Rivera, *op. cit.,* I, 264.

set aside for maintenance and construction of the churches, would be used.[168]

In the law of guarantees drawn up by Juan José Aycinena at the command of the Assembly two articles referred to religion and pointed to more religious freedom:

Article 6—All men by nature have the indisputable right to offer worship to Almighty God according to the dictates of their conscience, whether in private or in public, with the sole restriction that they do not disturb others in the free exercise of their worship, nor the public peace and tranquility.

Article 7—The civil power has no right to dominate the conscience of any individual; nor to prescribe limits to religious belief, nor to prohibit any assembling which has for its object the worship of God, nor to forbid to anyone the right to give, while living or as a legacy, the whole or part of his goods to perpetuate the solemnity or maintenance of the religion which he professes, or to provide according to his beliefs for the perpetual intercession for the welfare of his soul . . . [169]

The final and intolerable blow at the Church was the decree declaring that marriage was a civil contract which could be dissolved.[170] This so displeased the people in general that it was revoked in July, 1838.[171]

Gálvez had overstepped the bounds of prudence by his decrees on marriage and divorce, as Mecham states,[172] and the discontent of the people was increased to a high pitch by the deadly ravages of a cholera epidemic which swept the country.[173] Although the government did all in its power to

168 *Ibid.*, II, 78.

169 *Ibid.*, p. 434; August 18, 1837.

170 Pineda de Mont, *Recopilación de Leyes de Guatemala*, III, 300, Book IX, Title V, Law I.

171 Marure, *Efemérides*, p. 40; Pineda de Mont, *Recopilación de Leyes de Guatemala*, III, 309, Book IX, Title V, Law 3.

172 Mecham, *Church and State in Latin America*, p. 372.

173 Williams, *op. cit.*, p. 142.

combat the plague, the Indians were panic stricken and readily believed rumors that the government had poisoned the waters.[174] Revolt spread through the villages and the Indians gathered around Rafael Carrera, a young mestizo of the hills. The revolution might have ended early but for the excesses of the government troops sent to stifle it, which made all conciliation impossible.[175] The insurrection soon became general, strengthened by guerrilla bands. Meanwhile the ranks of the Liberals were weakening; Mariano Gálvez had been forced to resign and moderate Conservatives were installed on November 13, 1837. Soon the semi-Conservative government of Guatemala was calling on Carrera for assistance in putting down a revolt against it on the part of Liberals who sought the return of Gálvez and his ministers. While there were still Liberals in the Assembly, on May 1, 1838, that body passed a decree forbidding the election of any ecclesiastical candidate for a political office:

> The Legislative Assembly of the State of Guatemala, considering that the separation of Church and State and the incompatibility of the ecclesiastical ministry with secular employments can be deduced from the very nature of things, and that it is fitting and even necessary for the public liberty and peace and for the progress of religion; that such a separation, happily established in free, cultured and religious nations where it assures national well-being and purity of faith, should be established especially among us as necessary in the present circumstances to calm the fanaticism and conflicts which strive to encourage the union of sacerdotal prestige and temporal power, governing civil institutions and affairs and disturbing consciences and popular ignorance; and, finally, that the precepts of the Gospel and canon law as well as the spirit of the Church forbid to priests all intervention in public affairs, as

174 García, op. cit., III, 134-136.

175 Stephens, John L., Incidents of Travel in Central America, New York, Harper's 1852.

foreign to their sacred ministry, has been pleased to decree
and decrees:

1—No minister of religion, of whatever religious sect, may
be elected or designated for any political office.

2—The Constitution of the State will be changed in conformity with the above.[176]

While Morazán was at his post as President of the Federation of Central America, he was a check on the growing
Conservative power in Guatemala, but when he left in August,
1838 to put down a rebellion in El Salvador, Carrera seized
the opportunity to reinstate the Conservatives firmly in control. Under Mariano Rivera Paz, a moderate Liberal, a new
conciliatory government had been established.[177]

From the moment Rivera Paz became Chief Executive of
the State, reaction set in. The Conservatives undid all that the
Liberals had done under Gálvez. On July 26, 1838 a decree
granted amnesty to all who had opposed the government since
September, 1821.[178] There were suspended, likewise, the decrees on civil marriage and divorce, freedom of all to bequeath
property, the reduction of the number of holidays and the
further admission to religious vows. Rivera Paz also supported the petition of the clergy that a bishop be named for
the diocese, and public funds were to be used to defray the expense connected with the measure.[179]

On April 17, 1839 the State of Guatemala left the Confederation and declared its complete independence.

On May 29, 1839 the Second Constitutional Assembly was
installed in the capital and presided over by Fr. Fernando
Antonio Dávila.[180] The Assembly had a considerable number
of ecclesiastics among its members. Besides the President of

176 Montúfar y Rivera, op. cit., II, 96.

177 Crowe, op. cit., p. 145.

178 Montúfar y Rivera, op. cit., III, 190.

179 National Archives of Guatemala, No. 25144.

180 Marure, Efemérides, p. 49.

the Assembly, Fr. Dávila, there were the Vice-President, Fr. Juan José Aycinena, and the Secretary, Fr. Manuel Salazar, as well as the Deputies Canon Inquisitor Father Viteri, Father Quirós, Fr. Bernardo Piñol and Fr. Herrarte. The first act of the Assembly was to dictate the motion " that the Government request the Ecclesiastical governor of the archdiocese to appoint a day of public prayer for the success of the Constitutional Congress and for the preservation of peace throughout the country." [181]

A memorial was read to the Assembly on the occasion of its first meeting by Mariano Rivera Paz, who was concluding his term of office. It was a summary, really, of the religious and political events of his administration and of the needs of the country, as can be seen from the following excerpts:

To the Deputies:

The solemn installation of the Constituent Assembly of the State of Guatemala is the hope of the people who confide in its powers and who have put an end to the authority which the laws deposited accidentally in my hands. My last duty is to inform you of what has occurred during the time when I have been entrusted with the government, and of the condition in which you find the State, pointing out to your attention the matters which in my opinion should be called to it immediately ...

No. 8—Governed in this way, our people came to find themselves without any of the bonds which form human society. Attacked in their customs and in their religion, with no guarantees for their persons or properties, insecure even in the bosom of their families, receiving public example of immorality, without justice or judges, exasperated by heavy taxes, they saw in the authority which should protect them a hostile power which oppressed them and they felt at the same time the necessity and the sufficiency of their own force to resist it ...

No. 30—The government tried to satisfy as much as its faculties permitted another of the more general and vehement of the demands of the people; they ask constantly for the return of the legitimate and virtuous head of our Church, who

181 Montúfar y Rivera, *op. cit.,* III, 371.

ten years ago was unjustly exiled and separated from his flock. From then on there have arisen a thousand questions and difficulties for the clergy, and the consciences of the faithful have been tormented by doubts and privations which are consequent on it . . .

Stressing the moral needs of the people, he concluded, " Declare, then, solemnly that the Government of the State professes and respects the Catholic religion which is that of all the inhabitants, and that it will protect its worship." [182]

On June 21, 1839 the Assembly issued a decree declaring null and void the decree of June 13, 1830 in regard to Archbishop Casáus y Torres, restored to him his rights as Metropolitan and as citizen of the State, and arranged a petition for his return.[183] On the same day another decree revoked the decree of July 28, 1829 suppressing the religious orders.[184]

On December 14th of the same year the Church scored a notable victory—the Conservative government ceded to it the business of collecting tithes. It may be recalled that the grant to collect these tithes was given to the Spanish Crown in 1456 by Pope Callixtus.[185]

Once more we witness the pattern of interblending of Church and State. On October 14, 1839 the Government requested the Vicar General to have a portable altar located in front of the Cathedral for the solemn blessing of the banners of the country.[186] And, finally, on December 30th, the Vicar General received a notification from the Supreme Government to the effect that the members of the Government would attend services at the Cathedral on January 1st.[187] Carrera was the chief power in the country in 1839, ruling behind the throne and, at first at least, the Church appeared to be profiting by the régime.

182 *Archives of the Archbishop's Palace,* Guatemala.

183 Montúfar y Rivera, *op. cit.,* III, 373.

184 Pineda de Mont, *Recopilación de Leyes de Guatemala,* III, 262 Book IX, Title I, Law 18.

185 *Supra,* p. 18.

186 *National Archives of Guatemala,* No. 25157, Oct. 14, 1839.

187 *Ibid.,* No. 25161, Dec. 30, 1839.

CHAPTER II

THE CONSERVATIVE INTERLUDE
1839-1871

LONG before taking actual possession of the office of President on January 1, 1845, Rafael Carrera had been determining Church-State relations in Guatemala.[1] Drawn from obscurity to be a tool in the hands of the aristocracy and clergy, who had recognized his influence over the vast Indian population and the military forces, he proved before the end of his long rule of thirty years to be a veritable thorn in the side of the Conservative Party. Though allied with the aristocracy and higher clergy who had brought him into power, he showed himself, as Dunlop has aptly put it, " pretty cool to both." [2] When the clergy pressed for the restoration of their ancient privileges, he did not return all of them, refusing to create a power which soon would have overwhelmed him.[3] Again, he blocked the efforts of the Conservatives to return to the church its former revenues, preventing the passage of legislation which would have called for " a restoration of sacred property, sacrilegiously obtained," [4] which would likewise entail depriving those possessed of the lands and houses formerly belonging to the church, without any recompense.[5]

A chronological study of the thirty years Carrera was in power indicates that, while in general during this period the Church enjoyed the favor of the government, it was a spas-

1 Montúfar y Rivera, *op. cit.*, III, 537.

2 Dunlop, *op. cit.*, p. 89.

3 *Ibid.*, p. 210.

4 *Ibid.*, p. 214.

5 It is interesting to note that Carrera himself had received from the Government the large hacienda of Palencia, the former property of the Dominicans, and that in 1847, when he ordered it restored to the lawful owners, he sold it back to the government at his own price. (Bancroft, *op. cit.*, III, 272).

modic favor, granted and withdrawn according as it coincided with or hindered Carrera's schemes. For example, in urging his troops on to a last final effort against the enemy, he offered to reestablish the Church and its institutions, "which the impious hand of our mortal enemies has destroyed." [6]

In the case of the restoration to the Dominicans of their *hacienda* " Palencia ", already mentioned, Carrera was moved solely by the desire of gaining the cooperation of that Order in conciliating the Indians then in Sacatepéquez, over whom they had exerted great influence since their appointment to that mission by the Spanish Cortes.[7]

Again, in 1840, when the public treasury was exhausted, Carrera ordered his troops to be paid from church funds, which were being replenished periodically from the payment of the tithes he had restored.[8]

On September 24, 1840, there was ordered restored a project dear to the Conservatives, the Economic Society of the Friends of Guatemala, whose installation took place for the fourth time, under the direction of the ecclesiastic, don José María Castilla. This society had followed the vicissitudes of the Conservatives. Created by royal decree October 21, 1795, at the instance of Fr. don Jacobo de Villa-Urrutia, it was suppressed by the Crown on November 23, 1799 when it showed too " advanced " a policy, reestablished again in December, 1810 and in September, 1829 and suppressed once more by the Liberals in 1837.[9]

The Constituent Assembly under Carrera passed other legislation in favor of the Church. On Oct. 15, 1840, the laws

---

6 *National Archives of Guatemala*, Address of General Rafael Carrera, Commander in Chief of the Armed Forces, to the Army, Guatemala, Dec. 5, 1839.

7 On April 1, 1813, it was decreed by the Spanish Cortes that the Dominicans should undertake the conversion of the Indians of that province. (Cortes, *Diario*, 1813, XIX, 392).

8 Bancroft, *op. cit.*, III, 265.

9 Marure, *Efemérides*, p. 53.

relative to civil marriage and divorce passed in 1837, and suspended in 1838, were now definitely rescinded. By decree of Oct. 16, 1840, the funds from ecclesiastical chaplaincies which had been turned over to the Public Treasury were to be henceforth applied to the object for which they had been originally destined. On Oct. 28, 1840 a decree restored to ecclesiastics, in conformity with civil and canon law, " the privileges of their state " which had been taken away by the decree of the radical Cortes of Spain on Sept. 26, 1820.[10]

Another decree of Oct. 28, 1840 established once more in Guatemala the *fuero eclesiástico,* or special exemption from civil trial, suppressed by Article 153 of the Federal Constitution of the new Republic in 1824.[11]

On November 9, 1840 the Vicar General of the Archdiocese was notified that the Assembly had decreed to grant him all the faculties of ecclesiastical authority necessary for the improvement of public morals, just then at low ebb, with the right to use civil sanctions as well as ecclesiastical, if there were need.[12]

In a letter to the citizens of Guatemala dated Dec. 12, 1840 the dictator declared it necessary for the public well-being to fill the vacancy in the Metropolitan See, due to the absence of Archbishop Casáus y Torres:

> ... bearing in mind that the people have complained from the year 37 to the year 39 because the Archbishop has not been brought back, and that I, as leader since the beginning, have not ceased to solicit his return since April of 1839 when I took command of this city, availing myself of all the means which reason and judgment have suggested, working for this end with the greatest good faith, and persuaded that those who should help me would do so and that, with the efforts of all, the project would be accomplished; but it has not been

10 Montúfar y Rivera, *op. cit.,* III, 53.

11 Marure, *Efemérides,* p. 53.

12 *National Archives of Guatemala,* No. 25332, Oct. 28, 1840; Nov. 9, 1840.

so, because some have opposed rather than aided. . . . Since it is clear that the Archbishop would not be willing to return, it seems better that there should be substituted in this Diocese the present Vicar General, because alarming letters and other obstacles have prevented the legitimate pastor from coming. . .

It is very evident that the presence of an Archbishop is necessary and urgent; and the Government believes that it is its duty to learn definitely whether it is possible or not for our Metropolitan to return, and to urge the ecclesiastical chapter to prepare its *ternas* (list of three nominees) and notify the Roman Curia of the need of naming an auxiliary or a temporary occupant of the See who might be chosen according to his merits and aptitudes . . . [13]

In the appointment by Carrera in 1840 of Fr. don Juan Aycinena as Rector of the reestablished University of San Carlos,[14] he was exemplifying by one stroke what Bancroft has called " his favoring of the ultramontane priests, aristocrats and reactionaries," [15] for Aycinena, who was to hold this office until 1854, belonged in all three categories. He was permitted, with his sister doña Luz Batres de Aycinena, to establish an orphan asylum, and a free school in the Colegio de Belén for poor girls, to be conducted by the Sisters of Charity.[16]

Among other decrees abrogated by Carrera was that which had been issued by the Liberals on May 1, 1838, declaring that " no minister of religion, of whatever sect, may be elected or designated for any political office." [17] Thus, at the Con-

13 Montúfar y Rivera, *op. cit.*, III, 551.

14 *National Archives of Guatemala*—"Apuntes biográficos del Ill. señor don Juan José Aycinena, obispo titular de Trajanopolis," *Gaceta Oficial*, No. 66, p. 11.

15 Bancroft, *op. cit.*, III, 265.

16 *National Archives of Guatemala*, "Apuntes biográficos del Ill. señor don Juan José Aycinena, obispo titular de Trajanopolis," *Gaceta Oficial*, no. 66, p. 16.

17 Montúfar y Rivera, *op. cit.*, III, 96.

stitutional Assembly of Guatemala in 1841, there was the Deputy Father Anselmo Llorente, future Bishop of Costa Rica,[18] and the Minister of State, Father Jorge Viteri y Ungo, future Bishop of San Salvador. When Viteri protested against the high-handed actions of Carrera, the latter had him arrested, together with the nominal President, Rivera Paz.[19] Yet, when Fr. Viteri resigned on December 24, 1841 to act as Envoy Extraordinaire to the Pontifical Court on behalf of Salvador, the government of Guatemala requested him to present its ecclesiastical problems to the Holy See at the same time.[20]

On Sept. 13, 1841 the Constituent Assembly issued an order regulating the ceremony which had to be observed when the Supreme Authority of Guatemala attended ecclesiastical services.[21]

On Oct. 5, 1841 Carrera requested the Constitutional Assembly to report on the steps taken for the restoration of the convents of religious.[22]

By a decree of the National Assembly of Oct. 16, 1841, books which were objectionable to the Church because they promoted liberal ideas on social or religious matters were placed on the forbidden list, and the Church was authorized to proceed against those who violated the measure.[23]

The relations between the civil and ecclesiastical authorities grew even more friendly as the years passed.

On Jan. 14, 1842 th Supreme Government, in a letter to the Vicar General Antonio Larrazábal, approved his appointment of Fr. José María Barrutia y Croquer as Vicar Capitu-

18 *Boletín Oficial*, I, 13.

19 Montúfar y Rivera, *op. cit.*, III, 536-7.

20 Vilanova Meléndez, *op. cit.*, p. 139.

21 *National Archives of Guatemala*, No. 25190, Sept. 13, 1841.

22 *Ibid.*, No. 25197, Oct. 11, 1841.

23 Bancroft, *op. cit.*, III, 627.

lar and Auxiliary governor of the Metropolitan See, and the latter took the necessary oath of allegiance to the government before assuming office.[24]

On July 28, 1842 the President, Mariano Rivera Paz, issued an order to all the chief officials of the departments, municipalities and towns of the State to aid and cooperate with Juan Manuel Rodríguez, who was collecting alms for the completion of the Church of the Recolección and of the Colegio de Cristo Crucificado.[25]

Morazán's execution on Sept. 15, 1842 in San José caused much satisfaction to the ruling powers in Guatemala, who ordered High Mass and other religious ceremonies celebrated to commemorate the downfall of their enemy.[26]

On July 4, 1843 the government of Rivera Paz issued a decree permitting the return of the Jesuits and authorized the officials of the government to assist in their reestablishment in the country.[27] On Jan. 11, 1844 the government requested the commissary of the Belgian Company of Colonization, which had been granted land in Guatemala for settlement, to turn over 1,900 *pesos* of the sum due in July of that year, to don Rafael Batres, Treasurer of the Commission appointed to facilitate the return of the Jesuits.[28] A circular was sent on Feb. 12, 1844 to the chief civil officials by the Secretary of State asking them to cooperate with the Commission established by the government for the erection of a school to be conducted by the Jesuits, and aid in the collection of funds for this work, initiated by the President, " who takes so much interest in the successful reestablishment of the Company of Jesus, because of his firm conviction of the benefits which

24 *National Archives of Guatemala*, No. 25214, Dec. 30, 1841; Jan. 3, 1842; Jan. 14, 1842.

25 Montúfar y Rivera, *op. cit.*, III, 656.

26 Bancroft, *op. cit.*, III, 223.

27 Aguirre Cinta, *op. cit.*, p. 121.

28 *National Archives of Guatemala*, No. 25422, July 4, 1843.

youth in general will derive from their religious and secular education." [29]

When the Coadjutor Archbishop, Dr. Francisco García Peláez, named as a result of the mission entrusted to Fr. Viteri y Ungo by the government of Guatemala to the Roman Court, was to take possession of his new office early in 1844,[30] the government arranged the ceremonial to be carried out for his reception.[31] On March 3rd the new Coadjutor Archbishop entered Guatemala in solemn procession. A vast assemblage went to meet him and accompany him to the Cathedral where they sang a *Te Deum*. Then he was conducted to the Government Building where the President and his Council awaited him. Many speeches were made and " the relations between the civil and ecclesiastical governments could not be more intimate."[32]

This friendliness was shown by a petition of the government on March 16, 1844 to the Coadjutor Archbishop asking for prayers for the needs of the country:

> The Reverend Coadjutor Archbishop is urged to dictate the necessary dispositions in order that in the Cathedral as well as in the other churches of this Archdiocese there be held nine days of public prayer in order to implore the aid of the Almighty for the necessities of the State.[33]

On May 30, 1844 the executive asked the Archbishop Coadjutor to name Father Francisco González Lobo as Chaplain of the expeditionary forces.[34]

29 *Ibid.*, No. 25423, Feb. 12, 1844. In the Archives there are also many replies to the government from the various officials, among them those of Chiquimula, Totonicapán, Mazatenango, Sacatepéquez, Chimaltenango, promising cooperation in this matter.

30 Vilanova Meléndez, *op. cit.*, p. 139.

31 *National Archives of Guatemala*, No. 25240, Feb. 26, 1844.

32 Aguirre Cinta, *op. cit.*, p. 121.

33 *National Archives of Guatemala*, No. 24792, March 16, 1844.

34 *Ibid.*, No. 24796, May 30, 1844.

A second request for public prayers for the country was addressed to the Coadjutor Archbishop by the Ministry of War on June 8, 1844.[35]

Shortly after, on June 20th, the Coadjutor Archbishop called the attention of the government to the insults offered to the pastor of Escuintla, at the hands of the local commandant;[36] and on July 10, 1844 he reported the provision of pastors for Jutiapa, Santa Rosa and Jalapa.[37] These were insignificant matters, perhaps, but they show the constant friendly contact between the two powers.[38]

But clouds were gathering. Carrera had manoeuvered the dissolution of the Assembly, and on December 8, 1844 he installed a Council to take its place. Rivera Paz resigned and, at last, on December 11, 1844, Carrera assumed publicly the office he had really controlled since his seizure of Guatemala on April 13, 1839. His new council, including many Liberals, was especially displeasing to the aristocrats and Conservatives, and they plotted his overthrow.[39]

By February, 1845 the State of Guatemala was under the absolute dictatorship of Rafael Carrera and his henchmen, Sotero Carrera and Brigadier Gerónimo Paiz.[40] Some attempts by the Congress to pass liberal laws were checked through pressure by the aristocrats and clergy, and through fear of Carrera, who threatened all who resented his power.

35 *Ibid.*, No. 24797, June 8, 1844.

36 *Ibid.*, No. 24799, June 20, 1844.

37 *Ibid.*, No. 24798, July 10, 1844.

38 *Ibid.*

39 Bancroft, *op. cit.*, III, 268; Montúfar y Rivera, *op. cit.*, IV, 662. Frederick Crowe wrote that in a more decided stand against ecclesiastical influence, Carrera sent an order to the eastern ports, as the Jesuits from Belgium were about to arrive to assist in the new college decreed by the legislation, forbidding the authorities to permit one Jesuit to land, and intimating that if they attempted it, it would be at peril of their lives (*op. cit.*, p. 163).

40 Bancroft, *op. cit.*, III, 269.

No opposition was tolerated and this, naturally, led to violence.[41]

During the elaborate funeral services for Archbishop Ramón Casáus y Torres, who died in exile in Havana and whose body was brought back to Guatemala for burial in June, 1846,[42] an attempt to assassinate Carrera as he was leaving the Cathedral failed. The conspirators were captured, the more prominent being exiled, and the rest imprisoned.[43]

On January 14, 1847 Carrera sent two letters to Pope Pius IX, one congratulating him on his election to the pontifical See and the other asking him for bishops for Central America.[44]

In August of the same year there were new uprisings and the Archbishop was asked by the government to instruct his priests to preach obedience to the authorities and laws.[45]

When all efforts to check the revolution failed, Carrera, fearing his overthrow, called a Constituent Assembly and placed the executive power provisionally in the hands of Vice President Cruz on Jan. 25, 1848. The Conservatives, alarmed, begged Carrera to resume his office. He did so, organizing a new Congress composed mostly of Conservatives, and revoking the decree calling for a Constituent Congress. However, on Aug, 15, 1848, he was forced by the growing discontent to call the Assembly, send in his resignation and retire to Chiapas. The new president, Juan Antonio Martínez, kept Carrera's officers in command. Luis Molina organized a third party, the Moderates, which most of the Liberals joined,

41 In April 1846, at the instigation of the Archbishop Coadjutor, Frederick Crowe, English Baptist missionary admitted during Morazán's rule, was expelled from Guatemala. (Dunlop, op. cit., p. 82); Cf. Montúfar y Rivera, op. cit., V, 12-13, 19-25.

42 Vilanova Meléndez, op. cit., p. 145.

43 Dunlop, op. cit., p. 248.

44 Montúfar y Rivera, op. cit., V, 12-13, 19-25.

45 Gaceta Oficial de Guatemala, Aug. 14, 1847.

leaving their own party itself weak. The Church-State relations remained practically the same. Morelet, who traveled through Guatemala in 1848, found that, while the religious bodies had never regained the wealth and prestige they lost in the revolution of 1829, their influence was still evident, especially in the outward display of religious festivals.[46]

When Martínez, unable to maintain peace, resigned, José Bernardo Escobar took office, November 28, 1848, only to meet instant opposition from both the Moderate party and the aristocrats and clergy. He resigned and was succeeded on January 1, 1849 by Mariano Paredes, who was to prove but a tool of the Conservatives to bring Carrera back into power.[47] On April 13, 1849 the latter was once more given control and made Commander-in-Chief of the Armed Forces of Guatemala. The aristocracy and clergy proposed to give him prestige and make him appear indispensable. Paredes had not satisfied them. They did not believe themselves secure under his protecting sword. They needed Carrera. And to secure him they made Paredes believe that Carrera would be under his orders. These orders were not really dictated by Paredes, but by the aristocracy and clergy, who had Carrera well instructed, showing him the necessity of appearing submissive to a man who had been his subordinate and who had fought against him at Chiquimula.[48]

On February 2, 1851, when Guatemala established her independence definitely from the rest of Central America, Paredes published a decree declaring that on February 9th all the authorities and officials of the government would attend a Mass in thanksgiving, to be celebrated in the Cathedral with all religious pomp by the Archbishop, don Francisco de Paula García Peláez. He ordered, likewise, that all the in-

46 Morelet, Arthur, *Travels in Central America*, New York, Leypoldt, Holt & Williams, 1871, p. 401.

47 Bancroft, *op. cit.*, III, 277.

48 Montúfar y Rivera, *op. cit.*, VI, 218.

habitants of the Republic should give thanks for the triumph of Carrera's forces at Arada, where the latter were victorious over the combined strength of Salvador, Honduras and Nicaragua,[49] and on the first Sunday after the receipt of the decree, there should be a solemn Mass in the capital of each department at which all the officials should be present. Archbishop García Peláez not only said Mass, but also congratulated the government on its victory of Feb. 2nd, and there was a procession with the children from the schools and the Tridentine Seminary students singing litanies of the saints. Everywhere there were religious functions and the ringing of church bells.[50]

Significant of the friendly relations of the government toward the Church at this time are also the following passages from the proclamation of President Mariano Paredes to the Representatives on the opening of the Session, August 16, 1851:

> 9. There has been named, also, a public representative in Rome, not only as a just homage to the Holy Father, as Head of the Church and Universal Pastor of the faithful, but also for the purpose of soliciting a permanent arrangement of matters concerning the intervention granted to the government in the external affairs of the Church, and in order to remove all doubt in regard to privileges and juridical rights, because when these matters are dealt with without consultation of both authorities, harmony is disturbed, consciences are troubled, and the peace so necessary for the common well-being is lacking.
>
> 10. Fortunately, the Metropolitan to whom has been entrusted this flock by Divine Providence, has never failed in lending to the Government his respectful cooperation in the affairs of his ministry, aiding, like other zealous priests, in the pacification of the *montaña* (highland region of Guatemala), and it is now the occasion to manifest to the

49 Bancroft, *op. cit.*, III, 280.

50 Montúfar y Rivera, *op. cit.*, VI, 223.

Assembly the conviction of the government of the necessity of cooperation in the matter of worship, moral instruction as well as religious, because without these we cannot expect from our people either order or civilization, much less peace and complete security.

11. For these reasons, and because, moreover, it is a duty of governments to work in conformity with the desires of the majority of the people whom they rule, there is issued a decree permitting the reestablishment of the Company of Jesus in the Republic, which measure is entirely in conformity with what was adopted by the Constitutional Assembly in the year 1843, by a vote rarely seen in government bodies, and on the petition of the most respectable groups in the country, ecclesiastical as well as civil. For my part, gentlemen, I am very much satisfied with the measure and full of hope as to its beneficial results in favor of the well-being of the public and the progress of education of our youth in whom lies the hope of the nation; and so I do not doubt that it will meet with your worthy approbation.[51]

The Constitution drawn up by this Assembly on Oct. 19, 1851 likewise shows close alliance with the Church. Article 10 declared that the Councillors of the State have a voice and vote in the Executive Council, and that there might be called to it by the President of the Republic the Archbishop, Bishops temporarily administering the archbishopric. . . the head of the Ecclesiastical Chapter and the Rector of the University. Article 11 declared that the President must take his oath with the Archbishop presiding. In Section 3 of Article 16, on the Oath of Office, to the question: "Do you promise to maintain with all your strength the laws of God, to have the Catholic religion kept pure and unaltered, and to protect its ministers?" the new President was to respond, "I promise."[52]

51 *National Archives of Guatemala*, "Informe dirigido por el Presidente de la República de Guatemala al Cuerpo Representativo en la Apertura de las sesiones, el 16 de agosto de 1851."

52 *Ibid.*, "Constituyente de 1851—'En el Nombre de Díos Todo Podoroso.'"

On September 16, 1852 there was issued a decree referring to public instruction, which was called the Pavón Law. Each village was to have at least two schools, one for boys and the other for girls, the program consisting of " Primer, First Reader, Conduct and Manners, Christian Doctrine according to the Catechism by Fr. Ripalda, Writing, and the first four operations in Arithmetic." The inspection of the schools was entrusted to a committee composed of the pastor, one member of the municipal government and one of the leading citizens, who were likewise to choose the teachers. As for the reward offered to the outstanding students, it was indicated that the children who showed capacity, application and improvement, as well as good conduct, might be employed in the service of the church by the pastor, as acolytes or cantors. For this purpose, after school hours, they were to go to the house of the pastor and receive the necessary instructions, being in all matters subject to the pastor.[53]

It was during the Carrera administration, on Oct. 7, 1852, that the first Concordat which the Vatican negotiated with any Latin American republic was approved.[54] It was signed by His Eminence don Jacobo Antonelli, Cardinal Secretary of His Holiness, Pope Pius IX, and the marquis of Belmonte, don Fernando de Lorenzana, Representative Plenipotentiary of the Republic of Guatemala, and solemnly ratified by Carrera on December 24, 1852.[55] By this Concordat the Republic recognized as the only and exclusive religion the Roman, Catholic, Apostolic; gave to the clergy all kinds of privileges; permitted their control in matters of education and authorized them to censor all books and writings which were related to dogma; promised to preserve the payment of the tithes, and in addition to pay to the Church the sum of 4,000 *pesos*

53 Aguirre Cinta, *op. cit.*, p. 141.

54 Eyzaguirre, José Ignacio, *Los Intereses católicos en América*, Paris, Garnier Frères, 1859, II, 412.

55 Aguirre Cinta, *op. cit.*, p. 233.

each year from the Public Treasury. In exchange for these and many other concessions, the President received from the Pope the right of *Patronato*.

After the Concordat was signed the clergy were, naturally, favored and enjoyed all the prerogatives granted them in that document. By Brief of December 20, 1853 the Pope decorated Carrera with the Grand Cross of the Order of Saint Gregory the Great, in the military class, as a recognition of his efforts for the preservation and prosperity of the Catholic religion. By the same Brief, the Pope absolved him from any excommunication, interdict or other censure of which he might have been guilty.[56]

Carrera used his new title in a decree issued on March 31, 1854 clarifying Articles 15 and 16 of the Concordat, treating of the ecclesiastical privileges:

> Rafael Carrera, Captain General of the Armed Forces, Knight of the Cross of the Pontifical Order of Saint Gregory the Great, military class; Knight Commander of the Order of Leopold of Belgium; President of the Republic of Guatemala;
>
> Decrees:
>
> Article 1—The ecclesiastical authorities will continue to try cases of ecclesiastics in civil matters, whenever both parties are ecclesiastics, and those cases alone will be entrusted to the ordinary jurisdiction which involve disputes over temporal interests between ecclesiastics and seculars, and all those concerning the right to the enjoyment of chaplaincies and other pious foundations which have not been canonically instituted and the capital of which has not been converted into spiritual goods, in conformity with canon law.
>
> Article 2—In regard to criminal cases, no change will be made for the present, and ecclesiastics will continue to enjoy the existing privileges; but even in the more serious cases, no sentence involving corporal or defaming punishment, or the death penalty, will be executed without the approbation

56 Aguirre Cinta, *op. cit.*, p. 143.

of the President, or the compliance of the respective bishop with the regulations required by canon law in such cases.

Article 3—The Government reserves to itself the rights stipulated in Articles 15 and 16 of the Concordat, whenever the public welfare requires it.

Given in the Palace of the Government, in Guatemala, March 31, 1854.   —   Rafael Carrera.

The Minister of Government, Justice and
Ecclesiastical Affairs.   P. de Aycinena.[57]

On October 21, 1854 Carrera was proclaimed by an assembly of higher authorities President for life, the nomination being aided, according to Bancroft, by propaganda of parish priests as well as of military officials in the departments. The announcement of his appointment as Chief Executive for life ended with the words:

> On expressing this unanimous sentiment all those present hope that the Almighty will continue his protection of Guatemala, and will grant Your Excellency the strength necessary to fulfill the duties entrusted to you, and the light and prudence necessary to govern the Republic with benevolence and justice.

After the signing of the proclamation, amid the ringing of bells all the officials went to the house of Carrera to congratulate him; the Archbishop handed him the Act containing his election, and all then passed to the Cathedral for a solemn *Te Deum*.[58]

On January 12, 1858 a contract was drawn up between the government of Guatemala and the Superior of the Sisters of Charity of Saint Vincent de Paul, whose motherhouse was in Paris, to arrange for the religious to take over the direction of some hospitals in Guatemala.[59] On November 27th of the same year there arrived from Belgium seven nuns of

57 Montúfar y Rivera, *op. cit.*, III, 524.

58 Aguirre Cinta, *op. cit.*, p. 148.

59 *National Archives of Guatemala*, Jan. 12, 1858.

the Order of Sisters of Notre Dame, who, through the negotiations of the Archbishop and other interested persons, had
come to direct a school for young ladies. They were welcomed
with a solemn *Te Deum* sung in their honor.[60]

In the year 1863, Fr. Juan José Aycinena was commissioned, together with don Pedro Valenzuela, Councilor of
the State, to draw up a treaty of recognition, peace and
friendship between Spain and Guatemala.[61]

Still another evidence of the relations between the government and Church was shown by a document found in the
National Archives—a letter from the Archbishop to Carrera,
rejoicing that the latter had recovered from an illness and
was again in good health.[62]

Carrera continued to favor the Church to a considerable
degree until his death on March 14, 1865. The funeral ceremonies in the Cathedral were most elaborate. The highest
ecclesiastical as well as civil honors were paid to his remains.[63]
He had died in the full conviction that he had been an in-
strument of Providence in saving society and good order in
Guatemala. He had been so assured by his supporters and had
come to believe it, in the face of the fact that he had been
guilty of heinous crimes and notorious immorality. "So,"
continues Bancroft, "die those who pass hence from the
murderer's gallows under the banner of the cross, and with
priestly consolation."[64]

The last judgment of Carrera, according to Bancroft, is
not left in doubt. It might have been better to have left the
matter to Carrera's Maker, but it is a congenital weakness
of historical writers that they judge men and periods by
their own standards and often forget that in areas where

60 Aguirre Cinta, *op. cit.*, p. 160.

61 *National Archives of Guatemala*, "Apuntes biográficos del Ill. señor
don Juan José Aycinena, obispo titular de Trajanopolis," p. 16.

62 *National Archives of Guatemala*.

63 Aguirre Cinta, *op. cit.*, p. 171.

64 Bancroft, *op. cit.*, III, 284.

the physical and social climate is violent, men of all characters and kinds live violently—and so in like manner, die.

When Carrera died, the Foreign Minister, Pedro de Aycinena, summoned the Assembly to choose a successor, who proved to be Vicente Cerna. He took the oath of office in the presence of Archbishop García Peláez, on May 24, 1865.

Cerna, who had actually been designated by Carrera as his successor, continued Carrera's policy in regard to the Church. In fact, his attitude was more conciliatory than that of Carrera, who had sometimes strained at the leash.[65]

On the occasion of Cerna's inauguration religious festivals were celebrated everywhere. On a general tour of the country he was received cordially by ecclesiastical as well as civil officials, who gave elaborate banquets and conducted solemn religious functions in his honor.[66]

Throughout his term of six years he showed himself very favorable toward the Church, of which he was an active member, devoting much time, as his enemies lamented, to religious practices in the various churches.[67] Batres Jáuregui, describing the capital during Cerna's rule, wrote:

> Before the Revolution of 1871, which gave life to the country, there existed in the capital of Guatemala a monastic and funereal atmosphere; at the tempered and monotonous sound of the bell of some monastery, one saw pass by, silent and melancholy, a monk in his hood, approaching the monastery at the hour for dining; or some ecclesiastic with voluminous cloak, loose conscience and regulation habit, going to visit unhappy nuns enclosed within gloomy walls—unfortunate prisoners in the midst of the civilization and progress of the world.[68]

65 Díaz, Victor Miguel, *Barrios ante la Posteridad*, Guatemala, Tipografía Nacional, 1935, p. 46.

66 Aguirre Cinta, *op. cit.*, p. 172.

67 Díaz, *Barrios ante la Posteridad*, p. 46.

68 Batres Jáuregui, *op. cit.*, p. 17.

Cerna was a very close friend and constant associate of the Jesuits,[69] who had been reestablished in Guatemala during Carrera's term for educational as well as religious purposes. Their schools, as well as those of other repatriated religious orders, were flourishing, according to statistics published in *La Semana* in 1866 with the following optimistic note:

> The University is developing an enlightened youth which will take the place of the generation now retiring, and there will yet come about the complete reorganization of the religious orders which spread learning from the pulpit and in the schools.[70]

On January 25, 1867, when the Archbishop, don Francisco de Paula García Peláez, died, to the sincere regret of all, the President, giving evidence of the close bonds which existed between the Church and State, ordered all public officials to wear mourning for three days and full military honors accorded.[71]

Church questions continued to be favored and the clergy enjoyed all the privileges they had obtained under Carrera. So it is no matter for wonder that on March 1, 1868, at the solemn entry of the new Archbishop of Guatemala, don Bernardo Piñol y Aycinena, there should be showered upon him the most expressive demonstrations of welcome on the part of the Municipal Government, which cooperated by all the means in its power with the Ecclesiastical Chapter to increase the brilliance of the ceremonies. They proceeded in a body to the port of Buenavista where they received the new Archbishop with an address of welcome delivered by the head of the Executive Council.[72]

69 Bancroft, *op. cit.*, III, 413.

70 Díaz, *Barrios ante la Posteridad*, p. 298.

71 Aguïrre Cinta, *op. cit.*, p. 174.

72 And yet it would not be giving a complete picture if mention were not made of others, not sympathetic with solemn Masses, public prayers and sermons, who dreamed rather of liberty—that handful of patriots led by

Cerna was reelected, with a close margin over the Liberals under Miguel García Granados, in 1869. On May 24th, in the presence of the General Assembly formed by the Chamber of Deputies, the Council of State, the Department of Justice, the Municipal Government, delegates from the University and the Ecclesiastical Chapter, the Archbishop seated himself in the presidential chair and Cerna entered, knelt before the Archbishop, and took the oath for his second term as President of the nation. After the customary eloquent addresses had been given, all retired to the Palace, where the President received the government officials. Then all passed to the Cathedral where a solemn Te Deum was chanted.[73]

The election of 1869 foreshadowed the fall of Cerna. Carrera had left him the tremendous burden of saving the Conservative party from defeat. But Cerna did not have the political genius of his predecessor. The extreme Conservatives no longer had capable statesmen like Pavón, Aycinena and Batres; the Conservative press had lost its force; the people were becoming deaf to the voices from the pulpit and the private counsels of the clergy. The government was sleeping, lulled by the thirty years of almost undisturbed power.[74] Almost one third of the territory of Guatemala was in the hands of the Church and the upper class. Commerce was insignificant, communication almost unknown.[75] Finally, on June 29, 1871, the administration of Cerna fell from its own weight,[76] and with it, the privileged status the Church had enjoyed for so many years.[77]

Justo Rufino Barrios who were surprising Col. Camilo de Batlle of the government forces at Malacatán at this same time, only to be defeated. (Aguïrre Cinta, *op. cit.*, p. 175).

73 *Ibid., op. cit.*, p. 179.

74 Zeceña, Mariano, *La Revolución de 1871*, Guatemala, Tipografía Sánchez & de Guise, p. 57.

75 *Ibid.*, p. 23.

76 Bancroft, *op. cit.*, III, 425.

77 *Ibid.*, p. 14.

CHAPTER III

THE RETURN OF THE LIBERALS

ON June 30, 1871 there was yet another about-face in the conflict between Church and State in Guatemala. The government, remaining for a decade after the independence of 1821 under the influence of the Church, with the higher clergy and the aristocracy trying to maintain the colonial status, then passing in 1831 to the control of the Liberal party under Morazán and don Mariano Gálvez, then back again in 1839 to that of the ecclesiastics and Conservatives who were to support Carrera and his successor, Cerna, for the next thirty years, finally passed into the power of the Liberals, Miguel García Granados and Justo Rufino Barrios. García Granados was the orator who protested the violation of laws and liberties; Barrios was the force and action behind him.[1]

Barrios had commenced his revolutionary movement against the Conservatives on August 3, 1867 with an attack on the barracks of San Marcos. In 1869 he had united with General Serapio Cruz to attack the town of Huehuetenango, where he was wounded and had to retreat. While the government strove to suppress these and other insurrections, the Liberal opposition in the Assembly was gradually becoming more and more powerful,[2] and its mouthpiece, Miguel García Granados, was actively agitating against the Conservatives who dominated the country. This party, composed largely of the clergy, the aristocracy and the higher military class, had aspirations which were really monarchical, was bent on maintaining the status quo, and wished to direct society according to colonial traditions. Any feeble attempts of the opposition at reform were combated by the press, the court and, above all, from

1 Aguero, Raúl, *Guatemala: La Revolución Liberal de 1871*, San José, Costa Rica, Imprenta Alsina, 1914, pp. 10-12.

2 Bancroft, *op. cit.*, III, 417.

the pulpit, difficult to attack because in the eyes of the people it represented divine power.[3]

In January, 1870, there was a revolt against Cerna in the section of Guatemala known as the *Oriente,* supported by many of the important people of the capital. Among those taking part were Miguel García Granados and General Villa Lobos. Cerna ordered them arrested and imprisoned in the fort of San José. However, García Granados escaped and found shelter, first in the British Legation and later in Mexico. Barrios communicated with him there, having gathered together a force of well-armed Liberals. García Granados was appointed Supreme Commander of the movement and returned secretly to Guatemala. The active revolt came on March 17, 1871.[4] On June 1st, Barrios, with García Granados, entered Antigua.

On June 3, 1871, in drawing up the famous Act of Patzicia, proclaiming the establishment of a Constitutional Assembly and naming García Granados as Provisional President, there was much discussion. Two separate acts were drawn up. The first treated of religious fanaticism and of the ultra-conservative influence. Some of the leaders present declared it inadvisable to issue acts which might wound the religious sentiment of the people, and so a second one was drawn up with no reference whatsoever to religion, and this one was signed without objection.[5]

On June 23, 1871 the Ultra-Conservative forces of Cerna were overthrown and, on the 30th of the same month, he was forced to cross the border into Salvadorean territory. García Granados was handed the keys of the city of Guatemala and, accompanied by Barrios, marched triumphantly into the cap-

3 Zeceña, Mariano, *La Revolución de 1871*, Guatemala, Tipografía Sánchez & de Guise, 1898, p. 37.

4 Aguero, *op. cit.*, pp. 34-35.

5 Díaz, *Barrios ante la Posteridad*, p. 67.

ital.[6] On the same day the victors proceeded to the plaza opposite the palace, where Granados, having been previously invited to attend a *Te Deum* at the Cathedral, found the Archbishop, Dr. Bernardo Piñol y Aycinena, at the center door waiting, dressed in his robes. Approaching the revolutionary leader, the prelate said, " Miguel, I recommend my church to you," and García Granados answered jovially, " Don't worry, Bernardo." [7] All pleasant enough—but soon clouds were hovering once more over the Church-State relations in Guatemala.

Barrios and Granados were to find the task of organizing the government an arduous one. The heads of the important departments had fled, the treasury was empty, and certain of the more radical Liberals, mainly artisans and mechanics, wished to dictate the measures to be adopted. Above all, they manifested a most violent feeling toward the Jesuits and other Religious Orders.[8] On August 16, 1871 the Archbishop sent a petition to the Provisional President asking security for the Jesuits thus threatened.[9] The next day Bruno Samayoa presented a motion at a meeting of the *Junta Patriótica,* organization of the radicals or Patriots, as they called themselves, asking the government for the expulsion of the Jesuits. The members of the club, about eight hundred in number, sent a committee to García Granados to communicate this request to him. He answered that he would consider the matter promptly.[10] His decision was hastened by revolts arising at the end of that month in Santa Rosa, which the

6 Aguero, *op. cit.,* p. 34.

7 Díaz, *Barrios ante la Posteridad,* p. 102.

8 Bancroft, *op. cit.,* III, 424. *Cf.* also García, *op. cit.,* II, 375: " In the Patriotic Club which took upon itself the prerogatives of an authentic national representative body, there was great agitation for the expulsion. Night after night mobs of men and women who belonged to that club marched through the streets with seditious shouts, heaping insults on the Jesuits."

9 *Ibid.*

10 Díaz, *Barrios ante la Posteridad,* p. 108.

Jesuits, with others, were accused of instigating.[11] A periodical of San Salvador, " *La Verdad* ", gave a graphic account of the events in that crisis:

> ... The Patriotic Clubs were beginning to clamor for the expulsion of the Company of Jesus and to solicit signatures for that purpose. Petitions were also being circulated seeking signatures protesting their expulsion. The circulars and the orders of the government requesting the inhabitants to sign the petition against the Fathers finally reached Santa Rosa, capital of the *Oriente*. They aroused the people to such an extent that they seized their arms with the cry " ¡ *Viva la religión* ! " and thus commenced disastrous warfare in the *Oriente*. At this, the Provisional President, García Granados, wrote on a scrap of paper, without an envelope, these few words to the Archbishop: " Bernardo, it is urgent that I see you this afternoon at five o'clock."
>
> His Excellency don Bernardo Piñol y Aycinena, Archbishop of that See, taking his hat and cane, set out for the house of the Provisional President. The latter said to him, " The people have revolted against the government because they believe that it is persecuting religion. The only way to pacify them is for you to write a Pastoral saying that the government is not persecuting the Church; rather that, zealous for its well-being, it is expelling the Jesuits, who are an evil influence. I beseech you to write a Pastoral declaring this." The prelate answered, " I cannot do so. The Jesuits are exemplary priests. They have done much good in Guatemala, instructing the young and evangelizing those very towns. They are the honor and glory of the Church. To write such a Pastoral would be a betrayal, unworthy of a prelate of the Church. I cannot do it."
>
> On the following day the prelate received another note to the same effect. Once more he went to the house of the Provisional President and again heard the same request. Then García Granados said: " Yesterday I begged you to write the

11 *Ibid.*, p. 116.

Pastoral; now I command you to do it." The prelate replied: "Yesterday I told you I could not do it; now I tell you that I will not do it."

On the third day the Archbishop was summoned by means of another little note like the preceding. This time the Provisional President said, " The first time I begged you to write a Pastoral; yesterday I commanded you to write it, but you would not do it. Now I tell you that if you do not write it, there will be repeated the scenes of the year 1829." At this threat the Archbishop answered with unbroken calm: " I have told you that I cannot do it, that I will not do it; now I add that I am not afraid, no matter what you may do." [12]

In a decree dated August 31, 1871, García Granados issued a warning to those " who attempted to disturb the public peace by positive acts, or who brought about or aided such disturbances by word or writing " that they would be " judged summarily and officially as traitors to the country." [13] But his appeal to the insurgents to submit was disregarded.

On September 4, 1871 seventy-three Jesuits were expelled from Guatemala.[14] The previous day the Superior had received a communication signed by the Commandant-General, don Manuel Cano Madrazo, manifesting the order of the Ministry of War of Guatemala that at dawn on the 4th, at four o'clock, all the priests, novices and lay brothers of the mission should be assembled in the *Colegio Tridentino*, pre-

12 *La Verdad*, June 13, 1900. Because of his conservative sympathies, Piñol y Aycinena, then a young ecclesiastic, had emigrated in 1829 to Havana, where he had been denounced for having among his books a copy of the celebrated Constitution of 1812. This sufficed to cause him to be carried prisoner by the Spanish authorities to the *Castillo del Morro*, where he had remained until some friends exerted their influence. Years later he used to say: " They expelled me from Guatemala for being a conservative and religious; and in Havana, they imprisoned me for being a liberal, and partisan of the Constitution of Cadiz." (Batres Jáuregui, *op. cit.*, II, 365).

13 Decree No. 16, August 31, 1871 (*Recopilación de Leyes de Guatemala*, I, 16).

14 The *Boletín Oficial* for September 25, 1871 contained a list of the Jesuits expelled, their office and status in the Society.

pared to take their places in conveyances which would take
them to the port of San José, where they would embark on the
ship leaving the 5th, bound for foreign parts.[15] At the hour
cited carriages and horses appeared in front of the Convent
of *La Merced* and the *Colegio Tridentino,* together with a
military escort which treated the Jesuits with every consideration. They departed immediately for Amatitlán where they
lunched at the home of an ex-seminarian, Juan Mejicanos.
They continued their journey and spent the night at the
Hacienda " *Mauricio* ". They arrived at the port of San José
on the following day. Some were placed aboard the North
American ship " San Salvador " which left on September
10th, the rest on a ship bound for Corinth leaving on the
11th. The greater number of the Jesuits expelled were foreign:
Italians, Spaniards, Irish and others from the different countries of South America.[16]

The government of Guatemala prevailed upon the government of El Salvador to refuse hospitality to the banished
Jesuits, even going so far as to have included in the Arbizu-
Samayoa Treaty drawn up between the two countries on
January 25, 1872, Article XII, which expelled from the territory of El Salvador those Jesuits who had taken shelter there
after having been driven from Guatemala. This Article, which
did not appear in the copy of the Treaty published in El Salvador, but which was printed in full in the *Gaceta de Guatemala,* read as follows:

The Government of Guatemala having expelled the Fathers
of the Society of Jesus, it being well known that their presence
in the country is harmful to the interests of the Republic, and
it being evident that the Government of Salvador might be
disturbed in the same manner and find in them an obstacle
to the firm establishment of the liberal institutions proclaimed
in both Republics, and considering, moreover, that the Con-

15 Díaz, *Barrios ante la Posteridad,* p. 110.

16 Pineda de Mont, *Recopilación de Leyes de Guatemala,* III, 290.

stituent Congress of El Salvador declared that the said Fathers should not be admitted to this Republic, both Governments agree to prohibit in the future in any part of their respective territories the Fathers of the aforementioned Society, either organized or in any other manner.[17]

García Granados, in an address to the people of Guatemala on September 5, 1871, assured them that he had never harbored the least intention of attacking religion nor any of its ministers, but that he had been forced to expel the Jesuits in order to preserve the public peace: [18]

The Provisional President of the Republic of Guatemala to his fellow-citizens:

My dear Fellow Citizens:

The recent occurrences oblige me to address you once more.

Ever since the Constituent Assembly in 1851, already purged by means of terror of many of its liberal members, decreed the admission of the Society of Jesus into Guatemala, I protested against this measure, persuaded as I was and still am, that its preponderant influence is incompatible with liberty and that, sooner or later, it would be a cause of agitation and perhaps of civil war.

In spite of this protest, when, last June, I overcame the administration of Cerna, desiring to reestablish the peace and tranquility which the revolution had destroyed, I did not judge it opportune to bring up this question which could be put off to a more propitious time. But pens more passionate than prudent began to arouse public opinion and the occurrences of Quezaltenango increased the disturbance.

The conquered party of the Reactionaries, believing the time favorable, began openly and actively to conspire, and, directing itself to the department of Santa Rosa, whose inhabitants were disposed to revolt, but ignorant, they maliciously calumniated the government, believing that the latter had resolved on the expulsion of all the religious communities

17 Vilanova Meléndez, *op. cit.*, p. 193.

18 *Boletín Oficial*, I, no. 9, Guatemala, September 12, 1871.

of men as well as of women, and that of the Archbishop and other individuals, which has not been nor will be the intention of the present government.

This party, which unfortunately comprises men as ungrateful as they are disloyal, has finally succeeded by means of its calumnies in arousing a part of that department, and has inundated in blood this capital on the first of this month. The Jesuits, so skillful in handling the truth, instead of dissuading their co-partisans from carrying out their evil intention, and acting boldly to put an end to all civil warfare, did all in their power to have them demand that the Jesuits remain in the country, even though for that end torrents of blood would be shed.

My first duty as head of the Nation is to preserve the peace and tranquility of the country. Persuaded that this was impossible while the Society of Jesus remained in the Republic of Guatemala, I resolved on its expulsion, not in a violent manner, as has been done in other places, but warning them some days in advance, in order that they might prepare for their departure, supplying carriages which would take them as far as the port of San José and paying their passage as far as Panama.

Fellow-Citizens: The enemies of order and of liberty have interpreted this step as an attack on religion, assuring the public that in a short time there will follow the expulsion of the other religious. I protest that these are false calumnies which they themselves spread, rising out of hatred and spite over having been defeated.

Fellow-Citizens: You well know that I am not accustomed to lie. Well then, I assure you that I do not harbor, nor have I ever harbored, the least intention of attacking religion or any of its ministers. But you will also understand that I have, not only the right, but also the duty of preserving public peace. Up to now I have been tolerant. May God grant that in fulfilling my obligations I may not be forced to use severity, because I confess that I desire more to be considered clement than harsh.

The following day, September 6, 1871, Barrios addressed the nation from Quezaltenango on the same subject but in a far stronger tone, declaring that the enemies of the Liberals had deceived the people, making them believe that the Provisional Government intended to destroy " the sacred religion of our fathers which all Guatemalans will defend ardently when they see it attacked." He made a bitter tirade against the Jesuits, whom he accused of rousing hatred and discord. " No, my fellow-countrymen," he assured them, " let us not be deceived by false prophets! We Liberals do not attack religion; on the contrary, we desire that its holy law be the norm of our conduct as it has been up to now." He then urged revenge on those who had instigated the revolt.[19]

On September 13th, García Granados, in a proclamation to the inhabitants of the province of Santa Rosa, told them that the enemies of the administration, taking advantage of their credulity and simplicity, had led them to take up arms against the government. Knowing their adherence to the religion inherited from their forefathers, they had made them believe, he continued, that it was being attacked and that there was being decreed the expulsion of religious orders, a calumnious accusation aimed at arousing anarchy in the Republic. The Provisional President ended with a plea for their loyalty to the administration and a threat against those who did not conform.[20]

Accused, along with the Jesuits, of inciting the insurrections in Santa Rosa and other towns of the *Oriente,* were the Archbishop, don Bernardo Piñol y Aycinena, and Bishop Mariano Ortiz Urruela. In a proclamation of September 29, 1871 the Patriotic Club of Amatitlán directed bitter complaints to the Provisional President for the clemency he was showing toward the ecclesiastics in not having yet punished them for what he had on September 5th openly called their disloyalty. To the Archbishop himself they protested:

19 *Ibid.,* p. 2.

20 *Boletín Oficial,* I, no. 10, Guatemala, Sept. 20, 1871.

... And you, Reverend Archbishop, whom public opinion accuses, rightly or wrongly, of being one of the principal instigators of the rebellion now taking place in the departments of *Oriente*? Does not your conscience tell you, even though public opinion be deceived, that you are responsible for the evils we are suffering, since you could have prevented them by speaking to those misguided sheep, making them understand that the Provisional Government is not attacking our holy religion? Does not your exalted position, your ministry of peace, and even your duty as a simple citizen, impose upon you this obligation? Or perhaps the blood, the lives and, above all, the eternal salvation of the souls of these misguided sheep are nothing to you, in comparison with the satisfying of that thirst for power and domination which devours your party.[21]

At this accusation, the Archbishop protested to the Government in the following letter, dated October 2nd:

Palace of the Archbishop of Guatemala, October 2, 1871. To the Minister of Government, Justice and Ecclesiastical Affairs:

Yesterday I received the enclosed printed copy of a manifestation addressed to the public by the Patriotic Club of Amatitlán. In this paper, charges are made against me as serious as they are calumnious, in connection with the insurrection in the towns of the *Oriente* against the present Provisional Government; and in making the said charges they invoke with manifest hypocrisy the Catholic religion and Christian charity, which they pretend to wish to interpret in their own way.

I deny, my dear Minister, with all the energy which I owe to my own dignity, and more than all, to that given me by the episcopal character, these unjust accusations with which I am wounded by men whom I count among my flock and who thoughtlessly join in injuring their pastor. As citizen and as man, I pardon them these injuries; as priest, as bishop and as their pastor, I have the duty to reveal the

21 García, *op. cit.*, V, 431.

calumny and save the rest of my flock from the evil which such a publication might cause.

Since the outbreak of the present civil war for causes which the Government knows perfectly, I have deplored and will continue to deplore the fatal consequences of this revolt, which are far from weighing on my conscience, and only on that of those who have prepared its causes. No word of mine directed to my flock in such circumstances (a thing never done before in analogous cases) would have been able to avoid touching the origin of that question; I would have been obliged to show myself a partisan, causing me to lose the impartiality necessary to a pastor who loves and ought to love all his sheep, whatever be the errors into which they may have by chance fallen; and, what is more, it would have caused me to contradict the principles which I declared in my petition directed to the Government, in junction with the head of the Ecclesiastical Chapter, on August 17th last, a petition which merited no written reply, and which was, in fact, disregarded, as is well-known by all.

I beg you, my dear Minister, to call this matter to the attention of the Supreme Government in order that, if it sees fit, it may take some action to repair the scandal caused by the publication to which I refer.

But, above all, I beg you to inform me as soon as possible of the decision of the Government in this matter, so that, making use of the freedom of the press, as the aforementioned Patriotic Club has done, I may make public this communication and its results.

I reiterate to you the protestation of my deep consideration and appreciation.

May God grant you many years,
Bernardo, Archbishop of Guatemala.[22]

In reply to this protest the Archbishop received a note the same day telling him that the Minister of Ecclesiastical Affairs was ill, but that he had directed his secretary to get in touch with the publishers who had distributed the proclama-

22 *Ibid.*, p. 432.

tion of the Patriotic Club and inform them that, since the city was in a state of siege, they could not publish anything without first having the imprimatur of the government.

On October 12th the Archbishop received a letter from the government, not only refusing to reprimand the Patriotic Club for its proclamation against the Archbishop, but seconding the said organization in its accusations, saying, among other things:

> The Government has reread the publication to which you have referred and, not without deep grief, has recognized that the statements you make lack the exactness and impartiality which should be expected from your elevated position and intelligence.
>
> The Patriotic Club of Amatitlán, like all citizens whether friendly or unfriendly to the present administration, was deeply moved by the necessarily tragic results of the rebellion of some of the departments of the *Oriente*; it lifted its voice, interpreting the sentiments of all; and, realizing the beneficial results which would arise from the intervention of the Archbishop, persuading the inhabitants of the rebelling towns that the expulsion of the Jesuits did not imply an attack on the religion of the Republic, it found in the refusal of the Archbishop to intervene an unjustifiable omission, which could only be considered as evidence of a strong spirit of partisanship, as a forgetfulness of the sacred duties of the priest, as the indifference of a citizen to the victims of Fraijanes and Santa Rosa.... The President himself, recognizing the power of religion, asked, supplicated, begged you to issue the Pastoral, not because he doubted of his own power to crush the rebellion, but because, although accustomed to the hardships of war, he could not be indifferent to so much bloodshed...
>
> All of these considerations did not move you to take this humanitarian step; and, listening perhaps to the voice of personal interests, you refused to comply with a duty prescribed by your episcopal ministry, called for desperately by the circumstances, and implored repeated times by the President of the Republic.

It is, then, neither just nor logical for you to criticize so severely the judgments of the Patriotic Club of Amatitlán; it is neither just nor logical to deny with a word the charges made against you in that publication; it is neither just nor logical to request the Government to dictate a special order to repair a scandal which, if it exist at all, is certainly not in the publication alluded to . . . [23]

The Archbishop's reply to the preceding letter, dated October 17th, was a reiteration of his innocence of the charges and a protestation that he had acted according to his conscience in refusing to write the Pastoral demanded, and had had the unanimous approval of his ecclesiastical councillors in the matter.[24]

The government's answer was the decree of expulsion, issued that very day, and instructions to set out the next morning, October 18th, for the port of San José in the carriage which would be at his door at four o'clock.[25] The decree summed up the complaints of the government in the following terms:

Ministry of Government, Justice and Ecclesiastical Affairs.

The Provisional President has been pleased to issue the following decree No. 23: Miguel García Granados, Captain General of the Army and Provisional President of the Republic of Guatemala, considering: that the Archbishop Dr. don Bernardo Piñol y Aycinena, involved in the revolutionary movements, has not only intervened in a direct manner in the revolution, but, showing open hostility to the government, has refused to depose pastors who are working in favor of sedition; that he has refused to fill vacant parishes, in spite of the repeated complaints of the people; that, in spite of the reiterated demands of the government, he has refused to publish a pastoral which would have for its object to put an end

23 *Ibid.*, p. 434.
24 *Ibid.*, p. 435.
25 *Ibid.*, p. 436.

to the calumnies which have been spread for seditious purposes in certain towns, imputing to the government the project of destroying religion; and that this unjustifiable refusal
has been the cause of the bloodshed and the numerous victims
of the war; that, besides, he has directed toward the government threats for trifling causes and with the sole purpose of
provoking a rupture which would serve as a pretext for the
continuation of civil war; that the government has tried by
mild means to avoid these difficulties which hinder the administration and has not been successful, in spite of the deference and consideration it has shown in its official relations;
that this lack of harmony between the ecclesiastical government and the civil cannot continue without causing real and
irreparable harm: therefore, using the full powers which the
people have invested in me, and in accord with the counsel
of my ministers, I decree: that there be expelled from the
Republic Archbishop Dr. don Bernardo Piñol y Aycinena,
who must embark on the next ship which leaves for Panama,
and may not return to the country without previous permission from the government. Given in the Palace of the
Government, Guatemala, Oct. 17, 1871 — Miguel García
Granados.[26]

On October 19th García Granados issued a decree granting
amnesty to all those who had taken up arms in the department
of the *Oriente*, " in view of the consideration that:

... the Metropolitan Archbishop and the Bishop of Teya, on
whom rests the charge of having instigated the revolt and
having declared themselves openly hostile to the government,
thus failing in the duties of their ministry of peace and conciliation, and, instead of working for obedience to the constitutional government, have aroused the people against the
authorities, fomenting error and ideals which gave rise to
the civil war which has just been happily ended; these having
been expelled from the country, the responsibility for those
occurrences must not be imputed in all its gravity to those
who must be excused because of their ignorance, which pre-

26 *National Archives of Guatemala*, Decree No. 23, Oct. 17, 1871.

vented them from resisting the powerful insinuations of the persons who instigated the revolution.[27]

In the *Boletín Oficial* for October 24, 1871, the Liberal government defended at length its expulsion of the Jesuits, of Archbishop Piñol y Aycinena, and of the Bishop of Teya, don Mariano Ortiz Urruela,[28] against the accusation that it was attacking religion,[29] and declared that, not only would it fulfill its obligation toward all citizens, but it would grant special protection to all religious communities and ecclesiastics who would obey the orders of the government, "carrying out the duties imposed upon them by their holy ministry in conformity with the precepts of the Gospel."

From León, Nicaragua came the final protest of Archbishop Piñol y Aycinena to the government of Guatemala, written in that city December 1, 1871 and published in the periodical *La Verdad* on January 13, 1872:

To the Provisional President of the Republic of Guatemala:

On October 17th last at eight o'clock in the evening I received the official communication containing the decree expelling me from the Republic, and declaring that on the following day at four o'clock in the morning I was to enter the carriage which would be placed at my disposition. With peace of mind, although with the deepest sorrow over the sad lot of my beloved Church in Guatemala, I received this communication and proceeded to comply with it.

The short space of eight hours allowed me to prepare for my departure did not permit me, as is easily understood, to do more than gather together the things most necessary for a voyage. Thus it was that I did not answer the accusations made against me in that decree. I reserved my right to

27 *Ibid.*, No. 20, October 19, 1871.

28 Decree No. 24, dated October 17, 1871, expelling the Bishop of Teya, accused him of forgetting his sacred duties, and sowing discord among the people by accusing the government of persecuting religion.

29 *Boletín Oficial*, vol. I, Nov. 15, p. 4, October 24, 1871.

protest for the first opportunity, and now I am going to use it, hoping that you who have wounded me so deeply will at least listen to my just vindication.

The first consideration listed in the decree accuses me of having instigated a revolution directly. To instigate a revolution means to arouse the people thereto by writing or speech, to support them materially, and to hold with them some communication in order to urge them on to revolt; but where are the proofs that I have acted thus? There are none, nor can there be any, since deeds which have not occurred cannot be proved. Even if one knew so little of my character as to believe me capable of conduct so unworthy of a bishop, it would be most evident that in no event could I consider it beneficial to my position or to my interests. I know very well, my dear President, what I owe to my dignity and to my conscience . . . My error lay in thinking that the Government would be far from demanding from me what in conscience it ought not to expect, far from permitting itself to be led astray by evil counsel to the point of expelling me without any justification, since to make charges is not to prove them, and to hurl accusations is not sufficient to condemn.

That I showed myself hostile to the Government by refusing to remove pastors who were working in favor of revolution is another charge made against me in the decree, a charge entirely false, as can be seen from the official correspondence between the Government and the Ecclesiastical authorities during the three and a half months that the former have been in power. There it can be seen that I have never been requested to remove a pastor, and if there be any case of this nature, I beg of you to specify it. The only nomination of a pastor requested of me was that of Fr. don Rafael Contreras for the parish of Sonsonate; but I granted that request on Oct. 6th, ceding to the desires of the Government, notwithstanding the fact that I was well informed that, if Fr. Contreras had had contact with the insurrectionists when he was serving the parish of Mataquescuintla, it would certainly be inevitable if he were in that parish in the very center of the faction, even though he cooperated with it in no way of his own will. I remember no other cases to which could be applied the accusation made against me in this particular.

The same is true for the neglect ascribed to me in filling vacant parishes and correcting the abuses of pastors of whom the parishioners were complaining. If the scarcity of suitable priests has been the cause of delay in providing for some parishes, I have never refused to fill them; rather have I striven to my utmost to take care of the needs under the circumstances. As proof, there are those of don García, San Martín, Amatitlán and many others recorded in the Archives of the Ecclesiastical Government. As for the complaints of the parishioners against their pastors, I could not nor should not in justice accede to them without investigating the causes, especially since, as a general rule, these complaints are invented by a few malcontents who pretend to act in the name of the whole parish, and also because it is not strict justice to remove a pastor without hearing his side of the case and examining the matter. This charge, then, is as empty as the previous.

But what shows most clearly the unjust prejudice which unfortunately has predominated in the dictating of this decree is the accusation that I refused to issue a Pastoral which would have for its object to dissipate the calumnies spread through the towns imputing to the Government the project of destroying Religion, adding that this unjustifiable refusal has been the cause of the bloodshed and numerous victims of the war.

My dear President, the facts are clearly visible and speak more eloquently than the publications of a press dominated by the Government. The uprising in the departments of Santa Rosa, Jutiapa and Chiquimula was caused by the imprudent, unjust and violent expulsion of the Fathers of the Society of Jesus which, existing under the safeguard of a law which called them to the country twenty years previous, without having committed the slightest fault, without previous judgment and against the will of almost the entire intelligent and prudent part of the population, was banished from the Republic by the Government, without a previous decree, ignoring all the petitions and representations of the region in which they worked, corrupting the municipal governments of the towns to make them request this unjust measure, and, in fine, violating every human and divine right.

And is it not attacking Religion to outrage its ministers in such an unjustifiable manner? Does not this act cause scandal throughout the country, and even in the minds of those who always remain aloof from public affairs? I, as Prelate of the Church of Guatemala, in union with my Chapter, begged in writing; by word of mouth in private I entreated you and urged you to withdraw from an undertaking so hateful that it would draw down upon your administration an indelible stain in the eyes of all men of feeling; but nothing of this prevailed to prevent it. I suffered in silence this blow to the Church of Guatemala and to Religion, which has always been the support of governments, and I feared that the consequences would not delay in manifesting themselves.

A step so daring was sufficient to arouse the discontent of the people, so that there was no need of the calumny which you claim was spread among them against the government. The good sense of the people made them understand that there where the ministers of worship were submitted to such treatment, there was no respect for Religion and the Church; and the history of modern revolutions shows clearly, with no room for doubt, that the false application of liberal principles begins with the persecution of this Order which constitutes the bulwark of the Catholic Church, and soon follows with an attack on all the other sacred institutions.

Now, the government wished me to issue a Pastoral declaring that the expulsion of the Jesuits was not an attack on Religion; that, notwithstanding the injustice of this measure, they should hope for the most ample protection of the Church and Religion on the part of the Government; and that neither the former nor the latter should consider itself offended by the outrage perpetrated on its worthy ministers. This is what I was asked to tell the people. But with what conscience, with what dignity, could I incur the guilt of such a lie? To call evil good—would that not be for me, who have as Bishop the strictest obligation to teach my flock sound doctrine, would that not be to contract a fearful responsibility? This, then, was my position; there was nothing, nor is there anything in me of the spirit of partisanship, of hostility towards the Government, for which I pray to God every day of my life; neither is there any lack of humanity in my omitting what might have avoided the shedding of blood. No, there was nothing of this; God knows that if it were not for the interests of truth and of conscience, superior to all human interests, I should have been glad to accede to the supplications of the Government, as I acceded to those which you made me by word of mouth in the name of the Government, authorizing the missions of the Franciscans, Recollects and Dominicans to procure peace.

The blood, then, which unfortunately has been shed in the campaign of Santa Rosa will fall only upon those who brought about the uprising in those towns, and not upon me who in no way instigated it, nor was it in my power to prevent it by betraying truth and justice.

Finally, my dear President, I do not know what could have been the threatening communications which I directed to the Government for trifling reasons, according to the decree. Neither my character nor my principles would ever permit me to use a threatening style and much less in my relations with the Government. On making such charges against me it would have been not only fitting, but also of strict justice, to prove them, and to listen to my explanations.

In view of all this, I protest most solemnly against the unjustifiable violence of which I have been the object, that of expelling me from my Diocese; I protest, likewise, against the great harm and the real and irreparable evils caused by this act to the sacred rights of my Church and my person; and I beg you to consider this protest and to give it the publicity which justice requires.

I am, notwithstanding all this, with true Christian charity and paternal affection,

Very attentively yours,
Bernardo, Archbishop of Guatemala.

On December 1, 1871 the Archbishop in exile also sent a circular letter to the clergy and faithful of Guatemala, including all the documents of the case, so that they might vindicate the rights of the Church. After reviewing the events briefly, he declared it to be his opinion that the expulsion had been predetermined and that the Government had made use of the events and circumstances described to justify its actions. He closed with the assertion: " This we say with all the certainty which a clear conscience gives, and with no fear of being contradicted." [30]

García Granados' reiterated insistence that the Government intended no hostility toward religion seemed strengthened by an official announcement of the funeral services to be held for don Felipe Gálvez, Minister of Foreign Affairs:

> The *Junta Política* of this capital, desiring to offer a slight testimony of its appreciation of the memory of señor Gálvez, and of recognition of the important and disinterested services which he performed in the cause of liberty as one of its most enthusiastic collaborators, requests you to recommend his soul to God and attend the services which will be celebrated tomorrow at nine o'clock in the Cathedral.[31]

These services, carried out with the greatest solemnity, were attended by the government officials, as well as the Diplomatic Corps and the religious communities.[32]

But, in spite of their many protestations of innocence, the Liberals of 1871 continued in their efforts to remove all vestiges of Church influence, and they followed almost the same pattern as those of Mariano Gálvez' time. The latter had on April 12, 1831 prohibited burial within the towns, a measure rescinded October 25, 1839 by decree of the Conservatives when they had come into power. Now, once more, in a decree dated November 10, 1871, García Granados forbade all burial within the confines of the towns, with the exception of that of

30 García, *op. cit.*, V, 437.

31 Díaz, *Barrios ante la Posteridad*, p. 120.

32 *Boletín Oficial*, vol. I, Nov. 7, 1871.

the Metropolitan prelates, Bishops of the diocese, and the religious of both sexes whose rules demanded that they be buried within the walls of their convents.[33]

Following again the precedent set by the earlier Liberals, the legislators of 1871 passed laws involving the financial status of the Church in Guatemala. On September 4, 1871 the property of the Jesuits was confiscated. On September 16th the Provisional President entrusted to don José María Escamilla the administration of the goods which had belonged to this Order, the incomes from which were to be placed at the disposal of the Government, while the final disposition of the property and goods was being decided.[34] Later, on November 24th, the Government ordered that, while the authorities were determining this disposal, there should be handed over to Canon José Antonio Urrutia the estate called "Nubes", in order that its income might be applied to the upkeep of the Church of La Merced, of which he was in charge.[35] Still another measure striking at the wealth of the Church was the decree issued Dec. 22, 1871 abolishing the tithes,[36] which, however, declared that any deficit experienced by the Church because of this suppression should be paid out of the public treasury. As a preliminary to this action, the Minister of the Exchequer had interviewed the Vicar General, manifesting to him the inconveniences of the tithes because of the expenses encountered in its collection and the antagonism it aroused, and urging him to approve, in substitution for it, the sum of 20,000 pesos annually from the National Treasury. The Vicar General, having consulted the Chapter, replied that no arrangement could be made without consulting the Holy See, according to Canon Law. However, the Provisional President, taking the consent of the Pontiff for granted, decreed the suppression, to take effect Jan. 1, 1872.

33 Ibid., vol. I, no. 18, Nov. 10, 1871.

34 Ibid., vol. I, no. 11, Sept. 25, 1871.

35 Ibid., no. 20, December 6, 1871.

36 National Archives of Guatemala, Decree No. 43, December 22, 1871.

The Reactionary party had once more raised its revolutionary standard and the government felt itself obliged to take energetic measures. On Feb. 7, 1872 there was issued a decree limiting the freedom of the press.[37] On March 10, 1872, when the Constitutional Assembly met, it contained no ecclesiastics, a striking contrast to those of 1821 and 1839. Article 5 of Decree No. 39 on the election of Deputies to the Constituent Assembly, issued December 11, 1871, had stated quite definitely:

> No religious may be elected Deputy ... Neither may pastors nor curates be elected Deputies for the District in which their parishes are located.[38]

This Assembly found itself hampered by the fact that don Mariano Ortiz Urruela, Bishop of Teya, living in Honduras since his exile from Guatemala, had found a sympathetic protector and support in the person of José María Medina, President of Honduras. García Granados put himself at the head of his troops to wage war against Honduras, delegating his powers during his absence to Lieutenant General Justo Rufino Barrios.[39]

On April 4, 1872 a decree was issued declaring that any person who, in discourses, sermons or any other public act, would arouse the people to rebellion against the authorities constituted by law, or produce any subversive activity whatsoever against the public order, would be expelled from the territory of the Republic of Guatemala without any formality whatsoever.[40]

On May 24, 1872 a decree abolished in the Republic of Guatemala the Society of Jesus, forbidding the entrance into

---

37 *Recopilación de Leyes de Guatemala*, I, 95, Decree No. 48.

38 *Ibid.*, I, 76.

39 Díaz, *Barrios ante la Posteridad*, p. 133.

40 *Ibid.*, p. 166. *Cf.* also article entitled, "A Grandes Males, Grandes Remedios", in *El Crepusculo*, April 13, 1872, vol. I, no. 22.

the country of any of its members, either organized or in any other manner.[41] The decree likewise confiscated their possessions and ordered them sold at public auction, " in view of the needs of the public treasury and the expenses involved in conducting the said Fathers out of the country." On May 27th, another decree abolished the Congregation of St. Philip Neri, nationalized its property also, and placed all the sacred vessels at the disposal of the Vicar General of the Archdiocese.[42] On May 28th, the ancient property of the Dominicans, *Palencia,* taken from them in the first upheaval and restored in Carrera's régime, was once more confiscated, to be divided into small plots which were distributed to the Indians of the region.[43] On May 31, 1872, the Vicar General don Francisco Apolinario Espinosa protested vigorously against the expulsion of the religious from the Archdiocese.[44] The government's reply was a summons to appear before a jury,[45] to answer, not only for his protest against the last decrees of Barrios,[46] but also for implication in the frustrated conspiracy against the fort of San José.[47] The government continued the expulsion of the religious. On June 3, 1872, the Capuchins of Antigua, thirty-nine in number, were taken in carriages to the port of Champerico, placed on board the " Sacramento ", and conducted to San Francisco, California.[48] Finally, on June 7, 1872, General Barrios declared the extinction of all religious communities in the Republic of Guatemala, because he considered, among other things, " that the afore-

41 *National Archives,* Decree No. 59, May 24, 1872.

42 *Ibid.,* Decree No. 61, May 27, 1872.

43 *Recopilación de Leyes de Guatemala,* I, 107.

44 García, *op. cit.,* V, 474.

45 " La Verdad ", León, Nicaragua, No. 57, June 28, 1872.

46 García, *op. cit.,* V, 447.

47 Díaz, *Barrios ante la Posteridad,* p. 142.

48 García, *op. cit.,* V, 443 ; Aguero, *op. cit.,* p. 30 ; Díaz, *Barrios ante la Posteridad,* p. 140.

mentioned institutions were by their very nature a handicap to the reforms of modern civilization which proscribes theocracy in the name of liberty, of progress and of the sovereignty of the people." [49] On June 10, 1872, a decree declared that the confiscated goods of the religious orders would be dedicated preferably to support and develop free education, and forthwith ordered public schools established in each of the convents of the abolished Orders.[50]

All these decrees had such a profound effect on the people that Barrios felt constrained to issue a proclamation on the matter, which was published in the *Boletín Oficial* for June, 14, 1872, justifying his action in the following terms:

> Having firmly resolved to bring to a successful end the democratic revolution which, at the cost of so many sacrifices, has triumphed in our nation, I do not hesitate, nor will I ever hesitate, to take any measures to make such a triumph positive and productive of practical results. I proceed in this way because the ideals proclaimed to redeem the people, if not realized in deeds and institutions, will remain only vague theories which, today or tomorrow, will fall into shameful discredit at the risk of the direst reactions.
>
> A proof of these ideals, a clear testimony of my intentions, is the decree which I have issued declaring the secularization of religious communities and the nationalization of their goods, the proceeds of which the government will dedicate to free education, the only means of bringing about effectively the progress and liberty of the people.
>
> My fellow citizens: the disposition which I have taken is worthy of progressive and cultured countries. Even well-inspired monarchies have decreed the extinction of religious orders and the nationalization of their temporal goods. Why, my fellow citizens, why should we not take this step, we who are republicans and who cannot permit the civil death of the

49 *Boletín Oficial*, vol. I, no. 35, June 14, 1872.

50 *Ibid.*, Decree No. 64, June 10, 1872; *Recopilación de Leyes de Guatemala*, I, 139.

individual, we who aspire to reform our institutions in order to bring about the well-being of our country?

My fellow-citizens: let us not cover our eyes with the bandage of fanaticism and of ancient prejudices. Let not those who are discontented with the government use the decree of secularization as a party weapon to create difficulties and disturb the public order. Let the national clergy and the religious themselves, treated with benevolence and respect, not occupy themselves in stirring up imprudent citizens to promote discord, because, if such a thing should happen, for those religious who show themselves instigators there will be expulsion instead of secularization, and for all those who cause scandal and oppose the law—bear in mind, my fellow-citizens, that I have sufficient power and energy to repress them and apply severe punishment, in compliance with orders, and that I am able to enforce respect for the law and the principles which determine the ends of my administration.[51]

Among the documents for the remainder of the year 1872 there were three which, though of little import, yet give a brighter picture of the Church-State relations. On June 21, 1872, the anniversary of the coronation of His Holiness Pope Pius IX, the banner of the Republic was ordered raised in the tower of the Palace of the Government, in celebration of the event.[52] On July 13th, in response to a request of the Vicar General, the Provisional President ordered all ecclesiastical students exempt from military service.[53] Finally, in the regulations drawn up for the National Guard of Guatemala, declared in force Dec. 7, 1872, among the duties of the officials was that of calling a priest for any person who might need him because of illness or other circumstance.[54]

Early in 1873 fresh insurrections broke out among the inhabitants of Los Altos. According to the Chaplain, Fr. Sebas-

51 *Boletín Oficial*, vol. I, no. 35, June 14, 1872, p. 3.

52 *Ibid.*, No. 67, June 27, 1872.

53 *Recopilación de Leyes de Guatemala*, I, 128.

54 *Ibid.*, p. 148.

tian Váldez, the Indians were demanding the return of the Archbishop and the Recollet and Franciscan Fathers who had worked among them.[55] In a proclamation dated February 12, 1873, Barrios expressed his determination to put down this revolt at whatever cost:

> ... On the other hand, let not the conspirators here, nor the revolutionaries in the highlands, have any illusions, taking my words as empty phrases of oratory, for I am going to prove to them what measures I am ready to take in order to combat and put down the savage revolution which, under pretexts of religion, seeks to destroy the Liberal cause, which is the cause of righteousness, of justice and of the progress of the people.
>
> My Fellow-Citizens: I am aware of the deep responsibility which weighs upon the Government; and in order to deal with public disorders, I shall hesitate before no obstacle, nor shall I distinguish between classes or persons. Do not be surprised, then, at my measures; for great evils, radical and extreme remedies are necessary.[56]

The nationalization of the goods of the ex-religious proceeded in earnest during the year 1873. Barrios consolidated the property, furnishings, valuables, investments, inheritances, etc. of all the churches, monasteries, convents, sanctuaries, brotherhoods, confraternities and all ecclesiastical communities, secular as well as religious. He expropriated, likewise, the goods of the hospitals, hospices, orphanages, charitable institutions of all kinds, schools, retreat houses—regardless of the end to which they had been destined. The sum total of the proceeds of the consolidated goods was being placed in a special treasury or bank, established for the purpose of loaning money to farmers at low rates of interest and for long periods of time.[57] On January 2, 1873, the Polytechnical

55 Díaz, *Barrios ante la Posteridad*, p. 153.

56 *Ibid.*

57 Aguilera de León, Carlos, *Libro-Centenario de Guatemala*, Guatemala, Tipografía Nacional, 1935, p. 54.

School, under the direction of officers brought for the purpose from Spain, was opened in the old Convent of the *Recolección.*[58] The old School of San José Calasanz, founded by royal decree in the time of Archbishop Cayetano Francos y Monroy, was converted into a school for boys called *El Progreso,* under the guidance of a close friend of Barrios, Buenaventura Murga, who had been a pupil of Frederick Crowe, Protestant missionary from England.[59] The old School for Orphans, conducted formerly by nuns, became the *Colegio La Esperanza* for girls, in charge of don Trinidad Nuñez de Rendón.[60] On Aug. 27, 1873, Decrees No. 104 and 105 respectively formally nationalized the goods and property of churches and religious orders and placed the proceeds in the aforementioned bank.[61] Among the considerations offered by the government for the issuing of these decrees were the complaint that one of the greatest obstacles to the prosperity of the nation was the existence of so much property in mortemain, and that the establishment of an institution of credit would give greater impulse to the industry and agriculture of the country.[62] Because the nationalization was proceeding very slowly, Barrios issued an order on Nov. 25th[63] and a decree, No. 107, on December 15th,[64] to expedite the matter.

Nor did the government stop here. All ecclesiastical privileges in both civil and criminal cases were done away with on March 12, 1873.[65] Freedom of worship was decreed on March 15, 1873, after the Government had considered " that such freedom would aid in attracting immigrants to Guate-

58 *Recopilación de Leyes de Guatemala,* I, 162, Decree No. 86.

59 Díaz, *Barrios ante la Posteridad,* p. 262.

60 *Ibid.,* p. 257.

61 *Recopilación de Leyes de Guatemala,* I, 210, 213.

62 *Boletín Oficial,* No. 27, Sept. 27, 1873.

63 *National Archives of Guatemala,* November 25, 1873.

64 *Ibid.,* Decree No. 107, December 15, 1873.

65 *Ibid.,* Decree No. 92, March 12, 1873.

mala; and that competition might cause Catholicism to be
practiced more carefully, as in other countries having the
same freedom of religions." Among the articles of this decree
was one declaring that the exercise of all religions was free,
and therefore those who professed them might build churches
and hold public worship, and another insisting that, in spite of
the above, the Catholic religion remained on the same status,
by virtue of the existing laws and the Concordat.[66]

The advanced age of the Provisional President, the activity
of the reactionaries, the vagueness of the ideas of the revolutionaries, now made it advisable to replace García Granados.
Although an enlightened and able man, according to Bancroft,
García Granados was too easy-going and kind-hearted for the
place he had been called to fill at a period demanding great
energy and inflexible will. Another drawback was his connection by family ties and early association with many of the
Conservatives. The reactionaries took advantage of his good
nature to keep the country in a turmoil, hoping to restore
the old régime. " But," concludes Bancroft, " they defeated
themselves, bringing into existence the iron power of Barrios,
who tolerated no opposition to his will, nor overlooked sedition in any form." [67]

There was no doubt of the outcome of the popular elections
called by García Granados to choose his successor, and on
May 7, 1873, General Barrios was informed by the National
Assembly that he had been elected President.[68] One of his
first acts was the expulsion of the Vicar General, don Francisco Apolinario Espinosa y Palacios, with whom he had had
constant friction. The Vicar General had not only protested
repeatedly against the anti-clerical measures of the government, but had obstinately opposed the action of the latter in
naming ecclesiastics to the Cathedral Chapter to replace Dr.

66 *Ibid.*, Decree No. 93, March 15, 1873.

67 Bancroft, *op. cit.*, III, 430.

68 *Boletín Oficial*, No. 10, May 17, 1873.

don Pedro García and Dr. don Juan C. Cabrejo, whom it
had banished perpetually from the country.[69] The Vicar General based his objections on the grounds that the civil government could not assume the rights of the *patronato,* since
such rights were conceded only under condition that the Holy
See be first consulted; and, furthermore, even if it possessed
such right, it would permit only nomination to vacant offices,
and not the rendering of them vacant, since those offices
cannot be made vacant at the wish of the patron (supposing
the President to be such), but rather by the renunciation of
the dignity by the prebend himself, or by some canonical
cause.[70] General Barrios in his reply cited Article VIII of the
Concordat, in which His Holiness had conceded to the President of Guatemala the privilege of naming in each Chapter
six prebendaries, the first always excluded, and ended with
these words:

> ... Thus, then, the President being up to this very day in
> uninterrupted possession of his rights as patron of the Church
> in Guatemala, and of his other privileges, no authority, not
> even that of the Pontiff, can nullify the acts he has performed
> by virtue of it. Even supposing, then, that in the future, a
> thing which is not likely to happen, there should arise conflict
> between the Holy See and the Government of the Republic,
> because of past acts or future difficulties, so that both powers
> should declare the Concordat broken, this decision would have
> no retroactive effect on acts previous to the declaration of
> the rupture.[71]

When the Vicar General suggested submitting the matter to
the Holy See, the Government refused, and requested the
Ecclesiastical Chapter to remove the Vicar General from office,
since he had repeatedly refused to resign when requested to
do so by Barrios. The Chapter remained loyal to Espinosa,

69 *Recopilación de Leyes de Guatemala*, I, 199, Decree No. 100.

70 García, *op. cit.*, V, 454.

71 Díaz, *Barrios ante la Posteridad*, p. 170.

and the Government, its patience at an end, dictated the expulsion.[72]

From his place of exile in California, the Vicar General sent the following protest on August 19, 1873:

San Francisco, California, Aug. 19, 1873

To the Minister of Government, Justice and Ecclesiastical Affairs of the Republic of Guatemala:

In order to protest, as is my strict duty, against the unfounded accusations of the Decree dictated by the President, in which I am banished perpetually from my country, and although deprived of the documents which would justify my conduct in the government of the Church of Guatemala, because of the violence and absolute state of incommunication in which I was hurried to exile, I take advantage of this opportunity which is the first I have had, in order to raise my voice to that Supreme Government through your office. I do not attempt to vindicate myself in detail in regard to the accusations made against me, for that would require documents which are not in my possession, but in the Archives of that Metropolitan Curia; but I do deny, in the most absolute and energetic manner, all the accusations mentioned in my condemnation.

The only resemblance to truth, in the fundamental part of the Decree, is the reference to my relationship to don Enrique Palacios, one of the leaders whom it declares to have been working against that administration; but as for this, I call on the good faith of the Minister, on the conscience of the President himself and on the judgment of the people of Guatemala to say whether any one of my acts while at the head of the Church could ever be interpreted as connivance with or partiality towards Palacios and favoring of the Revolution, and not the strict fulfillment of my duty as Prelate, a fact which I glory in affirming, because it was always the only norm of my conduct.

I protest, then, my dear Minister, against the false accusations made against me in the said decree; I protest against

72 *Ibid.*, p. 167.

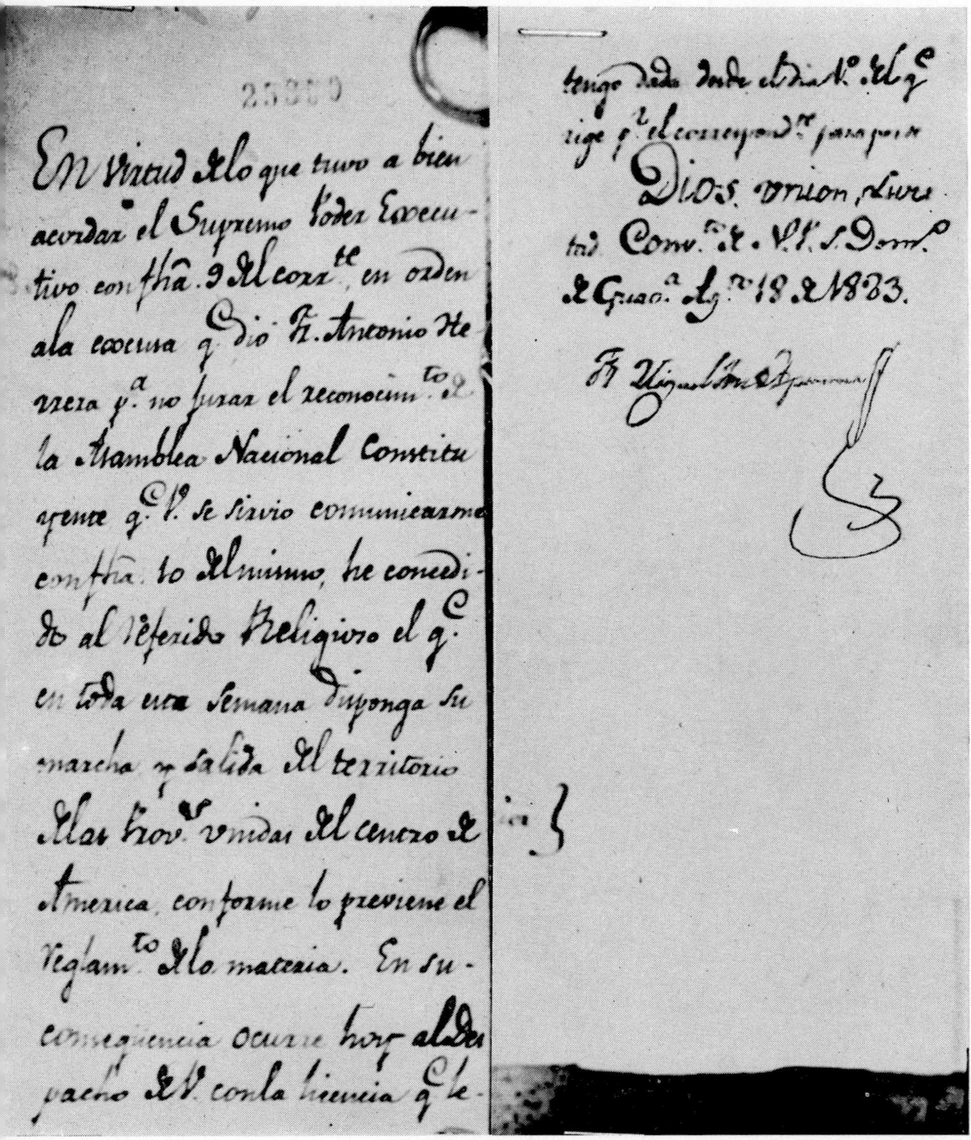

FIG. 1.—Order of Government dated Aug. 18, 1823, declaring that Fr. Antonio Herrera is to leave the country within one week for refusing to take the oath of allegiance to the republic. (See p. 78.)

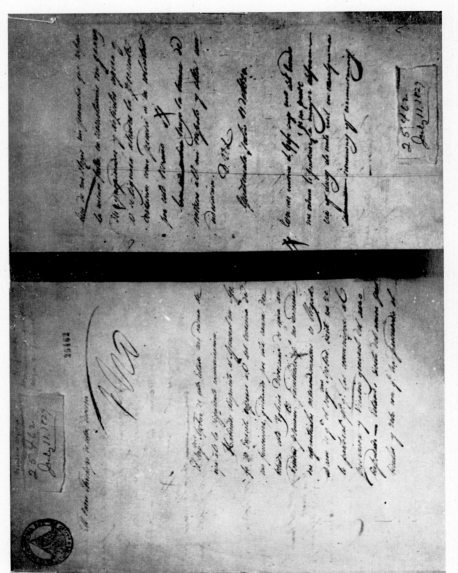

Fig. 2.—Letter of July 11, 1829, in which the Government of Guatemala requests the exiled Archbishop Casáus y Torres to delegate his faculties to the Vicar General. (See p. 108.)

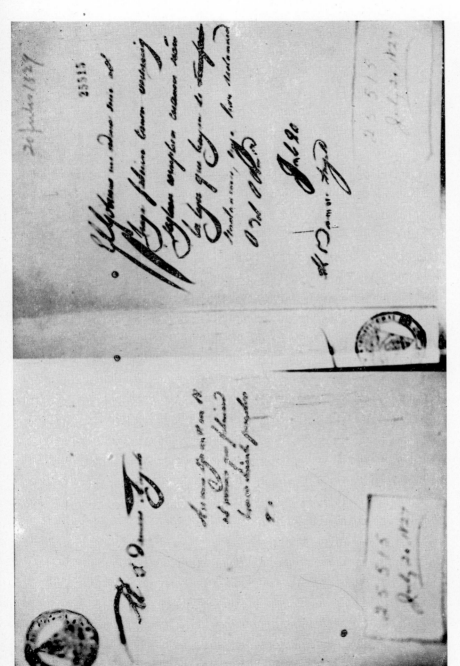

FIG. 3.—Orders of Government dated July 20, 1829, for the making of secular clothes for the religious expelled from their convents. (See p. 110.)

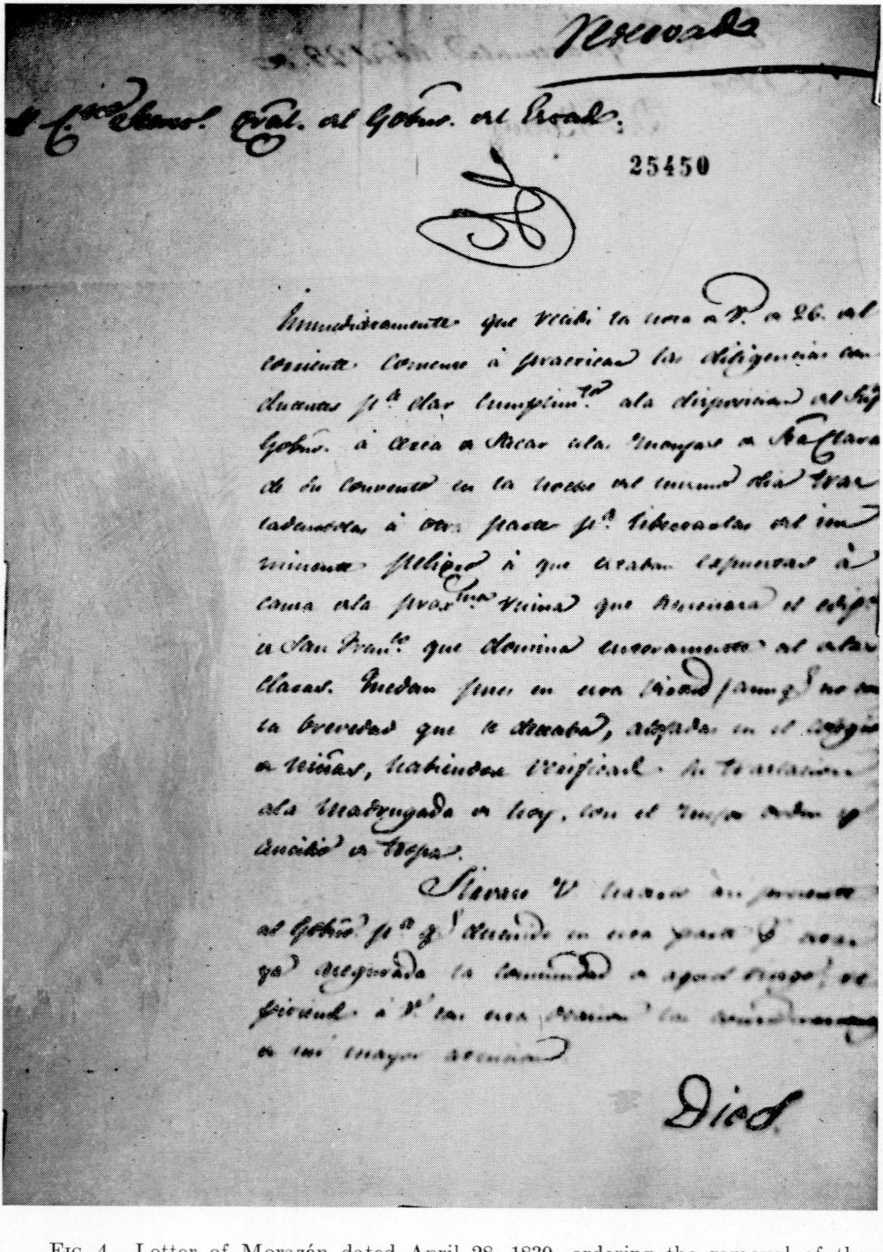

FIG. 4.—Letter of Morazán dated April 28, 1830, ordering the removal of the nuns from the Convent of Santa Clara with the greatest secrecy. (See p. 113.)

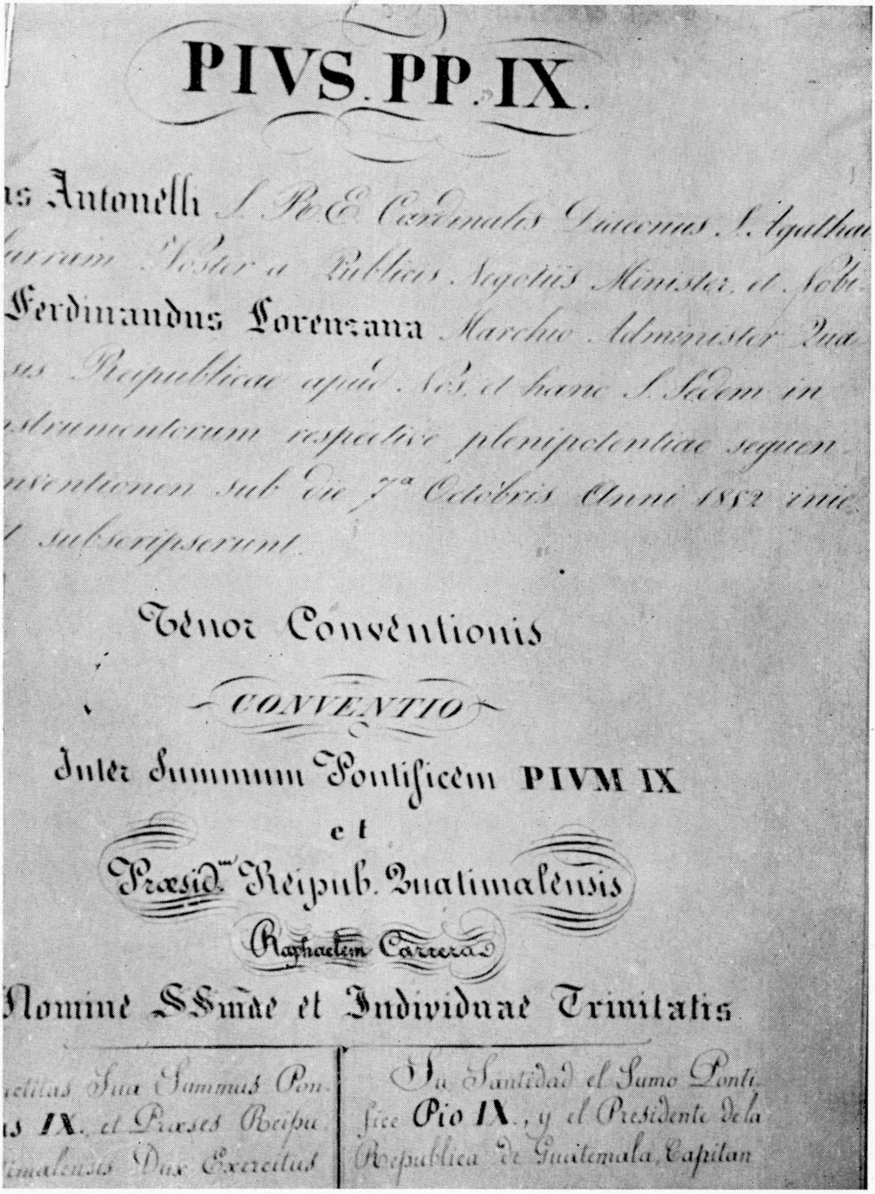

PIVS PP. IX.

...s Antonelli S. R. E. Cardinalis Diaconus S. Agatha...
...arum Noster a Publicis Negotiis Minister, et Nob...
Ferdinandus Lorenzana Marchio Administer Qua...
...us Reipublicae apud Nos et hanc S. Sedem in
...strumentorum respective plenipotentiae sequen...
...nventionem sub die 7a Octobris Anni 1852 ...
...t subscripserunt.

Tenor Conventionis

CONVENTIO

Inter Summum Pontificem PIVM IX

et

Praesid.em Reipub. Guatimalensis

Raphaelem Carrera

Nomine SSmae et Individuae Trinitatis

...ctitas Sua Summus Pon-	Su Santidad el Sumo Ponti-
...s IX. et Praeses Reipu-	fice Pio IX., y el Presidente de la
...imalensis Dux Exercitus	Republica de Guatemala, Capitan

FIG. 5.—First page of Concordat of 1852 drawn up between Pope Pius IX and Carrera. (See p. 140.)

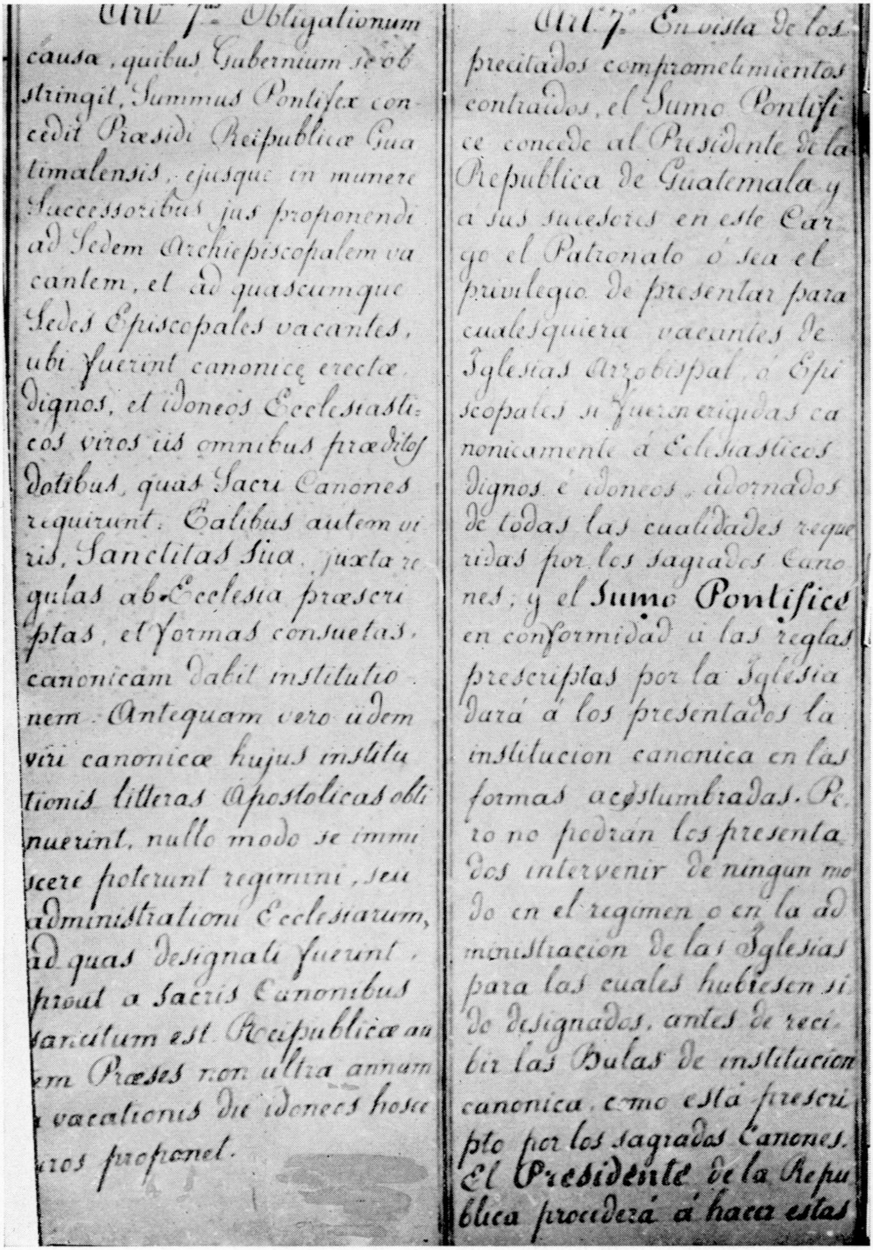

Art. 7us Obligationum
causa, quibus Gubernium se ob
stringit, Summus Pontifex con
cedit Præsidi Reipublicæ Gua
timalensis, ejusque in munere
Successoribus jus proponendi
ad Sedem Archiepiscopalem va
cantem, et ad quascumque
Sedes Episcopales vacantes,
ubi fuerint canonicę erectæ
dignos, et idoneos Ecclesiasti
cos viros iis omnibus prœditos
dotibus, quas Sacri Canones
requirunt. Talibus autem vi
ris, Sanctitas Sua, juxta re
gulas ab Ecclesia præscri
ptas, et formas consuetas,
canonicam dabit institutio
nem. Antequam vero iidem
viri canonicæ hujus institu
tionis litteras Apostolicas obti
nuerint, nullo modo se immi
scere poterunt regimini, seu
administrationi Ecclesiarum,
ad quas designati fuerint,
prout a Sacris Canonibus
sancitum est. Reipublicæ au
tem Præses non ultra annum
a vacationis die idoneos hosce
viros proponet.

Art. 7. En vista de los
precitados comprometimientos
contraidos, el Sumo Pontifi
ce concede al Presidente de la
Republica de Guatemala y
á sus sucesores en este Car
go el Patronato ó sea el
privilegio de presentar para
cualesquiera vacantes de
Iglesias Arzobispal ó Epi
scopales si fueren erigidas ca
nonicamente á Eclesiasticos
dignos é idoneos, adornados
de todas las cualidades reque
ridas por los sagrados Cano
nes; y el Sumo Pontifice
en conformidad á las reglas
prescriptas por la Iglesia
dará á los presentados la
institucion canonica en las
formas acostumbradas. Pe
ro no podrán los presenta
dos intervenir de ningun mo
do en el regimen ó en la ad
ministracion de las Iglesias
para los cuales hubiesen si
do designados, antes de reci
bir las Bulas de institucion
canonica, como está prescri
pto por los sagrados Canones.
El Presidente de la Repu
blica procederá á hacer estas

FIG. 6.—Facsimile of Article VII of the Concordat of 1852 in which Carrera is granted the right of *patronato* over the Church in Guatemala. (See p. 141.)

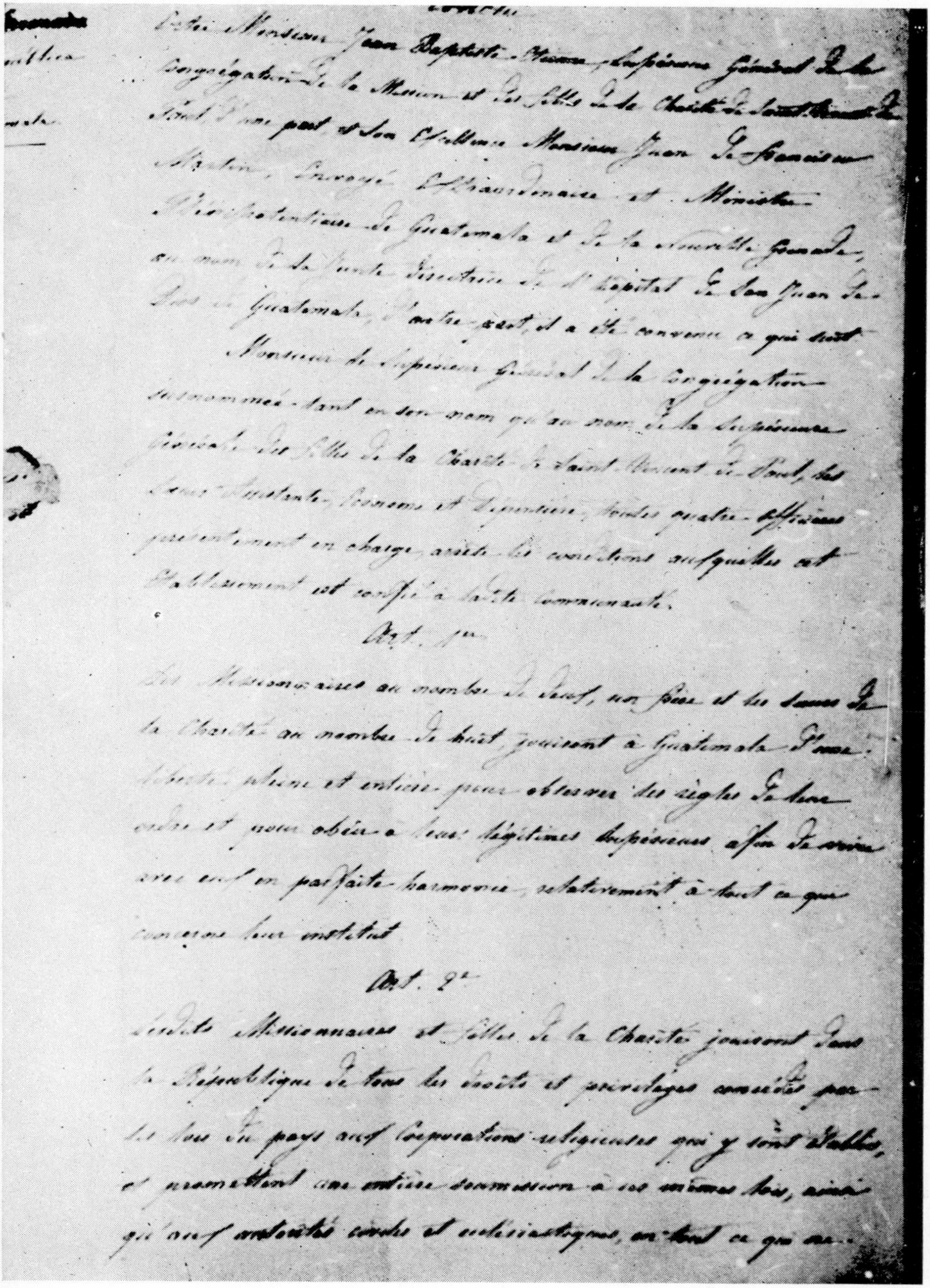

conclu

entre Monsieur Jean Baptiste Etienne, Supérieur Général de la Congrégation de la Mission et des Filles de la Charité de Saint Vincent de Paul d'une part et Son Excellence Monsieur Juan de Francisco Martin, Envoyé Extraordinaire et Ministre Plénipotentiaire de Guatemala et de la Nouvelle Grenade, au nom de la Junta directrice de l'hôpital de San Juan de Dios de Guatemala, d'autre part, il a été convenu ce qui suit.

Monsieur le Supérieur Général de la Congrégation susnommée tant en son nom qu'au nom de la Supérieure Générale des Filles de la Charité de Saint Vincent de Paul, des Sœurs Assistante, Économe et Dépensière, toutes quatre officières présentement en charge, arrête les conditions auxquelles cet établissement est confié à ladite communauté.

Art. 1er

Les Missionnaires au nombre de deux, un Frère et les Sœurs de la Charité au nombre de huit jouiront à Guatemala d'une liberté pleine et entière pour observer les règles de leur ordre et pour obéir à leurs légitimes Supérieurs afin de vivre avec eux en parfaite harmonie, relativement à tout ce qui concerne leur institut.

Art. 2e

Lesdits Missionnaires et Filles de la Charité jouiront dans la République de tous les droits et privilèges concédés par les lois du pays aux corporations religieuses qui y sont établies, et promettent une entière soumission à ces mêmes lois, ainsi qu'aux autorités civiles et ecclésiastiques, en tout ce qui con...

FIG. 7.—Partial Facsimile of Contract drawn up in 1858 between the Government of Guatemala and the French Sisters of Charity of Saint Vincent de Paul. (See p. 142.)

EL PARTIDO CONSTITUCIONAL

HA TENIDO CONOCIMIENTO DE LA MANIFESTACION POPULAR QUE SE VE-RIFICARA EL DOMINGO 25 DEL CORRIENTE, PARA EXPRESAR LA INCONFORMIDAD DEL PUEBLO DE GUATEMALA:

1o.—POR LAS DISPOSICIONES INCONSTITUCIONALES QUE CONTIENE LA LEY ELECTORAL, QUE LIMITA LA ORGANIZACION Y LIBRE ACTIVIDAD DE LOS PARTI-DOS POLITICOS,

2o.—POR LA INCONSTITUCIONALIDAD DEL ACUERDO GUBERNATIVO DE 20 DE MAYO DEL CORRIENTE AÑO QUE SUPRIME LA LIBERTAD DE LA PRENSA;

3o.—POR LAS DECLARACIONES DEL MINISTERIO DE GOBERNACION, AMENA-ZANTES A LA LIBRE EXPRESION DEL SENTIMIENTO RELIGIOSO DEL PUEBLO DE GUATEMALA.

EL PARTIDO CONSTITUCIONAL SIMPATIZA CON ESA EXPRESION DEL SENTI-MIENTO PUBLICO E INVITA A SUS AFILIADOS A PARTICIPAR EN ELLA.

GUATEMALA, AGOSTO DE 1946.

EL CONSEJO DIRECTIVO

Unión Tip.-Castañeda, Avila y Cía.

Fig. 8.—The political party called the "Partido Constitucional" urges its members to participate in the demonstration of Aug. 25, 1946, in order to protest against what they consider violations of the Constitution and threats to the freedom of religion. (See p. 214.)

EL PARTIDO DE LA REVOLUCION

En vista de la gran Manifestación Popular que tendrá lugar el 25 del corriente a las 10 horas, para patentizar la enérgica protesta del Pueblo de Guatemala:

1o.—Por las disposiciones violatorias de la Constitución que contiene la Ley electoral, que limitan arbitrariamente la organización y libre actividad de los Partidos políticos.

2o.—Por la inconstitucionalidad del Acuerdo Gubernativo fechado el 20 de Mayo de este año, que suprime la libertad de Prensa.

3o.—Por las declaraciones oficiales del Gobierno de la República, que amenazan la libre expresión del sentimiento religioso del Pueblo de Guatemala.

EL PARTIDO DE LA REVOLUCION, plenamente identificado con tal sentimiento público, invita a todos sus afiliados a participar en dicha manifestación.

Guatemala, Agosto de 1946.

LA JUNTA DIRECTIVA.

FIG. 9.—The political party called the "Partido de la Revolución" invites its members to participate in the demonstration of Aug. 25, 1946, enumerating the abuses against which they are to protest. (See p. 214.)

AL PUEBLO CATOLICO DE GUATEMALA

Los que suscribimos, ciudadanos guatemaltecos en pleno ejercicio de nuestros derechos constitucionales, en vista de la invitación que los diferentes partidos políticos organizados han hecho a sus afiliados para tomar parte en la gran manifestación popular que se llevará a cabo el próximo domingo 25 del corriente, para pedir:

1o.—La reforma de la Ley Electoral para que los ciudadanos puedan ejercer sus actividades lícitas.

2o.—La derogación del Decreto Gubernativo que congela el papel de imprenta para que pueda existir la libertad de prensa.

3o.—Que se respete el sentimiento católico del pueblo de Guatemala, sin amenazas ni coacciones de parte del Gobierno.

CONSIDERANDO: que los dos primeros puntos de la petición de los Partidos y del pueblo no sólo no se oponen en nada a nuestros sentimientos de patriotas y de católicos, sino que son dignos de ser apoyados por todo guatemalteco consciente, ya que la libertad no puede circunscribirse a determinado campo.

CONSIDERANDO: que el punto tercero atañe directamente a los intereses de nuestra Religión que ha venido siendo maniatada y denigrada desde hace más de setenta años.

Hemos acordado acuerpar a los Partidos y al pueblo en su gran manifestación de protesta.

En esa virtud, invitamos por este medio a todos los católicos de Guatemala para que concurran a la referida manifestación el próximo domingo 25 del corriente a las 10 en punto de la mañana.

Guatemala, 22 de agosto de 1946.

Antonio du Teil	Miguel Camacho L.	Alberto Castejón B.
J. Víctor Molina L.	Alejandro Poggio L.	Joaquín Barnoya
Enrique de la Riva	Francisco Cordón Horjales	Ricardo Rivas
Antonio Matta V.	Julio de la Riva	Carlos Castillo S.
E. Fernández G.	Juan F. Porras	Rafael Muñoz Peralta
Luis E. Porras	Juan Echeverría Lizaralde	Julio Gómez
Alejandro Rivas	José Luis Samayoa	Pedro Solé S.
Alfredo Colmenares P.	Herlindo Arbizú	Abel Vargas
J. L. Estrada de la Hoz	Salvador Falla C.	Roberto A. Díaz
Angel Barrera G.	Arturo Oliva	Ramiro Araujo
Francisco Castillo A.	Salvador Gaitán R.	Julio Gaitán
José Bonatto	José Luis Penedo de León	Héctor Gaitán C.
Carmen de León Cofiño	Irene de Peyré	Beatriz Molina S.
Emilia Barrios S.	Adela Rivas M.	Blanca v. de Castellanos
Berta S. de Castejón	L. Castellanos de Solé	María Castellanos de del Vecchio
Concha Estrada de la Hoz	Angela P. v. de Iriondo	María Teresa Sempé
Berta Castejón de Porras	Concha C. de Falla	Cecilia v. de Linares
Isabel Cuevas	Luz Figueroa	Concepción Cuevas
Ruth Juárez C.	María del Pilar Castillo A.	Eugenia Taracena
Luz Petrona Lemus	Aurora C. Piedrasanta	Rosario Balcárcel
Olga de Ochoa	Carlota U. de Ochoa	Elena Salazar
Piedad v. de Ubico	Lulú Ochoa U.	Carmen del Cid O.

FIG. 10.—Invitation to the Catholics of Guatemala to take part in the demonstration of Aug. 25, 1946. (See p. 214.)

El Gobierno Constitucional

HACE SABER:

QUE CONSIDERA el ejercicio de los cultos religiosos como una forma superior en la vida de los pueblos.

QUE POR SU ESPIRITU ALTAMENTE DEMOCRATICO, a pesar de estar integrado por funcionarios católicos, respeta la absoluta libertad de cultos, como lo establece nuestra Constitución revolucionaria.

QUE LOS ESTABLECIMIENTOS DE ENSEÑANZA NO OFICIAL, gozan de toda libertad para impartir enseñanza religiosa en horas especiales y bajo la inspección del Estado, para evitar abusos.

QUE EL GOBIERNO no hace distinción entre sacerdotes nacionales y extranjeros cuando todos ellos se consagran exclusivamente al ejercicio de su culto.

QUE LA REVOLUCION DE OCTUBRE es un movimiento de liberación nacional, destinado a recuperar en manos guatemaltecas la conducción de la política nacional e internacional.

POR TODO ESO:

Llama la atención del público en general, respecto a la existencia de un peligro de que extranjeros bien recibidos y bien tratados entre nosotros se dediquen a hacer propaganda en contra de la Revolución de Octubre y en favor de gobiernos o doctrinas extranjeros, con el exclusivo fin de impedir el gran programa de reivindicaciones históricas y sociales que la Revolución y sus hombres se han impuesto para grandeza de Guatemala.

Guatemala, agosto de 1946.

Reg. No. 162 Seg. hno.

FIG. 11.—Declaration of Government of Guatemala dated Aug. 23, 1946, protesting that it in no way restricted the freedom of religion or the work of foreign priests in the country, but at the same time calling attention to the danger of propaganda in favor of foreign governments and doctrines on the part of foreigners, well-received in Guatemala. (See p. 214.)

FIG. 12.—Manifestation of Aug. 25, 1946. Demonstration in the Square between the National Palace and the Cathedral. (See p. 215.)

FIG. 13.—Manifestation of Aug. 25, 1946. Section of parade passing the Palace of the Archbishop who appears in background. (See p. 216.)

FIGS. 14, 15.—Two Views of Counter-Manifestation of Sept. 8, 1946. (See p. 217.)

LAS DOS MANIFESTACIONES

Canción sin palabras

Fig. 16.—Cartoon from "La Hora" of Sept. 9, 1946, depicting the artist's concept of the two demonstrations. (See p. 217.)

Figs. 17, 18.—Indians at Mayan shrines. (See p. 231.)

FIG. 19.—Momostenango—annual observance of the Indian rite of the Guajxaquip Báts. (See p. 239.)

Fig. 20.—Members of *Cofradia* within the church. (See p. 232.)

Fig. 21.—Indians at prayer within the church. (See p. 233.)

Fig. 22.—Church and Plaza at Chichicastenango. (See p. 233.)

FIG. 23.—Leader of *Cofradia* with insignia. (See p. 232.)

Fig. 24.—Procession on Feast of All Saints. (See p. 228.)

Fig. 25.—Dance of the Conquest performed in front of the church on the Feast of All Saints. (See p. 228.)

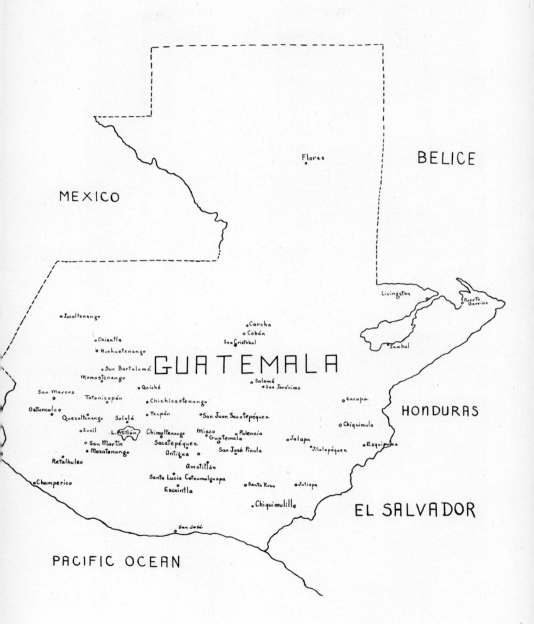

BELICE

MEXICO

Flores

Livingston

Puerto
Barrios

Izabal

HONDURAS

Jacaltenango

Carcha
Cobán
San Cristobal

Chiantla
Huehuetenango
San Bartolomé
Momostenango

GUATEMALA

Salamá
San Jerónimo

Zacapa

San Marcos
Totonicapán
Quiché
Chichicastenango

Ostuncalco
Quezaltenango
Solalá
Tecpán
San Juan Sacatepéquez
Chiquimula

Zunil
L. Atitlán
Chimaltenango
Mixco
Palencia
Jalapa

San Martín
Sacatepéquez
Guatemala
Jilotepéquez
Esquipulas

Mazatenango
Antigua
San José Pinula

Retalhuleu

Amatitlán

Champerico

Santa Lucia Cotzumalguapa
Escuintla
Santa Rosa
Jutiapa

Chiquimulilla

EL SALVADOR

San José

PACIFIC OCEAN

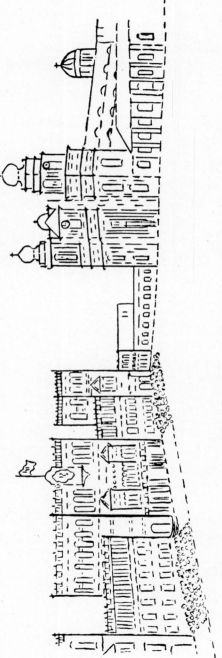

The Symbols of Church and State

Left—National Palace

Right—Cathedral, Guatemala City

the lack of judgment and justice which caused the Government to dictate it; I protest against the other calumnies which have been circulated to reflect on my honor, and I protest, finally, in the most solemn and strongest manner, against the outrages and vexations of which I was the victim on the night of the 3rd of July and the following days until the moment when I was placed aboard ship.

With expressions of my most distinguished consideration, I am, my dear Minister, yours most attentively,

Francisco A. Espinosa.[73]

On October 2, 1873 Barrios issued a decree recognizing the validity of marriages between foreigners celebrated in accord with a religion other than that dominant in the Republic, believing, as he said, that this would conduce to encourage immigration, as well as express the tolerance of the régime.[74]

Not satisfied with secularizing the religious of the country, Barrios attempted to lessen the influence of the secular clergy by forbidding them to wear clerical clothing in public, in a decree of February 25, 1874.[75]

In the year 1874 it came the turn of the nuns to feel the effects of secularization. On February 9, 1874 a wedge was driven by a decree ordering the confiscation of all the convents of nuns in the Republic save that of Santa Catarina in Guatemala City, and the concentration of all the nuns in that one convent.[76] This decree also provided for the suppression of all congregations and the secularization of those nuns who wished it, with a monthly pension of twenty *pesos*. On the publication of this decree there were protests not only from ecclesiastical authorities, but also from the nuns them-

---

73 *La Verdad, León*, Nicaragua, No. 108, Oct. 31, 1873.

74 García, *op. cit.*, V, 454.

75 *National Archives of Guatemala*, Decree No. 118, Feb. 25, 1874.

76 *Ibid.*, Decree No. 115, Feb. 9, 1874.

selves.[77] These were ineffective, however, for the government, on February 28, 1874, went a step further and declared that the religious congregated in the Convent of Santa Catarina by the decree of February 9th should not be isolated from their families and friends, that they should be permitted to see them openly whenever they wished (without the companion or *escucha* required by rule), and that once a month the government would make a visitation of the convent, " to inspect sanitary conditions, prevent corporal punishment or close confinement of the inmates, and report on what was observed." [78]

Finally, on March 3, 1874 came the last blow to the religious orders of women in Guatemala.[79] The government, exasperated by the protests of the Church and the Conservatives against the decrees of February 9th and 28th,[80] and especially by the action of the ecclesiastical government in threatening with excommunication anyone who, by carrying out the official inspection ordered by the last decree, would violate the enclosure of the convent,[81] issued a new decree closing the convent of Santa Catarina and expelling within twelve hours all the religious living there.[82] Their property having been confiscated by the government, each of these ex-nuns, over one hundred and forty in number, was to be allowed a life pension of twelve *pesos* monthly.[83]

The Sisters of Charity of Saint Vincent de Paul, with whom the government of Carrera had made a contract for serving in the hospital, were excepted from all legislation against the religious orders. When Barrios, on coming into

[77] García, *op. cit.*, V, 457 ff.; "La Verdad", No. 131, April 11, 1874.

[78] *Recopilación de Leyes de Guatemala*, I, 261.

[79] Díaz, *Barrios ante la Posteridad*, p. 385.

[80] *La Verdad*, León, Nicaragua, March 28, 1874, No. 129.

[81] *Ibid.*, March 21, 1874, No. 128.

[82] *National Archives of Guatemala*, Decree No. 120, March 3, 1874.

[83] *Recopilación de Leyes de Guatemala*, II, 64, 65.

office, had named Roderico Toledo as Director of the Hospital of Guatemala, all feared for the results, as he was known for his enmity toward religion. But he had promptly bettered conditions, not only in the hospital itself, but also in the living quarters of the Sisters, did nothing to oppose their austere rule and customs, and showed the utmost interest and tolerance in all his dealings with them.[84]

Meanwhile the nationalization of the property of the religious orders and the Church continued, not without protest after protest on the part of the ecclesiastical authorities.[85] On January 29, 1874 a part of the Convent of Santo Domingo was granted to the *Junta de Misericordia,* a lay organization which gave moral and financial support to many of the charitable institutions of Guatemala, to be used for a school attached to the Asylum.[86] On February 25, 1874, by order of President Barrios in Decree No. 117, the *Colegio Tridentino* was added to the University, with all its possessions, and the Major Seminary, in charge of the Vincentian Fathers, was converted into a Normal School for the preparation of primary teachers.[87] On April 18, 1874 the government consolidated the possessions of the Hospital of San Juan de Dios, the Hospice and the Orphan Asylum into a common fund to be directed by the National Bank and for which a tax on inheritances would be levied in the future.[88] A decree of May 19, 1874 reiterated the declaration of nationalization of the buildings and property of the secularized orders in the following terms:

National Palace, Guatemala, May 19, 1874.
For the purpose of clarifying doubts which have arisen concerning Article 4 of the Decree of February 9th of this year,

84 Díaz, *Barrios ante la Posteridad,* p. 385.

85 García, *op. cit.,* V, 457.

86 *Recopilación de Leyes de Guatemala,* I, 246.

87 *National Archives of Guatemala,* Decree No. 117, Feb. 25, 1874.

88 *National Archives of Guatemala,* Decree No. 123, April 18, 1874.

which orders nationalized the buildings and lands which formerly belonged to the nuns, *beatas*, sisterhoods, orders, etc. the
President considers it well to declare:

That there are also nationalized the goods belonging to
those institutions which were consolidated by Decree of
August 27, 1872.[89]

On June 9, 1874, the *Beaterio de Belén,* which was considered more appropriate for the school which was to be erected
in the old Convent of Santo Domingo, was ceded by the Government for that purpose.[90] The latter building was thereupon
used for a conservatory of music and headquarters of the
Philharmonic Society.[91]

It has been noted that the Government offered compensation in the form of pensions to the religious whose goods it
confiscated. Likewise, it subsidized services in the churches
of the religious orders when it took them over, wishing,
as a matter of policy, to supply the people with the devotions
to which they had been accustomed.[92] Thereupon the chap-
lains of these churches were ordered to draw up an estimate
of the probable expenses for the services in their respective
churches and send it to the Minister of the Interior for approval. The latter would then send it to the National Treasury which would make the necessary payments.[93] The government also granted subsidies to poor parishes on the request
of the Archbishop, though it is to be noted, in one case at
least, that the aid extended was in consideration of the
" services which with loyalty and constancy had been lent in

89 *Recopilación de Leyes de Guatemala,* I, 277.

90 *Ibid.,* p. 279.

91 Díaz, *Barrios ante la Posteridad,* p. 257. This author relates how
Barrios, a lover of music, used to order the Military Band to give a concert
in front of the Episcopal Palace for his good friend, the Vicar General Fr.
Juan Bautista Raúl y Bertrán.

92 *National Archives of Guatemala,* Aug. 4, 1874.

93 *Recopilación de Leyes de Guatemala,* I, 302.

the past and were still being lent toward the pacification and punishment of the insurrectionists." [94]

While the government thus sometimes aided the Church financially after the nationalization, it also at times interfered with the taxation imposed by the Church on its members. On February 4, 1875 the Executive, declaring that complaints had been received frequently regarding the forced contributions of the *primicias* or first fruits to the pastors, ordered that in the future only the pastors might receive these offerings, and not agents hired by them. He stated, furthermore, that the offerings must be voluntary, without any recourse to law for their collection. Finally, they could not be sold, nor transferred nor collected by others to whom the privilege had been ceded.[95] Again, on May 18, 1875, Barrios, because of the complaint of the muncipality of Amatitlán connected with the heavy expenses of the festivities of Holy Week, Corpus Christi, St. John and the Rosary, exempted the inhabitants from contributing to the support of these feasts.[96]

Once the education of the Republic had been taken out of the control of the Church by abolishing the religious orders and nationalizing their schools, the government set about in earnest to " reform " it. By decree of January 2, 1875 the government reduced to a single, uniform system the organization, direction and inspection of primary education, and made it obligatory, free and secular in character. At the same time, it declared and guaranteed the principle of the freedom of private schools.[97] At the earliest opportunity schools were opened on Sunday for the working class, of which large numbers of artisans took advantage. In that established in the old buildings of the Franciscan Convent, there was an en-

94 *National Archives of Guatemala*, Order of Government, June 13, 1873.

95 *Ibid.*, Feb. 4, 1875.

96 *Recopilación de Leyes de Guatemala*, I, 368.

97 *National Archives of Guatemala*, Decree No. 131, Jan. 2, 1875.

rollment of over three hundred. Classes in Physiology and Hygiene, Natural Science and Civics, Penmanship and Gymnastics were set up in the Convent of the *Recolección* and in a section of the old school of the Dominicans.[98] By decree of January 19, 1875 a central Normal School was instituted in the confiscated *Colegio Mayor,* whose object was to prepare teachers for the normal schools which were to be established in each of the departments of Guatemala, according to the plans of Barrios, and directors for the primary, elementary and secondary schools.[99] In the outline of studies for this institution there is no mention of religion or Christian doctrine.[100] On January 20, 1875 Barrios established in the old convent of *La Concepción* the National School for Girls, including both primary and secondary branches.[101] On April 2nd, in response to a request for a school of manual arts for those boys in the Orphan Asylum who had reached the age of twelve years and needed a man's direction, rather than that of the Sisters of Charity, the government opened in the old convent of the *Beaterio de Belén* a school of arts and crafts where the boys were instructed in such trades as would enable them to earn a living later.[102] In reply to a request from the municipality of Tejutla, in the province of San Marcos, for schools in that locality, the government ceded to it the convent of San Francisco for the purpose.[103] On July 1, 1875, Barrios issued a decree abolishing the Pontifical University of San Carlos Borromeo, and establishing in its place the University of Guatemala. There were to be stressed now in this institution in which the ecclesiastical studies had always

98 Díaz, *Barrios ante la Posteridad,* p. 259.

99 *National Archives of Guatemala,* Decree No. 132, Jan. 19, 1875.

100 *Recopilación de Leyes de Guatemala,* I, 341.

101 *National Archives of Guatemala,* Decree No. 133, Jan. 20, 1875.

102 *Ibid.,* Decree No. 138, April 2, 1875.

103 *Ibid.,* Order of Government, April 8, 1875.

predominated, the natural sciences, Law, and Letters.[104] On
September 15, 1875 Barrios opened in the suppressed academy of the Sisters of Notre Dame, established in 1859 in the
old Convalescent Home of the expelled Bethlemites (one sees
here the historical cycle in action), a National Institute for
girls,[105] equivalent to the secondary school for boys, the
Instituto Nacional Central de Varones.[106] When the latter
school had opened, the government withdrew the allotment of
ten *pesos* monthly which it had been paying to the former
scholarship pupils who had to leave the *Colegio Mayor* and
the Seminary of the Vincentian Fathers when the latter were
closed, and declared that those pupils could now attend the
new Institute free of charge.[107] The state domination of education is clearly demonstrated in the reply of Barrios to the
inquiries of the Vicar General of the Archdiocese regarding
the status of the courses given at the *Colegio de Infantes* and
that of *San Ignacio,* still in the hands of the Church, that such
courses were valid, provided the students matriculated in
the National Institute and passed the examinations required
by the law of January 28, 1875.[108]

Regulations drawn up on December 7, 1875 for the Faculty
of the Ecclesiastical Sciences in the new University also il-
lustrated the degree of government supervision. This Faculty
was required to have at least nine members named by the
government. The members had to be trained according to the
new organic law on higher education and be in conformity with
it. They were to submit to examinations provided for in that
law. In the same regulations, the Vicar General of the Arch-

104 *Ibid.*, Decree No. 140, July 1, 1875.

105 Díaz, *Barrios ante la Posteridad*, p. 275.

106 This historic building had been the meeting place in 1813 of the
conspirators of Belén who worked for independence and the prison in 1829
of the state prisoners before being exiled by Morazán.

107 *National Archives of Guatemala*, Decree No. 117, Feb. 25, 1874.

108 *Ibid.*, p. 404.

diocese was requested to demand that candidates for Holy
Orders certify to their regular attendance at classes at the
University, and that, in the provision of benefices, those hav-
ing degrees were to be given preference.[109]

Not all the property confiscated from the religious orders
was used for educational purposes. The Convent of Santa
Teresa was converted into a prison for women by government order of August 16, 1875.[110] The Convent of Santa
Catarina became a house of correction, or reformatory, on
June 15, 1877, by decree of Barrios. The latter institution, in
charge of Col. Ambrosio García, was to have workshops for
the teaching of arts and trades useful to the inmates on their
return to society.[111]

A question arose before the committee assigned to the
nationalization of the religious property as to whether there
should be considered included the offerings left by will for
Masses to be said for the soul of the deceased. The problem
was settled by a governmental order declaring that such
money should be placed with the consolidated goods, handed
over to the National Bank, and disposed of by the latter in
conformity with the wishes of the deceased.[112] This was but
one more example of the thoroughness of the measures of
Barrios.

On August 3, 1876, in a new treaty, Guatemala and El
Salvador ratified the agreement that they had made on Jan.
25, 1872 that "both governments promise never to permit
the presence in any part of their respective territories of the
Fathers of the Company of Jesus, neither organized nor in
any other manner." [113] A singular event, relating to this
agreement, occurred in the year 1881. Father Henry Gillet, a

109 *National Archives of Guatemala*, Decree No. 140, July 1, 1875.

110 *Recopilación de Leyes de Guatemala*, I, 390.

111 *National Archives of Guatemala*, Decree No. 188, June 15, 1877.

112 *Recopilación de Leyes de Guatemala*, I, 347.

113 *Ibid.*, I, 474.

Jesuit who had been teaching in the parochial school system in British Honduras and who had been stationed at Stann Creek, took advantage of the Easter vacation to pay a visit to the Izabal lagoon. He had scarcely landed on Guatemalan soil at Livingstone, when a telegram notified Barrios, President still, of the arrival of a Jesuit and asked for instructions. The next day the priest was arrested and taken under escort to Guatemala City, a journey of five days. As soon as he arrived, he was put into a dungeon used for those condemned to death and, after two days without food, he was subjected to a strict interrogation. Although the officials could find nothing against him, he was transferred to the public prison where he remained ten days, until he found the opportunity to communicate with the English consul at Guatemala. The latter sent his secretary to look into the case and when he learned what had happened, he went in person to the President and asked for the Jesuit's immediate release. On the following day Father Gillet was set at liberty and conducted back to Izabal from where he returned to Belize.[114]

In his message to the National Constitutional Assembly instituted on September 11, 1876, Barrios regretted that he had been forced to take so many drastic measures against religion, but insisted that the latter had been used as a pretext for revolt:

> ... I leave to your consideration the measure of my efforts to obtain order in the midst of the difficulties existing in the country; but I shall not refrain from speaking to you of the moral sacrifices, so grievously imposed upon me by my duty of conserving the work of the revolution.
>
> I refer to the extraordinary measures, harsh and severe, adopted against the disturbers of public order, against those who from this capital aided with money and elements of war the movements of the highlands; against those who, using the

114 Hopkins, Frederick C., S.J., "The Catholic Church in British Honduras", *Catholic Historical Review*, Oct. 1918, IV, pp. 309-10.

simplicity of the inhabitants of the *Oriente* as a weapon against the government, deceived them and made them fanatical, under pretext of religion, in order to lead them into misery or death in fraticidal war . . . [115]

On September 15, 1877 he was to carry out the measure which probably aroused more opposition than any preceding it, the law on civil marriage. Civil marriage was declared obligatory for the legal effects of the contract. The government regulated the formalities involved, as well as the causes for annulment and divorce.[116] When confusion arose over the law, because of the decree of Oct. 2, 1873, which had recognized the validity of civil marriages between foreigners in Guatemala, the President explained in a proclamation dated Dec. 4, 1878 that, while according to the law guaranteeing freedom of worship, marriages might be celebrated with religious ceremonies, the legal effects of the contracts depended on the registration before the civil authorities.[117] However, this announcement did not silence the objections, and the question was to arise again. On November 17, 1879 Barrios issued a decree to clarify the position of the government on the matter, declaring that " first, marriages had to take place before the civil authorities, and, second, marriages celebrated without the formalities expressed in Articles 139, ff., Title IV, Book I, of the Civil Code, would not be recognized as valid and legitimate for civil effects." [118] Next followed Decree No. 250 legislating on the procedure to be carried out by those who wished to contract matrimony, and on the causes for declaring null and void any marriage, as well as on the granting of divorce.[119]

115 Díaz, *Barrios ante la Posteridad*, p. 217.

116 *Ibid.*, p. 325.

117 *Recopilación de Leyes de Guatemala*, I, 224.

118 *National Archives of Guatemala*, Decree No. 249, Nov. 17, 1879.

119 *Ibid.*, Decree No. 250.

On April 6, 1881, there was read in the Assembly a proposition requiring a civil marriage previous to the celebration of the religious ceremony, and an amendment of Fr. Dr. Angel María Arroyo, in which he proposed that the law should respect the freedom of all the inhabitants of the country to celebrate the religious marriage with the usual ceremonies, and that there should follow within three days after the religious ceremony a civil one, under pain of a fine of from 50 to 500 *pesos*. This motion was violently opposed by Dr. Lorenzo Montúfar y Rivera, bitter anti-clerical, who wanted no religious ceremony celebrated before the civil one—in fact, no religious ceremony at all. He declared that he opposed Dr. Arroyo's proposal because his intelligence, the enlightenment of the times, the benefit, growth, and progress of the country demanded it. He said that if Dr. Arroyo opposed the project, it would be because he was a priest, and a Roman priest (this brought an outburst of laughter from the gallery); but that he, Montúfar, was a Liberal. He concluded by citing other republican nations which had destroyed the power of the Church in temporal affairs, in particular Austria and Spain. He exhorted the Assembly, in the name of Liberalism, to accept the initiative of the Government in instituting civil marriage, declaring that in no way did it attack liberty of conscience.

Dr. Arroyo, in answer, declared that the new ordinance was an attack on the Constitution which guaranteed public liberties, because it curbed the liberty of marriage; that in thus legislating the government was wounding popular sentiments, since the entire population of Guatemala was Catholic, and that, while the Church respected the dispositions of the government, the latter should not interfere in religious matters. He then considered at length the inconveniences of such a law in regard to the principles of Canon Law, and declared that if he were combating the measure, it was in his capacity of statesman, and not that of ecclesiastic.

Dr. Fernando Cruz then rose to refute what Dr. Arroyo had said, declaring that the proposal in no way attacked liberty of conscience, since it began by stating that the government recognized and held sacred the liberty of all individuals to solemnize their marriage by a religious ceremony, that the opposition the clergy were making to the law was inspired by fear of harm to their purses (here again there was prolonged applause), that the clergy had not objected before to the civil marriage, as long as those contracting marriage had been able to evade it, and for that very reason, this new law was necessary in order to prevent such evasion. (The new decree declared that the civil ceremony must take place first, and the minister presiding over the religious ceremony must not do so until he had first seen certification of the former ceremony). Dr. Cruz ended by begging the Assembly to approve the new bill in the name of public liberty, the peace of the family, order in society and the maintenance of the law.

Although Dr. Arroyo again protested vigorously, the projected legislation was approved in its entirety by the Assembly, with but two dissenting votes, those of Dr. Arroyo and Dr. Aguïrre.[120] The debate preceding the voting showed the strong anti-clerical feeling in the government, with every allusion to the Holy See or the clergy meeting with derision; with Dr. Angel María Arroyo, leader of the opposition group, although one of the most brilliant orators of the Assembly and a close friend of Barrios, being the object of constant innuendos and ridicule.

Following again the pattern of Gálvez' reform during the previous Liberal régime, Barrios insisted on ordering on November 15, 1879, the construction, administration and inspection of all the cemeteries of the Republic in the exclusive charge of the respective municipal authority, thus once more touching upon one of the principal grievances in the Church-State conflict.[121] However, the decree was accompanied by a rider stating that, after bodies had been reduced

120 Díaz, *Barrios ante la Posteridad*, pp. 374-5.

121 *National Archives of Guatemala*, Decree No. 248, Nov. 15, 1879.

to bones, they might, at the wish of friends, be transported to any of the churches or chapels, upon payment of a sum specified, according to the age, rank and status of the deceased. The Treasury of the Cemeteries was to be responsible for furnishing all required information.[122]

In his message to the National Constitutional Assembly on its opening on March 15, 1879, Barrios did not overlook the religious issue:

> ... The relations of the State with the Church have shown no change whatsoever. I have continued to develop the principles of liberty which civilization supports in religious matters, attentive only to suppress the aspirations of fanaticism. Civil marriage having been established and recognized by our Codes, some Guatemalans have been married directly before the departmental authority with the formalities necessary to make it valid.[123]

And the Congress in its reply to the Message of the President, referring to the aforementioned comment, said:

> ... It is a satisfaction to know that the relations between the State and the Church have presented no difficulties, once your political program has adopted full religious liberty, the repression of fanaticism, and the institution of civil marriage in accord with modern civilization.[124]

From these days when the Constitutional Assembly was in session, it would be interesting to take a sampling of the speeches of the delegates which illustrate views in connection with the Church-State question.[125] Once again it is to be noted that the extremists on either side were most articulate and that there is no evidence to indicate that a moderate program,

122 *National Archives of Guatemala*, "Arancel de los derechos que deben pagarse a la Tesorería de los Cementerios", p. 320.

123 Díaz, *Barrios ante la Posteridad*, p. 319.

124 *Ibid.*, p. 323.

125 *Ibid.*, pp. 348-356.

a *modus vivendi,* could have been worked out. As an example of the discussion on Article 24, of Title II, On Guarantees, " The State recognizes no official Church, but the exercise of all religions within the interior of churches is guaranteed to Guatemalans and to foreigners residing in Guatemala ", the following excerpts may be noted:

> ...Dr. Lorenzo Montúfar: ... I am going to speak of the article in question and at the same time I shall permit myself to answer some observations made in the session of Thursday last by Dr. Arroyo and by *señor* Machado. Dr. Arroyo agrees, agrees perfectly with many of the points I had the honor of presenting to the Assembly. I said then: ' The dogmas of a religion, although they may be true in themselves, cannot be proved, and if they cannot be proved, they cannot be imposed as a religion on a State.' Dr. Arroyo rose and said: ' That is true; the dogmas of a religion cannot be proved.' Therefore, Dr. Arroyo agrees with me on the premises and, as a consequence, he should do so likewise on the conclusions; because it is logical, very logical, to respect the precepts of logic, as he has so often demonstrated to us and counseled us in his discourses in the Chamber.
>
> Dr. Arroyo condemns, as I condemn, all the crimes perpetrated in the world in the name of an official religion, in the name of a religion with preeminence, a religion with privileges, in the name of a State religion. Dr. Arroyo praises, as I praise, the principles, the great principles of 1789. (Here Dr. Arroyo rises and asks for the floor) This gentleman, my dear Representatives, has told us: ' These principles are an emancipation, an emanation of those great doctrines which were enunciated almost nineteen hundred years ago in the admirable Sermon on the Mount.' Gentlemen, I did not say that night anything more in favor of liberty, I did not say as much, nor is it in my power to touch the human heart with such exalted accents. I confess that his words moved me; I believed myself transported for the time being to other happier days of my life, and to another country, and I believed that I was listening once more to the penetrating voice of Montalambert.

Dr. Arroyo condemned, as we all condemn, those deeds which blackened the name of the great revolution of 1789 and he deplores, as we all deplore, those crimes which took place in the name of liberty in 1793. Note well, my dear Deputies, how many are the points of contact and agreement which exist between Dr. Arroyo and the majority of the members of the Committee on the Constitution. The Representative condemned that night, and very severely, the French Convention for having established a State religion, the religion of the goddess Reason. Dr. Arroyo had risen to combat us, and he was supporting my ideas. I am not an enemy of the French Convention, nor can I be; much has been said against this Convention, much has been written against it; but, on the other hand, much has been said and written in favor of it. My dear Deputies, I am going to try to present to you some of the vindications which have been made in its favor. That Assembly cannot be judged by itself; it cannot be judged unless in view of the circumstances and the time ...

Dr. Arroyo has spoken to us of another religion established then. It is true, another religion was established then by Robespierre; but that was one of the many inconsistencies of which Robespierre was guilty. In order to be a French citizen it was necessary to profess that religion ...

Napoleon, an eminent warrior, but not always an eminent statesman, reestablished the official religion, the official religion which France had formerly professed. Napoleon wanted the aid of the French clergy and the latter gave him that support, and so he could say: 'With my soldiers, my police and my priests, I can do everything.' The Pope, Pius VII, blessed him, and, leaving Rome, went to Paris to anoint the new Charlemagne in the Cathedral of Notre Dame. Concordats had given the Emperor the right to lay hands on the censer; he could even touch the Ark of the Covenant without becoming guilty of death. But these distinctions and prerogatives were granted in exchange for obligations, of many obligations for France; and when Napoleon realized it, he declared war on the Pope, and the latter, who had previously anointed him, now excommunicated him.

Meanwhile, gentlemen, the North Americans had accomplished their great work; in the United States there was drawn

up the Constitution which Washington ordered put into execution, and in those laws there was no official church, there
was no State religion, there was no church with privileges;
and those laws, which were dictated for four million inhabitants, now govern a Nation of fifty million inhabitants, whose
extraordinary accomplishments and admirable progress amaze
the entire world ...

Dr. Arroyo told us: ' I do not wish a religion imposed by
the State, even though that religion be the holy, the august
religion of Jesus Christ.' These words are liberal, they are
very liberal. Dr. Arroyo does not wish a religion imposed by
the State, even though that religion be the one to which he
has consecrated his studies, his life, and on whose altars he
daily offers the smoke of incense to the Supreme Being. So,
therefore, if I could prove that a religion of State is a religion
imposed by the State, Dr. Arroyo would vote with me this
evening.

The history of Spain is our history up to the year twenty-
one. Let us see, then, what it teaches us. ... Gentlemen, how
different would be the fate of the Spanish Nation; how different would be the lot of those who in the old world and the
new speak the beautiful language of Cervantes if doña Isabel
of Castile could have dictated a law similar to the article which
we are now discussing! Then, the Jews ... then, the Moors, if
they had all been united under the standard of the Cross and
around it, that would have strengthened it, and Spain would
not have fallen from her grandeur, but, on the contrary, would
have risen, and today we would not see the English flag flying
over the Rock of Gibraltar. But the Queen, Isabel I, had to
render tribute to her times and, dominated by Cardinal Jiménez
Cisneros who received his orders from Rome, decreed the
expulsion of entire towns of Jews who went away with their
industry, their skills, their science and with the great wealth
they possessed, to enrich other nations, enemies of Spain.

At that time, the expulsion of the Moors from Spanish
territory could not be brought about by means of an official
religion. ... But that influence dominated the unfortunate
Philip III and there fell the second great blow suffered by
the Spanish Nation. Whole populations of Moors were ex-

pelled. . . . More than a million persons, weakened by the cold, by misery, by hunger, driven from the Spanish territory in the name of an official religion. . . . See, gentlemen, the cruelty, see the tyranny of official religions, whether they be Catholic or Mohammedan!

But, what has *señor* Machado said in his splendid discourses which attacked the ideas proposed by me that night? . . . *Señor* Machado told us that he wished freedom of worship, but with an official church, with a State religion, with a religion having privileges and preeminence. I congratulate *señor* Machado, I congratulate him most sincerely, because he wishes freedom of worship; but he wants what is impossible, what is absolutely impossible, because there cannot be freedom of worship where there is a State religion. In order to have freedom of worship it is necessary that all religions be equal before the law, just as for civil liberty it is necessary that all men be equal before the law; and all religions cannot be equal before the law if one of them is supported by income from the State, is supported by the authorities of the State, by the laws of the State. (*Señor* Machado here rises and asks for the floor) When there is an official religion, an official church, there is no freedom of worship; there is only simple tolerance.

Señor Machado told us that night that he is a Catholic. This assertion does not affect my ideas; this assertion has nothing to do with my discourse. *Señor* Machado is a Catholic! Then I congratulate him most sincerely for his Catholicity (laughter greeted this), as I would congratulate him if he were a Lutheran or a Calvinist, because there is nothing more worthy or respectable than religious sentiments expressed in good faith. But what connection is there between this article we are discussing and the Catholicism of *señor* Machado? If this article is in force, *señor* Machado may go to Mass every Sunday and holy day of obligation. He may even hear Mass every day in the week, since his Masses are guaranteed by this article we are discussing. *Señor* Machado may confess once a year, during the Easter time, or before it, if he expects to be in danger of death. (great outburst of laughter and applause) He may receive Communion every month, every week, every day, and he may receive Com-

munion under the two species if the priest permits it, for
the Government does not oppose it. (Laughter again) In no
way does this article, I repeat, oppose the Catholicism of
señor Machado. If this law is in force, he may fast whenever
Holy Mother Church orders it, and he may abstain every
Friday and the other days of the year, because his meals are
guaranteed by the Constitution. He may even do more; he
may cover himself with hair-cloth and do penance, like a
second St. Jerome, because the Constitution guarantees all that.

Señor Machado has told us also that the article we are
discussing must be defeated, because the majority of
Guatemalans are Roman, Catholic, Apostolic. But how is this
article opposed to the Catholicism of the Guatemalans? Even
if all the people of Guatemala were Catholics, there can be
an article in the Constitution which says there is no State religion. I would be glad to present this amendment; but I do
not present it, because I do not think the assertion of *señor*
Machado is true. The argument of *señor* Machado, if I am
not mistaken, rests on this proposition, on this thesis. Then
the Representative should have presented us with the statistics
on which his thesis rests; and if he does not present them,
his argument lacks foundation. How many inhabitants has
Guatemala? It has a little more than a million inhabitants.
Of these, you know positively that more than two-thirds
are Indians. Now, I wish that *señor* Machado would tell me
whether or not the Indians are Catholics. The Indians are
not Catholics; they are idolators.

Señor Machado, who has traveled so much among our
villages, must have seen, on Saturdays at sunset, the officials
calling the Indians on drums or bells to warn them that on
the following day they must go to the church to hear Mass,
and the governor orders them to be present. The Indians go
to Mass; if they don't go they must pay a fine or be put in
jail. Now, I ask you, are men who go to Mass to escape the
payment of a fine or a day's imprisonment Catholics? And
those governors, why do they compel the people to go to Mass?
Is it, by chance, because they know that the Mass is an un-
bloody renewal of a cruel Sacrifice? No, gentlemen, the Indians
know nothing of all this. Those governors compel the Indians

THE RETURN OF THE LIBERALS

to go to Mass in order to comply with a decree issued by don Manuel Francisco Pavón at the beginning of the 'thirty years'... And have you seen what the Indians do on coming out of Mass? They go to the house of a sorcerer, whom they all believe a priest, and then they march into the woods to worship their primitive divinities. See, my dear Deputies, the Catholicism of two-thirds of our population!

Now, it is necessary to consider the Catholicism of the cultured portion, the upper level of our society. I cannot penetrate very far, but I can judge many of the persons who boast of being Catholics, and I can judge them by their official acts, which may be discussed, which are evident to all.

Señor Machado has signed this project of the Constitution which we are discussing. But this project has come under the disapproval, the anathema of many Supreme Pontiffs, and not in the part to which *señor* Machado has not subscribed, but in the part which he has signed and which he helped to draw up. One article of this Constitution says that 'the Government of Guatemala is popular.' But this proposition was condemned by Pope Boniface VIII. This Pontiff said: 'No government comes from the people; all governments come from God.' This other article of the Constitution says that 'the government of Guatemala is free, sovereign and independent.' This proposition is likewise condemned by two Popes, Gregory VIII and Innocent III. These Supreme Pontiffs say that all authority comes from the Church; that there is no other authority than that of the Church; that kingdoms, that republics are usurpations of the ecclesiastical power.

Señor Machado wishes freedom of worship. But this proposition is condemned by Clement VIII. My dear Deputies, permit me to repeat the words of that Pontiff. He says, 'If anyone should say that it is permitted to worship God in the manner that he sees fit, let him be anathema.' But what need is there of referring to Pope Clement VIII when we have in the Encyclical of Pope Pius IX, dated December 8, 1856, a severe condemnation of freedom of worship?

Señor Machado has subscribed to the article on freedom of thought. But this article is under the condemnation of encyclicals, of the Syllabus and the Council of the Vatican.

If *señor* Machado, who boasts of being a Catholic, could have been guilty of so many faults in the eyes of the Supreme Pontiffs, if he could have fallen under the anathema of an Ecumenical Council, what shall we say of all those who do not boast of being Catholics and of those who have not been, like the Representative, in a school directed by the sons of St. Ignatius Loyola? What shall we say of that youth which is today educated in liberal schools and of all those Guatemalans who are more liberal than *señor* Machado? But I have already taken up too much time. I must conclude, my dear Deputies; there remains to me only to urge you in the name of liberty, in the name of the Nation, that you do not decree a religion with privileges, a State religion. (Strong and prolonged applause)

The Constitution which the Assembly finally drew up after this discussion and debate, on December 12, 1879, contained many of the anti-clerical measures existing today. In order to hold any office, whether it be that of President,[126] or *Designado,* one named before hand to take over the office of President, should it become vacant during a term,[127] the Secretary of State,[128] Judge or Prosecuting Attorney,[129] Supreme Justice,[130] or even a simple Notary Public,[131] it was necessary to be "*del estado seglar*"[132] (of secular status), so that all ecclesiastics were kept from power.

There was to be complete separation of Church and State, according to Article 24 of the Guarantees:

126 Rodríguez, José Ignacio, *American Constitutions,* International Bureau of the American Republics, Government Printing Office, Washington, D. C., 1906, pp. 238-258; *Constitution of Guatemala,* Title IV, Article 65.

127 *Ibid.,* Article 69.

128 *Ibid.,* Article 72.

129 *Ibid.,* Article 86.

130 *Ibid.,* Title V, *Del Poder Judicial,* Article 10.

131 *Ibid.,* Chapter II, *Del Notariado,* Article 2.

132 Article 50 of the Law of Guarantees prohibits ecclesiastics from being elected Deputies.

The practice of all religions, without preference for any particular one, is guaranteed in the interior of temples; but this freedom shall not be extended to the performance of acts which are subversive or inconsistent with public peace and order, nor shall it give the right to oppose the fulfillment of civil and political obligations.[133]

The suppression of monastic life was ratified in Article 25 which declares the "right of association and of peaceful assembly without arms," but adds, "the establishment of convents and all kinds of monastic institutions or associations is forbidden." [134] Primary instruction was declared compulsory, and that to be furnished by the government was to be secular and gratuitous, according to Article 18; [135] while that furnished and supported by individuals might be according to their preference.[136] However, the latter was to be under the control of the government, as stated in Section 2 of the "Duties and Attributes of the Executive":

He has also the supreme inspection of schools and other institutions of learning, even when they are not supported by national funds.[137]

and again in Article 3 of the *Organic and Regulatory Law of Public Instruction*, which reads:

Private schools are encouraged by the Government, the latter exercising over them only that vigilance demanded for the preservation of order, morals and the laws.[138]

The Assembly ratified once more the freedom of thought which had been decreed on October 15, 1877, giving the

133 *Ibid.*, Title II, Article 24.

134 *Ibid.*, Article 25.

135 *Ibid.*, Article 18.

136 *Ibid.*, Artice 27.

137 *Ibid.*, Title IV, *Del Ejecutivo*.

138 *Recopilación de Leyes de Guatemala*, II, 358.

right to publish without previous censorship even criticism of the acts of the government.[139] However, this liberty of the press, guaranteed in the Constitution by Article XXVI, was illusory. Of more than fifty-five new periodicals, mostly of short duration, published in Guatemala during the time of Barrios, only one, "*El Avisador*", was an opposition paper. Outside of the official "*El Horizonte*", "*El Progreso*", "*El Redentor*" and some few others, all controlled by Barrios and dedicated to singing his praises while attacking his enemies and religion, not one could publish without danger of prosecution.[140] No single paper in the country, according to Otto Stoll, a German traveler in Guatemala between 1878 and 1883, "would dare to convey anything other than foreign reports from fifth or sixth hand sources, and along with these the most loathing and fawning flattery of the current régime."[141] Among the most anti-religious of these periodicals was "*El Crepúscolo*". At times it attacked the Jesuits in such articles as that which described the fabulous possessions supposed to have been confiscated at the time of the suppression of the Order in Spain on April 3, 1767,[142] and another article justifying that suppression, as well as the one carried out in Guatemala, by means of a letter of Cardinal Ganganelli, later Pope Clement XIV, which declared that temporal sovereigns have the right to admit or prohibit religious communities and that, since these were not of divine origin, there was no attack on dogma when they were abolished for the tranquility of the state.[143] Still another article related the revolutionary activities being instigated by

139 *National Archives of Guatemala*, Decree No. 193, October 15, 1877.

140 *Cf.* Díaz, *Barrios ante la Posteridad*, pp. 682-690; García, *op. cit.*, V, 303.

141 Stoll, Otto, *Guatemala: Reisen und Schilderungen aus den Jahren 1878-1883*, Leipzig, F. A. Brockhaus, 1886, p. 322.

142 "El Crepúsculo", vol. I, no. 31, June 12, 1872.

143 *Ibid.*, No. 32, June 15, 1872.

the Jesuits who had sought refuge in Nicaragua when expelled from Guatemala.[144] Again, the editors of "El Crepúsculo" published lurid accounts of scandalous occurrences in convents,[145] or incidents ridiculing religious practices—a silly letter supposed to have been addressed to a patron saint on the advice of a confessor,[146] a cynical line or two aimed at a point of dogma.[147]

As was to be expected, the Constitution prevented the holding of property by the Church. Article 21 of the Law of Guarantees declared, after granting the free disposal of goods to all, that: "Entailed estates, however, are absolutely forbidden, and all alienation of land in favor of corporate bodies (mortmain), excepting only that destined for charitable institutions."[148] On February 14, 1880, Barrios declared liquidation of all funds reserved in favor of chaplaincies of whatever type, "the present holders of such benefices to receive only the interest accrued to date."[149]

The power of the Church had been definitely destroyed by 1880. Legislation affecting it after that date was concerned with minor matters, such as the order to all pastors to report to the government all baptisms taking place in their parishes,[150] or the order of Barrios that all processions were prohibited on the streets, as well as any ceremony in connection with accompanying the priest carrying the Viaticum.[151]

The property taken from the religious orders was still changing hands. On March 15, 1881 a Military Hospital was

144 Ibid., No. 18, March 16, 1872.

145 Ibid., No. 25, May 4, 1872.

146 Ibid., No. 47, Aug. 7, 1872.

147 Ibid., No. 48, Aug. 10, 1872.

148 National Archives of Guatemala, Dec. 12, 1879.

149 Ibid., Decree No. 255, Feb. 14, 1880.

150 Recopilación de Leyes de Guatemala, II, 470.

151 Díaz, Barrios ante la Posteridad, p. 415.

opened by General Barrios in the buildings which had been occupied by the Ursuline Academy.[152]

In May of that same year the former convent of San Pedro Carcha was converted into a theatre by the government " in order to develop the civilizing element of good taste in the population." [153] Some previous attempts to establish a theatre had been hindered by ecclesiastical authorities. Even when the first theatre had been erected in Guatemala in 1794, one of the regulations read: " No comedy, tragedy or other dramatic production may be presented without the previous examination and approbation by the Chief Justice and by the Diocesan Censor, don Antonio García Redondo." [154]

On October 2, 1881 police barracks and headquarters were set up in the ex-convent of Santa Catarina, where there was also an asylum for the insane, as well as in the ex-monastery of the Capuchin nuns. The latter was later transferred to the Convent of La Merced.[155] In 1882 the Chapel of the Third Order was converted into a General Post-Office, and the Cloister section of the convent of San Francisco into a primary school for boys.[156] On March 15, 1882 a school for Indian boys was opened in the former convent at Cobán.[157]

Although the Concordat drawn up between Carrera and the Holy See was still nominally in force, the government legislation during these latter years had left it meaningless. Therefore, in 1884, Barrios sent Dr. Angel María Arroyo as Envoy Extraordinaire and Minister Plenipotentiary of Guatemala to the Holy See to negotiate a new treaty. Arroyo was well received and was the object of outstanding proofs of deference on the part of Pope Leo XIII and the members of

---

152 Aguilera de León, *op. cit.*, p. 179.

153 Díaz, *Barrios ante la Posteridad*, p. 420.

154 Salazar, *op. cit.*, I, 259.

155 *Ibid.*, p. 382.

156 Díaz, *Barrios ante la Posteridad*, p. 411.

157 *Ibid.*, p. 416.

the Sacred College. With his diplomatic ability he was able to obtain from the Holy See the most liberal agreement which up to then had been granted in favor of Guatemala.[158] The new Concordat cleared many issues:

1. The Pope was insured the right of communicating freely with the prelate, clergy and faithful of Guatemala.
2. The Metropolitan Prelate was insured the right to govern the clergy, regulate church matters and maintain discipline.
3. The Seminary for the training of clergy was to be reopened under the administration and direction of the Metropolitan Prelate.
4. The head of the Metropolitan See of Guatemala was to be appointed by the Pope of his own accord.
5. The Ecclesiastical Chapter had the right to elect any of its members whenever a vacancy occurred.
6. The clergy were exempted from military service.
7. In compensation for the property of the Church which had been confiscated by the government, the latter was to pay to the Church 30,000 *pesos* yearly.
8. The Pope agreed not to molest those who were now in possession of the property which had been confiscated from the Church.[159]

Thus, both Church and State abandoned pretensions to any privileges in each other's domain. Yet, as Mecham states, the Church in Guatemala is to this day very much under temporal restraint.[160] The government has always interfered in the nomination to the Metropolitan See, as well as in its administration, as is evident from the fact that the French Archbishop Durou y Sure and the present Archbishop are the only occupants of the See since the time of Archbishop Casáus y Torres who were not exiled by the government. It should be

158 *Ibid.*, p. 657.

159 Mercati, Antonio, *Raccolta di Concordati su Materie Ecclesiastiche tra la Santa Sede e la Autorità Civile*, Roma, Tipografía Poliglotta Vaticana, 1919, pp. 1018-1020.

160 Mecham, *Church and State in Latin America*, p. 378.

remembered that Archbishop Rivera y Jacinto was removed by the Holy See.

While in Rome, Dr. Arroyo was delegated to draw up the canonical process previous to the naming of Dr. Juan Bautista Raúl y Bertrán, Vicar General of the Archdiocese, as the new Archbishop, to succeed don Bernardo Piñol y Aycinena,[161] who had died in exile in Havana on June 24, 1881.[162] This move was a diplomatic one, as Raúl y Bertrán was a very close friend of Barrios. When the relations between Church and State had been very strained after the exile of Archbishop Piñol y Aycinena, the Vicar General Raúl y Bertrán had published a pastoral, had communicated with President Barrios, and all difficulties ceased. For eleven years he governed the diocese during the exile of the Archbishop, taking advantage of his influence with Barrios to do good. He went directly to the President when he wished a favor and never left without obtaining his request. He used to advise Barrios whenever it appeared just and opportune to do so, and the latter never became angry with him.[163] Such gestures as a greeting to the President's wife on her return from Europe,[164] a pastoral circulated on August 6, 1883 in which the Vicar General urged cooperation with the government in its recent enterprise, the new Northern Railway, dear to Barrios' heart,[165] or the manifestation of approval of the clergy of Guatemala after Barrios' proclamation of the Confederation of Central America on February 28, 1885—[166] all tended to better relations between the government and the Church.[167] The Vicar General was the object of constant attention on the part of the Presi-

161 Díaz, *Barrios ante la Posteridad*, p. 657.

162 Batres, Jáuregui, *op. cit.*, p. 365.

163 Díaz, *Barrios ante la Posteridad*, p. 659.

164 *Ibid.*, p. 530.

165 *Ibid.*, pp. 466-467.

166 *Ibid.*, pp. 505-507.

167 *Ibid.*, p. 659.

dent and of members of the government, and he suffered real grief when Barrios died on the battlefield, April 2, 1885. The Vicar General published at that time a pastoral in which he appealed for obedience to the legitimately constituted authorities who would succeed Barrios.[168]

> We, Father Juan Bautista Raúl y Bertrán, Administrator Apostolic of the Archbishopric of Guatemala, and named by His Holiness Leo XIII to the Metropolitan See. To the Venerable Clergy and the Faithful of the Diocese, health, peace and charity in Our Lord Jesus Christ.
>
> A few days ago, Venerable Brothers and Dear Sons, we exhorted you to adhere to the Union of Central America, and urged you to the conservation of peace and public order. Now that a great calamity weighs upon our country because of the unexpected loss of the first Magistrate of the Republic, the distinguished President don Justo Rufino Barrios, who has just died on the field of battle, we urge you again with all our might, with all the zeal which love of country inspires in us, animated by the divine religion of Jesus Christ, to fulfill your great duties of submission, respect and obedience to the legitimately constituted authorities, which, in these solemn circumstances, the Church and the Republic have a right to expect from you.
>
> With our heart deeply grieved over such sad news of a friend, we can do no less than to remind you that, according to the Constitution, there is already determined the authority which shall rule over the destiny of the Republic and to which we must give our respect, obedience and support, as we are obliged to do as Christian citizens.[169]

At the funeral services for Barrios, all civil, with no single religious note,[170] Father Angel María Arroyo, as President of the National Assembly, gave the funeral oration.

168 *Ibid.*, p. 539.

169 *Ibid.*, p. 540.

170 *Ibid.*, p. 541. The remains of Barrios lie in the crypt of the Cathedral. As I gazed at the tomb I had occasion to wonder about the strange twist of fate which would cause this man's mortal remains to rest in an institution which personifies so much that he opposed.

Little is known of Barrios' personal attitude toward religion. He showed a certain tolerance toward several ecclesiastics, above all, as has been mentioned, to Fr. Raúl y Bertrán (one of the two persons permitted to address the President in the second person familiar form), and also to Dr. Angel María Arroyo, Representative of the National Assembly, and Father Alberto Rubio y Pilona, Rector of the *Colegio de Infantes*.[171] He had been married in a religious ceremony, in the Chapel of the Rosary of the parish church of Espíritu Santo at Quexaltenango, on August 3, 1874 by Dr. Silverio J. Santizo.[172] At the birth of his first child, in response to the request of his wife, he had the child baptized in the Church of the Sagrario, choosing a humble tailor, José Francisco Quezada, to act as godfather. When Quezada's son was born, Barrios acted as godfather in the ceremony held in the tailor's home, with Fr. Arroyo presiding.[173] At least one of the sons of Barrios was baptized in the Cathedral of Guatemala, with the ringing of bells and firing of rockets accompanying the service.[174] When García Granados lay dying, Barrios went to visit him for the last time and, after Granados had asked for the latest news, Barrios said, " Now, let's come to something else—have you examined your conscience? Have you gone to Confession? Have you had Extreme Unction? " The sick man answered, " As I have lived, so I die. Already it is time to begin the last journey. . . . ." [175] Barrios permitted his son Antonio to act as godfather at the confirmation of the son of Tomás Melgar, ex-revolutionary and member of the opposition group.[176] When the consolidation of ecclesiastical goods took place, don Valerio Irungaray, head of

171 Díaz, *Barrios ante la Posteridad*, p. 659.

172 *Ibid.*, p. 198.

173 *Ibid.*, p. 705.

174 *Ibid.*, p. 536.

175 *Ibid.*, pp. 309-10.

176 *Ibid.*, p. 701.

the commission in charge of nationalizing the church property, a very intelligent and energetic man, went to report to Barrios that he was going to send to the Church of St. Dominic for the statue of the Virgin of the Rosary, long venerated by the Guatemalans, in order to melt it down, for it would yield much silver. On hearing the proposal, President Barrios exclaimed, "Don't you dare touch my Virgin of the Rosary!" Batres Jáuregui, who relates this incident, comments: "Perhaps don Rufino was remembering that he had dedicated his degree of Bachelor of Philosophy to Our Lady of the Rosary when he was very young." [177]

Immediately after the death of Barrios, the *Primer Designado,* don Alejandro Manuel Sinibaldi, occupied the Presidential seat, but he was too weak to confront the abnormal situation of the time, and he renounced the office April 5, 1885, in favor of the *Segundo Designado,* or second named to succeed the President, Manuel Lisandro Barillas. The latter arranged for an early peace. When his interregnum was approaching its close, his friends and co-religionists wished to raise him to the presidency by election, but certain articles of the Constitution forbade such procedure. An Assembly was called for the purpose of changing these articles, and on October 23, 1885 a decree declared the desired reforms in the Constitution. The obstacles overcome, Barillas was elected to office for six years, from March 15, 1886. When the Legislative Power opposed his actions, he dissolved the Assembly and assumed supreme power over the nation in a decree of June 26, 1887.[178] He named an ecclesiastic, Dr. Angel María Arroyo as his first Minister of Foreign Affairs and Public Instruction, but the latter had to resign because he could not reconcile the constantly changing and disoriented policies of Barillas with his own.[179]

177 Batres Jáuregui, *op. cit.,* p. 109.

178 Aguïrre Cinta, *op. cit.,* p. 209.

179 Díaz, *Barrios ante a Posteridad,* p. 857.

On September 3, 1887 the Archbishop Ricardo Casanova y Estrada, who had been named to the See of Guatemala on the death of Dr. Raúl y Bertrán, was expelled violently and illegally, with no formal process, by the government of Barillas. The Legislative Assembly went even further; it ordered, on October 25, 1887, that, without its permission, the Archbishop could never return to the territory of Guatemala.[180]

When his term ended in March, 1892, Barrillas handed over the reins of government to the popularly elected don José María Reina Barrios, who like his predecessor, belonged to the Liberal school and continued the reforms begun by García Granados and Rufino Barrios.[181]

Reina Barrios was to prove a dictator whose despotism made him hateful to the people. He wished his rule prolonged and forced the Constitutional Assembly to extend it for four years. Although the people protested and two revolutions broke out, in San Marcos and the *Oriente,* the President remained master of the situation.[182]

While his attitude toward the Church was, in general, that of his predecessors, he made some concessions. The Major and Minor Seminaries, on which the diocese depended for the formation of the clergy, and which had been closed twenty-three years before by J. Rufino Barrios, were reopened on Jan. 15, 1896.[183]

Reina Barrios, likewise, permitted the return of the exiled Archbishop Casanova y Estrada. On February 16, 1897 the latter wrote from Havana to one of his friends, appealing to him, now that the authorities had changed, to intercede for him with the government so that he might return to Guatemala. The letter was shown to President Reina Barrios who

---

180 Aguirre Cinta, *op. cit.,* p. 209.

181 Aguero, *op. cit.,* p. 43.

182 Aguirre Cinta, *op. cit.,* p. 210.

183 Ramírez Colóm, José M., *Reseña biográfica de don Ricardo Casanova y Estrada,* Guatemala, Sánchez & de Guise, 1912, pp. 23, 24.

was well disposed and said, "The banishment of *señor* Casanova was certainly not legal. On my part, I offer my influence to facilitate his prompt return." [184] On the initiative of the President, the National Assembly on March 13, 1897 issued a decree granting full amnesty to all Guatemalans outside the Republic.[185] Under this decree, signed by President Reina Barrios that same day, the Archbishop was able to return to his country. At his arrival at the port of San José the Commandant, who had had instructions from the President to receive the Archbishop and show him every consideration and respect, entertained him, together with the committee of ecclesiastics who had been sent to welcome him home.[186] With great public joy, according to " *La República* " of Guatemala for Saturday, March 20, 1897, the Archbishop returned to the capital in the midst of a solemn and spontaneous ovation.

Meanwhile, when the national treasury became weaker, so that even the schools had to be closed for lack of funds, discontent grew and, finally, on February 8, 1898, President Reina Barrios was assassinated by a certain Oscar Zollinger on the Calle Poniente in Guatemala.[187]

Don Manuel Estrada Cabrera, first of those designated beforehand to succeed him in an emergency, took office, and for sixteen years continued the reforms of 1871—reopened the schools, made improvements in transportation and communication, established medical centers, hospitals, and asylums.[188] The Church-State relations remained practically the same.[189] It is interesting to note that President Cabrera sent

184 Batres Jáuregui, *op. cit.*, II, 366.

185 *National Archives of Guatemala*, Decree No. 351, March 13, 1897.

186 Batres Jáuregui, *op. cit.*, II, 366; Ramírez Colóm, *op. cit.*, p. 7.

187 Aguero, *op. cit.*, p. 38.

188 *Ibid.*, pp. 43-48.

189 Ramírez Colóm, *op. cit.*, p. 20.

a letter of congratulation to Archbishop Casanova y Estrada on the twenty-fifth anniversary of his consecration, July 25, 1911.[190] When the Archbishop died, on April 14, 1913, while making a visitation of the western part of his Archbishopric, he was buried with the greatest honors [191] in the capital from which he had been expelled twenty-six years before as the figurehead of the Conservative element which had opposed the government of Barrillas.[192]

One year after the death of Archbishop Casanova, there was consecrated in Rome by Cardinal Merry del Val, the twelfth Archbishop of Guatemala, Fr. Julian Raymundo Riviera y Jacinto.[193] However, he was soon removed by the Holy See and died in New Orleans in 1931.

On April 14, 1920 Estrada Cabrera was forced to resign and was followed in office by three leaders with terms so short that the Church status remained practically unaffected. However, on September 6, 1922, during the term of Gen. José M. Orellana, Archbishop Luis Muñoz y Capurón, S. J., less than one month after his consecration in the Church of La Merced, was expelled from Guatemala,[194] as a result of the political upheavals of August of that year, together with all those who belonged at that time or who had ever belonged to the Society of Jesus, and certain secular priests accused of opposing the government. Among the accusations brought against the expelled ecclesiastics were those of urging the masses to disobey and rebel against the dictates of authority, of perpetrating crimes against life, honor and property, of using the pulpit for propaganda against the government, of distributing leaflets bearing a prayer asking God to spare the flock from the government then ruling it, of participating in revolts in San

190 *Ibid.*

191 Batres Jáuregui, *op. cit.*, II, 366.

192 García, *op. cit.*, III, 361.

193 Batres Jáuregui, *op. cit.*, II, 365.

194 *Mediodía*, September 21, 1946.

Lucas, San Bartolomé, Taxisco, Chiquimulilla, San José Pinula, among others, and of lacking in zeal for the bettering of
the moral conditions of the people. Finally, it reproached the
Archbishop for not having brought about an agreement between the Church and the State. In his protest to the President, written from Colombia, the Archbishop reminded Orellana that on December 20, 1921, just after his succession to
the Presidential office, the new Minister of Government and
Justice had sent to the Archbishop a note containing in brief,
on the part of the new government, a statement of their stand
toward the Catholic religion, condensed by the Minister of
Government in the formula, "A Free Church in a Free
State!"

With the banishment of Archbishop Muñoz y Capurón, the
Church in Guatemala was again without a head until 1928,
when, after extensive negotiations between the government
and the Holy See, an outsider, a man advanced in years, was
installed as Archbishop. This was Monsignor Louis Durou y
Sure, a French ecclesiastic from Havana, who ruled peacefully until his death in 1938.

In the interval between 1922 and 1928 one can pick up the
pattern of some of the old causes for conflict between government and Church. In 1923 the government refused the
petition of the Apostolic Administrator to keep the collection
of alms under his jurisdiction, rather than that of the General Director of Accounts.[195] In that same year a complaint
was made to the Administrator that a secret meeting had
been held in the Church of Calvario, called for the purpose
of criticizing the government.[196]

Early in 1924 the Vicar General was informed of repeated
complaints to the effect that the pastors of Santa Lucia
Cotzumaltenango, Tecpán and Patzicia, in the department
of Chimaltenango, had been trying to incite the faithful

---

195 *Archives of Archbishop's Palace*, Guatemala, No. 371, Nov. 16, 1923.
196 *Ibid.*, No. 328, Sept. 12, 1923.

against the civil order.[197] The pastor of Tecpán, Fr. Celso Narcisio Calebor, sent his answer to the charges to the Ecclesiastical Court of Guatemala, and the parishioners of Patzicia defended their pastor by letter when he was accused of bringing political matters into his sermons.[198]

In 1931 General Jorge Ubico became President of the Republic and furnished Guatemala with a strong man's rule until he was ousted in 1944. When he died in exile in New Orleans, the people followed their traditional line of behavior and had much elaborate mourning displayed and many requiem Masses said in his behalf.[199] As was to be expected, the announcements of public prayers for Ubico brought much comment. To a very strong criticism in an editorial in *La Hora* of Guatemala, July 19, 1946, the Auxiliary Bishop, don Miguel Angel García A., replied the following day: " From the point of view of the Church, there is nothing extraordinary in the fact that the Archbishop himself officiates at a Mass for the repose of the soul of a person who has died as a Christian, even though that person may have been the President of the Republic; but the fact does have significance for those persons and groups who, placing false and derogatory interpretations on his legitimate acts, would like to place the Church in difficult situations."

In the meantime, Mariano Rossell Arellano, a native of Esquipulas (the town in which is located the famous shrine of the " Black Christ "), was consecrated as the fifteenth Archbishop of Guatemala, on April 16, 1939. At the time of his elevation he was pastor of the Church of San Sebastian in Guatemala City. He is a quiet man, possessed of great kindness and simplicity, who labors against almost unsurmountable odds and terrific conditions. His Archdiocese is poor, the clergy, for the most part, foreign and scattered, many poorly

197 *Ibid.*, No. 334, Jan. 8, 1924.

198 *Ibid.*, No. 334, Jan. 13, 1924; Jan. 20, 1924.

199 *La Hora*, July 19, 1946.

trained and equipped, and the people divided by vast social and economic cleavages. Yet around this distinguished prelate swirls at all times the rip tide of political extremities.

Ubico made a few concessions. He gradually allowed a few members of various religious orders to return. Shortly before his downfall he gave permission to the Maryknoll Order to enter the country, but everything depended on his personal whim. In every case he made it clear that there was to be no political activity and no pronouncements made on political or social questions or issues. There are at the present time seven Maryknoll Fathers and one Brother in the country, all of whom except one are working in the northwest under the Bishop of Quezaltenango. The pastor of the Church of the *Beatas de Belén* in Guatemala City is the one exception.

Guatemala has, since the time of Rufino Barrios, made a distinction between *Hermanas* (Sisters) and *Monjas* (Nuns). The Sisters are those of Charity of Saint Vincent de Paul, who were allowed to remain in 1879 in order to work in the General Hospital. They were all at that time French, and a contract was renewed by the Guatemalan Government with the Motherhouse of the Order in Paris in order that they might continue the work.[200] They are often seen on the street and are allowed legally to wear the religious habit. The Nuns are those who would teach, but they are not officially allowed in Guatemala.[201] However, under Ubico, the Belgian Nuns entered the country, supposedly as lay teachers to conduct a private seccondary school. One can easily recognize them on the streets for, although they wear no habit as such, their long black skirts and shirt waists, the very plain black hats, are somewhat conspicuous. Then, there are the Ladies of the Sacred Heart from Salvador, who conduct a school in the city known as the *Colegio de Santa Teresita*. The government allowed

200 *Supra*, p. 142.
201 Constitution of the Republic of Guatemala, Article 25, Title II.

them to buy a school, but, because they refuse to take the
Guatemalan examinations, the actual teaching is done by
seculars. Except for the intense seriousness of the entire problem, certain aspects come to seem almost comical. On the
one hand, the government insists that the teachers' examinations be taken; on the other, these women resist, saying
that, if they consented, the questions would be made silly and
impossible, and they would not be given licenses anyway. And
so it goes. Consequently, all but two, who are residents of
Guatemala, have only tourist status, and there is an almost
constant shuttling back and forth from Salvador. Again, the
pattern of dispute is recognizable. These women wear black
dresses, heavy silver crosses and chains, little black veils;
there is a chapel in the school; occasionally they admit that
a Mass has been celebrated. The Inspector of Public Education has accused them of deception and of affecting dis-
guises. They insist that that are " persecuted ", that the
government is anti-religious, Communistic, that they are dis-
criminated against, that they are practically hunted by hostile
agents who are ready to pounce on them at any moment.

The government, however, has the upper hand at the
moment. Every private school must get permission each year
to open. If the school continues its program regardless of
consent, there is the little matter of the government examinations at the end of the year. If the school has been operating
illegally, how can its director apply for the examinations?
This was the status of the Marist Brothers' *Colegio de Infantes* in 1946. The Spanish clergy were involved in some
incidents which brought forth the charge that they were
Franco sympathizers and, although they had an enrollment
of 900 pupils, on all sides the question was being raised as
to what would happen when the examination days arrived.
After a number of articles had appeared on the subject in
the various periodicals of the capital, the government, in the
following article published in *Nuestro Diario* for August 23,
1946, warns against the abuse of the privilege of conducting

private schools on the part of "foreigners well received and well treated among us":

> The Constitutional Government announces: That it considers the exercise of religious worship as a superior need in the life of the people.
>
> That because of its strictly democratic spirit, in spite of its being composed in part of Catholic functionaries, it respects the absolute freedom of worship, as established by our revolutionary Constitution.
>
> That all unofficial educational institutions enjoy complete liberty to impart religious instruction during special hours and under the inspection of the State, in order to avoid abuses.
>
> That the Government makes no distinction between native and foreign born priests provided they consecrate themselves solely to the exercise of their ministry.
>
> That the Revolution of October is a movement of national liberation, destined to return to the people of Guatemala the control of its national and international policies.
>
> Therefore:
>
> It calls the attention of the public in general to the existence of a danger that foreigners well received and well treated among us may be devoting themselves to spreading propaganda against the Revolution of October, and in favor of foreign doctrines and governments, with the sole purpose of preventing the success of the great program of historical and social revindication planned by the Revolution and its supporters for the grandeur of Guatemala.

To return to the Sisters of Charity for a moment. There are now only thirty of them, three of whom are French and of advanced age. The Superior is still French, but, because of her age, she seemed to defer pretty much to the Assistant. As is the case with the clergy, they recruit few members from Guatemala. Several are from Costa Rica and other parts of Central America and are generally from the poorer social and economic levels. They are supposed to receive twenty *pesos* per person a month from the government, but the amount had dropped first to eighteen, then to fifteen *pesos,* and the payments were several months in arrears at the time that I spent several days at the Convent of the Sisters of Charity in Guatemala, photographing documents, visiting the hospital, interviewing the Superior and the Assistant.

At the time of the suppression of the religious orders, the Sisters of Charity refused to remain in Guatemala without confessors, so the *Paulinos,* who are also French-speaking, were given the necessary permission to remain. Today they number twenty in all, and are in charge of parishes in Sololá, where they have five Fathers, in Totonicapán and in Jutiapa. They attend to a number of the churches in the capital and have undertaken a school for working men.

A Provisional government succeeded that of Ubico, but this Ponce régime did not last long. However, while Ponce was in office, the official Catholic newspaper, " *Verbum* ", was suspended (July, 1944). It began operations again in January, 1945. It was again suspended in October, 1945, but after eight days, because of the uproar from the citizenry, the government begged the Archbishop to start it again. " *Acción Social Cristiana* ", which was started in January, 1945, was likewise suppressed in October, 1945. In 1946 both were being published and, although critical of the government, there seemed to be no agitation toward their suppression.

After Ponce, came the interval of the triumvirate of don Jorge Toriello, Major Arana and Captain Arbenz, and, finally, on October 20, 1944, the election of Juan José Arévalo, a Professor of Education, who had lived for many years in Argentina. His has been another of the so-called Liberal régimes, and his whole administration has been increasingly feared and suspected by the Church. The old lines of tension tightened throughout 1946, and once more the battle lines were drawn up. On August 25th, a Sunday, the opposition held a " manifestation ". It was a protest against the defects in the election laws, against government agreements which control the distribution of paper, and against acts which Catholics believed harmful to the free exercise of their religion.[202] Typical of the "Catholic" protest was a statement in *El Imparcial* on August 5, 1946 which carried 1,304 signatures and which read as follows:

> The Catholic people of Guatemala, deeply indignant, protest most energetically against the calumnies and insults heaped upon the noble Spanish clergy by both foreign and national elements, in the semi-official periodical *Mediodía* as well as in the Communistic demonstration of Sunday, July 28th, during which the Holy Name of God was profaned, and His doctrines given malicious and distorted interpretations for the purpose of confusing and disrupting the Guatemala people.
>
> As Guatemalans and as Catholics, and for the well-being of our country, we demand that, in conformity with the express injunctions of the Constitution, there be guaranteed in an effective manner the security and liberty of our religion and all its ministers; for, in attacking and insulting some, one attacks and insults all, since all, whether they be Guatemalans, Europeans, North Americans, etc., work in the same way and for the same end: "the love of God and of neighbor!" [203]

This device was copied by countless numbers who lived outside the capital, but who had the city papers carry their statements and the list of signers.[204] In all cases they were profoundly indignant that there had been an energetic campaign of calumny and insults carried on against the Spanish clergy.

The point of departure of the parade held on August 25th was the statue of Barrios, Father of Liberalism in Guatemala, which stands opposite the railroad station. At the feet of Justo Rufino, no less, there had been since 9:30 in the morning a poster reading, "Religion is the bulwark of Youth." [205]

202 *El Imparcial*, August 21, 1946.

203 The same protest was repeated on August 21, and 26th, with other lists of signatures of about the same length.

204 *Cf.* also *Acción Social Cristiana*, August 22, 1946.

205 *El Imparcial*, Monday, August 26, 1946, p. 1.

The demonstration had been preceded by a great deal of publicity. All of the newspapers had notices inserted by the various political parties and groups. Excitement ran high when rumor had it that the government was not going to issue a permit for the procession, but that turned out to be fallacious.

The day before, Saturday, August 24th, Archbishop Rossell Arellano published a letter which was noteworthy. It pointed out the error of identifying the opposition and Catholicism officially.[206] That well-meaning and sincere Catholics were identified with it was their own business, but the Church should not be embroiled or involved—it was not, and should not be, understood as a Catholic gesture.

That was surely a statesmanlike stand—but alas, when the crowd on Sunday morning was massed in the central square (the National Palace on the one side, the Archbishop's Palace on the other), the Archbishop appeared on a balcony and repeatedly raised his hand in blessing and benediction.[207] There would be counter-manifestations, surely, to keep the story going. And there were.

The manifestation of August 25th was scarcely over when it was announced that there would be another to protest against the first, that of the " Falangists " or " Reactionaries ", the opposition. Now it was the turn of the "Workers," the " Liberals " (and, of course, the " Communists "), the supporters of the government, the Arévalists. They would hold a demonstration of super-colossal proportions, to put the other one to shame. On Sunday, September 8th, it was to take place. For several days before, the publicity program flamed up anew. Freight-car loads of bare-footed Indians arrived in the city; railroad and bus fares were reduced to encourage a visit to the capital. It was a much larger and

206 *El Imparcial*, August 23, 1946.
207 See cut.

better organized affair. The posters of the marchers were elaborate and certainly numerous. In answer to the first one of August 25th, there were many signs to the effect that Religion and Politics must not be confused.[208]

In the central square, the President of the Republic, Juan José Arévalo, addressed the crowd. He apparently became excited and carried away with himself, because he made several statements which were judged to be quite imprudent. He had not appeared on the 25th of August; the Archbishop did not appear on September eighth!

On the 12th of September the protest of a group of citizens calling themselves the "Independent Political Party" was distributed in the form of a pamphlet. Concerned mostly with refuting statements of the President concerning the accomplishments of his administration, it also took offense at the fact that President Arévalo said that some Catholics (namely those opposing him and his government) were acting as if they were riding on the crest of the waves. The protest of Sept. 12th made the point that this reference only brought out the latent feeling of aversion toward Catholicism which from time to time escaped from the imprudent lips of the President.[209] Perhaps it is significant that in neither demon-

208 See cut.

209 *El Imparcial*, Sept. 9, 1946. The original text of President Arévalo's comment follows in part: "Y esta juventud del 20 de Octubre, muchachos de 14 a 20 años, saltaron como potros en las aceras para deshacer aquel menjurge hipócrita de liberales y conservadores. Fueron ellos, los chiquilines, los muchachos que tienen integras las vitaminas, los que son el fermento perpetuo de esta revolución, los que quitaron los estandartes de aquellas manos que se estaban dando unas a otras mezclados los liberales de 1871 con los sacerdotes y con algunos católicos que se creían en el mejor de los tiempos."

The original of the protest reads: "Y el doctor Arévalo no dice la verdad cuando afirma que en aquella manifestación se daban las manos los liberales de 1871 con los sacerdotes, porque ningún sacerdote del culto católico ni de ningún otro culto participó en ella. La alusión a 'algunos católicos que se creían en el mejor de los tiempos' solo acusa el sentimiento latente de aversión al catolicismo que de cuando en vez escapa a la imprudente palabra del señor presidente de la república."

stration was there violence; no attempt to settle the issues with bullets. Neither, as of this writing, are the great historical issues between Church and State in Guatemala settled. It is a fascinating story, with a tremendous plot, a persistent theme, uncompromising characters—one cannot write the dénoument.

The Roman Emperor, Antoninus Pius, once is supposed to have said, " Happy are the people whose annals are meager." It is self-evident, then, from the proportions of this volume that the relations between Church and State in Guatemala have not been Utopian in their character.

PART THREE

CHAPTER I

TODAY'S PICTURE

THERE is nothing more difficult to measure or evaluate than such intangibles as influence or status. The printed page has too often oversimplified complexities; statistics are often pyramided on hollow foundations. A handbook, a year book or a text book is often guilty (unintentionally) of creating false impressions. One reads, " Guatemala is thoroughly Catholic, 90% Catholic," or again one reads, " Guatemala is a country steeped in paganism." Before drawing any conclusions as to what extent any country is Catholic or Christian or pagan, a thorough analysis of all factors relevant to the situation should be made. No conclusions based on wishful thinking are in themselves valid.

In contemporary Guatemala the conflicting relationships between Church and State which I have discussed have had some results which in all cases are interesting, but which in many cases are tragic. The mistake is often made of discussing the Church and the State as abstractions or disembodied spirits, whereas neither can be separated from the social climate of the environment in which it has its existence. In no case can the State or the Church perform any better than the behavior of a cross section of its members and leaders warrants.

Nor can it be expected that a Church, gradually stripped of its political power and prestige through a period of over one hundred years, can exercise a substantial and healthy influence when existing behind a façade, a shell of its former self. Even though that Church continues to insist upon its former supervisory and regulatory rôles, it is apparent to all that it is actually playing a pantomine.

Indeed, the Church-State conflicts have been accentuated by the tremendous population cleavages which are so striking in Guatemala, the separate stratifications of whites (*blancos*), *ladinos,* and Indians.

Guatemala has an estimated population of 3,284,269,[1] 64.8% of which is Indian, 34.43% of which is *ladino.* The term *ladino* originally meant *mestizo* (racial mixture of Spanish and Indian). Now it has taken on a social significance, and any Indian who dons white cotton trousers and a colored shirt, (in other words, abandons the costume of his village), is classified as a *ladino* officially by the government.[2] However, when the term *ladino* is used in this treatise, it will usually carry its original connotation, namely that of mixed blood. Less than 1% (.77%) of the population of Guatemala is white,[3] and the foreign population is concentrated at the coast or in and around the capital.

It is necessary before proceeding further, to explain the character of these divisions in the population. Guatemala can be divided, like all Gaul, into three parts. On the coast is the foreign banana empire ruled by American capital, whose subjects are predominantly British and American negroes, a scattering of Chinese, and all that other flotsam and jetsam of humanity that is to be found in every port of the world. As soon as the traveler leaves the sea level and ascends by railroad to the capital (5,200 feet in altitude) and pushes even further upward by car or finally by mule or horse, the complexion of the inhabitants changes along with changes in physical geography. This is the Indian country where coffee thrives. The negro will not go up; he gets cold, ague, pneumonia, etc.; the Indian will not voluntarily go down where he contracts, he avows, tropical fevers of all kind. The third world is that of the *ladino,* the composite of both new and

1 *Statesman's Year-Book*, vol. LXXXIII, 1946, p. 985.

2 *Cf.* decree of Barrios granting to those natives of Sacatepéquez who would wear the costume of the *ladino* the right to assume that name. (*Recopilación de Leyes de Guatemala*, vol. I, Decree No. 165).

3 Jones, Chester Lloyd, *Guatemala: Past and Present*, Minneapolis, University of Minnesota Press, 1940, p. 271.

old world stock, who has a foot in both worlds. He is to be found in the towns and cities, and scattered here and there in the villages. Most of the municipal officials are *ladinos*. Even in the villages where an Indian is the *alcalde* (mayor), the town secretary is a *ladino*. In the village of San Martín Chiliverde, e.g., I went to interview the Indian *alcalde*, only to find him standing and the *ladino* secretary sitting at the desk, to all intents and purposes being the actual head, and telling the Indian what to do (and, incidentally, how to do it).

It is the *ladino* who has become ambitious, anxious to advance himself and to seek a large place in the sun for Guatemala. And yet, perhaps because the *ladino* is a racial mixture, blended of the old world and the new, possessing a split personality, he suffers more from an inferiority complex than anyone else, I think perhaps, in the world. He is an extremist in everything. It is practically impossible to carry on a reasonable argument with him, for, rather than face the inevitable and logical conclusions, he will change the subject and go off on a tangent.

Naturally, then, this whole Church-State conflict has had an interesting effect on the *ladino's* character. Being an extremist, as previously stated, he is either violently for or against the Church—in his own way of expressing it—either a "fanatical" or "cold" Catholic. Those who are "cold" have not to any appreciable extent been won over to any other denomination, nor are they for the most part "non-believers". They are indifferent, apathetic; sometimes, especially among the "intellectuals", they are openly scornful and contemptuous of the clergy.

The *ladino* man, for the most part, stays away from church services and leaves such things to the women. The women, on the other hand, are anxious to teach catechism and give religious instruction, but American Catholic missionaries with one accord state that, although these ladies are willing, they know little about the basic doctrines. Their reactions are founded on emotionalism and their practices shot through with Jansenism. Tumin, in his study of religion in the village of San Luis Jilotepeque, confirms numerous observations that I made in connection with the leading rôle played by women in church affairs.[4] They chant prayers in the church and maintain a certain order in processions. I have often seen them taking up the collections. The *ladino* boy—or here let us just say the Guatemalan boy—as he is growing up is taught (probably by the women) about the power and glory of the traditional Church. At about the age of sixteen he is faced with the very realistic challenge of the authority of the State. Although the Church continues to insist on its prerogatives and jurisdiction in many areas, such as morality, education, and welfare, the State also does its share of insisting. As has been shown in these pages the Church has been steadily and consistently weakened, and that weakness, in spite of a show of resistance and protests, becomes evident to the ambitious youth.

Much time and energy are devoted to display—and this is true of both Indian and *ladino*. On the occasion of several requiems celebrated for the late President Ubico, who died in exile in New Orleans, as previously noted, there were elaborate notices edged in black in the daily papers; the entire church was completely draped in mourning, a richly adorned catafalque was presided over by enormous statues of angels; every woman present (with the exception of myself) was dressed in complete mourning; the men wore black arm bands.

I attended many Guatemalan weddings, several of which were very fashionable with religious services executed in the most elaborate continental pattern. A beautiful silver chain was slipped over the heads of the bride and groom during part of the ceremony, and one corner of the bride's veil was draped over the groom's shoulder. At one of these weddings, place cards were set out in the pews for the guests. Yet it

4 Tumin, Melvin Marvin, *San Luis Jilotepeque: A Study in Social Relations*, Evanston, Ill., Northwestern University Press, 1944, p. 72.

was obvious that the large number of men witnesses were not at all accustomed to attending church services—though they did, however, kneel at the elevation of the Host. This attitude on the part of *ladino* men in the cities also holds over in the villages. Tumin, in the study cited above, declares:

> For all but *ladino* males, religion entails practice as well as belief. This means regular church attendance, amounting sometimes to twice-daily visits; regular participation in religious fiestas and processions; adoration of the saints; for not a few people the investment of their attitudes and behavior with a certain element of Christian love.[5]

There is always a large attendance in the churches for special occasions: processions, weddings, requiem Masses, ordinations, anniversaries and, of course, the fiestas. They have in Guatemala what is known as the *Jubileo Circular,* somewhat similar to the Forty Hours' Devotion in the United States. Each church in the capital is designated in turn to have Exposition of the Blessed Sacrament for three days. Crowds flock to the particular church in which the *Jubileo Circular* is being held, and in the immediate area of the church there is the appearance of a fair, with all kinds of vendors purveying their wares: candies, cakes, hot corn soup, juices, candles, cheap religious articles and jewelry. The majority going in and out of the churches on those days seem to be very poor.

As has been noted, the celebration of fiestas in the cities is observed principally inside the churches. Usually reference is made to the religious societies, or *cofradías,* among the Indians, but there are organizations in the cities and towns which are identified with the upper classes, e.g., the association which celebrates the Feast of the Seven Dolors, observed at the Church of Santo Domingo, in charge of the Dominican Fathers in the capital. A purple drop from the ceiling entirely obscures the main altar. In front of it is a

5 Tumin, *op. cit.,* p. 97.

long, hand-carved bier, the top of which is filled with earth and in which flowers and plants are growing. Above this is laid out a life-size Christus figure in white. Behind it is a second heavy hand-carved frame bearing a life-size statue of the Virgin wearing a gold crown and clothed in purple velvet trimmed with gold. Around the pedestal also real flowers are planted. I witnessed the celebration in 1946. At six o'clock in the evening the members of the *Cofradía,* all representatives of well-known families, gathered in the sanctuary. These men wore long black robes like cassocks with emblems on their arms; black skull caps with hoods down the back, long black gloves. About one hundred of them stood at attention with high, lighted torches at their sides. A priest recited the rosary; the choir sang parts; there was a half-hour sermon. The women in the body of the church wore black mantillas with purple ribbons around their necks. Little altar boys were dressed in the Dominican habit. After the side aisles had been cleared of pews, the men took turns carrying the bier around the church, fifteen on each side and, at the end of the ceremony, the bells of the church tolled endlessly for the entombment.

Only rarely now are processions held outside the church in the cities. One exception I noted on August 15, 1946, in connection with the feast of the Assumption of the Blessed Virgin. At the Church of that name, a priest accompanied the procession around the block, but I was told that such a thing had not happened in that area for many years.

The observance of fiestas in the city follows generally a similar pattern, whether it be for Our Lady of Mt. Carmel, Our Lady of Guadalupe, Our Lady of the Seven Dolors, St. John or St. Christopher. There are several Masses, processions, long sermons, etc. in the churches, and the carnival effect outside.

In fact, the manner of celebrating fiestas has not changed much since the time of Thomas Gage, who wrote in 1625 of a celebration at Chimaltenango:

The chief fiesta is upon the 26th of July (which they call St. Ann's Day) and then is the richest fair that ever my eyes beheld. ... It is set forth with Bull Baiting, Horse racing, Stage Plays, Maskes, dances, Musick and all this gallantly performed by the Indians of the Town.[6]

Later in the same work he refers to the fact that the Indians commonly become drunk, and in the fiesta sports " some venture, some lose their lives." [7]

There are many studies which have been made of Guatemalan villages, some emphasizing the economics, others the customs and symbols, still others, the general picture.[8] All have found it necessary to mention the extent to which the various phases are intertwined with religious significance. It is the purpose of this study only to mention these various customs in order to emphasize how these affect the status of the official church organization and ultimately the result of such phenomena on Church-State relations.

While I have tried to check carefully my own findings with those of earlier authors, I am taking the liberty, from time to time in this section, of citing my own experiences.

In setting my own observations over against those of earlier writers, the same conclusion is reached that the manner of celebrating the numerous fiestas has not changed materially from that of past centuries, either in the city, the

6 Gage, *op. cit.*, p. 117. Many other works in subsequent years may be resorted to for proof of the fact that the method of celebrating fiestas remains practically unchanged, e. g. Montgomery, *op. cit.*, pp. 67; 71-3; 76, 77; Thompson, *op. cit.*, p. 160; Domville-Fife, Charles W., *Guatemala,* London, Francis Griffiths, 1913, pp. 172-174; Wagley, Charles, "Economics of a Guatemalan Village", *American Anthropologist*, vol. 43, no. 3, pp. 29 ff.; La Farge, Oliver, *The Year-Bearers' People*, New Orleans, Tulane University Press, 1931, pp. 91-98; *Santa Eulalia, the Religion of a Cuchumatán Indian Town*, Chicago, Univ. of Chicago Press, 1947, pp. 250 ff.

7 Gage, *op. cit.*, p. 133.

8 Tumin, *op. cit.*, pp. 97, 99, 100, 134, 135, 139, 179, 180; Siegel, Morris, "Religion in Western Guatemala", *American Anthropologist*, vol. 43 (1941), pp. 71-75.

town or the village. The great National Fair held annually in Guatemala City is called the Fair of the Assumption (*Fiesta de Asunción*) and is held throughout the week of August 15th.

In the Indian villages the natives, worn out from endless dancing, shooting off fire crackers (home-made affairs consisting of long reeds to which dynamite is attached), drinking *aguardiente*, are often seriously hurt in all manner of accidents during the fiesta.

I took a long journey partly on mule back with a Guatemalan friend, doña María Matheu, in order to bring medicines of all kinds to the village of Todos Santos. An American woman, Maude Oakes, engaged in research for the Mellon Foundation, had wired for help, because so many Indians had been hurt in connection with the fiesta of Todos Santos. These two women rode long distances into the mountains to bring medical aid to many who had fallen, who had powder burns, etc. In addition, for days they vaccinated, inoculated, administered all manner of remedies to women and children who formed in line outside the one-room adobe house, where they had begun to arrive at daybreak.

In the taxis and in the buses one notices always over the driver's head an array of holy pictures, a crucifix or pleated palm. It is safe to say that it would not occur to most of the drivers that anything more could be required in the way of practising their religion.

It is not surprising that a people of such temperament and character, who are interested in the dramatic, should be ever hopeful of witnessing miracles. In the summer of 1946 even the newspapers which are openly hostile to the Church carried feature articles about the supposedly miraculous appearance of the Face of Christ on the statue in the parish church of Taxisco. The village was the birthplace of President Arévalo. He has been called by the 'fanatical' Catholics, a radical and a communist, an enemy of the Church. At the Countermanifestation on September 8th he attacked the Church, but approximately two weeks previously there had supposedly appeared on the statue of Christ over the main altar luminous features of a face. This phenomenon was apparently noticed by a village boy after a brother of the President had visited the church. Excitement ran high all over Guatemala and much publicity attended the fact that the passengers in a bus en route to the scene were killed. I made a trip to Taxisco on October 18, 1946. The village is situated about one hundred and ten kilometers from the old capital of Antigua, and was, without doubt, one of the most miserable, poorest and dirtiest places I ever saw. There were two priests in attendance at the run-down primitive *convento*. One was very young, getting a thrill out of everything; the other, Padre Eugenio Arango, had previously been a secretary at the Archbishop's Palace. He was very serious and anxious to be of assistance. The priests were in a small room with several men, some of whom turned out to be government agents who had come to " supervise the revenue ". The amount of cash was insignificant, but a dispute developed which was typical of the historic church-state feud, namely whether the clergymen or the civil agents should have control of the key to the strong box. The government officials were willing to have some one of each jurisdiction have a key, but Padre Eugenio was adamant— one key or nothing, and that key for himself. When I left the scene, having offered to provide Padre Eugenio with transportation back to his *convento* in Escuintla, the government agents were in control.

To return briefly to the church scene, I went with the priests to an entrance in the rear. They unlocked a door and I went up a steep flight of stairs which led behind the main altar into a glass-enclosed space beside the Christus statue. It was possible to make out the outlines of a face on the torso. Then I went into the main body of the church (the priests furnished me with a pair of binoculars) and I viewed the statue from every angle. The church was filled with Indians who were praying quietly. Many held lighted candles. It would be impossible to describe a more pathetic sight. Dogs were running in and out, some were sleeping on the floor; children were crawling everywhere—the whole picture evoked a reaction of pity and some degree of sadness.

This particular phenomenon, a second face appearing on a statue in the midst of such surroundings seemed very unreal indeed, but perhaps, after all, that is the kind of environment which would most need a miracle.

On the return trip to Escuintla, Padre Eugenio, attired in his cassock, with a burlap bag containing his luggage flung over his shoulder, made known the fact that his good friend, the Archbishop of Guatemala, had visited the scene. Then the Padre added, " The Archbishop told me about you and said that he had an idea that you would visit Taxisco soon ". Then he asked me my opinion about the authenticity of the apparition. I posed a counter question, " What did the Archbishop say? " And there followed these words which reflect the ·great wisdom of the prelate, " Not a word." Nor would any visitor, I think, be found following any other course.

In most of the villages which are predominantly Indian and which have only a scattering of *ladinos,* each group keeps pretty much to itself. On All Saints' Day, November 1, e.g. and on a few other occasions depending on the area,[9] both *ladinos* and Indians visit the cemetery and greet each other with considerable courtesy. In some cases I suspected this unusual friendliness was somewhat aided by the use of artificial stimulants.

Oliver La Farge, in his recently published study, *The Year Bearers' People,* cited above, writing about the Prayers for

---

[9] In many areas little attention was paid to All Saints' Day, but for several days before there were ceremonies in the cemeteries, e. g. music, eating, burning of incense and candles, elaborate floral displays, etc., in connection with All Souls' Day and remembrance of the dead. This kind of thing has led to criticism on the part of the Protestant missionaries that too much emphasis is put on the Dead Christ and not enough on Living Christianity.

the Dead, gives the following version and notes that it seems to be a direct address to the dead themselves as minor deities and suggests the possibility of definite ancestor worship; " Here we come to thee, let thy heart be big toward our souls. Let thy big heart forgive that we were unable to bring anything to thee. Help the health and welfare of our family; let there be no sickness in our souls, or in our children or in our family." [10]

There is no doubt but that the present Indian religion is a mixture of the old Mayan beliefs, based primarily on the *Popul Vuh,* their equivalent of a Bible, and Christianity .

The Indian recognizes a certain orthodox sphere in which the Catholic priest is competent to act, but seems to regard him as a complete outsider when he is concerned with his prayer rounds and performances peculiar to his traditional customs.

One of the most difficult things for the non-Indians to understand is that, to an Indian, there is no inconsistency in accepting the Christian God on the one hand, and continuing his Mayan rites on the other. For several days preceding the Feast of the Rosary, October 7th, I was in the village of San Juan Chamelco. The procession to carry the image of St. Dominic and that of the Virgin to the *ranchitos* (or little shelters) was to start at four o'clock in the afternoon. Only Indian men were making the preparations and as time went on I became more and more aware of the fact that they were " stalling ". I sent my driver, an Evangelical *ladino,* to inquire if some one would come and talk to me so that I could satisfactorily explain my presence. The one *ladino* present, the schoolmaster, Manuel Ramírez, advanced. He was truly a gentleman of distinction, kind, gentle and sympathetic. He stated that the Indians were fearful and suspicious of outsiders, and when I explained that I had a letter from the Archbishop of Guatemala, he went to the front of the church and

10 La Farge, *The Year Bearers' People,* p. 76.

read it aloud, while all gathered about him. Then, with *señor* Ramírez leading them, they all came down the aisle and bowed, and a spokesman thanked me for my courtesy and interest. The preparations continued and when it was almost dark all left the church. In the pouring rain, to the accompaniment of the usual rockets and drum beatings, the women following behind, we set forth. Slipping and sliding up and down narrow paths and then through the cornfields we went. At the first *ranchito* St. Dominic was left with a certain number of the company to provide music and prayers. At the second, after the Virgin was properly installed, the heads of the various *cofradías,* or religious societies, sat down on benches placed on either side of a long table. There the inventory was to be taken of all the various properties of the societies before the officers for the new year should be installed on the following day.

Before they began this considerable undertaking, the eldest of the group, the *padrino,* came forward and, bowing before the Virgin, prayed somewhat in the following fashion; he asked the God of the Hills to grant good health to all, and the God of the Plains to give His assistance to the common welfare. I turned to the schoolmaster and, in a tone which indeed betrayed the New England spirit, asked, "How do they reconcile a prayer like this with the teaching of Christianity?"

And the answer came ever so gently: "They see nothing inconsistent at all in their beliefs. An Indian spends his days close to the hills and the plains; it is not strange, then, that he would make a connection between them and divinity."

To much of what the official church says the Indian is apparently indifferent. This is in part due to the fact that there is such a dearth of priests; many villages see a clergyman only once a year and they have become accustomed to carrying on their own projects, independent of any supervision. Yet, even in villages in which priests are in residence, the Indians pay little attention to formal ceremonial. It seems absolutely necessary for each Indian to be doing something or saying something that makes him a personal participant in religious acts. I have attended countless services where Mass was in process of being celebrated, only to have the Indians going and coming constantly, lighting their candles, scattering their flower petals on the floor, visiting the saints' statues, murmuring prayers for their families, their crops, their animals, etc., oblivious of the sermon and the ritual. And yet the Indians are anxious for the padre to come down the aisle and bless each one and sprinkle holy water on petals and candles. Often whole groups of Indians approach a priest, their hats doffed and heads bent to receive a pat on the head and a blessing.

In contrast with the general indifference of the *ladino* men to church services, the Indian men are almost the only participants. Over and over again Indian men can be seen in a village to enter a church and emerge with a statue, and with drums beating, carrying the image from one place to another, returning to the church two or three hours later, while the women, with children on their backs, continue uninterruptedly their laundry work at the central washing place. This procedure is followed also on Sundays.

The official church with its orthodox teachings and regulations apparently has little or no effect on the Indians. In Cobán, it is customary, for example, for the statue of St. James to be carried through the fields in supplication for rain; also once a year to take the statue of the patron saint of the village to visit the patron saint of the neighboring village. The Bishop at Cobán a few years ago forbade the Indians to remove the images from the churches because they were church property. The villagers in this instance obeyed for about a year, and then resumed their traditional practice.

In the Cobán area, likewise, it has always been customary for the Indians to play stringed instruments continuously in the churches before certain feasts. The strumming effect seemed to me to be very monotonous, but not so to the Bishop.

One afternoon I was sitting in the cathedral watching the various activities—pine branches being strewn on the floor, elaborate floral decoration being arranged in preparation for the Feast of the Rosary on Sunday. The Bishop stopped the musical performance once; there was a pause; then the musicians began again. The Bishop protested a second time; the playing ceased once more—but the musicians still sat on their wooden benches. I left before the final outcome was known—which party's endurance was greater. But—next morning at High Mass, the Bishop (a native Spaniard, but resident in Guatemala over twenty years), addressed the congregation. He was soft spoken and apparently trying to " reason " with his children. He explained that the music was " profane ", of the dance hall type, not suitable for the House of God. I am sure that the Indian part of the congregation was entirely bewildered and unaffected by the appeal. As for the *ladinos,* they struggled atrociously with the unfamiliar Latin High Mass music. The net result was, I am sure, that the Bishop, the Indians, the *ladinos* and myself were all miserable. That very evening I had one of two interviews with the Bishop. He again explained his position. My own judgment was that, although he was sincere, he did not understand the psychology of his people, that after all these years in Guatemala, he had no realization that to ban and prohibit the performance of traditional customs gained nothing for the Church or for religion.

An attempt to account for the great gap that exists between the Church and the Indian brought to light several obstacles. There is no common ground on which the Spanish Bishop and his congregation of Indians, with an occasional *ladino,* may meet. Even with good intentions, the profound lack of understanding prevents real communication, and, strange as it may seem, there is little realization of the gap.

One obstacle is psychological. The Indian is a realist. He spends his days concerned with the concrete: his little house, the weaving of his clothes, the making of pottery, baskets, candles, incense cakes. He lives close to the soil. He has no idea of abstraction, no practice in generalization. Things figurative, symbolic, are foreign to him; if he has any symbolism, it is what he has worked out for himself, or something handed down by his ancestors.

Contrariwise, the European or the North American with a predilection for living in the world of make-believe has become a master of fantasy, picturing the world of the future, diverted and abstracted by the unknown, the distant, the obscure. While the European or the North American talks of the Holy Spirit, the Indian must have a dove decorated with red ribbons coming down upon the head of the priest in the church. He must have his statues, his candles, his flowers, his incense pots, his direct and personal participation, while the Spaniard deals with abstruse reasonings on immaterial beings, their nature, their attributes and all manner of philosophical ramifications.

A second impediment is the difference in language. The Bishops and many of the priests often speak only Spanish, while thousands of the parishioners talk only Indian dialects. It should be noted that there is a growing realization of the need for learning the language of the Indian.[11] A good deal of pioneer work in modern times has been done in this area by Protestant missionaries, especially the Presbyterians.

Another obstacle is the great dearth of priests. Guatemala with its population of over three million has only one hundred twenty Roman Catholic priests, about one priest to every 30,000 faithful. The province of Quezaltenango, with over 1,000,000 inhabitants, has only thirty priests. The parish of Huehuetenango, with 176,000 souls, has only two priests.[12]

11 One is reminded here of the work of the religious orders in the colonial period in this field, and of the royal decree of May 27, 1582 establishing a Chair of Native Languages at the Institute, later the University. (Pardo, *Efemérides*, p. 26.)

12 *Memoria del Segundo Congreso Nacional de Guatemala de Vocaciones sacerdotales*, Guatemala, Tipografía Unión, 1944, p. 17.

The number of priests has remained practically static since the administration of Barrios, when an inventory ordered by that executive showed there were, in 1872, one hundred nineteen priests.[13]

Included in the clergy of the present time are the following members of religious orders, mostly from Spain:

Jesuits—directing the Seminary	4 members
Friars Preachers (Dominicans)	3 members
Franciscans at La Recolección	2 members
at San Francisco	5 members
Paulinos	10 members
Salesians	4 members

Most of these Religious are stationed in the capital,[14] as are most of the secular priests.[15]

I visited a frail, elderly Spanish priest, Father Gaspar Jordan, who was stationed in the fairly remote village of Nabaz and was working alone, responsible for an area comparable to a small county, and whose eyes filled with tears as he told me things would be more difficult for him, because his horse had died a week previously.

With the exception of the Americans, the priests are very poor, and, although well-meaning and sincere, they are obviously ill-equipped to deal with the problems at hand, the exigencies of the time.[16] They have been brought up in an

13 Díaz, *Barrios ante la Posteridad,* pp. 139-140.

14 It cannot be too often stressed that statistics in Latin America generally are not too exact, nor can the condition be otherwise when all the difficulties are considered. Even a lengthy report furnished by the Archbishop's office was not too helpful, for although it was captioned " Status of the Church in Guatemala Today," the basic figures used were in some cases those for 1902, others 1909 or 1942, and the figures furnished for 1946 in regard to religious orders did not tally with those I made myself.

15 Archbishop's Report, September, 1946.

16 I do not mean to convey the idea that the American priests are wealthy, but that they have the advantage of being members of an Order which is responsible ultimately for financing their projects. They also receive help from contributions sent by individuals in the United States.

old world tradition. They are, without exception, courteous and willing to talk all day about the tragedy of the situation, and the plight of the poor people, but seem to be without the semblance of an idea of how to do anything to remedy matters.

The American Catholic missionaries, members of the Mary-knoll Order, as one might expect, have an infinite amount of good will, an impatient desire to be doing something about health and education, as well as formal religion. Their church in Guatemala City has been a boon to the English-speaking Catholics since 1944, and the Rev. Edmund McClear, now of Salamá, for two years did a superb piece of work with the small colony of his own compatriots. The majority of the congregation, however, were *ladinos* and Indians, and, although they attended services in fair numbers, only rarely did they hear any instructions even in Spanish. However, they sat patiently, though uncomprehendingly.

A fourth difficulty which complicates the situation is that even today the majority of the clergy are foreign. While the Archbishop and the Bishop of Quezaltenango are natives, the Auxiliary of the latter, and the Bishop of Cobán are Spaniards.

Of the foreign clergy, naturally, the Spaniards predominate, but I met and interviewed others who were Italian, German,[17] Mexican, Costa Rican and American.

17 Three of the most able priests of this nationality had died since I had made a previous visit to Guatemala in 1944; among them was Father Rossbach, who had labored for forty years in Chichicastenango. One might include an interesting commentary on him—he thoroughly, deeply and sympathetically understood and identified himself with the Indian mentality and psychology. He was beloved by the Indians. For three days in 1946 I watched them coming before All Souls' Day, to bring to his tomb every kind of tribute—flowers, candles, petals, incense and carved crosses. Paradoxically enough, it is the people from the United States, even Catholics and Catholic clergy, who hold up their hands in horror at the "pagan goings-on" of these people.

The other two German priests, both remarkable men, were brothers, the Fathers Knittel, who died within a few months of each other.

Often the native clergy is berated because it is ignorant, or dirty, or greedy—because the men live in squalor. The thing goes around in a circle—no matter what it might have been in the distant past, the Guatemalan Church is at present poor; the people are for the most part poor moneywise (the use of barter is extensive) and the clergyman cannot be, and is not, a more superior product than can be expected from that social and economic environment in which he is found.

A fifth obstacle is the mountainous terrain and the lack of means of transportation in a country which, in the middle of the twentieth century, still has only a few paved streets or roads outside the capital. The whole area has, from Zacapa to Puerto Barrios, no road connection. A single track railway joins the two towns. Other areas can be reached only on mule back, e.g. the whole Cuchumatán area, with mountains, unprotected *barrancas,* and steep trails. In other places the absence of bridges and the washing out of the roads in the rainy season make the villages wholly inaccessible at certain times of the year.

All these obstacles serve to isolate and insulate, not only the Indian from the *ladino,* but the Indian from the official Church.

Few people, I suppose, in history, have clung four hundred years after their conquest to their ancient customs as have the Guatemalan Indians. When the Spaniard came in the sixteenth century, he wanted to do two things, first, to make his new subjects good Europeans, and second, to make them good Catholics. In the first, the judgment of history is that he failed; in the second, the religion of the present day Indian is Roman Catholicism mixed with old Mayan beliefs and rites.

One of the unique annual ceremonies in the town of Momostenango has to do with the very ancient ritual calendar, to which the Indians of Guatemala, notwithstanding all, still cling tenaciously. Without going into a complicated exposition, it might be indicated that the Mayan year has 260 days, divided into shorter periods of twenty days, each day having its own name. Then a numerical sequence from 1 to 13 is coordinated with these twenty days.[18] When all these twenty names have passed through each number (20 x 13) the calendar year begins again on a certain fixed day.

The purpose of the calendar was, and still is, the regulation of religious acts and the secret interpretations of the happenings of life.[19] Only a certain number of initiated people know how to compute the days. They are the sooth-sayers, in Spanish " adivinos ", in Quiché " chuch-ka-jau ". They use seeds or grains of corn and polished stones to interpret happenings, and have a tremendous influence on the Indian from birth to death. The Indian is convinced that this ritual calendar is of enormous significance and that his destiny is influenced by the soothsayer's interpretations, because of the hidden significance of the days in relation to the numerical coordinate within the mechanism of the oracle.

Also, according to the religious concepts of the Indian, the day, in addition to being a division of time, is the personification of a god. Reference has been made in this study to the fact that the Indian mentality is concerned with the real and the concrete.[20] Consequently, some days are ruled for him by deities who make certain undertakings propitious, others unlucky. Some days are " mixed ". In the northwest around Huehuetenango, or more specifically, in Jacaltenango, the Indians revere the Year-Bearers, the four deities who sus-

18 Goubaud Carrera, Antonio, " El Guajxaquip Báts, ceremonia calendárica indígena," *Anales de la Sociedad de Geografía e Historia de Guatemala*, vol. XII, no. 1, 1935, p. 40.

19 Ludendorff, M., " Ueber die Entstehung der Tzolkin-Periode im Kalendar der Maya ", Preussischen Akademie der Wissenschaften, Berlin, 1930 (cited by Goubaud Carrera, *op. cit.*, p. 40).

20 *Supra*, p. 234.

tain the year.[21] In summation, the ideas of good and evil become incorporated into the computation of time.

Now to the particular all-Indian observance of the New Year called *Guajxaquip Báts* (it does not seem to be relevant here to discuss in detail whether literally it means Day of the Eighth Thread or of the Eighth Monkey) ; it is the day which is most propitious for the efficacy of prayer which human beings address to the divinity of the earth. In other words, the *Guajxaquip Báts* is a religious ceremony in which the spirit is purified, and all sins committed are confessed. Thanks are given for benefits received during the past year and, at this time, new *adivinos* or soothsayers are initiated into the business of interpreting human destiny.

Thousands of Indians feel that they must return from distant points to celebrate the occasion. In 1946 the ceremonies began on Sunday, September 29th, with increasing crowds pouring into the village and more especially into the church. I have often heard the buzzing of Indians at prayer as they put down their flower petals, place little lighted candles about on the floor—but at Momostenango it was different. There was a constant chanting resembling to some degree the High Mass chant.

On Monday, September 30th, in a drenching rain, guided by the shoemaker of the village and the *ladino* chauffeur, I started around 4:30 A.M. for the mountain called " *Chutimesabal* " or " Little Broom ", about three quarters of a mile west of the village of Momostenango. (The slithery mud, the cobblestones, the pitch blackness except for a little flashlight made it seem like three miles!) First I smelled incense, then saw candles flickering. I took shelter until daybreak in a tiny thatched-roofed *ranchito,* where there were eleven Indians sitting on an extremely low wooden bench. They were very kind, quiet, courteous. The men could speak Spanish; the women, speaking various dialects, could not, in some

---

21 Goubaud Carrera, *op. cit.,* p. 42; La Farge, *op. cit.,* pp. 157 ff.

cases, understand each other. They were huddled around a fire and they offered in turn soup, coffee, *aguardiente*. The women came silently to examine my watch, rings, and were entranced by a metal lapel vase. They even removed my shoes to dry them at the fire.

At daybreak, still in the rain, I moved out to inspect the many altars, some rising over thirty feet in height, constructed of clay pots. The soothsayers were both men and women—about one hundred seventy were men, eighty, women. I noticed that the women did not have nearly so many clients as their male colleagues.

The *adivino* was recognizable from the white bag that he wore at his side, in which he kept his stock in trade—beans, seeds, corn, stones. etc. As his clients approached, the soothsayer asked their names and the nature of their petitions. He got no more than a penny (if that) from each of the suppliants. Then he began, with the burning of incense and candles, the chant which was similar to, or at times, identical with those heard down in the village church.

I lingered some time beside an old Indian, shawl-draped, who wore lenseless tortoise-shell frames as he prayed. I caught occasional words in Spanish—*casita, vacas, huevos, niños*— then words in his own dialect and occasionally a " *Kyrie Eleison* ", or " *Pater Noster.*" I saw him later, in the afternoon, repeating the act in the church.

None of the procedure called for any set ceremonies or ritual. Each *adivino* acted seemingly independent of all the others.

Although I did not actually see this, it has been reported [22] that the soothsayer occasionally offers *aguardiente,* the native liquor, to the divinity and then drinks it himself. (I can affirm that I observed, in the course of time, the effects of this procedure). This is done to show that there exists between the two complete understanding and harmony of ideas.

22 Goubaud Carrera, *op. cit.,* p. 48.

In this instance, the divinity becomes a participant and accepts favorably the petitions. Naturally, as the *adivino* repeats the performance, he is released from ordinary tensions and believes that he is nearer the deities.

At various intervals, I would go down to the square and the church and return again to the hilltops. There was little change in the character of the celebration—it went on and on —continued according to ancient tradition, still oblivious to super-imposed cultures.

This illustration is given to dramatize the continued insistence of the Indian in executing religious rites connected with the beliefs of his Mayan ancestors, and his perfect willingness to integrate these customs with Roman Catholicism. It further serves, however, to accentuate the tremendous spiritual, psychological, and mental gaps that separate him from the various elements which constitute the Guatemalan hierarchy and clergy.

The phenomenon of anti-clericalism must be considered. Of all subjects this is the most enigmatic, complicated and difficult to explain. In the first place, very, very few seem to understand that, primarily and fundamentally, anti-clericalism is a civil conflict. It has reared its head and flourished historically in countries which have been referred to as being Catholic, e.g. France, Italy, Spain etc. It is a battle which has had arrayed on one side the clergy, and on the other, the lawyers. The government officials have always insisted, for the most part, that they are " believers ", but that they are inveighing against " political Catholicism." Name calling has been an inevitable concomitant on both sides. In some periods it has been " *los Fiebres* ", the Radicals, against their enemies " *los Moderados* " or the Reactionaries. In our present day nomenclature it is the Communists on the one hand, the Falangists on the other. North American Catholics seldom understand the situation—they quickly raise the cry of persecution, and, reacting emotionally, they want the United States government to intervene. The Church has often sought to explain the situation in terms of the activities of exterior agencies. In one era of history the Masons were to blame, in another, the Anti-Christ, in still another, Protestant proselytizing. Now, of course, the Communists are playing the rôle of the devil. It is not reasonable to think that a handful of outsiders are practically solely to blame for unsatisfactory conditions within an area which has had virtually a monopoly exercised by one institution for hundreds of years. Perhaps it is too much to expect, but it would seem that after all that time, cognizance would be taken of the lessons that history teaches. One of the greatest of these lessons is that when the Church acts like a political party it will be treated like one. When churchmen become politicians, they will be regarded as politicians.

As has been noted, the countries of Europe which have been traditionally known as Catholic, e.g. France, Spain, Italy, have been afflicted at times with the most violent forms of anti-clericalism. The seeds were transplanted to the New World and flourished, producing dissension, destruction, devastation, deterioration and degeneration.

In keeping with a previous point, namely that these people are extremists, either for or against, either friend or enemy, there has been considerable agitation in the press about the Spanish clergy because of their supposed sympathy with Franco's régime in Spain. This antagonism toward the Spanish clergy appears in the daily press, in public speeches and in manifestations like that of September 8, 1946, where placards were carried bearing such protests as " We want Guatemalan priests! " An orator on that occasion spoke in the same strain, revealing the antipathy smouldering against Spain, " The people no longer wish to live like pariahs; we wish a Guatemala free and worthy. . . . We want priests like Pedro de Bethancourt. . . . In the United States they can boast of an American saint, while in Rome they refuse to canonize our Hermano Pedro, in order to maintain favor with a powerful country. . . ." [23]

23 *Nuestro Diario*, September 9, 1946.

It has been noted that Guatemala has less than 1% (.77%) white population. Aside from the foreigners, the " *blancos* " are comprised of those who are very definitely of the upper social strata and who still mentally and culturally cling to " *Madre España*." They are the remnants of the *peninsulares,* that upper class group of civil and clerical officials, born in Spain, but who came to the new world. There is still a great gap between these descendants of the *peninsulares* and the descendants of the *criollos,* who were born in the new world of Spanish parents. Even now among the former group there is spirited defense of the Spanish clergy, whose presence is to a great extent resented. These clergymen are accepted socially in the homes, whereas, for the most part, except with members of the hierarchy, the native clergy are looked down upon because they come from a very poor background and are generally conceded to be quite untutored and ignorant.

Even the so-called " fanatical " Catholics of the upper class take cognizance of this social division as far as the clergy are concerned. Often when they refer to the possibility of a devout member of the family being ordained, they will say, " but, of course, not in Guatemala."

In connection with treating of the relations of the *ladino* and the Indian to the Church and each other, brief reference must be made to the subject of marriage. In Guatemala, there must be two ceremonies, the one civil, the other religious.[24] Neither the Church nor the State recognizes the jurisdiction of the other in this matter. For the white and the *ladino* much importance is attached to the double requirements. Mention has been made of the fact that even at the most elaborate weddings it is apparent that the participants find the church services unfamiliar—but they insist on having them. They may not be inside the edifice again until there is another wedding, requiem or fiesta observance.

24 *Civil Code of Guatemala*, Articles 123 and 182.

With the Indian, it is a different story. Each ceremony requires money and, for many of them, that is something with which they have very little acquaintance. Their dealings in the village market place are mostly on a barter basis. (In some parts of the country, the only item for which they give a few *centavos* is salt.) Consequently, among the Indians the large majority have not been formally married.

It is not just the money difficulty alone. Indians usually do not like the government officials and avoid dealing with them whenever possible. They are unfamiliar with preliminary procedures and that has given rise to a class of *ladino* agents who make such arrangements as procuring the license and arranging the time of service. But, again, that also requires money. The Indian becomes bewildered and just doesn't understand why he should make such an effort. Then, again, the priest only gets around about once a year, if that. I attended several weddings in Indian villages, where several couples were married at once. The *ladino* agent was impatient with them when relaying instructions and virtually shoved them around. After it was all over, one could not wonder that others would not be encouraged to follow their example. Estimates, of course, vary about the actual number of Indians formally married—it is said to be as low as 2% in some parts of Guatemala.

Mention must be made of the activities of the Protestant missionaries in Guatemala, which add complications to an already complicated and intricate story. To minimize confusion the Protestants, regardless of specific sect, are called Evangelicals, and no matter what the denomination, their meeting places are designated as Evangelical chapels (*Capillas Evangélicas*). The Protestants, too, by general consent, have divided the territory among the different sects. They have a rest home at Lake Atitlán, the facilities of which are open to all, and they hold once a year a general synod. Except for the Presbyterians, who, of course, are a very well known and substantial group in the United States, it seems a fair statement to make that almost all the others are relatively obscure in the States, e.g., the Nazarenes, the Primitive Methodists, Seventh Day Adventists. The Quakers do have a mission at Chiquimula, which it was impossible for me to visit because the roads were at the time impassable.

The Central American Mission was organized by some residents of Dallas, Texas, on November 14, 1890, as an independent, undenominational work. Two of their missionaries were in Guatemala City in 1896, but moved on to Honduras in less than a year. In 1899 Mr. A. E. Bishop and his family took up residence in Guatemala City and remained there until his retirement in 1943. This group conducts two Bible Institutes for the training of native pastors, one at Guatemala City and one in the village of Panajachel, Lake Atitlán. The Institute in the city concentrates on interesting *ladinos*; the one at the Lake is for Indians. At the latter, four tribes are now represented. The mission operates in three areas, Sololá, Huehuetenango and San Marcos. At Huehuetenango there is a boarding school open to the children of all Protestant missionaries. At Panajachel there were three Indian teachers on the Institute staff. It is always difficult to find out the number of actual church members, because the point is always made that there are a greater number of believers than members, because the latter must be baptized and married in order to be formally received.[25]

The Nazarenes are to be found principally in Upper Verapaz, Lower Verapaz and Petén. They have seventeen missionaries in Guatemala at the present time. Cobán is their center and they first came to the area in 1904, when they began to conduct a regular grade school. Although they still retain a few grades, they have to a large degree relinquished this work because the government has become increasingly

---

25 Information based on personal visits to the Institute, interviews with Miss May Butler, and pamphlets published by the Central American Mission, 3611 Congress Avenue, Dallas, Texas.

active about conducting grade schools. They have a girls' dormitory (seventeen enrolled in 1946) and boys' building (about twenty-two). The quarters were very simple and clean. An attempt was definitely being made to introduce a sports program, to teach cleanliness in connection with the cooking and housekeeping lessons. Like the Faith Mission, they aim to train theological students, but were frank in admitting that at this time very few seem able to go very far. In answer to the question about the number of members— " In the whole area less than one thousand, but there are many more believers who have not been formally baptized and received."

At Cobán there was a good sized chapel on the boys' school property. It was quite attractive, airy, light; had nice pews and a pulpit. I was impressed by the many vases of flowers set all around—I wondered if perhaps a slight concession had not been made to native love of color and display.[26]

Perhaps the best known of these Nazarene missioners is Reverend Paul Haymaker now at *El Rancho,* a village situated on the Matagua River. He is very old now and quite deaf. He seemed primarily and essentially a teacher rather than the so-called " fanatical " missionary. His attitude was much more tolerant than is generally the case. He did not follow the usual conversational pattern of referring to the " darkness in which these poor pagans dwell, their ignorance, superstition, etc." He spoke instead of his little library in the town, the attempts at giving simple lectures on diet, pre-natal care, cleanliness. The school is conducted in rooms in his house and has thirty-one pupils. Mr. Haymaker himself had made all the little benches and chairs for the kindergartners and was busy at his advanced age in making plans for the future. *El Rancho* was the only place in the country where there seemed to be any kind of intercourse between Catholics and

26 Information based on interview with Miss Lave and Mr. and Mrs. Hess at Cobán Mission, Oct. 9, 1946.

Protestants—there had been three Catholic teachers employed
in the school. In addition to the regular chapel there is a
small one in the village of San Agostino which is served
from *El Rancho*.

The aim of all these groups is to train native pastors, and
the Presbyterians started an Indian Institute in the village
of Santa María de Jesús which has been lately moved to
Quiché. The Primitive Methodists last year (1945) joined
the Presbyterians in conducting the Institute and they are
now looking for a location suitable for the erecting of permanent quarters. The school is open from January to
October and has an enrollment of about sixteen boys and ten
girls. The general age range is from fourteen to sixteen
years. One third of those enrolled are entirely illiterate at
first. One half day is given to industrial training and the
formal curriculum seems to take in everything. The teachers
peruse the *Popul Vuh* with the students; they get a bird's eye
view of the Old Testament, arithmetic, geography, grammar,
book-keeping and a little history! After three years they are
supposed to have a thorough Bible training.

As has been indicated, the Presbyterians are the most
extensively organized of the Protestant sects in Guatemala. Paul Burgess, the well known author of a book about
Justo Rufino Barrios, and his wife have been in Guatemala
since 1913. Their four children were born in the country,
and they now have nine grandchildren. One daughter is
married to the Rev. Zywulka, a Czechoslovakian missionary
who is stationed at San Rafaél. The Burgesses built the grey
stone mission which is in the center of Quezaltenango, across
from the National Theatre, and worked there for twenty
years. The adjoining Evangelical Library was established by
Mrs. Burgess because there was no Christian library. A Rev.
Mr. Peters and his wife are now in charge of the town mission and the Burgesses are located on the outskirts where
they have their home chapel and conduct some activities. The

Burgesses gave up the working with the *ladinos* fifteen years ago and have devoted themselves entirely to the Indians.[27]

The Presbyterians' activities are concentrated in the departments of Quezaltenango, Retalhuleu, Mazatenango and Sacatepéquez. They have a total of nineteen organized churches and every one of these has a regular number of preaching stations under it.

Rev. and Mrs. Dudley Peck, who have been in Guatemala twenty-two years, have their headquarters at San Juan Ostencalco. Their most remarkable work has consisted in translating the New Testament in the Mam dialect. They have made great contributions in working out charts for the teaching of grammar and in compiling of simple readers. They also publish a little paper for their village congregation. Because body lice is such a plague for the natives, and such insecticides as D.D.T. are financially out of the reach of these people, the Pecks are growing various plants which they hope will serve the same purpose as the more expensive products. This remarkable couple also conduct a little clinic which is very well equipped. They know the terrain thoroughly for miles around and can lead one easily to fairly remote areas where the Shamans or witch doctors still sacrifice chickens and turkeys to the gods and offer incense and candles to the idols.[28]

I must not neglect to mention what is undoubtedly the greatest single contribution of the Presbyterians. This is the American Hospital situated in the capital city which, under the administration of the remarkably capable Dr. Charles Ainslee, has done a magnificent work and has introduced a standard of medical care and service which will always be thought of as a model in that field.

27 Interview with Mrs. Burgess at Quezaltenango, 1946.

28 Interview of the author with Rev. and Mrs. Dudley Peck at San Juan Ostencalco, Nov. 9, 1946.

The Primitive Methodists at the present time have twenty churches in the departments of Totonicapán and Quiché. Their first mission was started by one Dr. Secord in 1902. He was known then as an Independent. He held services in the village of Chichicastenango and built a chapel there. He apparently became involved in politics and was exiled when Estrada Cabrera fell from power. Later he returned to the country and still resides in Guatemala City. The Rev. Mr. William Hayes and his wife Margaret have been in charge of the mission in Chichicastenango for about seven years. They reported about twelve hundred " believers " and again only about seven hundred communicants, i.e. baptized and married members. They conduct Christian Endeavor Meetings in the village and have about thirty members, of whom three are Indians and the rest, *ladinos*. One Indian family is reckoned to be in the classification of " believers ". These Methodists have an Indian chapel out in the fields at Chuwixa. There they have about sixty " believers " but only about fifteen to twenty baptized members.[29]

The Seventh Day Adventists are also to be found in Chichicastenango. Their chapel consists of a very poor bare room next door to a little shop. The *ladino* lady who keeps the shop seems to be in charge. She reported a membership of thirty-seven. They have head-quarters in Guatemala City and have been about ten years in the area. They had no North American workers. Their activities seemed to consist of holding services on Saturday and Sunday, with Sunday School classes for the children. From a report hung on the wall of the chapel it was indicated that the total money offerings made over a period of four weeks was $2.08!

What has been written so far about the Evangelical activities has not been for the purpose of treating completely their histories or programs in detail, but only to indicate

29 Information based on interview with Mr. and Mrs. William Hayes at Chichicastenango, 1946.

briefly and rapidly their general background. There is no doubt but that, even in the last two years or so, they have been spreading as far as organization is concerned. I was much more aware in 1946 of little buildings in Indian villages, especially in the *Lake Atitlán* area marked as Evangelical chapels than in 1944. On the bus running between Guatemala City and San Salvador there are often enthusiasts distributing tracts. And yet, numerically, there is not, even according to their own admission, much headway in permanent conversions. The *ladino* has not turned out generally to be a very satisfactory convert and it is to be noted that some of the Protestant sects are turning from that endeavor to the Indian work. The *ladino* is to be found in one camp after another; he may be even a Mason if he thinks it means improved business; he will be paying lip service to the Evangelicals while he is complaining about all that is wrong with the Catholic Church situation. The next day he will be in the middle of the fiesta celebration or found wending his way to the Calvario chapel.

There has been noted the distinction that the Evangelical ministers make between " believers " and " communicants ". The Indians are more apt to cling obstinately to those elements of Christian faith and worship which they accepted four hundred years ago and which they carry on even without the presence of a priest. Consequently Indian conversions to Protestantism must of necessity be slow and small in number.

Considering the history, temperaments and psychological characteristics of the Indian and the *ladino,* it is rather difficult to understand how either would be appealed to or won over by most of the programs or projects now used, which do not seem too well adapted to the particular social climate.

Between the Catholic and the Evangelical there is a chasm of separation deep and complete. There is no fraternizing between minister and priest, no common cooperational ground. To the padre, the Protestant missionary is an interloper, a usurper, an enemy. To the minister, the priest is only one step removed from the witch doctor—he is an agent of ignorance, idolatry and reaction. The minister decries religious monopoly; the priest bemoans proselytizing which would have his people exchange one brand of Christianity for another, as if it were an over-the-counter commodity.

Now there must be considered the attitude of the government. In recent years it has been comparatively easier for the Protestant missionaries to enter the country than for Catholics, because the Protestants come, of course, in secular clothing, with their families, and come primarily as teachers or, in some cases, as nurses. By and large it is probably fair to state that, although the national governments in recent years have not been too positively enthusiastic about Protesant missionaries, they have not discouraged them.

On the other hand, local governments have been known to be hostile. La Farge found that even the Shamans would ask anxiously whether the party were composed of " Christians ", warning that there was no place for " Evangélicos ".[30] In the village of Zúñil there is a chapel and the Presbyterians send an Indian boy there once a year to deliver tracts in the market place. The church is closed and there are no services, because of the hostility of the municipal government.[31]

To try to summarize the status of the Church today in the light of all that has been presented is far more difficult than putting together a patchwork quilt. There are, as has been noted, the elements of racial cleavages, divergent customs and traditions, obstacles of language, scarcity of priests, foreign economic, political and social influences and anti-clericalism. To all of these must be added in the physical deterioration of church property, which seems to stand as a symbol of the deterioration which has been social and spiritual as well as

30 La Farge, op. cit., p. 91.

31 Interview with Mrs. Paul Burgess, Quezaltenango, November, 1946.

political. This is violent country and much of the physical damage has been wrought by earthquakes and volcanic eruptions. In town after town the parishes are indicated as being vacant and, even where there is a clergyman in residence, his *convento* and church are often in a state of disrepair or practical ruin. Spiritually, the people have been too long left without adequate teaching and guidance; consequently and naturally, the moral tone has been definitely lowered. It is customary often to throw barbs of criticism at the United States as being a godless and immoral country, but nowhere in the United States could advertisements be run in newspapers, as they are in the capital city of Guatemala, offering without any notion of social restraint (to say nothing of the legal angle) every kind of birth control device.

The family has been, in all these countries, the nucleus of social life, and now that external influences have beaten at the door, there is almost a total lack of ability to deal with the change. Guatemalans, like others, are resorting to escapism, and their young are virtually invading the schools and colleges of the United States in order to obtain what is not provided at home.

In the days when the kings administered and supervised every phase of church building, the government had no thought of taking over the work of instruction or social welfare either in the moral or in any other field. Without making in any way a prejudicial statement, one can say without reservation that, in Guatemala's case, the expropriation by the Government of the various institutions and endeavors once administered (even with due regard to human weakness and frailty) by the Church has resulted to date in a deterioration, disintegration and devastation that is well nigh fatal.

One might observe that the transfer of administration of educational and charitable institutions from Church to Government has not resulted ipso facto in the last state being better than the first.

As Mecham states in his work on the Church and State in Latin America, the laws of 1879, drawn up in the time of Barrios, are still a part of the law of Guatemala. He points out that it is a most interesting phenomenon and unique, too, that these anti-clerical laws should persist so long without change. He questions whether or not the religious problem is settled in Guatemala, or whether the Conservatives are only waiting to marshal their forces for the reaction? He concludes very reasonably that the Church is dissatisfied with a status which impairs legitimate freedom of action.[32] And, from the story of the preceding chapter and the agitation and fomentation that continues, it would seem that the Church-State conflict is far from settled.

As was indicated in the introduction, this study is not final in its character, but at least one conclusion emerges from these pages, namely that the Church in Guatemala has never been, and is *not* now *free*. It might, in truth, be stated that the core of conflict has been this lack of freedom. Natural concomitants of this situation have been suspicion and distrust which have resulted in hostile expressions and actions on the part of the human elements involved on both sides, the civil and the ecclesiastic. Happily, it is not the function of this study to furnish a modus vivendi.

---

32 Mecham, *Church and State in Latin America*, p. 370.

APPENDIX

PART I

CHAPTER I

Decree issued September 13, 1589, to Captain General of the Philippine Islands, giving complete instructions regarding the ecclesiastical patronage of the Indies.

The King. To our viceroy of *Nueva España*, or the person or persons who shall, for the time being, be exercising the government of that country: As you know, the right of ecclesiastical patronage belongs to us throughout the realm of the Yndias— both because of having discovered and acquired that new world, and erected there and endowed the churches and monasteries at our own cost, or at the cost of our ancestors, the Catholic Sovereigns; and because it was conceded to us by bulls of the most holy pontiffs, conceded of their own accord (*de motu proprio*). For its conservation, and that of the right that we have to it, we order and command that the said right of patronage be always preserved for us and our royal crown, singly and *in solidum*, throughout all the realm of the Yndias, without any derogation therefrom, either in whole or in part; and that we shall not concede the right of patronage by any favor or regard that we or the kings our successors may confer.

Further, no person or persons, or ecclesiastical or secular communities, or church or monastery, shall be able to exercise the right of patronage by custom, privilege, or any other title, unless it be the person who shall exercise it in our name, and with our authority and power; and no person, whether secular or ecclesiastical, and no order, convent or religious community, of whatever state, condition, rank and preeminence he or they may be, shall for any occasion and cause whatever, judicially or extra-judicially, dare to meddle in any matter touching my royal patronage, injure us in it—to appoint to any church, benefice or ecclesiastical office, or to be accepted if he shall have been appointed—in all the realm of the Indias, without our presentation, or that of the person to whom we commit it by law or by letters-patent. He who shall do the contrary, if he be a secular person, shall incur the loss of the concessions that shall have been made to him by us in all the realm of the Indias, shall be unable to hold and obtain others, and shall be exiled perpetually from all our kingdoms and seigniories; and if he shall be an ecclesiastical person, he shall be considered as a foreigner, and exiled from all our kingdoms and shall not be able to hold or obtain any benefices or ecclesiastical office, and shall incur the other penalties established against such by laws of these my kingdoms. And our viceroys, audiencias, and royal justices shall proceed with all severity against those who thus shall infringe or violate our right of patronage; and they shall proceed officially, either at the petition of our fiscals, or at that of any party who demands it; and in the execution of it great diligence shall be exercised.

We desire and order that no cathedral church, parish church, monastery, hospital, votive church, or any other pious or religious establishment be erected, founded, or constructed, without our express consent for it, or that of the person who shall exercise our authority; and further, that no archbishopric, bishopric, *dignidad*, canonry, *ración, media-ración*, rectoral or simple benefice, or any other ecclesiastical or religious benefice or office, be instituted, or appointment to it be made, without our consent or presentation, or that of the person who shall exercise our authority; and such presentation or consent shall be in writing, in the ordinary manner.

The archbishoprics and bishoprics shall be appointed by our presentation, made to our very Holy Father (i. e. the Roman pontiff) who shall be at that time, as has been done hitherto.

The *dignidades*, canonries, *raciones* and *media-raciones* of all the cathedral churches of the Indias shall be filled by presentation made by our royal warrant, given by our royal Council of the Indias, and signed by our name, by virtue of which the archbishop or bishop of the church where the said *dignidad*, canonry, or *ración* shall be made, shall grant to him collation and canonical installation, which shall also be in writing, sealed with his seal and signed with his hand. Without the said presentation, title, collation, and canonical installation, in writing, he shall not be given possession of such *dignidad*, canonry, *ración* or *media-ración*; neither shall he accept the benefits and emoluments of it, under the penalty contained in the laws against those who violate our royal patronage.

If in any of the cathedral churches of the Yndias, there shall not be four beneficiaries—at least resident, and appointed by our presentation and warrant and the canonical installation of the prelate because of the other prebends being vacant, or if appointments to them have been made because the beneficiaries are absent (even though it be for a legitimate reason) for more than eight months, until we present them, the prelate shall elect four seculars to fill out the term of those who shall have been appointed as residents, choosing them from the most capable and competent that shall offer, or who can be found, so that they may serve in the choir, the altar, the church, in the curacies, if that should be necessary in the said church, in place of the vacant or absent prebendaries, as above stated. He shall assign them an adequate salary, as we have ordered, at the account of the vacant or absent prebendaries; and the said provision shall not be permanent, but removable at will (*ad nutum*), and those appointed shall not occupy the seat of the beneficiary in the choir, nor enter or have a vote in the *cabildo*. If the cathedral church has four beneficiaries, the prelates shall not take it upon themselves to appoint any prebendaries, or to provide a substitute in such post, whether for those that become vacant, or for those whose incumbents may be absent, unless they shall give us notice, so that we may make the presentations or take such measures as may be advisable.

No prelate, even though he may have an authentic relation and information that we have presented any person to a *dignidad*, canonry, *ración*, *media-ración*, or other benefice, shall grant him collation or canonical installation, or shall order that he be given possession of it, unless our original warrant of the said presentation be first presented; and our viceroys or audiencias shall not meddle by making them receive such persons without the said presentation.

After the original warrant of our presentation has been presented, appointment and canonical installation shall be made without any delay; and orders will be given to assign to him the emoluments, unless there is some legitimate objection against the person presented and one which can be proved. If there is no legitimate objection, or if any such be alleged that shall not be proved, and the prelate should delay the appointment, installation, and possession, he shall be obliged to pay to such person the emoluments and incomes, costs, and interests that shall have been incurred by him.

It is our desire that, in the presentations that shall be made for *dignidades*, canonries and prebends in the cathedral churches of the Yndias, lettered men be preferred to those who are not, and those who shall have served in cathedral churches of these same kingdoms and who shall have had most experience in the choir and divine worship, to those who shall not have served in cathedral churches.

At least in the districts where it can be conveniently done, a graduate jurist in general study shall be presented for a doctoral canonicate, and another lettered theological graduate in general study for another magistral canonicate, who shall have the pulpit with the obligations that doctoral and magistral canons have in these kingdoms.

Another lettered theologue approved by general study shall be presented to read the lesson of the holy scriptures, and another lettered jurist theologian for the canonicate of penitence, in accordance with the established decrees of the holy Council of Trent. The said four canonries shall be of the number of those of the erection of the Church.

We will and order that all the benefices, whether sinecures or curacies, secular and regular, and the ecclesiastical offices that become vacant, or that, as they are new, must be filled, throughout the realm of the Yndias, in whatever diocese it may be, besides those that are provided in the cathedral churches, as stated above, shall, in order that they may be filled with less delay, and that our royal patronage may be preserved in them, be filled in the following manner:

When a benefice (whether a sinecure or a curacy) or the administration of any hospital or a sacristy or churchwardship, or the stewardship of a hospital or any other benefice or ecclesiastical office, shall become vacant, or when it has to be filled for the first time; the prelate shall order a written proclamation to be posted in the cathedral church, or in the church, hospital, monastery where such benefice or office is to be filled within the suitable limit, so that those who desire to compete for it may enter the lists. From all those who thus compete, and from all the others whom the prelate shall believe to be suitable persons for such office or benefice, after having examined them and after having informed himself concerning their morals and ability, he shall choose two persons from them—those whom, in the sight of God and his conscience, he shall judge most suitable for such office or benefice. The nomination of the two thus named shall be presented to our viceroy or to the president of our royal government of the province where such benefice or office shall become vacant or must be filled, so that he may select one from the two appointees. He shall send that selection to the prelate, so that the latter in accordance with it, and by virtue of that presentation, may grant the appointment, collation, and canonical installation—by way of commission and not by perpetual title, but removable at will by the person who shall have presented them in our name, together with the prelate. And should there be no more than one person who desires to compete for such office or benefice, or the prelate shall not find more than one person whom he desires to receive the nomination to it, he shall send the name to our viceroy, president, or governor, as above stated, so that the latter may present him. Then by virtue of such presentation, the prelate shall make the appointment in the form above directed. But it is our desire and will that when the presentation shall be made by us, and we shall expressly state in our presentation that the collation and canonical installation shall be by title and not by commission, those presented by us be always preferred to those presented by our viceroys, presidents, or governors, in the form above mentioned.

And in the *repartimientos* and villages of Indians, and in other places where there shall be no benefices or any regulations for electing one, or any form of appointing a secular or religious to administer sacramentals and teach the doctrine, providing it in the form above directed, the prelate—after posting a proclamation so that if there shall be any ecclesiastical or religious person, or any other of good morals and education who may go to teach the doctrine at such a village—from those who shall compete or from other persons whom he shall deem most suitable and fitting, shall elect two, after informing himself as to their competency and good character. He shall send the nomination to our viceroy, president, or governor who shall reside in the province, so that the latter may present one of the two thus nominated by the prelate. If there shall be no more than one, by virtue of that presentation, the prelate shall appoint him to the mission, giving him installation, as he has to teach the doctrine. He shall order to be given to such person the emoluments that are to be given to ministers on missions, and shall order the *encomenderos* and other persons, under the penalties and censures that he shall deem suitable, not to annoy or disturb such person in the exercise of his duty and the teaching of the Christian doctrine; on the contrary, they shall give him all protection and aid for it. That appointment shall be made removable at the will of the person who shall have appointed him in our name, and that of the prelate.

We also will and order that the religious orders observe and maintain the right of patronage in the following forms:

First: No general, commissary-general, visitor, provincial or any other superior of the religious orders, shall go to the realm of the Yndias without first showing in our royal Council of the Indias the powers that he bears and giving us relation of them; and without the Council giving him our decree and permission so that he may go, and a warrant so that our viceroys, audiencias, justices, and our other vassals may admit and receive him to the exercise of his office, and give him all protection and aid in it.

Any provincial, visitor, prior, guardian, or other high official who may be elected and nominated in the realm of the Yndias, shall, before being admitted to exercise his office, inform our viceroy, president, Audiencia, or governor who shall have in charge the supreme government of such province, and shall show him his patent of nomination and election, so that the latter may give him the protection and aid necessary for the exercise and use of his office.

The provincials of all the orders who are established in the Yndias, each one of them, shall always keep a list ready of all the monasteries and chief residences (maintained there by his order) and of the members (resident in each) that fall in his province, and of all the religious in the province—noting each one of them by name, together with a report as to his age and qualifications, and the office or ministry in which each one is occupied. He shall give that annually to our viceroy, Audiencia, or governor, or the person who shall have charge of the supreme government in the province, adding to or removing from the list the religious who shall be superfluous and those who shall be needed; our viceroy, Audiencia, or governor, shall keep these general lists which shall thus be given, for himself, and in order that he may inform us by report of the religious that there are, and those of whom there is need of provision, by each fleet sent out.

The provincials of the orders, each one of them, shall make a list of all the religious who are occupied in teaching the Christian doctrine to the Indians, and the administration of the sacraments, and the offices of the *curas* in the villages of the chief monasteries. They shall give such list once a year to our viceroy, Audiencia, or governor, who shall give it to the diocesan prelate, so that he may know and understand what persons are occupied in the administration of sacraments and the office of *curas* and the ecclesiastical jurisdiction, and who are in charge of the souls for whom he is responsible; and in order that what is or must be provided may be apparent to him, and from whom he has to require account of the said souls, and to whom he must commit what is to be done for the welfare of those souls.

Whenever the provincials have to provide any religious for instruction or for administration of sacraments, or remove any who shall have been appointed, they shall give notice thereof to our viceroy, president, Audiencia, or governor who shall exercise the supreme government of the province and to the prelate; and they shall not remove any one who shall have been appointed, until another shall have been appointed in his place, observing the above order.

We desire, in the presentation and appointments of all the prelacies, *dignidades*, and ecclesiastical offices and benefices, that those most deserving, and who shall have been engaged longer and to better profit in the conversion of the Indians, and in instructing them in the Christian doctrine, and in the administration of sacraments, shall be presented and appointed. Therefore, we strictly charge the diocesan prelates, and those superiors of religious orders, and we order our viceroys, presidents, Audiencias, and governors, that in the nominations, presentations, and appointments that they shall have to make there, as is said in conformity (with this decree), they shall always prefer, in the first place, those who shall have been occupied, by life and example, in the conversion of the Indians, and in instruction and administering of the sacraments, and those who shall know the language of the Indians whom they have to instruct; and, in the second place, those who shall be the sons of Spaniards and who shall have served us in those regions.

In order that we may better make the presentation that shall become necessary of prelacies, *dignidades*, prebends, and the other ecclesiastical offices and benefices, we ask and charge the said diocesan prelates and the provincials of the religious orders, and we order our viceroys, presidents, audiencias and governors, each one of them, separately and distinctly by himself, without communicating one with another, to make a list of all the *dignidades*, benefices, missions and ecclesiastical offices in his province, noting those of them that are vacant, and those that are filled. Likewise they shall make a list of all the ecclesiastical and religious persons, and of the sons of citizens and Spaniards who are studying for the purpose of becoming ecclesiastics, and of the good character, learning, competency, and qualities of each one, stating clearly his good parts and also his defects, and declaring, so that prelacies, *dignidades*, benefices and ecclesiastical offices shall be suitably filled, both those that shall be at present found vacant, and those that shall become vacant hereafter. Those relations shall be sent to us closed and sealed, in each fleet, and in different ships; and what shall be deemed advisable to add or to suppress from the preceding ones that shall have been sent before, shall be added or suppressed; so that no fleet shall sail without its relation. We charge the consciences of one and all straitly with this matter.

In order that we may not be deceived by those who come or who send to petition us to present them to some *dignidad*, benefice or ecclesiastical office, we desire, and it is our will, that he who shall thus come or send, appear before our viceroy, or before the president, the Audiencia, or before the one who shall have charge of the supreme government of the province; and, declaring his petition, the viceroy, Audiencia, or governor shall make the relation officially, with information concerning his standing, learning, morals, competency, and other details. After it is made, he shall send it separately from those persons. Likewise the approval of their prelate shall be obtained, and warning is given that those who come to petition for a *dignidad*, benefice or ecclesiastical office without such investigation shall not be received. (Clevens, N. Andrew, *Readings in Hispanic American History*, pp. 250-8.)

Brief of Pope Pius VII, dated January 30, 1816, exhorting the Bishops of Spanish America to obedience and loyalty to the King.

Pius VII. Venerabilibus Fratribus Archiepiscopis et Episcopis ac dilectis filiis Cleri Americae Catholicae Hispaniarum Regi subjectae.

Pius Papa VII. Venerabiles Fratres ac dilecti filii salutem. Etsi longissimo terrarum ac marium intervallo dissiti a nobis sitis, vestra tamen pietas vestrumque religionis colendae praedicandaeque studium, satis, venerabiles Fratres dilectique filii, compertum nobis est. Cum igitur inter loculenta et praecipua sanctissimae quam profitemur religionis praecepta, illud sit quo omnis anima potestatibus sublimioribus subdita esse jubetur, vos, in seditiosis cordique nostro acerbissimis istarum regionum motibus eorumdem firmo sapientique animo abhorrendorum, assiduos gregi vestro fuisse hortatores persuasum habemus.

Nihilo tamen minus; cum illius vices in terris geramus qui Deus pacis est, quique redimendo a demonum tyrannide humano generi nascens, pacem per angelos suos hominibus nunciari voluit; apostolici quo immerentes fungimus muneris esse duximus, vos magis per nostras hasce litteras excitati, ut funestissima turbarum ac seditionum zizania, quam inimicus homo isthic seminavit, eradicare penitusque delere omni ope contendatis.

Quod facile, venerabiles Fratres, consequemini, si teterrima ac gravissima defectionum damna; si praestantes eximiasque carissimi in Christo filii nostri Ferdinandi Hispaniarum vestrumque Catholici Regis, que nihil religione et subditorum suorum felicitati potius habet, virtutes; si denique illustria et nullo unquam aevo interitura hispanorum Europae exempla, qui fortunas vitamque suam projicere non dubitarunt, ut se religionis fideique erga Regem retinentissimos ostenderent, ob oculos gregis quisque sui, quo par est zelo, posueritis.

Agite ergo, venerabilis Fratres dilectissimique filii, paternis exhortationibus studiisque nostris morem ex animo gerentes, debitamque Regi vestro obedientiam et fidelitatem ennixe commendantes, bene de populis vestrae custodiae traditis meremini; nostram Regisque vestri quam jam fruimini gratiam amplificate, promissam curis laboribusque vestris ab eo mercedem, qui beatos Deique filios appellat pacificos, in coelo consequuturi.

Interim, tam praeclari, tamque frugiferi operis feliciter a vobis perficiendi auspicem, apostolicam benedictionem, vobis, venerabiles fratres dilectique filii peramanter impertimur. Datum Romae die 30 Januarii 1816, Pontificatus nostri anno. XVI. (Leturia, Pedro, S.J., *El Ocaso del Patronato Real en la América Española.* Madrid, 1925, pp. 281-282.)

Correspondence between Pope Leo XII and Ferdinand VII of Spain during the final struggle of the latter to retain the rights of *patronato real* in the New World.

After Leo XII had named bishops for the vacant sees of Colombia, omitting the *patronato real*, he wrote to Ferdinand VII: " The sincere affection which the outstanding merits of Your Majesty have won from our paternal heart oblige Us to speak to you upon a matter of the greatest importance. . . . We have heard with great affliction of the state of the churches in America because of the lack of pastors, and there immediately was brought to our mind the unfortunate series of evils resulting from such a lack, which, if it is so harmful in places very near us, is certainly an irreparable loss in places so distant from the center of Catholicism. This grievous consideration persuaded Us very soon of the indispensable necessity of delaying no longer the choosing of pastors as the only remedy for so many evils. In such circumstances, our solicitude has not been unaware of the claims of justice toward a prince like Your Majesty, so loyal to the faith, to the Holy See and to Us, but we feel that where there is a question of spiritual necessities, it is not in our power to delay the action which God has entrusted to us. . . . Convinced as Your Majesty must be of the truth of this, we do not doubt that you will regard with joy those faithful liberated in this way from the horrible abyss to which they would have been led by a longer privation of pastors. We trust, then, that these sentiments expressed to you with sincere affection will be acceptable to you as a sincere testimony of our constant affection which, following the example of our predecessors, we have and always shall have for Your Majesty and His August Family. . . . "

In reply, Ferdinand VII wrote on July 30, 1827, declaring that he was disposed to show his submission to the Church, to the Apostolic See, and his affection for His Holiness, but, at the same time, he declared that he would preserve the rights of the Crown, whose integrity he could not fail to consider himself bound to defend. Meanwhile, the Papal Nuncio had been forbidden entrance to Spain in protest to the naming of Bishops by the Pope without consulting the King.

On July 4, 1827 Leo XII had written a reproach to the King: "Your Majesty: While we have been sincerely believing that we were fulfilling our duty, serving likewise the cause of Your Majesty in the nomination of the Bishops of America, since the bonds of religion will always be the only ones capable of calling those wandering subjects back to your obedience, we see with the greatest grief that you have conceived our action as an outrage to Your person, and that you have wished to take revenge, which humiliates Us, as well as the Holy See. We have learned that by order of Your Majesty our Nuncio has been forbidden to enter Your states, and, realizing that there can be no other motive for such violent procedure, we submit our conduct relative to the naming of Bishops of America to the justice characteristic of Your Majesty, asking at the same time for the reparation which so grievous an injury demands.

Your Majesty is not ignorant of all the efforts of the Americans in order that, recognizing their separation from Spain, we should discuss political problems with them, as well as grant spiritual favors. Our constant opposition to the first petition is well known throughout Europe and also by Your Majesty. We have not wished to admit any delegation under any title, nor any recognition, even of a commercial character; but, when they have approached us to seek only spiritual favors, and particularly to beg for the provision of pastors for those churches, without whom religion would be in danger of being lost completely, after protesting that we would have made this choice of our own free will, how could we have refused to do so, in view of the necessities of those faithful, in our position as Head of the Church which obliges us to render an account to Jesus Christ, the Divine Founder, of even one lost sheep? Your rights, Sire, have been harmed in no way, and, if God wishes to return to you, as we hope, the authority over those places, your rights will rise again, and you will then be able to exercise them without contradiction; but, meanwhile, we cannot sacrifice our duties and lose our soul to prevent the suspension of those rights which Your Majesty can in no way exercise under the present circumstances. We have not taken into consideration any of the candidates proposed to us by the present governments in America, but rather we have chosen those suggested by the worthy Archbishop of Merida, and of whom, besides, we have received excellent references from Spain. If heretofore we would have consulted Your Majesty concerning these candidates, we should now certainly have run the risk that the Americans would not have accepted them under those circumstances, and this is the reason which explains our not having done as we should have desired. Finally, before presenting them in the Consistory, we notified Your Majesty in a letter containing the most lively sentiments of our obligations, the most tender considerations inspired by our affection for Your Majesty, and then, just when we were awaiting a reply, we received the sad news of Your Majesty's great indignation which led You to so injurious a step towards this Holy See and one so humiliating for Our Person. . . . We ask, consequently, once more from Your Majesty's loyalty and justice that reparation which a good son of the Church owes to a loving Father; from a sovereign full of faith to a sovereign working only for the former's welfare, trying to preserve the faith in a people who, if they lose it, will surely never again think of submitting themselves to their legitimate sovereign; to a Father full of the most bitter affliction on seeing that a son so beloved could have interpreted so poorly what he has done for the son's own good. . . ."

To this reproach of Pope Leo XII, the Spanish King replied: " Dear Holy Father: Sad are the duties of a Catholic King when the unfortunate sequence of events brings with it a conflict between the affection of a loving son of the Church and the obligations of a temporal Sovereign. The former prevents me from speaking directly to Your Holiness of a matter concerning which the latter prevents me from using any other language than that consistent with the dignity of my Crown. Therefore, in answer to the letter of Your Beatitude I shall limit myself to assuring You that my conduct has been regulated by necessity and not by my desires, and that I foresaw a protest which would prohibit the presentation of the Nuncio in my Court. Your Beatitude may rest assured that I am disposed to give You unalterable proof of my loyalty and affection; that I beg God fervently to grant you good health, and ask humbly for myself and for my family Your apostolic benediction. . . . "

The Bull "Sollicitudo Ecclesiarum" of Gregory XVI, dated August 5, 1831.

Gregory, Bishop, Servant of the Servants of God . . .

The ecclesiastical solicitude with which the Roman Pontiffs occupy themselves tirelessly with the care of the Christian flock confided to them by Divine Power, impels them also to continuous efforts to bring to the entire world, among all peoples, all that is necessary for the administration of sacred things and the salvation of souls. Nevertheless, such are the conditions of the times, such are the vicissitudes of the state and the government of nations, that often the said Pontiffs find themselves hindered from ministering promptly and freely to the spiritual necessities of those peoples. Its authority can, in effect, give rise to envy, especially among those whose standards are based on the principles of the world, as if they were judging of the rights of persons with partiality, above all when in the struggle of different rivals for power, they accord something to the churches of those regions, especially in what concerns the nomination to their bishoprics, after having consulted those who have the greatest power. In almost all ages, the Roman Pontiffs have shown themselves above this harmful and obnoxious suspicion. As they have at heart their eternal salvation, it is obligatory for them to root out this evil and refuse their support for once and all.

Our predecessor, Clement V, of happy memory, judged wisely on this matter. In the General Council of Vienna, in a constitution showing great prudence, he established that if the Sovereign Pontiff named anyone or accorded to him the title to any dignity whatsoever, verbally, by letter, or in any other manner, the recipient must not consider it as the approbation of or granting of any new right.

John XII, brilliant in his declarations, when for the purpose of bringing about harmony, wrote to Robert Bruce, who was attempting to assume the rôle of King of the Scots, giving him a royal title, knew well that, according to the regulations of the Clementine Constitutions, he was taking nothing from the rights of the King of England and that he was granting no new right to the former. He declared this distinctly in a second letter to Robert, and in a letter full of loyalty, he informed Edward, King of England, during the fiercest part of the struggle over the domination in Scotland, that, naturally, he could not think that there could have been in this title anything which would increase the rights of one to the prejudice of the rights of the other.

Pius II acted in the same manner at the time of the conflict between the Emperor Frederick and Mathias, the son of Janos Hunyadi, in regard to the throne of Hungary. In effect, he answered then that, according to custom, he who occupied the throne was called King by him, and he himself did not think that there was in that anything that could cause any grievance.

The Apostolic See has retained this manner of acting, as we well know, from the earliest times. Sixtus IV, of happy memory, like our predecessor, ratified it in a Constitution in which he declared that it would be valid, perpetual and irrefutable.

He confirmed especially that if any person had been established as king or clothed with a dignity, who had been received, named or treated as such by the Roman Pontiffs themselves or by their Nuncios, who have named themselves, or been named by others, or if they or their representatives have been received in Consistory or in other ceremonies, even in the presence of the Pope, the fact itself of these ceremonies gives them no license to obtain or acquire any right in what concerns royalty and its dignities, and those who already possess this right will receive no injury therefrom.

Furthermore, in compliance with the rules prescribed in a preceding century by the said Constitutions, Clement VI, Pontiff of immortal memory, not only gave the title of Catholic King to the Archduke Charles of Austria, but also declared in Consistory that he recognized in favor of that monarch the use of the rights inherent in all that concerned the authority he possessed. He declared that he would not refuse absolutely these rights to his posterity, and he approved the Constitutions of his predecessors and renewed the rights which were being discussed in regard to

the succession to the throne of Spain which would likewise remain intact. But if the custom and the traditions of the Apostolic
See directed toward a proper administration of sacred things have
always been carried out in such a way that no disposition can be
considered as a sanction in what concerns the recognition and
granting of powers, there would be still greater motive for doing
so in the case of so great an unrest in the different states and
of so many revolutions. We must in no way permit the abandon-
ing of the cause of the Church because of human affairs.

For this reason we have sought the opinion of our venerable
brothers, the very holy, reverend and eminent cardinals united in
congregation comprehending the plenitude of apostolic power,
following the example of our predecessors John XXII, Sixtus IV,
and Clement VI, of our own free will and after a mature consideration we have adhered to their declarations and approved them
and fully sanctioned the said Constitution of Clement V, of happy
memory, our predecessor, which they themselves approved and
renewed in regard to disputes relative to power in analogous
circumstances. Even for future occasions we declare that whenever anyone with the object of obtaining the solution of questions
relating to the spiritual regulation of the churches of the faithful
is, by Us or by our successors, granted the title to any dignity,
even the royal dignity, let him be accorded the honors verbally,
by constitution or by any other method, and let such dignity be
recognized; and if it should happen that they find themselves in
charge of the government of a State in any form whatsoever,
these acts, these ordinances, these agreements establish in no way
whatsoever in favor of that person the grant, acquisition or approbation of any right, and he may not and should not act in any
way prejudicial to the rights and privileges of the others, in what
concerns the changes in authority which have taken place. We
affirm, then, that we declare and ordain, that there is to be, as a
consequence of these acts, no change in the condition of things;
We repeat this in our own name and in the name of the Roman
Pontiffs, Our Successors. In times like these, in circumstances
where there will be a repetition of these relations between places
and between persons, one should seek nothing except that which
belongs to Christ; one should have no object nor contemplate any-

thing, except that which leads most easily to the spiritual and eternal well-being of the people.

We declare that this letter is to be observed in its entirety, its fullness and efficacy; it should always produce its full effect; it is to be observed inviolably by those who have this duty, and when they have it, in spite of all who would work to the contrary, no matter what dignity they may possess, whether expressed, specific or individual. (Vatican Library, cited by Ayarragaray, *op. cit.*, pp. 306 ff.)

CHAPTER II

SECTION 2

Articles in the Acts of Independence of September 15, 1821, relating to the Church

Artículo Décimo: Que la religión católica, que hemos profesado en los siglos anteriores, y profesaremos en los siglos sucesivos se conserve pura y inalterable, manteniendo vivo el espíritu de religiosidad que ha distinguido siempre a Guatemala respetando a los Ministros eclesiásticos, seculares y regulares, y protegiéndoles en sus personas y propiedades.

Artículo Undécimo: Que se pase oficio a los dignos Prelados de las Communidades religiosas, para que cooperando a la paz y sosiego que es la primera necesidad de los pueblos, cuando pasen de un gobierno a otro, dispongan que sus individuos exhortan a la fraternidad y concordia a los que estando unidos en el sentimiento general de la independencia deben estarlo también en todo lo demás, sofocando pasiones individuales que dividen los ánimos, y producen funestas consecuencias.

Artículo Décimo Cuarto: Que igual juramento preste la Junta Provisional, el Excelentísimo Ayuntamiento, el Illustrísimo señor Arzobispo, los Tribunales, Jefes Políticos y militares, los Prelados regulares, sus Comunidades religiosas, Jefes y empleados en las rentas, autoridades, corporaciones y tropas de la respectivas guarniciones.

Artículo Décimo Octavo: Que se cante el día que designe el señor Jefe Político una Misa solemne de gracias, con asistencia de la Junta Provisional, de todas las autoridades, corporaciones y Jefes, haciéndose salvas de artillería y tres días de iluminación.

(García, *op. cit.*, vol. I, p. 62.)

PART TWO

CHAPTER I

Decree of June 10, 1826 forbidding entrance into Convents under twenty-three years of age, and profession under twenty-five.

La Asamblea Legislativa del Estado de Guatemala, deseando que los conventos de religiosos que profesan clausura se vean practicar las virtudes que en otros tiempos han florecido con utilidad pública, y considerando que para esto es necesario que los individuos que han de entrar en ellos, hagan sus votos con toda la libertad y discernimiento que exijen la prudencia y crédito de nuestra santa religión; ha tenido a bien decretar y decreta:

Artículo 1°—En ningún convento de religiosos podrán entrar jovenes con menos edad que la de veintitres años, ni profesar sino hasta la de veinticinco cumplidos.

Artículo 2°—Antes de entrar a dichos conventos deberán presentarse ante el gefe departamental, para acreditar su edad, conducta y modo de vivir conocido.

Artículo 3°—El gefe del departamento remitirá copia de la partida de bautismo que se le haya presentado, a la autoridad local respectiva, para que en unión del párroco la confronte con el original, informando a la mayor brevedad, si está o no arreglada.

Artículo 4°—Todos los individuos que actualmente existan en los conventos de ambos sexos, sin profesar, no podrán verificarlo sin la referida edad de veinticinco años.

Artículo 5°—Los prelados, seculares o regulares, que otorgasen licencia para entrar o profesar en dichos conventos, contraviniendo a lo dispuesto por esta ley, sufrirán las penas de destitución de su prelatura, y de inhabilidad perpetua para obtener otra.

Artículo 6°—Si los prelados de que habla el artículo anterior fuesen arzobispos u obispos, por la primera vez se les impondrá una multa de la cuarta parte de sus rentas de aquel año, por la segunda la mitad de éstas, y por la tercera la pena del estrañamiento del territorio del estado.

Artículo 7°—Los gefes departamentales velarán sobre la observancia de esta ley, cuidando de restituir a la casa de su padre, tutor o curador a toda persona que contrariendo alguna de sus disposiciones se hallará en los espresados conventos. (*Recopilación de Leyes de la República de Guatemala*, vol. III, p. 252.)

Law requiring permission of Chief Executive for all Pastorals and other notices of the Ecclesiastical Government.

Libro IX, Título I, Ley 5—

1°—No podrán expedirse ni circularse las pastorales, edictos, y cualesquiera otras circulares del gobierno eclesiástico, sin que hayan obtenido el pase del gefe del estado; que deberá darlo o negarlo en los mismos casos en que por las leyes vigentes debía darse dicho pase, o mandarse retener, las bulas pontificias.

2°—Para dar o negar el pase procederá el gefe con consulta del consejo representativo; y mientras este no se halle instalado, con la del congreso. (*Recopilación de Leyes de la República de Guatemala*, vol. III, p. 250.)

Decree of December 6, 1828 upholding ecclesiastical censures against certain books.

Decreto

1°—que se ruegue y encargue al P. Arzobispo que proceda, conforme a los canones, contra los contumaces, que sin respeto a sus edictos ya publicados, introducen o retienen los libros o estampas que se han prohibido en aquellos.

2°—que las autoridades civiles y militares, requeridas que sean por la eclesiástica, recojan los mismos libros y estampas del poder de sus respectivos súbditos.

3°—que sin otra justificación que la aprehensión real, se aplique a los tenedores la multa de diez pesos por primera vez, veinticinco por la segunda y cincuenta por la tercera; y en defecto de medios para pagar la multa, otros tantos días de arresto en la misma proporción.

4°—que el producto de estas multas, se destine a beneficio del hospital militar; y los libros y estampas se quemen en presencia de los ministros de ambas autoridades.

5°—El ministro de policia queda encargado de la ejecución de este decreto y lo mandará imprimir, publicar y circular. (Marure, *Bosquejo histórico*, p. 88.)

Reply of Archbishop Casáus y Torres refusing request of the President of the Republic that he withdraw his opposition to the irregular appointment of Dr. Delgado as Bishop of San Salvador.

" Ciudadano Secretario del Gobierno del Estado:

Con la nota de Vd. de 7 de corriente, he recibido copia de las que dirigió el Jefe del Estado, por el Secretario de Relaciones en 27 de diciembre último comunicándole, que el Presidente de la República, conformándose con el consejo del Senado, se sirvió acordar se me excitara a suspender mis operaciones en orden a la erección de obispado en San Salvador, elección de obispo, y posesión que se ha dado al electo. Me es muy sensible no poder complacer al Supremo Executivo, en el informe que pidió sobre esta materia. Soy Arzobispo, y sería necesario dejarlo de ser y abandonar la grey que Dios ha puesto a mi cuidado y bajo mi jurisdicción pastoral. No está en mis facultades el desatar este vínculo, ni hacer a favor de nadie este sacrificio. Estoy estrechamente ligado, y soy responsable a Dios y a toda la Iglesia de Jesucristo de los derechos de mi dignidad episcopal y metropolitana. Nadie puede ignorar aquí, lo que mi conciencia me ha obligado a contestar ya repetidas veces, que lo hecho en San Salvador, sobre este particular, es un exceso y abuso de la potestad divina para el gobierno de la Iglesia. La tranquilidad y seguridad de las conciencias, la pureza de la religión, el valor y lícita administración de los sacramentos de que depende la salvación eterna de las almas que Dios ha puesto bajo mi responsabilidad, se interesan en este negocia. ¿ Cómo puede, pues, un Obispo prescindir de sus resultados? ¿ Podrá tolerar se autorice directa o indirectamente a ningún intruso en el gobierno espiritual de las almas, y que un Jefe nombre curas y les dé facultad para confesar y para administrar los demás sacramentos? El silencio y disímulo sobre estos errores puestos a ejecución, sería en un Obispo el prevaricato más escandaloso. Mi conducta en este particular es manifiesta a todos. Desde el principio podía haber cortado este asunto de raíz, para lo cual tenía espeditos unos medios que la potestad temporal ni me ha dado ni puede quitarme. Sin embargo, si he cometido alguna falta, es la de no haberlos puesto en ejecución con la energia con que debe defenderse la causa de Dios. He llevado el asunto por todos sus trámites legales; he lamentado su conclusión, esperando un arbitrio que pudiera escusarme el dolor de usar de las armas espirituales de la religión, contra unos sujetos que al fin han sido individuos de mi Clero y de cuya seguridad y obstinación compadezco.

Lejos de mover y exitar a los curas a que dejasen sus parroquías, como calumniosamente se me imputa, les he mandado espresamente que no las abandonen, hasta que la violencia los arrojase de ellas. Ha llegado este caso, los pueblos no tienen ya pastores; en vez de ellos se les ha sustituído hombres sin moralidad, sin jurisdicción y sin religión. Si los pueblos se resisten a sufrir este mal, el mayor que puede sobrevenirles, si al fin conocen que los mismos a quienes ellos erigieron para promover su felicidad se ocupan en oprimirlos por la parte más sensible, por lo más caro y sagrado de sus intereses, si tratan ellos mismos de sostener su religión y sus derechos, y sucede en San Salvador, lo que en todo pais oprimido por los tiranos, yo no soy culpable de estos funestos resultados; lo son y lo serán los mismos que los han causado, y la autoridad que está constituída para mantener el orden, la paz y la religión, si sus medidas no se dirigen a este objeto.

La propiedad más sagrada y respetable de esta nación católica es la de la religión que profesa, y ejercicio libre de ella, con la conservación de sus ministros legítimos. Perseguirlos es procurar la anarquía y el cisma, las guerras civiles y religiosas. Los innovadores, en cuanto a lo concerniente a la autoridad de los obispos y su misión canónica, son los que no se espantan de las consecuencias de su ambiciosa temeridad. Les digo a ellos que son sacerdotes, lo que un profeta de otro semejante, 'no he alborotado yo a Israel, sino tu y la casa de tu padre, porque habéis dejado los mandamientos del Señor y habéis seguido a los Boales.' Los que turban el Estado no son los que defienden las leyes del Señor Díos y de su Iglesia, sino los que las quebrantan y las atropellan. He dicho antes y lo repito ahora. Estoy dispuesto y

pronto a adoptar todos los medios religiosos y políticos de con-
ciliación que estén en mis facultades, y sean conformes a las
leyes de la Iglesia. El verdadero y el más justo y necesario, sería
que comprometiéndose a no vejar a los curas legítimos, se les
dejase volver a sus parroquías, interin la Santa Sede resuelve
sobre la erección de mitra en San Salvador. Y si se ha de instruir
el expediente, como corresponde, y si conduce mi súplica al Papa,
la haré para que tenga el efecto; pero abandonar mi alma, honor
y autoridad, por servir a la ambición de algunos eclesiásticos,
suspender mis operaciones indispensables para cubrir mi responsabilidad en orden a lo hecho en aquel Estado, y reconocer y
aprobar directa ni indirectamente las infracciones de las leyes
canónicas y de la disciplina general eclesiástica, que allí se han
perpetuado, es cosa que no está en mi arbitrio; ni dar indicio el
más leve de que tengo erigida por bien, tal mitra en mi Diocesis;
ni de que reputo por obispo a un párroco que se apropia de esta
jurisdicción usurpándomela con los diezmos; así como no está
en él de las altas facultades del Presidente de la República, permitir que San Salvador mudase de constitución política que ha
jurado con todos los habitantes de ella. Es cuanto juzgo del caso
exponer este punto cardinal, desatendiéndome de otros con que
se me ha provocado, injuriado y amenazado en varios impresos
y notas de San Salvador, porque no apruebo y aplaudo los des-
aciertos y errandas máximas de algunos eclesiásticos. No temo
amenazas injustas, olvido y perdono agravios, e injurias infe-
cundas. Haga Vd. el favor de manifestar al Gobierno mi respuesta, con las protestas de mi respeto y consideración. Díos,
Unión, Libertad, Palacio Arzobispal de Guatemala, enero 18 de
1826. Es copia fiel. Secretario eclesiástico de Guatemala, José
Mariano Herraste." (Vilanova Meléndez, *op. cit.*, pp. 63-65.)

Circular sent on June 12, 1829 to the heads of all the Departments of Guatemala ordering them to send all the religious in
their territory to the motherhouses.

Circular

12 de junio, 1829

Al Jefe Departamental de ——————

El P. E. ordena que al hacer V. cumplir la orden que se le
comunicó previniéndole que hiciese venir a sus casas matrices a

todos los religiosos residentes fuera de ellas cualquiera que fuese su título, cuide muy particularmente que no se demoren en los pueblos del tránsito, vigilando así mismo que ninguno salga ni viaje sin pasaporte.

> D. L. Guatemala, junio 12/29. (*National Archives*, No. 25502, June 12, 1829.)

Protest of the Vicar General of the Archdiocese against one of the appointments of General Morazán of an ecclesiastic to a parish, dated June 16, 1829.

Al Ciudadano Secretario General del Supremo Gobierno del Estado:

Con la apreciable comunicación de V. del 10 de corriente se propone para servir la parroquía rectoral del Sagrario de esta Santa Iglesia Metropolitana mientras viene el doctor Méndez al Presbítero Estevan Solorzano.

Este eclesiástico sirvió la parroquía y Vicaria Provincial de San Miguel por comisión del Dr. Delgado; ha conocido también los oficios de Gefe político y comandante militar.

El gobierno eclesiástico, que en todos casos debe manifestar al del Estado su armonia, no puede prescindir en este caso de estos obstáculos para deferir en todo a los deseos del Gobierno Supremo.

Sírvase Vd. elevarlo a su conocimiento, y aceptar las protestas de mi consideración.

> D. U. L., Guatemala, junio 16 de 1829.
>
> José Antonio Alcayaga, Palacio Arzobispal.
> (*National Archives of Guatemala*, No. 25502, June 16, 1829)

Decree of July 9, 1829 which granted the extraordinary faculties which Francisco Morazán claimed to have used in the expulsion of Archbishop Casáus y Torres and the Religious from the territory of Guatemala.

La Asamblea lejislativa del Estado de Guatemala, considerando: que es de absoluta necesidad dictar las más prontas y energéticas providencias para conservar el orden y proceder contra sus perturbadores, ha tenido bien decretar y decreta:

1°—Se faculta extraordinariamente al Gobierno por el término necesario al restablecimiento del orden, para ocurrir a todos los casos en que tenga que obrar para asegurarlo.

2°—Esta facultad podrá delegarla por el tiempo que estime conveniente a persona de su confianza. Dado en Guatemala, a 9 de julio de 1829.

(*National Archives of Guatemala*, July 9, 1829)

Letter of the Government to the Vicar General asking him to urge the Archbishop to delegate his faculties to him before leaving for exile.

Al P°. Provisor del Vicario General:

El Supremo Gobierno atendiendo a los particulares del día, ha acordado que Vd. sin perdida de tiempo disponga que el Secretario del P°. Arzobispo y el Notario Gavarrete asociados del Presb°. José Antonio Albarado pasen al punto donde se halle dicho Prelado, le entreguen la adjunta nota y lo exciten a que se sirva delegar sus facultades en Vd. para atender en su ausencia a las necesidades de este diocesís. (*National Archives of Guatemala*, No. 25465, July 11, 1829.)

Letter of the Government to the Archbishop requesting him to delegate his powers to the Vicar General of the Archdiocese during his exile, July 11, 1829.

Al P°. Arzobispo de esta Diocesís:

El Supremo Gobierno de este Estado me ordena dirigir a Vd. la siguiente comunicación:

Habiendo dispuesto el General en Jefe del Ejército separar a Vd. del ejercicio de sus funciones, quedando por esta causa destituta esta iglesia diocesana de una autoridad plenamente facultada a sus necesidades espirituales extraordinarias, ha llegado el caso de que el Supremo Gobierno excite dicho pastor para que les comunique al provisor y Vicario General del Arzobispado estando excito del amor particular y zelo con que ha procurado el bien de sus ovejas sin permitir que entren la menor falta, en circunstancias tan graves, desynopinados y difíciles, y espera que Vd. se dignará atender la presente excitación como pronta en su solicitud por este rebano.

Tengo la honra de reiterar a Vd. mi respeta y alta consideración.

D. U. L.

Con este motivo el Gefe Supremo del Estado me ordena le participa de su parte la mayor deferencia y deseos de serle útil en cualquiera situaciones y circunstancias. (*National Archives of Guatemala*, No. 25462, July 11, 1829.)

Reply of Archbishop Casáus y Torres, complying with request of government that he delegate his faculties to the Vicar General, July 12, 1829.

Al Ciudadano Secretario del Gobierno Supremo del Estado:

Conviniendo con la excitación que el Gobierno Supremo se sirve hacerme por medio de V. en su nota de ayer, y para que mis ovejas no queden destituídas con mi separación del socorro espiritual que necesitan, doi y delego las facultades de sólitas y extraordinarias mientras yo no esté en el territorio de mi arzobispado con mi vicario general don José Antonio Alcayaga; en falta de este, el Dr. Pedro Bustamante, y en su defecto en el P. Diego Batres.

Las facultades extraordinarias están concedidas por el mismo término que las sólitas, y siendo difícil ocurrir a Su Santidad. El término de su concesión era de diez años y expirará ya en este año. He pedido su renovación y, según un declaratorio del señor Pr°. G., yo podía usar de ella como he usado aún antes de llegar la contestación de S.S. Pero dudo si podía comunicarlas, debiendo presumir con más que probabilidad que la mente de S.S. no será de prorrogarlas, en caso de hacérseme salir de esta manera de mi diocesís.

Deseo sin embargo hacer todo el bien posible a mis ovejas y que mi separación no les hace perjuicio alguno; y en este concepto si pudiera, pero dudo que puedo las delegar en los sujetos expresados baxo el orden dicho.

Todo este debera entender mientras yo viviese, o su Santidad no me admitiera la segunda remisión que hizo ya desde Mayo del año pasado; pero en cualquiera de los dos casos el gobierno pasa según derecho al Cabildo y cesan las facultades delegadas.

Agradezco las espresiones y ofrecimientos que el Gobierno ha querido hacerme en esta ocasión; y usaré de ellas opportunamente, prestándole por mi parte los mejores sentimientos y consideraciones.

> D. U. L., Ponteruelas, julio 12, 1829. Fr. Ramón, arzobispo de Guatemala. (*National Archives of Guatemala*, No. 25466, July 12, 1829.)

Report of Committee appointed by the Government to determine the pensions for the Archbishop and Religious, expelled from Guatemala July 11, 1829.

La Comisión encargado para dictaminar sobre la consulta del gobierno relativo a las rentas que deba gozar el Prebítero Arzobispo desde el día de la separación de esta Iglesia y sobre la pensión que debe asignarse a los religiosos que por perjudiciarles a la tranquilidad pública se han mandado exilir de la república, examinado el punto con la detención que permite un asunto deliberado del momento y en vista de las disposiciones que rijan en la materia, opina se diga al gobierno que aunque por las leyes civiles y eclesiásticas los pastores separados de sus iglesias solo gozan un tercio parte sobre sus rentas, atendiendo que esta separación es permanente, económica y governativa, ya que el gobierno se halla investido de la facultad necesaria, se sirva declarar que el Presbítero Arzobispo gozará desde este día los dos tercios de la renta que le convenga conforme los quadrantes el cuyo considerando para que le abonará anualmente.

Con respeto a los religiosos el gobierno podría tracer la asignación que pague proporcionados en vista de los bienes que de estos religiosos entraren en Tesorería en virtud de su expulsión.

> Guatemala, julio 11, 1829 (*National Archives of Guatemala*, No. 25461, July 11, 1829.)

Decree of July 11, 1829 granting pensions to the Archbishop Casáus y Torres and the banished Religious.

El Gefe Executivo con vista de la consulta del consejo motivada por la iniciativa del mismo gobierno y en uso de las facultades extraordinarias que le son delegadas por la Asamblea ha tenido a bien decretar:

1°—que el Padre Arzobispo gozará en lo sucesivo las dos terceras partes de su renta eclesiástica, fixándose por el cuadrante y las gozará tanto que obtenga el mismo Padre Arzobispo otro beneficio.

2°—que los religiosos expulsados del territorio de la república gozarán también una pensión vitalicista, fixándose ésta según el costado de sus rentas y bienes comprobados con el inventario mandado hacer de ellos. (*National Archives of Guatemala*, No. 25461, July 11, 1829.)

Letter of Government to Archbishop Casáus y Torres informing him that he is to receive a pension.

Al Presbítero Arzobispo de esta Diócesis:

El Supremo Gobierno del Estado, de acuerdo con el Consejo representativo ha tenido a bien acordar asignar a Vd. para su decente subsista las dos terceras partes de las rentas que ha disfrutado en estos últimos años, dando al mismo tiempo las ordenes necesarias para su liquidación y recaudación. Lo convenimos a Vd. de órdenes del mismo Supremo Gobierno para su inteligencia y para que libre contra esta tesorería general el importe de dichas dos terceras partes que le serán prontamente pagadas. De Gª., julio 11, 1829. (*National Archives of Guatemala*, No. 25460, July 11, 1829.)

Letter of Government to the Exiled Religious informing them that they are to receive a life pension.

A los religiosos expulsados del territorio:

El P.E. con consulta del consejo ha tenido a bien decretar en favor de V.V. una pensión vitalicia que se fijará según el estado de las rentas y bienes existentes de sus respectivas casas— Lo comunico a V.V. para su inteligencia.

Tengo la satisfacción de protestar a V.V. mi estimación y aprecio. (*National Archives of Guatemala*, No. 25482, July, 1829.)

Order of the Government to the Vicar General to make an inventory of the possessions of the Archbishop's Palace.

Al Presbítero Provisor del Vicario General:

El P. E. ha acordado pase V. con los comisionados al Palacio Arzobispal e inventoriado los muebles y alhajas se pase los que sea de uso personal del prelado y a esto agregue mil pesos del dinero efectivo que se encontrase, remitiendo todo lo demás a esta tesorería general.

El General del Gobierno lo suministrado, ofreciendo mis consideraciones. D^e Gua^a., julio 11/29 (*National Archives of Guatemala*, No. 25459, July 11, 1829.)

Order sent to General Morazán to make an inventory of all the religious houses of the State, and take into custody all religious not yet expelled.

(Reservados algunos artículos)

El Gefe Executivo en consecuencia de haverse decretado y verificado la expulsión de los regulares de los conventos de Santo Domingo, él de los Franciscanos y Recolección, haviendo también salido el arzobispo, tiene a bien decretar:

1°—que se inventarse y que pongan en depósito todas las temporalidades.

2°—que para verificarse en esta ciudad un municipal nombrado por el Gefe Político y un eclesiástico por el Provisor pasen a cada uno de los expresados conventos acompañado de un escribano y registran al sacerdote que ha quedado en ellos para que les va poniendo de manifiesto todos los bienes y papeles del convento y de los individuos.

3°—Los papeles sean luego dados y sellados sin reconocerse.

4°—Los bienes y acciones y dinero serán aún antes de inventoriarse puesto en un departamento seguro, sellándose las arcas y puertas procurándose que sea donde han quedado los coristas a quienes se harán los encargos convenientes. Luego se irá procediendo al inventario de todo y sellando las puertas en que se dejase lo inventariado, y se den esto al gobierno.

5°—El provisor por medio de una persona de su confianza acompañado de un notario y dos testigos formarán el inventario de la casa Episcopal y proveerá como halle por conveniente a su seguridad y mantenimiento interior.

6°—También proveerá al de los conventos.

7°—En defecto de escribanos dos testigos de toda excepción cumplirán a sus veces.

8°—A los nombrados en comisión y a los escribanos se admitirán excepciones de ningún género y serán obligado al servicio por mientras al arbitrio del Gefe Político.

9°—En los otros departamentos se comete la ejecución de lo provenido para esta ciudad a los comandantes militares.

10°—Las fincas rurales serán también puestas luego en depósito y formarán inventarios de los depositarios que el gobierno se reserva nombrados.

11°—Los comandantes militares de los departamentos procederán a asegurar a los regulares, no laicos y coristas, que hayan en ellos y sin molestarlos, con el mayor sígilo, les harán salir custodados sin tocar en cita capital ni en la Antigua, conduciéndolos a la Villa de Sonsonate.

12°—Los curas provistos de doce de Abril para acá, no serán comprendidos en la providencia contenida en el artículo anterior que será executado con el más inviolable secreto y precaución.

Guatemala, julio 13, 1829. (*National Archives of Guatemala*, No. 25458, July 13, 1829.)

Decree of July 14, 1829 secularizing the coristas and lay brothers of the Dominicans, Franciscans and Recollets.

Ga.ª 14.

El P.E. teniendo en consideración 1° que el P°. Arzobispo de esta diócesis ha delegado sus facultades y sólitas en el P. Provisor y Vicario General José Antonio Alcayaga; 2° a que por la expulsión de los regulares de Santo Domingo, San Francisco y la Recolección verificada de orden del general en Gefe del Ejército, no debiendo continuar el regimen y disciplina bajo lo cual vivían estos individuos; 3° y ultimamente a que el Gobierno deve remover todo motivo de inmoralidad, ha tenido a bien decretar y decreta: que el P°. Provisor en uso de las facultades que se le han suministrado proceda a la secularización de los coristas y religiosos legos de las comunidades religiosas de Santo Domingo, San Francisco y la Recolección, de quienes quedan en esta ciudad y en este departamento aún algunos ... (*National Archives of Guatemala*, No. 25466, July 14, 1829, B83.12).

Decree of July 15, 1829 suppressing monastic establishments of men throughout the province.

La Asamblea legislativa del estado de Guatemala, considerando:

1°—Que los establecimientos monásticos por su misma naturaleza y odiosos privilegios son opuestos a la libertad e igualdad, bases fundamentales de toda constitución republicana.

2°—Que aunque el objeto primordial de sus institutos es solamente el regimen espiritual y la propagación del evangelio, con la palabra y el ejemplo, como ageno de los negocios políticos; sus individuos ingiriéndose en ellos han dado pruebas en todo tiempo y en todas naciones del influjo que ejercen en los pueblos para sumirlos en la anarquía y envolverlos en sangrientes y horrorosas revoluciones.

3°—Que la mayor parte de los que componen las corporaciones regulares del estado, desde el pronunciamiento de nuestra independencia han dado constantes y repetidas pruebas de aversión y desafecto al sistema adoptado, oponiéndose al juramento de la ley fundamental de la república, desobedeciendo y contrariando las disposiciones, tanto de la asamblea nacional constituyente, como las del mismo estado.

4°—Que haciendo causa común con les enemigos del orden, contra el espíritu y lenidad de su ministerio, se han valido de la predicación para insureccionar a los pueblos contra las legítimas autoridades, y fascinándolos con pretesto de religión, los han impelido a sublevarse y a cometer los más atroces asesinatos, como el ejecutado en la ciudad de Quezaltenango en la persona del vicegefe supremo ciudadano Cirilo Flores, y han fomentado en todo el estado el incendio de la guerra civil.

5°—Que sin embargo de haberse terminado ésta felizmente por los triunfos del ejército aliado contra los facciones y haberse restablecido la paz a costa de inestimables sacrificios, aún intentaban a alterar de nuevo la tranquilidad pública tramando conspiraciones contra las legítimas autoridades y encender otra vez la guerra en el estado.

6°—Que la Orden de Belemitas es un instituto fundado en Guatemala, cuyo piadoso objeto es en favor de la humanidad, por el cuidado y asistencia que prestan sus individuos a los enfermos convalescientes, al mismo tiempo que dan a los niños la enseñanza primaria, y que estos religiosos, lejos de haberse mezclado en los asuntos políticos, han dado en todas épocas pruebas de subordinación a las autoridades constituídas.

7°—Que en el mismo caso se hallan los establecimientos monásticos de mujeres pero que sin embargo los votos y profesiones solemnes son contrarios, no solo a la libertad civil, sino a la que se requiere para el ejercicio de las virtudes morales; ha tenido a bien decretar y decreta:

Artículo 1°—Quedan estinguidos en el estado los establecimientos conocidos bajo la denominación de domínicos, franciscanos, recoletos y mercedarios.

Artículo 2°—Subsistirá él de hospitalarios belemitas.

Artículo 3°—Igualmente subsistirán los conventos de monjas y beaterios, y se prohiben para lo sucesivo las profesiones de votos solemnes.

Artículo 4°—Todos los individuos existentes en el estado que pertenezcan a cualquiera de los monasterios estinguidos por le artículo 1°, podrán solicitar su secularización ante el gobierno, quien no podrá negársela sino en caso de que se justifique al que la solicite, haber cooperado directamente a la revolución.

Artículo 5°—Los individuos que no sean secularizados deberán salir del territorio del estado dentro de un breve término que señalará el gobierno, y no podrán pasar a ninguno de los estados de la unión, sin previo permiso de sus respectivos gobiernos.

Artículo 6°—Los religiosos legos de los conventos estinguidos que no quieran secularizarse o salir del estado, podrán continuar sus votos en el convento de Belén bajo el instituto de esta orden.

Artículo 7°—Cada uno de los ordenados *in sacris* que por no querer secularizarse o por haber sido comprendido en la espulsión verificada por el gobierno, tuviese que salir fuera de la república, disfrutará una pensión vitalicia de ciento cincuenta pesos anuales pagaderos del producto de sus temporalidades, reglamentándose por una orden particular el modo y forma de satisfacerla. (Pineda de Mont, *Recopilación de Leyes de la República de Guatemala*, vol. III, p. 253.)

Letter from the Supreme Government of the State of Honduras to the Government of Guatemala approving the action of the latter in expelling the Archbishop and religious.

Ministerio General del Gobierno Supremo del Estado de Honduras.

A los Ciudadanos de la Asamblea General del Gobierno Supremo del Estado de Guatemala:

Se ha enterada mi Gobierno por la nota de V. el 22 del presente de la providencia dictada por ese digno Gefe Supremo para espulsar de esa Corte al Padre Arzobispo y a los regulares por la parte activa que tomaron en la Revolución abrazando la causa de los enemigos de los liberadores públicos y que esta providencia fué exercitado por el General en Gefe de los Ejércitos aliados protectores de la Ley en la noche del 10 del propio mes.

El mismo General había ya comunicado esta medida con extraordinario y tengo el honor de decir a Vd. que ella fué aprobada y celebrada por mi Gobierno, que previó los bienes que va a producir en los pueblos infelices que llevaban sobre si el peso de mantener y sostener una porción de hombres que solo se creían con derechos sin conocer obligaciones.

Mi gobierno da a Vd. las individuas gracias por tan heróica resolución y ofrece contribuir en cuanto esté de su parte para proteger a Centro-América de sus enemigos y asegurarla su independencia y felicidad.

Por su Exm. lo digo a Vd. grato que se sirva elevar al alto conocimiento de su Supremo Gefe y en respuesta a su citada nota.

Quiera V. Ciud°. Laio. (*National Archives of Guatemala*, No. 25458.

Letter from the Supreme Government of the State of Costa Rica to the Government of Guatemala approving the expulsion of Archbishop Casáus y Torres and the Religious, dated September 3, 1829.

Ministerio General del Gobierno Supremo de Costa Rica.

Al Ciudadano Ministro General del Gobierno Supremo del Estado de Guatemala:

Por la apreciable nota de V. dirigida en julio último, sin anotarse el día, mi gobierno se ha enterada de los sólidos fundamientos que impelieron al de ese Estado a ponerse de acuerdo con el General en Gefe del Ejército aliado, protector de la Ley, y decretar la expulsión del Arzobispo y Clérigos regulares como agentes de la revolución. Igualmente está impuesta ya por comunicaciones oficiales del General que semejantes medidas havía comprendido a los prisioneros por aquella causa que havía ganado a costa de tan duras y inmensos sacrificios.

Mi gobierno creía que los autores de tamaño males desengañados por la útil y repetida experiencia que hemos recibido en los sucesos anteriores habiendo desistido de sus maquinaciones y dado lugar por conveniencia propia y de toda la república en que debían cifrarla a curar pacificamente las profundas heridas y enjugar las lágrimas que por un interés privado ha derramado escoriosamente, contribuyendo a afianzar la paz, el orden y marcha constitucional de la república y cooperando a reintegrarla de tan estimables y preciosas dones, pero convencidos ya de lo contrario, y que una vez que sus esperanzas han sido frustrados por el genio del mal y de la discordia no había quedado otro recurso que el adoptado para alejar los riesgos de hincar a la república a nuevo en la anarquía y asegurarla de este modo en las instituciones que hemos jurado observar irrevocablemente.

Lo digo a Vd. a ordenes de este Gobierno en contestación a su citada nota para conocimiento del Gobierno si bien con admitir los reiteraciones de mi verdadero aprecio y respeto acia Vd.

Díos, Union, Libertad, San José, septiembre 3,
1829. Ig. V. G. Calvo (*National Archives
of Guatemala*, No. 25458, Sept. 3, 1829, B83.12)

Measure dictated by the Government of Guatemala to ascertain whether or not the exiled Archbishop Casáus y Torres had left Havana for Spain, dated February 23, 1830.

A los individuos de la Comisión de Hacienda del Cuerpo legislativo:

Acompaño a VV las diligencias mandadas inscrivir por el Gobierno ecc°. a averiguar si el Padre Arzobispo fra Ramón Casáus ha marchado a España, cuya averiguación necesita la comisión que VV forman.

Gª. febrero 23/30 F.M. (*National Archives of Guatemala*,
No. 24787, February 2, 1830)

Decree of February 27, 1834 declaring that all nuns are free to return to the world, and to take with them the dowry which they brought.

Libro IX, Título 1, Ley 16:

1°—Las autoridades del estado no retendrán a ninguna monja que quiera no continuar en el convento a que pertenezca por su profesión, antés por el contrario si se les privase su libertad para volver al siglo el supremo gobierno las deberá protejer.

2°— Las que por su propia voluntad salieren de los conventos tienen derecho de recojer de sus administradores el dote que hubiesen introducido en proporción del estado que tengan los fondos ... (Pineda de Mont, *Recopilación de Leyes de Guatemala,* vol. III, p. 261)

Decree dated April 16, 1834 declaring secularized religious eligible to inherit and to enjoy all the rights of citizenship.

Libro IX, Título III, Ley 1 :

Las personas que antés pertenecieron a las comunidades regulares pueden adquirir bienes, disponer de ellos en vida o por testamento, adquirir del mismo modo o ab-intestado y gozar de todos los derechos civiles que las leyes conceden al resto de los habitantes, sin más limitaciones que las que imponen su estado a los eclesiásticos seculares.

Se declaran firmes y valederas las ventas, donaciones o enajenaciones de toda especie que en cualquiera tiempo hayan hecho los regulares, de bienes que habían adquirido con su trabajo, y sobre los cuales sus estatutos les prohibían tener propiedad.

En consecuencia se habrán por lejítimos duenos a los poseedores actuales de tales bienes, adquiridos de los regulares por títulos onerosos o lucrativos. (Pineda de Mont, *Recopilación de Leyes de Guatemala,* vol. III, p. 292.)

Letter of the Holy See, dated February 24, 1836, approving the faculties granted to don Diego Batres as Vicar General of the Archdiocese of Guatemala.

Decreto: De Guatemala, en la América Septentrional—De Sanción y Confirmación del Vicario Capitular.

Hace pocos días representaron a nuestro Smo. Padre Gregorio, por la divina Providencia Papa XVI, algunos individuos del Cabildo de la Iglesia Metropolitana de Guatemala, como, habiendo sido el actual Arzobispo de la misma Iglesia separado de su grey por las turbulencias políticas, y hallándose en la Habana; juzgó dicho Cabildo, atendidas las circunstancias y principalmente la distancia de los lugares, deber proceder a la elección de Vicario capitular; y que ésta recayó en el doctor Diego Batres, designado en tercer lugar entre los que había nombrado el Arzobispo, cuando iba a apartarse de Guatemala, para que en su ausencia hiciesen sus veces. Pero como se suscitó duda sobre la lejitimidad de la misma elección, acordaron consultar a la silla apostólica, así para que les dejase tranquila su consciencia, como para que oportunamente les prescribiese lo que debería hacerse en este asunto. Por tanto, despues de un madura examen de todo, su Santidad a quien di cuenta yo, el infrascito Secretario de la Sagrada Congregación destinada a los negocios consistoriales, acojiendo benignamente esta súplica, y sanado previamente, en cuanto sea necesario lo que el mismo Diego Batres haya practicado como vicario capitular de la referida Iglesia Metropolitana le ha confirmado con la autoridad apostólica en este cargo, con las facultades que por derecho o costumbres competen a los Vicarios capitulares; concediendo además al Cabildo la potestad de subrogarle otro, cuantas veces aconteciese que falte, sin que obste en contrario cosa alguna. Y mandó que sobre esto se estendiese el presente decreto y se insertase en las actas de la misma Sagrada congregación. Dado en Roma, el día 24 de febrero del año del Señor de 1836. Lugar del sello. Luis Tregia, Arzobispo de Calcedonia, Secretario de la misma Sagrada Congregación. (Montúfar y Rivera, *op. cit.*, vol. I, p. 264.)

Decree of April 10, 1837 declaring that marriage was a civil contract which could be dissolved.

Libro IX, Título V, Ley 1: La Asamblea Legislativa decreta:

1°—La ley solo considera los matrimonios como un contrato civil, y en consecuencia pueden rescindirse.

2°—Todo el que se declare divorciado, con las solemnidades del decreto de agosto del año pasado, queda hábil para contraer nuevo matrimonio.

Comuníquese al Consejo representativo para su sanción. Dado en Guatemala, a 10 de abril de 1837—Mariano Sánchez de León, José B. Valenzuela, diputado secretario—José María Flores, diputado vice-secretario. (Pineda de Mont, *Recopilación de Leyes de Guatemala*, vol. III, p. 300.)

Decree issued in July, 1838 revoking all previous decrees declaring marriage a civil contract which could be dissolved.

Libro IX, Título V, Ley 3:

Se suspenden los decretos de 20 de agosto de 1836, 10 de abril y 19 de agosto de 1837, 20 de febrero de 1834, y el artículo 3 del de julio de 1829. (Marure, *Efemérides*, p. 40.)

Decree dated July 26, 1838, issued by the Conservatives, granting general amnesty to all who had opposed the government since September, 1821.

Article 1—No measures, decrees or resolutions dictated by any authority whatsoever, and by virtue of which there have been expatriated or deprived of their rights any persons whatsoever, any longer exist or hold in the State. Therefore, all those persons who by virtue of such decrees or resolutions have been expelled may freely return to the country.

Article 2—From this moment on there are restored all political and civil rights to those who have been deprived of such at different times, without any obligation of a special rehabilitation.

Article 3—A general oblivion will be observed in regard to all political occurrences from the 15th of September, 1821, up to the present time; and it is forbidden absolutely to recall them for any reason whatsoever. (Montúfar y Rivera, *op. cit.*, vol. III, p. 190.)

Decree of June 21, 1839 declaring null and void the decree of expulsion of the Archbishop Casáus y Torres, dated, June 13, 1830, and restoring to him his rights as Metropolitan and as citizen.

La Asamblea Constituyente del Estado de Guatemala ha decretado:

1°—Se declara nulo y de ningún valor el decreto que espidió la Asamblea del Estado en 13 de junio de 1830 contra la persona, carácter y dignidad del muy reverendo arzobispo, doctor y maestro Frai Ramón Francisco Casáus.

2°—Por tanto, queda desde luego espedito para el ejercicio de los derechos que le corresponden en concepto de prelado metropolitano, y como ciudadano del Estado.

3°—Por una comunicación que dirijirá el Presidente de la Asamblea al mismo digno Prelado, le presentará los votos de los representantes que la componen, y de los pueblos sus comitentes, por su más pronto y feliz regreso a su diocesís.

Pasa al Gobierno para su publicación y cumplimiento.

Dado en el salón de sesiones—Guatemala, a veintiuno de junio de mil ochocientos treinta y nuevo—Fernando Antonio Dávila, Presidente — J. Mariano Vidaurre, Secretario—Manuel F. Pavón, Secretario.

Casa de Supremo Gobierno—Guatemala, junio 21 de 1839. Por tanto, ejecútese, Mariano Rivera Paz, (Montúfar y Rivera. *op. cit.*, vol. III, p. 373)

Decree of June 21, 1839 revoking the decree of July 28, 1829 which had suppressed the religious orders.

Libro IX, Título 1, Ley 18. Decreto de la Asamblea:

1°—Se declara nulo e insubsistente el decreto de veinte y ocho de julio de mil ochocientos veintinueve, contraído a la supresión de las órdenes religiosas de San Francisco, Santo Domingo, Merced y Colegio de Misioneros de Propaganda fide.

2°—En consecuencia, el gobierno del estado, poniéndose de acuerdo con el gobierno eclesiástico, y oyendo a la municipalidad de esta capital proveerá lo conviniente para que desde luego tenga efecto el restablecimiento del colegio de misioneros de propaganda fide, proporcionando a los religiosos la devolución de su iglesia y convento; y haciendo para ello las indemnizaciones que fueran de justicia.

3°—Para el restablecimiento de las otras órdenes religiosas, el gobierno también de acuerdo con el ordinario eclesiástico y oyendo a la corporación municipal, dispondrá lo conveniente; consultando a la asamblea cuando fuese necesario alguna resolución legislativa. (Pineda de Mont, *Recopilación de Leyes de Guatemala*, vol. III, p. 262.)

Chapter II

Address of General Carrera to his soldiers urging them on to a last effort against the enemy, and offering them as an incentive the reestablishment of the institutions of the Church, December 5, 1839.

"El General Rafael Carrera a sus soldados: Compañeros: habéis cumplido con vuestro deber a la última campaña del acan-

tonamiento de Jutiapa, y demás expediciones que se han ofrecidos:
habéis estado ausentes de vuestros hogares; separados de vuestras
caras familias, vuestros campos y labores abandonados, y sufriendo
privaciones de todas clases. Mientras tanto, nuestra Asamblea
Constituyente y Gobierno, con toda seguridad y libertad, se han
ocupado de arreglar la administración del Estado en todos sus
ramos. Han hecho leyes ya, adecuadas a nuestras exijencias y
peculiares circumstancias, y ha restablecido la Religión y muchas
de sus instituciones que la mano impía de nuestros mortales
enemigos había destruido. A ellos solo se les debe la miseria en
que estamos, en una Patria que por sus producciones naturales,
debía ser la primera en Centro América. . . .

Estos dos contactos que tenemos de San Salvador y Quezaltenango son los únicos embarazos que retardan el regreso deseado
a nuestros hogares. Mientras desaparecen esas nubes que aún im-
piden el disco a nuestro orizonte, tened paciencia, y completad
la obra que empezastéis. Os doy las gracias a nombre del Gobierno
y de la Patria, y no olvidéis que la moderación y disciplina son
la divisa con que se distingue el soldado guatemalteco. Guatemala,
diciembre 5, de 1839 — Rafael Carrera." (*National Archives of
Guatemala*, December 5, 1839.)

Decree of October 28, 1840 granting the Vicar General of the
Archdiocese all the faculties necessary for the improvement of
public morals in the absence of the Archbishop.

Impuesta la Asamblea de la nulidad a que había quedado re-
ducida la autoridad eclesiástica, en la perversión de costumbres
que se nota en la generalidad de los pueblos, ha tenido a bien
declarar:

Que están expedidas las facultades de la autoridad eclesiástica,
para promover por los medios que le son proprios la mejora de
costumbres con respecto a todos los fieles, valiéndose al efecto
de las penas espirituales y aún de las temporales en los casos en
que ha podido hacerlo por las leyes aún vigentes al tiempo de la
independencia, y con las calidades que en ella se esponen. . . . —
Casa del Supremo Gobierno de Guatemala—Cúmplase—(*National
Archives of Guatemala*, No. 25332, Oct. 28, 1840.)

Decree dated March 31, 1854 in which Carrera clarifies
Articles 15 and 16 of the Concordat with the Holy See, treating of the ecclesiastical privileges:

Rafael Carrera, capitán general del ejército; Caballero Gran Cruz de la Orden Pontificia de San Gregorio Magno, en la clase militar; Comendador de la de Leopoldo de Bélgica; Presidente de la República de Guatemala.

Decreta:

Artículo 1°—La autoridad eclesiástica continuará conociendo de las causas de los eclesiásticos, en materia civil, siempre que se versen entre solo eclesiásticos, y solamente pasarán a conocimiento de la jurisdicción ordinaria las causes de intereses temporales entre legos y eclesiásticos, y todas aquellas sobre derecho al goce de capellanías y demás fundaciones piadosas que no hubieron sido canonicamente instituídas, ni convertidos los capitales en bienes espirituales, conforme al derecho canónico.

Artículo 2°—En materia criminal no se hará por ahora ninguna novedad, continuando los eclesiásticos en el goce del fuero, tal como existe; pero aún en los casos de desafuero, las sentencias que contengan condenación a pena capital, aflictiva o infamante, no serán ejecutadas sin la aprobación del Presidente, y sin que el respectivo obispo haya cumplido previamente con cuanto en tales casos se requiere por los sagrados canones.

Artículo 3°—El Gobierno se reserva hacer uso de lo estipulado en los artículos 15 y 16 del Concordato, siempre que el buen servicio público lo requiere.

Dado en el Palacio del Gobierno, en Guatemala, a treinta y uno de marzo de mil ochocientos cincuenta y cuatro.

Rafael Carrera

El Ministero de gobernación, justicia, y negocios eclesiásticos,

P. de Aycinena.

(Montúfar y Rivera, op. cit., vol. III, p. 524.)

CHAPTER III

Petition of the Archbishop to the Provisional President García Granados asking security for the Jesuits who were threatened by the more radical Liberals, August 16, 1871.

Palacio del Arzobispo de Guatemala. Señor Presidente Provisorio de la República. Hace algunos días que hubo no poca inquietud en el vecindario de esta capital, por haberse sabido que algunos individuos trataban de recoger firmas para solicitar al Gobierno provisorio la espulsión de los padres de la Compañía de Jesús, y en reuniones públicas se procuraba concitar los ánimos e indisponerlos contra ese instituto, que durante veinte años ha prestado y sigue prestando, como es notorio, importantes servicios a la Iglesia y a la sociedad. Hoy se han visto llegar espulsos de la ciudad de Quezaltenango a algunos de los padres que estaban en aquella residencia y se sabe con certeza que todos los que la ocupaban tuvieron igual suerte. Si las personas que, por preoccupación o por ignorancia abrigan aún opiniones poco favorables a los padres de la Compañía de Jesús, se limitasen a permanecer adictos a su propia convicción, está aunque muy lejos de ser justa e ilustrada, no caería bajo la acción de la autoridad, ni podriá dar margen a reclamaciones de ninguna especia. Por esta consideración, y confiado en la lealtad de las autoridades que hoy nos rigen, me había abstenido de hacer gestión de alguna manera sobre el particular. Mas viendo yo que no solamente trata de estraviar la opinión pública y aún de haver peticiones contrarias a los principios de orden y libertad recientemente proclamadas sino que se procede de hecho a infringirlos violando la seguridad personal, atropellando a los padres y lanzándolos de su domicilio, no me es posible guardar silencio sin contraer la más grave responsabilidad. Es por esto que en unión del cabildo de esta santa Iglesia Metropolitana, cuyos individuos también subscriben la presente, he resuelto acudir a Vd., cumpliendo con un deber sagrado; pues lo es en efecto para nosotros y para todo el pueblo católico interesarnos por una sociedad que pertenece a nuestro gremio, que es una parte muy principal del clero católico y que contribuye a formarlo con su doctrina y con ejemplo. Sabemos, Señor Presidente, que no se puede ocultar a la penetración e ilustrado juicio de Vd. cuan grave es bajo todos respetos la inguria que se acaba de infligir a la casa de la Compañia de Jesús establecida en Quezaltenango, y cuanto compromete ese hecho el honor y buen nombre de la Nación, y el orden público, puesto que envuelve la violación de todo principio de justicia y de verdadera libertad. Por esto omitimos descender a más detalladas consideraciones y nos limitamos a pedir que el Gobierno provisorio a más de tomar todas las medidas necesarias para reparar esa desgracia, se sirva dictar también las que corresponden con el fin de dar plena seguridad a los padres que residen en esta capital, y que acaso pueden ser víctimas de una violencia semejante. Hacemos esta súplica con todo el respeto debido pero también con toda la energia que inspiran los intereses de la Religión, de la justicia y del honor del país; y esperamos de la justificación del Gobierno provisorio, se digne obsequiar nuestros votos que, podemos asegurarlo, son también los de la gran mayoría de la República. Con estos sentimientos protestamos a Vd. nuestros respetos y distinguida consideración. Guatemala, agosto 16 de 1871, Bernardo, Arzobispo de Guatemala, Manuel Francisco, Obispo de Caristo—Francisco A. Espinosa, Francisco W. Jaracena, Pedro García, Juan Cabrejo, José Antonio Urrutia Jáuregui. (García, *op. cit.*, vol. II, pp. 375 ff.)

Warning of the Provisional President García Granados to all those who attempted to disturb the peace that they would be treated as traitors, dated August 21, 1871.

Decreto Número 16:

1°—Los departamentos de Guatemala y Santa Rosa quedan declarados en estado de sitio.

2°—Los que con actos positivos procuren trastornar la tranquilidad pública o conciten a ello de palabra o por escrito, serán juzgados sumaria y militarmente como traidores a la patria.

> Dado en Guatemala a treinta y uno de agosto de mil ochocientos setenta y uno.
>
> Miguel García Granados.
>
> (*Recopilación de Leyes de Guatemala*, vol. I, p. 16)

Article XII of the Arbizu-Samayoa Treaty drawn up between Guatemala and El Salvador, in which the two republics agree to exclude from their territory all members of the Company of Jesus, dated Jan. 25, 1872.

Habiendo expulsado el Gobierno de Guatemala a los Padres de la Compañía de Jesús, por ser notorio que su permanencia en el país es nociva a los intereses de la República, y siendo evidente que el Gobierno del Salvador puede ser contrariado de la misma manera y encontrar en ellos un obstáculo para el restablecimiento definitivo de las instituciones liberales proclamadas en ambas Repúblicas, y teniendo presente además que el Congreso Constituyente de la del Salvador dispuso que no se admitiesen en esta República a los referidos Padres, se convienen ambos Gobiernos en no permitir que existan en lo sucesivo en ninguna parte de sus respectivos territorios los Padres de la Compañía antedicha, ni organizada en sociedad ni de otra manera. (Vilanova Meléndez, *op. cit.*, p. 193.)

Document issued October 24, 1871 by the Provisional Government of Guatemala defending its expulsion of the Archbishop and the Bishop of Teya against the accusation that it was attacking religion:

Reasonable persons in the Republic understand the just motives impelling the Provisional Government to expel the Fathers of Company of Jesus from the country.

This measure, necessary for order and for the security of our new institutions, was used by certain discontented persons, enemies of that administration, to start an insurrection in Guatemala, Chiquimula, Santa Rosa and Jutiapa, whose inhabitants are, for the most part, simple and ignorant, and who readily accept the idea maliciously spread by the enemy of the government that in the said expulsion the government was attacking the religion of the Republic.

As soon as the Government learned of the revolt, it took prompt measures to put it down. It declared martial law in those provinces, requested the religious of the different orders to exercise their ministry of peace in order to restore the order and tranquility which had been lost, and, finally on September 13th, it issued the decree offering amnesty to all who would within eight days present themselves before the government. But these conciliatory measures, these prudent dispositions, were in vain. Religious fanaticism took possession of simple minds and the revolt, nourished and favored by influential persons of the capital, took on colossal proportions, forcing the government to send large numbers of troops to put down the rebellion. In this state of affairs, and with the conviction that the expulsion of the Jesuits, considered as an attack on Religion, was the pretext of those who took up arms against the government, the latter requested the Archbishop to issue a pastoral explaining that Religion and a community of religious which disturbed the public order should not be confused, and assuring the people that the government, in expelling the said community, was attacking in no way the religion of the Republic.

But the Archbishop, indifferent to the innocent victims of the revolution, and guided by personal interests foreign to his ministry, refused openly to issue the said pastoral, under the feeble pretext that it would imply a contradiction of the desire he had previously manifested that the Jesuits be permitted to remain in the country.

But such a contradiction, if indeed it existed, was never the true cause animating the Archbishop's refusal to comply with the request of the Government. If he refused, it was because, instead of condemning the revolution, he desired its triumph, deceiving himself concerning the restoration of institutions now impossible in the country, and because he presumed that his pastoral would destroy a faction which he wished preserved.

And, unfortunately, not only the Archbishop, but also the Bishop of Teya, as is well known, encouraged the faction and urged on the overthrow of the provisional government; but all was useless. The reactionary forces recoiled before the powerful and valiant army which Lieutenant General Barrios commanded, and Providence, on the side of justice, gave a complete victory to the arms of the government.

And, in spite of the fact that the government had a right to punish the insurrectionists who were overthrowing the public order and tranquility, it did not exercise such a right, but rather granted an amnesty to those who would submit and lay down their arms.

And, certainly, why should there rest upon these simple, ignorant people the responsibility for the crime of those who exploited their religious zeal? No, it is not these who should be punished, but rather those who, abusing popular belief, introduced errors which gave rise to the revolt, and, with it, its fearful results.

But, notwithstanding, the government wishes to give a proof of its clemency, granting a general amnesty, with rare and justifiable exceptions, to all those who have taken part in the recent revolutionary movements.

But, likewise, the government, burdened with the imperious duty of maintaining peace and preserving intact the rights which have been entrusted to it by the inhabitants of the Republic, sees itself obliged to dictate certain dispositions, which, ensuring peace and tranquility, prohibit changes in the public order which might again involve it in bloody civil warfare. The expulsion of the Archbishop and the Bishop of Teya, who, abusing their lofty office as shepherds of the Church, and neglecting their duty as honorable and peaceful citizens, contributed to inflame discord, has been one of the dispositions weighed with deliberation and resolved upon with grief when it became apparent that it was necessary for the peace and well-being of the Republic.

In effect, let it be observed that, in a country like ours in which the Church forms a part of the State, it is indispensable for the government, in order to fulfil its delicate functions, to count on the cooperation of the head of the diocese; or, in other words, that the two authorities, in complete harmony in their duty, and reconciling their respective interests, proceed in perfect accord in all their dispositions. But, if the ecclesiastical authority bars the free course of the Administration, if, unfortunately, the two powers become hostile to each other, if even the lowest grades of the hierarchy of the Church, the vicars and the pastors, obeying their superiors or adhering, as is natural, to their opinions, and becoming the bulwark of the same interests, if these disagree with the departmental heads, the alcaldes and municipal governments, and, although the government asks that such grave errors be remedied, they refuse to comply, it is impossible to preserve internal tranquility, and civil war and anarchical chaos will be the deplorable result of such conflict.

Such was the embarrassing position from which the Government found itself obliged to rise, and such motives it had in mind when it decreed the expulsion of the Archbishop and the Bishop of Teya; and let it not be believed that this step wounds religion, because the latter does not subsist in the shadow of seditious prelates who have no care for the torrents of blood shed in order to revenge deeply rooted hatreds and satisfy material interests.

The reasoning public will judge this measure as a precaution, as a step counselled by prudence and the restoration of public order.

Moreover the government understands very well the duty it has of preserving the guarantees which common law and upright reason grant in favor of all the inhabitants of the Republic, and not only will it fulfil gladly its obligations to all citizens, but it will likewise dispense special protection to all religious communities and ecclesiastical persons, who, subscribing in what concerns them, to the prescriptions of public order, fulfil the requirements imposed on them by their holy ministry, in conformity with the precepts of the Gospel. (*Boletín Oficial*, vol. I, no. 15, p. 4, Oct. 24, 1871.)

Decree issued December 22, 1871 abolishing the tithes.

Ministry of Government, Justice and Ecclesiastical Affairs: The Provisional Government has considered it well to issue the following decree No. 43: Miguel García Granados, Captain General of the Army and Provisional President of the Republic of Guatemala, considering: that some municipalities have requested the government to suppress the tithes; that all the people resist the payment of this tax which has been recognized as unjust because it burdens one single class of society, and odious because its collection causes constant and unjustifiable vexation; that, in consequence, the civil authorities cannot give the necessary help to try to make the taxation effective; that, on the other hand, the Church and other participants in this income have current expenses which do not permit the giving up of the tithes unless they have some other income; that nevertheless, the Venerable Ecclesiastical Chapter has agreed with the government that the proposed project is under its jurisdiction according to Article V of the Concordat:

Article 1—While His Holiness and the Government of the Republic are regulating the manner of suppressing and of substituting for the tithes, these will be considered suppressed and there will be assigned for the same objects of that contribution 20,000 *pesos* annually, which, with the 4,000 *pesos* which the Church must contribute, according to Article V of the Concordat, will be paid by the General Treasury, in payments of 2,000 *pesos* monthly.

Article 2—This disposition will begin to take effect on January 1, 1872, at which date there will be considered cancelled all debts on tithes which proceed from a formal contract. These will be liquidated until the last day of the present month of December.

Given in the Palace of the Government of Guatemala, Dec. 22, 1871. Miguel García Granados.

Ministry of Government, Justice, and Ecclesiastical Affairs.

Francisco Albúrez—And by disposition of the Provisional President let this be printed, published and circulated.

(*National Archives of Guatemala*, Decree No. 43)

Article entitled "A Grandes Males, Grandes Remedios" in *El Crepúsculo* for April 13, 1872, commenting on the threat of the Government to expel from the country any person inciting to rebellion, by discourses, sermons, etc.

La conducta injustificable de los enemigos de las instituciones liberales entre los cuales se cuenta cierto número de individuos del clero, al tratar de concitar a la rebelión con sus escritos y discursos, ya en reuniones o en el púlpito, a los recalcitrantes y a los fanáticos, ha puesto el gobierno en la imperiosa necesidad de separarse del espíritu de política moderada y conciliadora que hasta aquí ha seguido, expidiendo un decreto severo, que es de esperarse hará entrar en razón a los que se muestren dispuestos a abusar de la bondad con que se les ha venido tratando. Para el bien del país y de los mismos sobre quienes pudiese caer la mano fuerte de la autoridad, confiamos en que no volveremos a oir las especies subversidas que en estos últimos días han llamado a la atención pública, con asombro de los buenos ciudadanos. He aquí el decreto a que aludimos: 'Toda persona que en discurso, sermones o en cualquier acto público, concite a su auditorio a la rebelión contra las autoridades constituídas, o produzca especies subversivas contra el orden público, será extrañada del territorio de la República sin forma ni figura de juicio. (*El Crepúsculo*, April 13, 1872, vol. I, no. 22)

Decree of May 24, 1872 formally abolishing in the Republic of Guatemala the Society of Jesus and confiscating its property.

Decree No. 59, May 24, 1872:

Artículo 1°— Se declara extinguida en la República la Comunidad Religiosa de los Padres de la Compañía de Jesus, no permitiéndose su ingreso a ella ni organizados en sociedad ni de otra manera alguna.

Artículo 2°—Se declaran nacionales los bienes que usufructuaban y que dejaban en la República, entre los cuales se comprende la hacienda de las Nubes, por no existir tampoco el Convento de la Merced a que pertenecía anteriormente.

Artículo 3°—Dichos bienes serán enagenados en pública subasta: los situados en este Departamento, por el Administración General de Rentas, y los ubicados en los otros, por los respectivos jefes políticos, como sub-delegados de Hacienda, quienes sacarán los bienes al asta pública por treinta días, y previo valuo, los venderán en el mejor postor, cuidando de que su producido entre en tesorería.

Artículo 4°—Si no hubiese licitador que haga una postura legal, los funcionarios antedichos pondrán en depósito los bienes y pedirán instrucciones al Ministro respectivo.

Artículo 5°—El apoderado y depositario que constituyeron los espresados Padres en esta ciudad al salir de ella, se pondrán de acuerdo con los funcionarios designados para la entrega por inventario de los bienes y productos que están a su cargo.

Dado en Guatemala, a veinticuatro de mayo de mil ochocientos setenta y dos, J. Rufino Barrios.

(*National Archives of Guatemala,* Decree No. 59, May 24, 1872)

Decree of May 28, 1872 granting to the inhabitants of the town of Palencia the former *Hacienda de Palencia* of the Dominicans, to be divided into small plots for each.

Palacio del Gobierno, Guatemala, 28 de mayo de 1872.

Habiendo la Comunidad de Santo Domingo devuelto al Gobierno la posesión de la hacienda de Palencia; y considerando que los habitantes de este lugar carecen de tierras para hacer sus sementeras; qué es conveniente formar centros de población y un deber de Gobierno proporcionarles los medios de que subsistan y progresen; el Teniente General, oídas las solicitudes que la Municipalidad y vecinos de Palencia le han elevado pidiendo el amparo del Gobierno; ha tenido a bien acordar:

1°—Se concede de ejido al pueblo de Palencia la legua cuadrada que señala la ley, en las tierras que componen la hacienda de este nombre, debiendo todos los habitantes de ésta reducirse a poblado dentro del menor término posible.

2°—Se comisiona al Agrimensor don Felix Vega para que haga la medida del mencionado ejido—Comuníquese—Rubricado por el señor Teniente General encargado de la Presidencia del Gobierno provisorio—Albúrez.

Protest of Vicar General Francisco A. Espinosa against Decrees No. 59 and 61, abolishing the religious orders and confiscating their goods, dated May 31, 1872.

Gobierno Metropolitano de Guatemala.

Señor Ministro de Gobernación, Justicia y Negocios Eclesiásticos:

Habiendo llegado a mis manos los Decretos números 59 y 61, expedidos por el Gobierno Provisorio, que sin comunicárseme oficialmente circulan ya impresos, y observando que en ellos se extinguen dos Comunidades Religiosas y se declaran nacionales sus bienes, el infrascito Gobernador del Arzobispado, de acuerdo con el Venerable Cabildo Metropolitano, a nombre de la Iglesia de Guatemala, protesta de la manera más solemne y terminante contra dichos Decretos, y contra los efectos que ellos produzcan, declinando toda la responsabilidad que pudiera resaltar en quien haya lugar, todo con arreglo a derecho, y especialmente a lo ordenado por el Santo Concilio de Trento. Espero que el Señor Ministro se sirva aceptar esta protesta, reservándome el derecho de publicar por la prensa los fundamentos que existen para hacerla.

Soy de Vd. muy atento S.S. Francisco A. Espinosa. Palacio Arzobispal de Guatemala, mayo 31 de 1872)

Decree abolishing all religious communities in the Republic of Guatemala, June 7, 1872.

The Secretary of Foreign Affairs, Ecclesiastical Affairs and Public Instruction. J. Rufino Barrios, Lieutenant General of the Army and in charge of the provisional government of the Republic:

Considering that the religious communities lack a purpose in the Republic, since they are not deposits of learning; that, being no longer able as in past centuries to lend important service to society, the transcendental defects inherent in associations of this

class have become all the more evident without being at all ex-
cusable; that the aforementioned institutions are by their nature
a handicap to the reforms of modern civilization, which proscribes
theocracy in the name of liberty, of progress, and of the sovereignty of the people; that, withdrawing themselves in the economic
order from the natural and beneficial laws of production and con-
sumption, they constitute an unjustifiable exception which weighs
down upon the producing class; that the aforementioned communities, owing their existence to the law, it is the right of the
latter to abolish them, and, consequently, to dispose of their goods
for the benefit of the public, and that, adhering to the principles
which govern the democratic revolution of Guatemala, it is an
inescapable consequence to order the extinction of the religious
communities, and in decreeing it, a duty of the government not to
provide these with the means of sustaining a new social position.

Therefore I have decreed and do decree:

Article 1—All communities of religious are abolished in the
Republic.

Article 2—The property and income which they possess are declared national.

Article 3—These goods and their income will be dedicated preferably to the maintenance and development of free public instruction.

Article 4—The secularized religious have absolute liberty to reside
wherever they wish or to leave the Republic if they so desire—
they may acquire possessions, dispose of them during their lives
or by testament; they may make contracts and enjoy all the rights
which the law grants to the other inhabitants, without any limita-
tions other than those imposed upon them by their state as secular ecclesiastics.

Article 5—As for the religious who wish to leave the Republic,
there will be paid their necessary expenses, and those who prefer
to remain become by that fact secularized, not being permitted to
wear any distinctive religious habit.

Article 6—The churches of the communities will be preserved with
their respective property and titles, as well as their sacred vessels,

jewels, ornaments and all that is destined to worship. In each one of the said churches there will be erected a parish to whose support the government will contribute.

Article 7—The libraries of the communities will be transferred to the library of the University.

Article 8—The public treasury will pay for one year to the secularized religious who have not yet been ordained as priests and to those prevented from exercising their ministry by old age or illness a pension of twenty-five *pesos* per month, the first monthly payment to be handed over on the day of the secularization.

Article 9—The aforementioned ministry is entrusted with the carrying out of this decree, giving the necessary instructions.

Given in Guatemala, in the National Palace, June 7, 1872.
J. Rufino Barrios.

Marco Aurelio Soto, Subsecretary of the Interior, in charge of the Ministry of Foreign Affairs, Ecclesiastical Affairs, and Public Instruction.

And by disposition of the Lieutenant General, in charge of the provisional presidency of the Republic, let it be printed, and published.   Guatemala, June 7, 1872—
—Soto—

Order of the Government dated Feb. 9, 1874 for the concentration of all the nuns in one convent, and the confiscation of their property.

Decreto Número 115:

Considerando que los principios que presidieron a la emisión del Decreto de 7 de junio de 1872, sobre comunidades de religiosos, demandan logica y convenientemente que se dicte una medida determinativa del estado y condición en que deben quedar muchos conventos de religiosas, beaterios, hermandades, órdenes, órdenes terceras y congregaciones existentes en la República:

Que el Gobierno si bien está en el caso de remover el obstáculo social y económico que ofrece la multiplicidad de conventos de monjas, debe consultar a las especiales consideraciones que merecen las religiosas profesas, por su sexo, y carácter contraído, para acordar una disposición concretada en cuanto a ellos, a la reducción de las localidades que ocupan y a la traslación consiguiente, en un solo local de las comunidades de religiosas que se rijen por reglas análogas:

Que tanto en la actualidad como para lo sucesivo, es necesario que quede reconocido y aplicado en absoluto, el principio de que el Estado no puede consentir nuevas profesiones con votos de perpetuidad, por entrañar éstas la renuncia de los derechos de la personalidad humana, suicidio moral que las sociedades y los Gobiernos no deben tolerar sino impedir resueltamente y sirviéndose de la autoridad basada en la ley;

Que la subsistencia de los conventos de comunidades de religiosas profesas, únicas que quedarán en atención a las consideraciones enunciadas, no obsta a que se aplique en todo su vigor al principio de libertad individual, por el que aún las personas vinculadas con los votos de la profesión, puedan desligarse de ellos por oponerse su perpetuidad a las leyes superiores e inviolables de la naturaleza; por tanto,

Decreto:

Artículo 1°—Dentro del término de diez y ocho días se verificará la reducción de los conventos de Religiosas, y se llevará a cabo la consiguiente traslación de las mismas al local que al efecto se designe.

Artículo 2°—Se declaran por completo suprimidos los Beaterios, Hermandades, Ordenes Terceras, y demás congregaciones de esta clase.

Artículo 3°—En consecuencia, se nacionalizan los edificios y sitios que desocupen las Monjas, Beatas, Hermandades y Ordenes, de que habla el artículo anterior.

Artículo 4°—Las religiosas que a virtud de la reducción de conventos y traslación decretada, prefieran su esclaustración, el Estado les reconocerá ese derecho y lo apoyará con su autoridad, proveyendo el Gobierno a la subsistencia de las religiosas que dejen el Convento, con la asignación a cada una de veinte pesos mensuales.

Dado en Guatemala, a nueve de febrero de mil ochocientos setenta y cuatro. J. Rufino Barrios.

El Secretario de Estado en los Despachos de Goberna-

ción, Justicia y Negocios Eclesiásticos.—Marco A. Soto.
(National Archives of Guatemala, Decree No. 115,
February 9, 1874)

PART THREE

Decree of Barrios granting to those Indians of Sacatepéquez who will wear the costume of the *ladino* the right to that name, dated Oct. 13, 1876.

Decreto Número 165:

Artículo único: Para los efectos legales, se declaran ladinos a los indíjenas de ambos sexos del mencionado pueblo de San Pedro Sacatepéquez, quienes usarán desde el año próximo entrante el traje que corresponde a la clase indiana. Dado en Guatemala, en el Palacio Nacional, a trece de Octubre del año mil ochocientos setenta y seis. J. Rufino Barrios — El Ministro de Gobernación, Justicia y Negocios Eclesiásticos, J. Barberena.

(Recopilación de Leyes de Guatemala, vol. I.)

Excerpt from Dr. Melvin Tumin's Study on Social Relations among the Indians:

Both ladino and Indian children are exposed at an early age to religious training, accompanying their parents to church and in the case of the Indians, to the religious clubs as well; joining in religious processions, attending Masses, learning catechism and other devotions, and sometimes going through preparation for confirmation. In later life it is expected that ladino women and Indian men shall take care of the important religious performances and the patterns of these expectations are laid down in early childhood. Ladino women and Indian men mutually respect each other's devoutness, and tend to view with regret the total absence of any overt manifestation of it in ladino men. They refrain, however, from comment on the religious practices of Indian women, from whom none too great involvement in such matters is expected. (Tumin, Melvin M., *San Luis Jilotepéquez, A Study in Social Relations*, p. 72)

Decree of Barrios dated April 26, 1881 requiring a civil ceremony for the legalization of every marriage.

"La Asamblea Nacional Lejislativa de la República de Guatemala decreta:

1°—La ley respeta y garantiza la libertad de todos los habitantes de la República para celebrar matrimonio religioso con las solemnidades del culto a que pertenezcan, y solo exije que previamente se cumplan las disposiciones civiles, contrayendo el matrimonio civil.

2°—El ministro de cualquier culto que proceda a las ceremonias religiosas de un matrimonio, sin que se le exhiba certificación competente de estar celebrado ya el civil, según las circumstancias debe pagar la multa conveniente.

3°—Los que sin haver verificado el matrimonio civil, contrajeren él que se reputo clandestino, sufrirán la pena del artículo 2; pero si hubiese intervención o participación voluntaria en aquel acto por parte del Ministro del culto, éste, lo mismo que todos los que resultarán ser instigadores, serán castigados con la misma pena que los contrayentes.

4°—Cuando el infractor de la ley fuese insolvente o se resistiese al pago de la multa, se hará aplicación de lo dispuesto en el artículo 443 del Código Civil.

5°—Las personas que pretendan contraer el matrimonio civil, pueden, a su arbitrio, presentar esposición escrita solicitando, u occurrir de palabra con el mismo objeto a la autoridad respectiva, la cual, deberá levantar una acta, y previo todos los demás requisitos y formalidades legales, proceder a la celebración.

6°—En caso de peligro inminente de muerte de uno o de ambos contrayentes, el funcionario ante quien debe celebrarse el matrimonio civil podrá autorizarlo sin observar las solemnidades que no sea posible llenar y que establece el decreto de 21 de noviembre de 1879, que es vigente siempre que no haya algún impedimento ostensible y evidente.

Pasa el Gobierno para su publicación y complimiento — Dado en el salón de Sesiones, abril 26, 1881. (*Recopilación de Leyes de la República de Guatemala*, vol. II, p. 571)

A SURVEY OF STATE AND CHURCH IN GUATEMALA

1524 *Conquest of Guatemala by Alvarado*
Accompanied by three priests, two Franciscans, one secular priest, don Juan Godinez, as Chaplain to the forces with the purpose of conquering " peacefully " the Indians.

1529 *Part of Viceroyalty of Mexico*
Church in Guatemala under jurisdiction of Mexican hierarchy.
Church, under *patronato real*, was an arm of the government, fostered obedience to king, who had absolute control of all ecclesiastical appointments.

1537 *Bishopric erected in Guatemala*
don Francisco Marroquín, first Bishop

1542 *Captaincy General erected in Guatemala*
Government had the powerful support of the clergy. High ecclesiastics met in the Assembly with the civil authorities.
Ecclesiastical authorities received copies of decrees, acts, documents, etc.
Government attended ecclesiastical functions in a body.
Government exercised authority in minutest details over Church.

1743 *Guatemala erected into Archbishopric*
On petition of Philip V.

1811 *Revolt in San Salvador and in Granada*
Some members of the clergy took great part in movement for independence. Archbishop Casáus protested against it.

1812 *Churchmen took part in Cortes in Spain*
Out of 13 nominees for delegate from Guatemala, 6 were ecclesiastics
The ecclesiastic, don Antonio Larrazábal, was named delegate—zeal led to his imprisonment by King.
Clergy helped to draw up resolutions to present for the Constitution to be promulgated.
Constitution sworn to by clergy in presence of Archbishop.

1813 *Conspiracy of Belén*

Members of clergy with leading civilians and military officials plan revolt; discovered and punished.

1814 *Second Uprising in San Salvador*

Under leadership of Fr. Nicolás Aguilar, ally of Dr. Delgado.

1818 *Movement for Independence accelerated*

Participation of some ecclesiastics in *Tertulia patriótica*, intellectual movement toward independence.

Opposition of Archbishop and certain higher ecclesiastics.

1820 *Spanish Revolution*

Radical Cortes convoked—adoption of measures obnoxious to Church.

(a) Inquisition abolished

(b) Tithes suppressed

(c) Much ecclesiastical property confiscated

Many of higher clergy felt that independence would be a lesser evil than submission to these radicals in power in Spain, and therefore joined the movement for separation from the Mother Country.

1821 *Declaration of Independence in America*

Many Spanish officials and members of the higher clergy joined with the *criollos*, in working for independence. Although the Archbishop had opposed the movement at first, he was named in the Act of Independence second only to the Provincial Deputation, and with him were named the Superiors of the Religious Orders and the Ecclesiastical Chapter.

Many eminent members of the clergy spoke in favor of independence at the Assembly and signed the Act.

The Act of Independence included the following articles referring to the Church:

(a) a solemn Mass of Thanksgiving to be offered with all honors and ceremonies at which the civil authorities will assist.

(b) The status of the Catholic Religion which has always been professed in the past, maintaining the strong religious spirit which has always distinguished

Guatemala, respecting the Ministers of the Church,
secular and religious, and protecting their persons and
property, was to remain unchanged.

(c) the Superiors and Prelates of the Religious orders
in order to maintain the peace so necessary when a
change occurs in the government, will exhort their
subjects to spread fraternity and concord among the
people and try to put an end to discord.

(d) that this Act of Independence be sworn to by the
Provisional Government, the municipal government,
the illustrious Archbishop, tribunals, political and military heads, the religious orders, officials and employees
of the government, corporations, and troops of the
respective garrisons.

1822 *Annexation of the Province of Guatemala to Mexico*
Among other provisions, the *Plan de Iguala*, set up by
the new empire in Mexico under Iturbide, offered preservation of the Roman Catholic religion and clerical
privileges, inducements which won the support of many
ecclesiastics in Guatemala.

1823 *Central American Confederation*
Catholicism was to be the state religion, and public exercise of all the others forbidden.

Clergy took active part in the Congress.

The President of the National Constitutional Assembly
was the ecclesiastic, don José Matías Delgado.

Gradually, the influence of the Church and clergy, always
outstanding heretofore, seemed to weaken and Liberals
were able to pass many anti-clerical laws:

(a) Order abolishing sale of *Bulas de Cruzada*

(b) All pastorals of the Archbishop must have approbation of the Chief Executive (reply to violently anti-
republican pastorals of Archbishop)

(c) all appointments of Archbishop to benefices must
first have approbation of the Chief Executive

(d) Pastors were deprived of service and rations which
they had enjoyed.

(e) Clergy were no longer important, to be exempted
from payment of *alcabala*, or import duty

(f) The tithes contribution was reduced by one-half.

(g) Superiors were forbidden to perform any acts of obedience to superiors-general in Spain.

(h) The reception of subjects under 23 years of age, and profession of subjects under 25 years of age were forbidden in all the convents of the Republic.

1826-29 Conflict between Liberals (*criollos*, professional men, less privileged under colonial system), and the Conservatives (higher clergy, colonial nobility, landowners and wealthy merchants).

1829 Many Conservatives, the Archbishop and religious were exiled, when Liberals came into power.

1830 *Régime of Francisco Morazán, leader of Liberals*
Program of anti-clerical reforms instituted by Mariano Gálvez, right arm of Morazán
(a) separation of Church and State—toleration of all religions
(b) suppression of religious orders and confiscation of their property
(c) establishment of civil marriage and divorce
(d) right of appointing to ecclesiastical office declared proper to the nation and to be exercised by President
(e) secularization of cemeteries
(f) restriction of number of church holidays
(g) nuns permitted to leave their convents with restoration of dowry

1837 *Revolution bringing Carrera to fore*
Uprising of Indians under Carrera
(a) Indians irritated by new penal laws
(b) Indians said to be influenced by interpretation of cholera as deliberately caused by existing government

1838 *Federal Government of Central America declared dissolved*
Complete independence of Guatemala
All laws of Gálvez suspended
Catholic religion was once more state religion

1839-65 *Rafael Carrera in power under Conservatives*
Strong government allied with aristocrats and high clergy, and landowners who desired peace and protection

Restoration of religious orders

Reestablishment, in part, of clerical privileges

Church granted representation in Congress in 1851 —

Chapter granted two delegates

Concordat with Holy See—1852

Gradual growth of dissatisfaction on the part of the Conservatives when Carrera refused to restore all the privileges of the clergy and opposed Church taxes.

1865-1871 *Rule of Vincent Cerna—Conservative*

Warm friend of Church

Accused of partiality toward the Jesuits.

Policy of Carrera continued for the most part

Overthrown by Liberals in 1871.

1871 *Liberals in power under control of Rufino Barrios*

Miguel García Granados, President — did bidding of Barrios

Measures against the Church

(a) Expulsion of Jesuits

(b) Suppression of tithes

(c) Expulsion of religious orders and confiscation of their goods

(d) Expulsion of Archbishop Piñol y Aycinena and Auxiliary Bishop Ortiz Urrutia

1873 *Justo Barrios as President*

(a) Complete separation of Church and State

(b) Abolition of all ecclesiastical privileges.

(c) Suppression of religious orders of women, confiscation of their goods, but pensions granted to expelled members.

(d) 1879—Constitution with anti-clerical laws still extant. The influence of the Church in Guatemala permanently destroyed.

1885 *Manuel Lisandro Barillas—Liberal*

No change in relations between Church and State

Continued policy as firmly established by Barrios.

1892-98 *José María Reyna Barrios—Liberal*
Despot whose attitude toward the Church was generally like that of his predecessors.
However, he made some concessions
(a) permitted the seminaries to be reopened
(b) permitted the return of the exiled Archbishop Casanova y Estrada.

1898-1920 *Manuel Estrada Cabrera—Liberal*
Church State relations remained practically the same

1920-21 *Carlos Herrera—Liberal*
Church—State relations the same

1921-26 *José María Orelana—Liberal*
Expulsion of the Archbishop, don Luis Múñoz y Capurón, one month after his consecration, together with all those who had ever had any connection with Jesuits
Constant complaints of Government to Ecclesiastic authorities of subversive activity on the part of pastors.

1926-30 *Lázaro Chacón—Liberal*
No important change in Church-State relations. Election brought about through intervention of the United States during his rule.

1931-1944 *Jorge Ubico*
Much material progress
Made a few concessions to the Church
Permitted a few members of religious orders to enter country

1944 *July Palace Revolution*
Gen. Federico Ponce became President—
October triumvirate which promised free elections — don Jorge Toriello, Major Arana and Capt. Arbonz
Oct. 20, 1944 — Juan José Arévalo — because President.
His administration accused of being opposed to Church

1638, Apr. 10. The President of the Audiencia, using the privilege of the *Vice Patronato Real*, granted permission to the Confraternity of the Holy Scapular of *Nuestra Señora del Carmen* to construct a hermitage. (Pardo, *Efemérides*, p. 53)

1651, Nov. 4. The Syndicate Procurator of the Municipal Government protested the permission granted by the Act of the *Audiencia* on Oct. 31, to erect in the city of Santiago a hospice of his order to Fr. Juan de la Plata y Aldana, Carmelite, because of a royal decree of September 14, 1588, prohibiting it, since said decree permitted in the Indies only convents of the Order of Discalced Carmelites. (Pardo, *Efemérides*, p. 62)

1675, June 22. A royal decree authorizing the convent of Discalced Carmelites under the protection of Santa Teresa de Jesús. (Pardo, *Efemérides*, p. 85)

1676, Feb. 13. His Majesty authorized the opening of the Convent of Discalced Carmelites. (Pardo, *Efemérides*, p. 85)

1682, Mar. 17. Decree of His Majesty ordered that the President and the Bishop should proceed to revise the accounts and lands assigned for the establishment of the University of San Carlos. (Pardo, *Efemérides*, p. 95)

1686, June 9. Royal Decree permitting the Franciscans to occupy the Chair for the study of Duns Scotus, *ad honorem*, in the University of San Carlos. (Pardo, *Efemérides*, p. 102)

1693, Sept. 12. Decree of His Majesty authorizing the foundation of the Convent of Santa Clara under the rule of St. Francis. (Pardo, *Efemérides*, p. 114)

1696, Aug. 16. The Audiencia carried out the royal decree in which His Majesty granted the circulation of the Pontifical Brief confirming the Congregation of *Nuestra Señora de Belén* in Guatemala. (Pardo, *Efemérides*, p. 118)

1696, Aug. 21. The Municipal Government received a letter from Fr. Rodrigo in which he declared that on March 17 His Holiness had confirmed the existence of the Congregation of *Nuestra Señora de Belén* (granted circulation by His Majesty August 9th). (Pardo, *Efemérides*, p. 119)

1700, July 16. Royal Decree permitting the foundation of the *Colegio de Cristo Crucificado de propaganda Fide*. (Pardo, *Efemérides*, p. 126)

1712, Sept. 7. Letter of the *Audiencia* to His Majesty, asking permission for Fray Juan de Medellín to build a hermitage dedicated to *Nuestra Señora de Guadalupe*. His Majesty, by Royal Decree of Jan. 19, 1714, did not authorize the erection of this hermitage, but did consent to the building of a chapel to *Nuestra Señora de Guadalupe* in the Cathedral. (Pardo, *Efemérides,* p. 139)

1717, April 12. Royal Decree approving the erection of the Chair of Philosophy in the University of San Carlos to be served by a Friar of the Order of St. Francis. Fr. Antonio de Lizarraga was named the first Professor to fill this post. (Pardo, *Efemérides,* p. 144)

1717, May 15. In a decree of this date the King spoke of the grave disorders which followed the increase in monasteries either because the regular clergy made themselves exempt and became a burden on the community, or because it lessened the number of workers in the colony. He ordered demolished the convent of the Franciscans in Mendoza which had been built without royal permission. He prohibited from that date the foundation of convents and hospitals by religious orders in the Indies and ordered the Captain-General of Guatemala, if any houses were built in that country by religious orders without royal permission, to have them destroyed, since his duty to the King demanded it. (Carrillo, *Historia de la América Central,* vol. III, p. 132)

1721, Aug. 13. The Municipal Government in Special Chapter carried out the royal decree of Nov. 17, 1720 asking for information concerning the advisability of the foundation of the Convent of *Nuestra Señora del Pilar de Zaragoza,* as the nuns of Madrid had requested. (Pardo, *Efemérides,* p. 150)

1725, May 5. Royal decree authorizing the foundation of the Convent of *Nuestra Señora del Pilar de Zaragoza* (Capuchin Nuns). (Pardo, *Efemérides,* p. 159)

1730, May 14. The Municipal Government in obedience to the ordinance of His Majesty began proceedings for the reconstruction of the Church of *Nuestra Señora de las Mercedes* and the erection of the Church and Convent of *Nuestra Señora del Pilar de Zaragoza.* (Pardo, *Efemérides,* p. 169)

1740, Jan. 31. Royal Decree ordering the *Audiencia* to suppress those confraternities erected without permission of the Ordinary and dictating a providence to avoid abuses on the part of the administration, to protect the natives in this way. (Pardo, *Efemérides*, p. 187)

1744, June 2. His Majesty ordered that the hermitage of San José be closed since permission was not obtained for its construction, according to the laws of the *patronato real.* He ordered, besides, that the *Fiscal* of the *Audiencia* who officiated in this matter be fined. (Pardo, *Efemérides*, p. 196)

1763, Oct. 6. Having finished investigations to determine whether or not the *Colegio de San Jerónimo* was founded with royal permission, the *Fiscal* asked that, since there was no such permission, the *colegio* be closed. (Pardo, *Efemérides, p. 225*)

1765, July 3. Royal Decree prohibiting the existence of the *Colegio de San Jerónimo*, erected by the Friars of the Order of *La Merced* without the permission of the King. (Pardo, *Efemérides*, p. 236)

1766, Nov. 4. Royal Provision declaring that only with the permission of the *Vice Patron Real* might buildings be erected destined as centers or institutions of religious character. (Pardo, *Efemérrides*, p. 232)

NO ECCLESIASTIC ORGANIZATION WITHOUT KING'S PERMISSION

1534, Dec. 18. Erection of Bishopric of Guatemala as suffragan of the See of Seville, by order of the Emperor. (Vilanova Meléndez, *Apuntamientos de Historia Patria Eclesiástica*, p. 16)

1602, May 15. His Majesty ordered that the Confraternities of Negroes, Indians and Mulattoes be always under the vigilance of the priest entrusted with the spiritual care of the villages. (Pardo, *Efemérides*, p. 36)

1607. In the year 1607 the King ordered the reincorporation of the diocese of Verapaz into that of Guatemala, the administration of the villages of that province to remain as heretofore in the hands of the Dominicans. (Milla, *Historia de la América Central*, vol. II, p. 239)

1624, July 14. His Majesty ordains that there be preferred for service in parishes those who had studied in the *Colegio de Santo Tomás de Aquino.* (Pardo, *Efemérides*, p. 46)

1732-1736. The Cathedral Church of *Ciudad Real* found itself lacking in funds, and, in order to obtain some, its Chapter wrote to the King, declaring that the income from the *diezmos* was insufficient for the necessities, as could be seen in the report from the period 1732-1736; it asked, therefore, that there be granted what was needed, in addition to a sum for the construction of altars and embellishments. (Carrillo, *Historia de la América Central*, vol. III, p. 75)

1742. A letter from the King asking information concerning the above from the Captain General of Guatemala. (Carrillo, *Historia de la América Central*, vol. II, p. 75)

1750, Dec. 15. A reply of the Captain General of Guatemala to the above letter of the King, declaring that what the Chapter had said of the matter was true, and it would be fitting to increase the income of the cathedral from 200 to 300 *pesos* for each prebendary and to add from 10 to 12 thousand for other exigencies—these funds could be taken from the *reales novenos*, and from the minor vacancies of the said cathedral. The matter hung in the air for a long time, but finally the King conceded the *novenos* of the *diezmos* of the province and besides 4,000 *pesos* from the treasury of *Ciudad Real*. (Carrillo, *Historia de la América Central*, vol. III, p. 75)

ROYAL PERMISSION REQUIRED FOR ALL CLERICS GOING TO THE INDIES

1571, July 20. The government of the city of Guatemala requested His Majesty to send Franciscans to augment the number already there. (Pardo, *Efemérides*, p. 20)

1736, April 20. The Municipal Government agreed to solicit His Majesty to send missionaries for the reduction and catechising of the infidels. (Pardo, *Efemérides*, p. 180)

1542, Nov. 20. The Council of the Indies proposed Bartolomé de las Casas for the bishopric of Chiapas when that became vacant. The Emperor Carlos V sent the decree naming him to that bishopric. (Milla, *Historia de la América Central*, vol. II, p. 18)

1596, Feb. 18. Esteban de Adarzo y Santandar, Procurator General of the Municipal Government of Madrid, announced that

His Majesty had named as the Bishop of Verapaz, Dr. Calderón, who had been filling the charge of Chancellor of the Cathedral of the *Nuevo Reino de Granada*. (Pardo, *Efemérides*, p. 33)

KING NAMED BISHOPS WITHOUT PAPAL CONFIRMATION

1641. There arose in the year 1641 a grave ecclesiastical question. The Chapter or *Cabildo* received notice of a royal decree naming as a bishop of Guatemala Dr. don Bartolomé Gonzales Soltero and ordering transferred to the See of Arequipa Dr. don Augustín Ugarte y Saravía. Without any delay the Chapter declared the see of Guatemala vacant—which announcement was declared null and void by the Bishop. He founded his protest on the fact that he had not yet received the Pontifical Bulls of his promotion to another diocese, and hence could not consider his connection with the see of Guatemala at an end. Angry, the Chapter requested the *Audiencia* to have recourse to force, and the latter, as was to be expected, decided against the protest of the Bishop, and declared that the latter had no case. (Milla, *Historia de la América Central*, vol. II, p. 287)

1641, May 28. The Venerable Ecclesiastical Chapter received and carried out the royal decree in which it was announced that the Illustrious señor don Augustín de Ugarte y Saravía was transferred from the bishopric of Guatemala to that of Arequipa. (Pardo, *Efemérides*, p. 55)

1668, Feb. 4. There departed from the city of Santiago Bishop Payo Enríquez de Rivera bound for Michoacán to take charge of the bishopric there—which office he never filled, because meanwhile His Majesty the King named him Archbishop of Mexico. (Pardo, *Efemérides*, p. 77)

1676, Sept. 21. The King presented Dr. don Juan de Ortega y Montañés as Bishop of Guatemala and the latter began to govern his flock by royal decree until the month of November when the pontifical bulls arrived. (Batres Jáuregui, *La América Central ante la Historia*, vol. II, p. 351)

1683, March 24. By royal decree Fray Andrés de las Navas y Quevedo took charge of the See of Guatemala, although the bulls did not arrive until December 27th of that year. (Batres Jáuregui, *La América Central ante la Historia*, vol. II, p. 351)

ECCLESIASTICAL TERRITORIAL BOUNDARIES SET BY KING

1538. His Majesty approved the separation of the territory of
Chiapas from the bishopric of Guatemala and its erection into the
new diocese of *Ciudal Real.* (Vilanova Meléndez, *op. cit.*, p. 19)

1539. The Emperor declared the separation of the territory of
Vera Paz from the diocese of Guatemala and its erection into a
diocese under Pedro de Angulo. (Fernández, Alonso, *Historia
Eclesiástica de Nuestros Tiempos*, p. 143.)

1542. When the sees of Oaxaca and Guatemala had a dispute
over boundaries, they had recourse to the royal authority. Carlos
V issued a decree defining the said boundaries with the admoni-
tion "... por ende yo vos mando que tornéis a ver los dichos
limites y si vieredes que están bien hechos, proveáis que se guarden
y, porque soy informado que entre los dichos obispos hay ciertas
diferencias sobre algunos pueblos, proveed en ello lo que vieredes
que más convenga." (Cuevas, *Historia de la Iglesia en México,*
vol. I, p. 352)

1608, June 23. His Majesty disposed that the bishopric of Vera
Paz, because of lack of income, be annexed to that of Guatemala.
(Pardo, *Efemérides*, p. 38)

1717, July 7. The Royal Audiencia obeyed the decree of His
Majesty requesting information as to the economic status, income, jurisdiction, etc. to determine whether it would be wise or
not to raise the Cathedral church of Guatemala to the rank of
Archbishopric. (Pardo, *Efemérides*, p. 145)

1740, August 17. Act of the Council of the Indies accompanying
documents concerning the erection of the Cathedral of Guatemala
to the rank of Archbishopric. (Pardo, *Efemérides*, p. 187)

1769. The government of Spain decreed in May, 1769 that the
ecclesiastical jurisdiction of *Ciudad Vieja* be divided in two. The
governor Salazar protested because of the financial hardships such
a division would cause the Indians. The King, impressed by the
reasoning of Salazar, suspended the execution of this law and
asked the *Audiencia* to study the matter and consult the bishop
in regard to it. (*Royal Providencia*, dated Feb. 6, 1772)

1786, Feb. 16. A royal decree ordered Petén added to the diocese
of Guatemala. (Batres Jáuregui, *La América Central ante la Historia*, vol. II, p. 88)

THE KING HAD POWER OF PRESENTATION

1530, June 3. Don Pedro Alvarado, in his capacity of *Vice Patron Real*, presented don Francisco Marroquín as pastor of the church of Guatemala. (Batres Jáuregui, *La América Central ante la Historia*, vol. II, p. 77)

1733, Jan. 20. The Municipal Government carried out the royal decree of Sept. 10, 1732, in which His Majesty asked to be informed of the number of clerics and number of missions served by the Dominicans in the Province of Tzendales. The King desired that these *doctrinas*, or missions and stations, be given into the charge of the secular clergy. (Pardo, *Efemérides*, p. 173)

THE KING CHASTISED RECALCITRANT CLERGY

1553, May 22. In a decree of this date the King requested the Bishop to inform him regarding the presence of religious and priests who were giving scandal, or who were refugees from other bishoprics and now in Guatemala. He asked him to treat the good friars better, to correct those whose lives were irregular and expel those known to be vicious and those who had deserted their monasteries elsewhere. (Milla, *Historia de la América Central*, vol. II, p. 111)

1567, Nov. 3. A decree of His Majesty reprimanding the Bishop, Bernardino Villapando, for having named clergy to serve in the *doctrinas* without previous presentation to the *Vice Patron Real*, who was the President of the *Audiencia*. (Pardo, *Efemérides*, p. 18)

1737, Sept. Bishop Pardo de Figueroa, as soon as he had arrived in the city of Guatemala, showed himself little disposed to manifest the necessary consideration for the *Audiencia*, scorning the *patronato real*, old customs, and even the courtesy expected from his office. The King sent a decree *May 7, 1740* reminding the bishop and the *Audiencia* of their respective duties, although according to the sovereign, the bishop had shown himself at greater fault. (Carrillo, *Historia de la América Central*, vol. III, p. 256)

1778, April 20. Decree of King ordering the Captain General of Guatemala to inform Archbishop Pedro Córtez y Lárraz that he was to return to Spain at once because of his opposition to the removal of the capital of the said province from Antigua, decreed by the King July 21, 1775. The king requested the Captain General likewise to watch the conduct of all ecclesiastics opposed to the transferral, in order to take the severest measures if necessary. (Vilanova Meléndez, *Apuntamientos*, pp. 19, 20)

THE KING ADMINISTERED THE TITHES AND ALLOCATED INCOME

1548, Jan. 16. His Majesty in view of the fact that the work on the Cathedral was not yet completed extended the grant of two *novenos* for six months more. (Pardo, *Efemérides*, p. 11)

1552, Jan. 31. His Majesty assigned new incomes for the construction of the Cathedral. (Pardo, *Efemérides*, p. 12)

1588, April 6. A royal provision established that no confessor to the Indians might be heir to the possessions of the penitents of his ministration, or of the relatives of his penitents. (Pardo, *Efemérides*, p. 31)

1598. In 1598 the Municipal Government wrote to the King telling him of the necessity of providing assistance to the *Seminario Tridentino* of Guatemala, and asking that there be assigned to it the *novenos* of the *diezmos* of the bishopric which had been vacant for seven years. (Milla, *Historia de la América Central*, vol. II, p. 211)

1602, June 16. His Majesty ordered that financial aid be given to the *Colegio Seminario de Nuestra Señora de la Asunción.* (Pardo, *Efemérides*, p. 36)

1658, Jan. 22. Royal provisions declaring that the expenses of the Ecclesiastical Visitors (*Visitadores*) must be taken from the funds of the native communities. (Pardo, *Efemérides*, p. 66)

1705, Nov. 15. Royal decree granting permission to the Brothers of the Order of *Nuestra Señora de Belén* to seek alms to cover the expenses of the beatification and canonization processes for Hermano Pedro. (Pardo, *Efemérides*, p. 133)

1758, May 18. Royal decree suppressing payment of *synods* to the priests in charge of the *doctrinas*, consisting of 50,000 *maravedis* for each group of 400 natives. There was to remain only the payment of 72½ *maravedis* for each tributary annually. (Pardo, *Efemérides*, p. 215)

1774, Oct. 19. Don Carlos, desiring obedience to the laws concerning the administration of the tithes of the churches of America, collecting and distributing them in the manner ordered and effecting successfully the collection of the *real novenos* and of the major and minor vacancies, despatched a royal decree dated from San Lorenzo Oct. 19, 1774, declaring that said churches could no longer continue to name *contadores de diezmos*, a faculty which the King reserved to himself, so that in no case would these employments be conceded to one's heirs, or be perpetual, purchasable or renounced. He declared that many times before attention had been called to this matter, but without result, the administration having been carried on with great loss to the royal treasury through the carelessness of those whose duty it was to defend the royal rights. Don Carlos manifested that the *diezmos* were patrimonial goods of the Crown. He also reminded the governors-general that, as *Vice Patrons*, they would name provisionally the *contadores*, while he provided the property and trusted the archbishops and bishops of *Nueva España*, Guatemala and the other provinces of the new world to see that what the King ordered in this matter was duly carried out. (Carrillo, *Historia de la América Central*, vol. V, p. 76)

THE KING FIXED RENTAL RATES OF BENEFICES

1560, Sept. 1. In view of the fact that the bishopric of Verapaz lacked sufficient funds for its maintenance, the King ordered that the Royal Treasury of Guatemala hand over to it annually 50,-000 *maravedis*. (Pardo, *Efemérides*, p. 16)

1572, Jan. 27. His Majesty declared that the royal officials would collect the emoluments assigned to the bishops from the day on which they took possession of their sees and not from the date of their nomination. (Pardo, *Efemérides*, p. 20)

THE KING AS AN ECCLESIASTICAL JUDGE

1600. In the cloisters even there were sides taken by the *peninsulares* and the *criollos*, the latter claiming the right to alternate with the former in the prelacies. Carried to the court, the matter was decided by the King in favor of the natives of the country. (Milla, *Historia de la América Central*, vol. II, p. 311)

1739. By a royal decree of 1739 don Felipe V ordered the *Audiencia* of Guatemala not to condemn women in the future to be enclosed in convents for crimes committed against civil law. The *Audiencia* of Guatemala had condemned one Tomasa Morán, accomplice in the murder of her husband, to ten years imprisonment in a convent, since there were no prisons for this purpose at the time in Guatemala.   (Carrillo, *Historia de la América Central,* vol. III, p. 257)

Section II—The Transitional Period

THE MUNICIPAL GOVERNMENT CONCERNED WITH PROTOCOL

1629, Jan. 16. The Municipal Government declared that in conformity with the act of the *Real Audiencia* the *alcaldes* and *regidores* should carry candles of one pound weight and bearing engraved the arms of the city, in order to assist at the festivity of *Nuestra Señora de Candelaria.*   (Pardo, *Efemérides,* p. 59)

1644, Feb. 16. The Municipal Government took San Francisco de Paula as patron and titular saint of the Armada of Barlovento to pursue the pirates and corsairs molesting the coast.   (Pardo, *Efemérides,* p. 57)

1654, July 17. The Municipal Government agreed to swear to defend and sustain the Mystery of the Immaculate Conception. (Pardo, *Efemérides,* p. 64)

1658, Dec. 1. The Municipal Government announced that, since notice had been received of the coming of the Bishop of the diocese, two members of the Chapter were to go to give His Lordship welcome.   (Pardo, *Efemérides,* p. 67)

1685, Dec. 26. The Municipal Government, in view of the fact that the Rev. Rector of the Parish of *Nuestra Señora de los Remedios,* José de Lara, declared in a sermon that this body did not cooperate in the propagation of the faith, agreed to protest to the authorities.   On this occasion the members of the Municipal Government left the Church edifice in protest.   (Pardo, *Efemérides,* p. 101)

1684, Jan. 4. The Municipal Government declared that it was not obliged to go in a body to the door of the Chapter Room to welcome and say goodbye to the Superiors of Religious Orders. (Pardo, *Efemérides*, p. 101)

1704, March 28. By motion of the Syndicate Procurator, the Municipal Government solicited His Majesty to intercede with His Holiness concerning the canonization of Hermano Pedro de San José de Betancour. (Pardo, *Efemérides*, p. 101)

1726, Sept. 27. The *Alcaldes* and Chapter members ordered that for the good success of all their business with His Majesty for the benefit of the citizens of Guatemala and the Province, the names of all the patron saints which they had should be placed in a hat and then one be drawn out, to be considered as a special advocate or intercessor for their intentions and that they order a mass said in his honor. . . . This being done, the name of St. Nicholas Tolentino was drawn out. (Pardo, *Efemérides*, p. 162)

1737, Sept. 10. From the year 1736 (Nov. 18), date of the taking possession of the bishopric by the *Chantre* Dr. Manuel Cayetano Fallo de la Cueva, in the name of Bishop Fr. Pedro Pardo Figueroa, the Municipal Government entered into strained relations with the Ecclesiastical Chapter because it refused to grant the places assigned in ceremonies to the former. Now, because the date was approaching for the receiving of Bishop Pardo y Figueroa himself, the Municipal Government declared that it would not attend unless the ceremonial be respected, the municipal government being placed at the left side of the Bishop's Chair and the members of the Ecclesiastical Chapter at the right. . . . These dispositions and others wounded the pride of Pardo y Figueroa, who did all in his power to place obstacles in the way of the projects of the Municipal Government. (Pardo, *Efemérides*, p. 182)

1738, June 3. The determination of the Municipal Government on refusing to attend functions when Bishop Pardo y Figueroa attended proved continuously the state of the relations between them. (Pardo, *Efemérides*, p. 184)

1738, July 18. The Municipal Government, considering the great distance between Guatemala and the Archbishopric of Mexico, the importance of these provinces and other things, agreed to move toward requesting the elevation of Guatemala into an archbishopric. This project was agreed upon, but at the end of the Chapter it seems to have been nullified in view of the fact of "haber reconocido que la ciudad no debe promover este negocio, respecto a que la cédula no habló con ella . . ." It is necessary to record that the relations between the Municipal Government and Bishop, don Figueroa were "*bastante frías*". (Pardo, *Efemérides*, p. 183)

1740, Nov. 18. Up to now we have seen the lack of harmony between the Municipal Government and Bishop Pardo de Figueroa, due to the slight felt by the former at not receiving certain seats at public functions. On this date, Bishop Pardo de Figueroa made a visit to the Municipal Government in order to invite it to attend a certain religious function "*sin asignar nada del ceremonial*", to which invitation the municipal government did not respond and the bishop was forced to cede to the request of the members of the Chapter—the placing of seats at the left side of the chair of the Bishop. (Pardo, *Efemérides*, p. 188)

THE CHURCH USED AS A WHIP BY THE MUNICIPAL GOVERNMENT

1723, July 23. The Municipal Government asked Bishop to impose ecclesiastical sanctions with the object of recovering the original manuscript of the *Recordación Florida*, work written by Captain Francisco Antonio de Fuentes y Guzman. (Pardo, *Efemérides*, p. 155)

1723, Sept. 7. The *Alcalde* Captain Miguel de Uria handed over to the Municipal Government two "*Libros Ystoriales que izo Capitán don Francisco de Fuentes* para que se guarden en el archivo . . ." (Pardo, *Efemérides*, p. 155)

1725, Feb. 16. Two manuscript copies of *Norte Político*, work of Captain Francisco de Fuentes y Guzman, were deposited in the archives of the Municipal Government. (Pardo, *Efemérides*, p. 158)

1735, July 29. The Syndicate Procurator presented a memorial before the *Audiencia*, asking that there be promulgated again the Bull of ecclesiastical immunity, in view of the fact that some criminal took shelter in holy places and then came out to commit new crimes.

1738, July 10. Letter of Municipal Government to the Superiors of Religious Orders requesting them to instruct the priests working among the natives to increase the ·production of wheat and send more supplies to the capital. (Pardo, *Efemérides*, p. 185)

1748, June 28. The Syndicate Procurator asked for authority to request the Archbishop to promulgate censures for the return of different books belonging to the Chapter and other documents of the secret archives. (Pardo, *Efemérides*, p. 200)

THE CHURCH AS A MEDIATOR

1659, Dec. 3. Solemn Procession, attended by the Bishop, President, *Oidores*, Ecclesiastical Chapter, Municipal Government, Superiors of the Religious Orders, and leading citizens, in accordance with the proposal of the Presidency of the *Audiencia,* to have a general procession bearing the image of San Sebastian, in view of the terrible death toll due to the epidemic of " *calenturas.*" (Pardo, *Efemérides*, p. 69)

1660, Aug. 13. The Municipal Government ordered a petition to the Bishop for a Procession of *Nuestra Señora del Socorro*, carrying said image to the Church of the *Concepción* for a novena begging for the cessation of the great drought afflicting the city and the towns of the surrounding valley. (Pardo, *Efemérides*, p. 69)

1663, May 18. The Municipal Government declared that on May 20th there would be a procession in honor of *Nuestra Señora del Socorro*, carrying the said image to the Church of the *Concepción* for a novena of prayer for those afflicted by the recent earthquakes. (Pardo, *Efemérides*, p. 71)

1666, July 9. In view of the fact that the city was suffering from an epidemic, the Bishop was asked to order special prayers. (Pardo, *Efemérides*, p. 73)

1702. Aug. 9. The *Audiencia* asked the Municipal Government to arrange for public prayers to *Nuestra Señora del Socorro*, imporing protection from the earthquakes which had continued. (Pardo, *Efemérides*, p. 129)

1707, Dec. 13. The Municipal Government solicited His Majesty for the complete liberty of commerce with Peru, and for this wished him to consult the advice of the Bishop, the President, and the Superiors of the Religious Orders.   (Pardo, *Efemérides*, p. 135)

1709, Mar. 15. The Municipal Government requested the authorities of the Bishopric, the Vicar General, the Superiors of the Religious Orders, the Licenciate Diego Gómez de Angulo, the Royal Officials and the Municipal Government of Habana to testify to the necessity of free commerce between Guatemala and the ports of Cuba.   (Pardo, *Efemérides*, p. 136)

1730, Jan. 13. The Municipal Government thanked the President and the Bishop for their assistance in persuading the powers in Spain concerning free trade.   (Pardo, *Efemérides*, p. 167)

MUNICIPAL JURISDICTION OVER ECCLESIASTICAL AFFAIRS

1717, Oct. 6. In the Palace and presided over by the Captain General Francisco Rodríguez de Rivas, there was held a general meeting of the authorities, civil and ecclesiastical, with leading citizens, to discuss the removal of the city of Guatemala.   (Pardo, *Efemérides*, p. 146)

1718, April 11. In the general meeting attended by the President, the *Oidores*, Bishop Ecclesiastical Chapter, Superiors of the Religious Orders, Members of the Treasury, the President, Rodríguez de Rivas, declared that there having been disagreement as to the moving of the city, and a lack of sufficient funds for such removal, they should consult His Majesty, and meanwhile await his decision.   At this point Bishop Fr. Juan Bautista Alvárez de Toledo asked the immediate removal to the valley *de las Vacas*; but the opinion of the President prevailed because the royal officials and the Treasurer declared there were no funds.   (Pardo, *Efemérides*, p. 149)

1774, Jan. 12. President Mayorga published an act declaring that seculars and ecclesiastics could freely discuss their opinions on the question of determining first, if the city of Santiago should be transferred, and second, to what site, the valley of Jalapa or that of *las Vacas*.   (Pardo, *Efemérides*, p. 252)

1775, Dec. 9. A notice was sent to the Reverend Superiors of the Convents of nuns and to the Cloister of the University of San Carlos ordering their speedy transfer to the valley *de la Virgen*.   (Pardo, *Efemérides*, p. 258)

1777, Feb. 14. The Director of Public Works, Vicente Cruz, announced that there was an abundance of material which could be used in the construction of the new city in the Palace, the *Colegio de Borja*, the Treasury building, the Customs House, etc. (Pardo, *Efemérides*, p. 260)

1777, April 23. By order of President Mayorga the Infirmary constructed years before was closed; for this reason on this date the parish priests of Guatemala Antigua asked for the building of a hospital. (Pardo, *Efemérides*, p. 261)

1777, June 28. The Captain General Martín de Mayorga issued a decree that the city of Guatemala be entirely removed within one year, the ruins still standing to be entirely demolished at the end of said period; that the Ecclesiastical Chapter, the University, the Ecclesiastical Curia, the Prelates and Communities of Religious, the inhabitants and their possessions be transferred from Antigua Goathemala to the New City without delay for any excuse, within two months from the time when the notice was received, and the town of Guatemala was to be entirely abandoned and deserted within a year from that date. And all inhabitants were commanded within the year to establish themselves in the new capital or its environs, with the understanding that if such establishment within the new city were not made within the time appointed, necessary measures would be taken. (Pardo, *Efemérides*, p. 261)

1777, Sept. 11. The President Martín de Mayorga wrote to his Majesty the King declaring that the Archbishop Cortés y Lárraz was interfering with the removing of the city of Guatemala to the new site, having declared that only with the express permission of the Pontiff could the new cathedral be built. (Pardo, *Efemérides*, p. 268)

1777, Nov. 30. Only the Augustinians had answered the request of the President Mayorga to abandon the old site of the city. The Congregations of Bethlemites, Franciscans, of *La Merced*, and the Propagation of the Faith—the Dominicans had begun to move—all were notified again on this date that the transfer must be made within the two months appointed, no exceptions nor excuses of any kind being permitted. (Pardo, *Efemérides*, p. 262)

1779, Jan. 17.   The Order of *Las Beatas Indias de Nuestra Señora del Rosario*, according to the command of the Municipal Government, was transferred on this date to the new site of Guatemala, called *Nueva Guatemala de la Asunción*.   (Pardo, *Efemérides*, p. 263).

1689, Nov. 7.   The *Vice Patron Real*, President Jacinto de Barrios Leal, approved the fiscal document declaring that the *Maestrescuela*, Dr. Lorenzo López, could not be elected Rector of the University because two positions were incompatible.   (Pardo, *Efemérides*, p. 107)

1699, May 4.   The President of the *Audiencia*, in his capacity of *Vice Patron Real* of the University of San Carlos, commanded the Rector to control the attendance of the students.   (Pardo, *Efemérides*, p. 123)

1747, Aug. 27.   Act or *"real acuerdo"* declaring that neither the President of the *Audiencia*, as *Vice Patron Real*, nor the Rector of the University of San Carlos, had the faculty of conferring dispensations of attendance to the students of said University.   (Pardo, *Efemérides*, p. 199)

1774, April 18.   Archbishop Cortés y Lárraz informed the Municipal Government concerning the need of building shelters for the care of the sick.   (Pardo, *Efemérides*, p. 254)

SECTION III—THE REPUBLICAN PERIOD

ASSUMPTION OF JURISDICTION IN ECCLESIASTICAL AFFAIRS BY THE REPUBLICAN OFFICIALS

1820, Dec. 7.   The *Jefe Político* of Guatemala, on the advice of the Provincial Deputation, made certain inquiries of the Archbishop of Guatemala concerning the tithes and incomes which might be affected by the proposed separation of the province of El Salvador from the archbishopric of Guatemala.   (Vilanova Meléndez, *Apuntamientos*, p. 56)

1821, Jan. 12.   The *Jefe Político* urged the Archbishop to reply to the request of Dec. 7, 1820, concerning the tithes and incomes, in the matter of the proposed bishopric of El Salvador.   (Vilanova Meléndez, *Apuntamientos*, p. 56)

1822, March 29. Among those who composed the Provincial Deputation of Guatemala, established March 29, 1822, in Nueva Guatemala, were His Excellency the Archbishop, representing the capital. (Díaz, *Guatemala Independente,* p. 5)

1822, April 1. The Provincial Government of Guatemala passed the resolution abolishing the attendance of the Deputation at functions in the Cathedral. (Díaz, *Guatemala Independente,* p. 10)

1822, April 25. At the sixth session of the Provincial Deputation of Guatemala, April 25, 1822, the Archbishop declared that the government of Mexico had taken measures to prevent the introduction into that country of books harmful to morals and religion, that Guatemala had many such books and that he made a motion that the Government should take action. This was agreed upon, and the *Jefe Político* was authorized to attend to the matter. (Díaz, *Guatemala Independente,* p. 23)

1822, May 20. The Pastor and Municipal Government of the town of San Cristóbal Amatitlán requested the Provincial Government of Guatemala in the 13th session of that body to be permitted to use the municipal funds in the treasury of said town for the repairing and redecorating of the church. (Díaz, *Guatemale Independente,* p. 50)

1822, June 3. The Chief Executive of Guatemala acceded to the petition of the Archbishop and decreed that the Indians be required to pay parochial fees since they had been exempted from offering rations and services. (Díaz, *Guatemala Independente,* p. 53)

1822, June 3. The Provincial of the Franciscans and *La Merced* were requested by the Provincial Government of Guatemala to report whether or not they were still collecting alms for the Holy Places and the Redemption of Captives, and, in case of an affirmative reply, to remit to the deputies a sworn report of the amounts which had been collected since the previous September 15, the use to which said funds had been put, and the amount on hand. (Díaz, *Guatemala Independente,* p. 105)

1822, June 14. Reply of the Reverend Provincial of *La Merced* to the request of the Provincial Government of Guatemala relative to the alms for the Redemption of Captives, reporting that, according to royal orders on this matter, they had stored in the main treasury in Guatemala all the funds collected in the past year, perhaps totalling 2,000 *pesos*. (Díaz, *Guatemala Independente*, p. 59)

1822, June 14. The Provincial Deputation of Guatemala, in view of the reply of the Provincial of the Order of *La Merced* regarding the funds collected for the Redemption of Captives, informed the said Provincial of *La Merced* that, while the Deputies were deciding on whether or not the collection should be continued, in view of the grave condition of the public treasury there should be deposited in the said public treasury with the greatest expediency all the funds now in the capital, and that as soon as possible the funds stored in other convents of Guatemala should be transferred likewise to the public treasury in the capital for the same purpose. (Díaz, *Guatemala Independente*, p. 60)

1822, June 17. The Pastor and Municipal Government of the town of Tecuaco requested the Provincial Government of Guatemala, met in session at the capital, that funds stored in their municipal treasury might be used for the repair of the parish church, and the said Provincial Deputies agreed and entrusted the said pastor and municipal government with the money to use as requested. (Díaz, *Guatemala Independente*, p. 63)

1822, June 17. The Provincial Deputies, met in session in Guatemala, ordered suspended at once the collection of alms for the Redemption of Captives. (Díaz, *Guatemala Independente*, p. 66)

1822, June 25. The Provincial of the Franciscans reported to the Provincial Government of Guatemala, concerning the request as to whether or not his Order were still collecting alms for the Redemption of Captives, that he did not know the amount collected since September 15, 1821, but he declared on oath that there was in the hands of D. Gregorio Urruela the sum of 2,255 *pesos*, 3-¾ *reales*. (Díaz, *Guatemala Independente*, p. 67)

1822, June 25. The Provincial Government of Guatemala ordered the Provincial of the Franciscans to hand over to the National Treasury of Guatemala the amount of 2,255 *pesos*, 3-3¾ *reales* which he reported on hand, and to issue orders to those Franciscans then soliciting alms to return to their convents, since they would be no longer permitted to seek alms, according to the resolutions of the Supreme Government. (Díaz, *Guatemala Independente*, p. 67)

1822, June 27. The Provincial of the Franciscans protested to the Provincial Government of Guatemala the order of that body prohibiting in the future the collection of alms for the Redemption of Captives. (Díaz, *Guatemala Independente*, p. 71)

1822, June 27. The Provincial Deputies of Guatemala, in their 21st session, inform the Franciscans of their assurance that up to that time, the collection of alms for the Redemption of Captives had been legitimate, but that, in view of the political circumstances of that time, the Deputies were still agreed upon the advisability of the suspension of the collections until the matter was resolved by the Supreme Government of Guatemala. (Díaz, *Guatemala Independente*, p. 71)

1822, Aug. 12. The Parish of San Lucas Sacatepéquez requested and received public funds for the repairing of the churches of San Bartolomé and San Mateo from the Provincial Assembly of this date. (Díaz, *Guatemala Independente*, p. 100)

1823, July 1. Decree of National Assembly of Guatemala establishing religious tolerance for private worship. (Montúfar y Coronado, *Memorias*, p. 76)

1823, July 2. The Congress of the United Provinces of Central America declared that the religion of the State was the Roman, Catholic, Apostolic, with the exclusion of all others. (Marure, *Bosquejo histórico*, p. 63)

1823, July 8. Decree of the National Assembly of Guatemala declaring that no action could be taken in regard to the election, presentation or proposal to prelacies without previous and express agreement with the Holy See. (Marure, *Bosquejo histórico*, p. 130)

1823, July 8. The Executive took advantage immediately of his right to remove political and military chiefs, magistrates and judges, without formality, by deposing twelve or fifteen employees on the civil list, some military officials, and several pastors, among those who had distinguished themselves by loyalty to the imperial system. (Marure, *Bosquejo histórico*, p. 68)

1823, July 21 ff. The Superior of the Order of *La Merced* acknowledged in a letter to the Government of Guatemala the receipt of various decrees and laws. (*Documents in National Archives*, B83.7, No. 25414, 25415, 25416)

1823, July 21 ff. The Guardian of the Order of *Recollets* ac-acknowledged the receipt of various decrees and orders. (*Documents in National Archives*, B83.6, No. 25396, 25398, 25399, 25400, 25401, 25402, 25403, 25404, 25405)

1823, July 22 ff. The Provincial of the Franciscans acknowledged receipt from the Government of Guatemala of various decrees and orders. (*Documents in National Archives*, B83.5, No. 25365, 25366. 25367, 25368, 25370, 25371, 25372, 25374, 25375, 25376, 25377)

1823, July 22 ff. The Ecclesiastical Chapter of Guatemala acknowledged receipt of various decrees and laws of the Municipal Government. (*Documents in the National Archives*, B83.3, No. 25243, 25244, 25245, 25246, 25247, 25251, 25253, 25258, 25259, 25260, 25261, 25262, 25263, 25264, 25265, 25266, 25267, 25268, 25269, 25270, 25271, 25272, 25273)

1823, July 23 ff. The Provincial of the Bethlemites acknowledged receipt of various decrees and laws of the civil authorities. (*Documents in National Archives*, B83.9, No. 25425, 25426, 25427, 25428, 25429, 25430, 25431)

1823, July 23 ff. The Provincial of the Dominican Order acknowledges receipt of various decrees and orders of the civil authorities. (*Documents in National Archives*, B83.4, No. 25342, 25343, 25344, 25345, 25346, 25347, 25349, 25350)

1823, July 24. The Archbishop Fr. Ramón Casáus y Torres acknowledged receipt of the order according to which the Secretary of State would use in the future " *media firma* ", or a simple closing to correspondence. (*Documents in National Archives*, No. 24704)

1823, July 30 ff. The Superior of the Augustinians acknowledged receipt of various decrees and laws of the civil authorities. (*Documents in National Archives*, B83.10, No. 25435, 25436, 25437, 25438, 25439, 25440, 25441, 25442, 25443)

1823, Aug. 1. The Archbishop forwarded to the Government the testimony of the oath sworn to by the members of the Ecclesiastical Court. (*Document in National Archives*, No. 24713)

1823, Aug. 3 ff. The Archbishop acknowledged receipt of various decrees and laws of the government of Guatemala. (*Documents in National Archives*, No. 24717, 24718, 24719, 24721, 24722, 24723, 24724, 24725, 24726, 24729, 24731, 24735, 24740, 24742, 24743)

1823, Aug. 6. The Archbishop acknowledged receipt of decree abolishing the distinctions and titles used during the Spanish régime. (*Documents in National Archives*, No. 24723)

1823, Aug. 7. The Provincial of the Franciscans, in reply to a request of the National Assembly, declared that he would give orders to have Fr. Pedro Contreras transferred from Sonsonate to the capital for his political conduct. (*Document in the National Archives*, No. 25369)

1823, Aug. 14. The Archbishop informed the Government of the State that he would order the priests named as delegates to the assembly who had not yet presented themselves to fulfill that obligation at once. (*Document in the National Archives*, No. 25350)

1823, Aug. 18. The Prior of the Dominican Order acknowledged receipt of the order of expulsion directed against Friar Antonio Herrera for refusing to recognize the Assembly. (*Document of National Archives*, No. 25351)

1823, Aug. 25. The Government requested that the Vicar General issue orders that the pastor of Mataquescuintla cooperate in preserving order in the said town. (*Document of National Archives*, No. 24817)

1823, Aug. 26. The *Jefe Político* requested the Archbishop to forward affidavits for the oath of obedience and recognition of the National Assembly which should have been sworn to by the personnel of the *Beaterio de Niñas* and the *Colegio de la Presentación*. (*Document in National Archives*, No. 24733)

1823, Sept. 5. Letter of the Dominican Prior to the Government containing certifications of the oath of recognition of the Assembly on the part of several friars of the Convent of Cobán. (*Document of National Archives*, No. 25351)

1823, Sept. 9. The Provincial of the Dominicans acknowledged receipt of order for the commemorating of the anniversary of the Independence. (*Document in National Archives*, No. 25352)

1823, Nov. 21. The National Constitutional Assembly abolished the sale of *Bulas de Cruzada.* (Marure, *Efemérides,* p. 9)

1824, Jan. 27. The Vicar General notified the government that Fr. Merida would be removed as requested by the Government from his parish. (*Document in National Archives,* No. 24809)

1824, Feb. 14. The government issued an order specifying qualifications for the obtaining of ecclesiastical offices. (*Recopilación de Leyes de Guatemala,* vol. III, p. 250)

1824, Sept. 15. The First Constitutional Congress was installed in the State of Guatemala under the presidency of Fr. José María Chacón. (Marure, *Efemérides,* p. 12)

1824, Nov. 8. The National Assembly of Guatemala issued a law abolishing the exemption of clergy from the payment of the *alcabala,* or tax on imported goods. (Marure, *Bosquejo histórico,* p. 161)

1824, Nov. 22. Article II of the Federal Constitution of Central America, decreed by the National Constitutional Assembly on Nov. 22, 1824, that the religion of the republic was the Catholic, Apostolic, Roman, to the exclusion of the public exercise of any other. (*Recopilación de Leyes,* vol. II, p. 251)

1824, Dec. 24. The Vicar General requested that the Executive approve the exchange of the pastors, Francisco Solís and Mariano Cabrera. (*Document in National Archives,* No. 24832)

1825, Jan. 31. The *Jefe Político* of Guatemala requested the Ecclesiastical Chapter to remove certain pastors. (*Document in National Archives,* No. 25619)

1825, Feb. 19. The Chief Executive of Guatemala ordered the Fathers of the *Propaganda Fide* suspended, and commanded the superior, before beginning his apostolic work giving missions, as a subject of the civil power, to swear obedience to the code of laws which the nation had adopted. (Marure, *Bosquejo histórico,* p. 120)

1825, June 13. The Vicar General informed the Government that Father José María Puente had been named pastor of Taxisco. (*Document in National Archives,* No. 24835)

1825, Aug. 14. The Government complained to the Rev. Guardian of the *Colegio de Misioneros,* of the *Recollets,* that the lay brother,

José María Viduarre, was insisting on collecting funds for Fernando VII. (*Document in National Archives*, No. 25409)

1825, Oct. 25. The Government issued order prohibiting Fr. José León Toboada from assuming the duties of pastor in Huehuetenango without the permission of the President. (*Document in National Archives*, No. 24766)

1825, Dec. 20. The Government informed the Ecclesiastical Chapter that it had no objections to the return of Fr. Miguel Merida to his parish of Retalhuleu. (*Document in National Archives*, No. 25626)

1825, Dec. 30. The Archbishop remitted a report, requested by the Government, of the number of parishes, pastors and incomes, which, however, was no more recent than 1815. (*Document in National Archives*, No. 24769)

1826, Jan. 18. The Archbishop acknowledged receipt of the declaration of the Supreme Government of the report of the Commission of the Constitutional Assembly relative to the statement of the specific incomes of the state. (*Document in National Archives*, No. 24770)

1827, March 6. The Ecclesiastical Chapter asked the Assembly of Guatemala for the derogation of certain laws. (*Document in National Archives*, No. 25274)

1827, March 16. The Government of the State of Guatemala ordered the continuation of and cooperation in the collection of tithes and the exact accounting therefor, and the protection and stimulation of donations and offerings for pious purposes. (*Document of National Archives*, No. 25632)

1827, March 27. The Vicar General notified the Government that the Church would exert its authority and influence for the enlisting of troops as requested. (*Document in National Archives*, No. 25633)

1827, March 30. The Metropolitan Prelate declared the causes preventing him at that time from appointing pastors to certain parishes, in a letter to the Government of that date. (*Document in National Archives*, No. 24771)

1827, April 25. The Government granted permission for the temporary appointment of Fr. Francisco Alcantara to the parish of Izapa. (*Document in National Archives*, No. 24772)

1827, May 25. The Ecclesiastical Chapter agreed that the funds from the collection of tithes be loaned to the State. (*Document in National Archives,* No. 25275)

1827, May 28. The Archbishop was informed that Fr. Goiburu had been appointed by the Government of Guatemala as Chaplain of the Expedionary Forces which had left Guatemala City. (*Document in National Archives,* No. 24773)

1827, Sept. 19. The Archbishop sent to the Government of Guatemala a translation of the letter of His Holiness to the Prelate himself, to the *Jefe* of the State of El Salvador, and to Father Matías Delgado, in regard to the episcopate. (*Document in* National Archives, No. 24774)

1827, Nov. 27. The Government requested the Archbishop to order public prayers for the triumph of Guatemalan arms. (*Document in National Archives,* No. 24776)

1827, Nov. 27. The Metropolitan Prelate informed the Government that he would proceed to order public prayers for the success of the operations of the expeditionary forces. (*Document in National Archives,* No. 24776)

1827, Dec. 5. The Archbishop asked the approval of the Government to the appointment of Fr. José Manuel López as pastor of San Antonio Suchitepéquez. (*Document in National Archives,* No. 24777)

1828. Memorandum of an official letter to the Vicar General and Assistant to the Archbishop of Guatemala from the Government requesting that the pastor of Jutiapa, Esteban López, be ordered to desist from arousing the population. (*Document in National Archives,* No. 24807, Leg. 1112)

1828, April 26. The Assembly decreed that in a proposed increase of the loan to the government, ecclesiastics would contribute their share. (Montúfar y Rivera, *Reseña histórica,* vol. I, p. 24)

1828, Sept. 4. Letter of the Archbishop to the Secretary General of the Government telling him that there would be public prayers for the welfare and the current necessities of the country; and promising to urge the clergy to influence enlistments for the defense of the nation. (*Document in National Archives,* No. 25466)

1829, April 27. The Executive announced to the Archbishop that he had circulated among the pastors the recommendation that they cooperate in the prevention of the spread of smallpox. (*Document in National Archives*, No. 24782)

1829, April 29. The Government declared that the clergy should all contribute financially to defray the expenses involved in the prevention of the spread of smallpox. (*Document in National Archives*, No. 24783)

1829, June 8. The Executive declared that, before a sermon could be delivered in any church, a copy must be presented to the executive twenty-four hours in advance. (*Document in National Archives*, No. 24785)

1829, June 9. The Government forwarded to the Provincial of the Franciscans documents relative to the secularization of the friars and the removal of pastors. (*Document in National Archives*, B83.13, No. 25502)

1829, July. The General in Chief of the Army, Francisco Morazán, reported that he had expelled the religious orders from the Republic of Guatemala, according to the special faculties granted him. (*Document in National Archives*, No. 25481)

1829, July 12. Order sent to Vicar General to prepare a list of the religious living in the Convents of Saint Dominic, Saint Francis and the *Recolección*, said list to be sent to the Government. (*Document in National Archives*, B83.13, No. 25506)

1829, July 14. The Government issued a decree secularizing the lay brothers and *coristas* still remaining in the capital. (*Document of National Archives*, No. 25466)

1829, July 15. The Vicar General was asked to make a list of the lay brothers, choir and regular monks who had been living in the convents of the capital. (*Document in National Archives*, B83.13, No. 25510)

1829, July 18. The Vicar General informed the Government that he would name pastors for the villages of Los Altos, as requested. (*Document in National Archives*, No. 24855)

1829, July 20. The Government ordered secular clothing made for the lay brothers who had been secularized. (*Document in National Archives*, B83.13, No. 25515)

1829, July 28. The Assembly of Guatemala decreed the extinction of all monastic establishments of men, with the exception of the Hospitallers of *Betlém* (*Belemitas*) and prohibited in the convents of women all professions and solemn vows, the State appropriating to itself the temporalities of the convents abolished. (*Document in National Archives*, No. 24858)

1829, Aug. 5. The Commander General of the Armed Forces was requested to issue an edict declaring that after 8 days no religious was to be permitted to remain in his respective community. (*Document in National Archives*, B83.13, No. 25539)

1829, Aug. 5. The Government advised the Vicar General to insist that the pastors whom he had named take possession of their parishes. (*Document in National Archives*, No. 24859)

1829, Aug. 8. The head of the Department of Guatemala reported that he had issued orders that no religious was to be permitted to travel. (*Document in National Archives*, B83.13, No. 25545)

1830, May 21. The Vicar General requested the Secretary of the Government of Guatemala to send him a copy of the document granting him faculties for the governing of the diocese. (*Document in National Archives*, No. 25466)

1831, March. The Executive of the Government of Guatemala informed the Vicar General that all ecclesiastical employees must be such as to be trusted absolutely by the Government. (*Document in National Archives*, No. 24901)

1831, March. The Vicar General declared, in reply to a complaint of the government, that always before filling any pastorate he had consulted the executive of the State. (*Document in National Archives*, No. 24891)

1831, April 6. The Government asked the Vicar General to remove Fr. Victor Castillo from the parish of Salamá. (*Document in National Archives*, No. 24906)

1831, May 13. The Government inquired of the Vicar General why he had not made a report and submitted it to the government. (*Document in National Archives*, No. 24926, Leg. 1113)

BIBLIOGRAPHY

Aguero, Raúl. *Guatemala, La Revolución Liberal de 1871*. San José, Costa Rica, Imprenta Alsina, 1914.

Aguilera de León, Carlos. *Libro-Centenario de Guatemala, 1835-1935*. Guatemala, Tipografía Nacional, 1935.

Aguirre Cinta, Rafaél. *Historia General de Guatemala*, Guatemala, Tipografía Nacional, 1899.

Arce, Manuel José. *Memoria de la Conducta Pública y Administrativa de ...*, Mexico, Imprenta Galvan, 1830.

Ayarragaray, Lucas. *La Iglesia en América y la Dominación española*. Buenos Aires, J. Lajouane & Co., 1920.

Baluffi, Gaetano. *L'America en tempo spagnuolo riguardata sotto l'aspetto religioso*. Ancona, Gustavo Sartori Cherubini, 1845.

Bancroft, Hubert Howard. *History of Central America*. San Francisco, History Company, vol. III, 1887.

Batres Jáuregui, Antonio. *La América Central ante la Historia*, Guatemala, Tipografía Sánchez & de Guise, 1920.

Blanco-Fombona, Rufino. *La Evolución política y social de Hispanoamérica*, Madrid, Bernardo Rodríguez, 1911.

Carrillo, Agustín Gómez. *Historia de la América Central*, Guatemala, Tipografía Nacional, vols. III, IV, V, 1905.

Castellanos, J. Humberto. *La Metrópoli Colonial Centro-Americana*, Antigua, Tipografía Azmitia, 1936.

Chapman, Charles. *Colonial Hispanic America*. New York, Macmillan, 1938.

Cleven, N. Andrew N. *Readings in Hispanic American History*, Boston, Ginn & Co., 1927.

Condor, Joseph. *The Modern Traveler: a popular description of Mexico and Guatemala*, Boston, Wells & Lilly, 1830.

Crosby, Elisha Oscar. *Memoirs:* Reminiscences of California and Guatemala from 1849 to 1864. San Marino, California, Huntington Library, 1945.

Crowe, Frederick. *The Gospel in Central America*. London, Charles Gilpin, 1850.

Díaz, Victor Miguel. *Guatemala Independente — Recopilación de Documentos Históricos*, Guatemala, Tipografía Nacional, 1932.

——. *Barrios ante la Posteridad*. Guatemala, Tipografía Nacional, 1935.

Domville-Fife, Charles W. *Guatemala and the States of Central America*, London, Francis Griffiths, 1913.

Dunlop, Robert Glasgow. *Travels in Central America*. London, Longman, Brown, Green, Longmans, 1847.

Dunn, Henry. *Guatimala*, or the United Provinces of Central America in 1827-8; being sketches and Memoirs made during a Twelve Months' Residence in that Republic, New York, G. and G. Carvill, 1828.

Eyzaguirre, José Ignacio. *Los Intereses Católicos en America*. Paris, Garnier Frères, 1859.

341

Fernández, Alonzo. *Historia Eclesiástica de Nuestros Tiempos.* Toledo, Pedro Rodríguez, 1611.

Frasso, Pedro. *De Regio Patronatu Indiarum,* Madrid, Blasii Roman, 1775.

Fuentes y Guzman, Francisco A. *Recordación Florida del Reyno de Guatemala,* Guatemala, Tipografía Nacional, 1933.

Gage, Thomas D. *A New Survey of the West-Indies,* London, B. Cotes, 1655.

Filísola, Vicente. *La Independencia de Guatemala.* Mexico, Imprenta Váldez, 1823.

García, Miguel Angel. *Diccionario histórico enciclopédico de la República de el Salvador,* San Salvador, Imprenta La Salvadorena, vol. III, 1929, vol. IV, 1932; Imprenta Nacional, vol. V, 1935.

García Peláez, Francisco de Paula. *Memorias para la Historia del Antiguo Reyno de Guatemala.* Guatemala, Tipografía de La Luna, 1852.

Genesis de la Reforma Constitucional de la República de Guatemala, Guatemala, Imprenta Nacional, 1927.

Gómez Zamora, P. Matías. *Regio Patronato Español e Indiano.* Madrid, Imprenta del Asilo, 1897.

Hernáez, Francisco Javier. *Colección de Bulas, Breves y otros Documentos relativos a la iglesia de América y las Filipinas,* Brussels, Alfred Vromant, 1879.

Herrera y Tordesillas, Antonio de. *Historia general de los castellanos en las islas i tierra firme del Mar,* Madrid, 1601-14.

Jones, Chester Lloyd. *Guatemala: Past and Present.* Minneapolis, University of Minnesota Press, 1940.

Juarros, Fr. Domingo. *Compendio de la Historia de la Ciudad de Guatemala,* Guatemala, Tipografía Nacional, 1937, 3rd edition.

Kelsey, Vera and Osborne, Lily de Jongh. *Four Keys to Guatemala.* New York, Funk & Wagnalls, 1539.

La Farge, Oliver. *Santa Eulalia: the Religion of a Cuchumatán Indian Town,* Chicago, University of Chicago, 1947.

——. *The Year Bearers' People.* New Orleans, Tulane University Press, 1931.

La Renaudière, Philippe F. *Mexique et Guatemala.* Paris, Firmin Didot Frères, 1843.

Leturia, Pedro, S.J. *El Ocaso del Patronato Real en la América española.* Madrid, Imprenta Razón y Fé, 1925.

Marure, Alejandro. *Bosquejo histórico de las revoluciones de Centro-América,* Guatemala, El Progreso, 1877.

——. *Efemérides de los hechos notables acaecidos en la República de Centro-América desde el año 1821 hasta él de 1842,* Guatemala, Imprenta de la Paz, 1844.

Mecham, John Lloyd. *Church and State in Latin America.* Chapel Hill, University of North Carolina Press, 1934.

Mercati, Antonio. *Raccolta di Concordati su Materie Ecclesiastiche tra la Santa Sede e la Autorità Civile,* Roma, Tipografía Poliglotta Vaticana, 1919.

de Mendieta, Fray Gerónimo. *Historia Eclesiástica Indiana.* Mexico, Librería Antigua, 1870.

Milla y Vidaurre, José. *Historia de la América Central.* Guatemala, Tipografía El Progreso, 1879.

Montgomery, George W. *Narrative of a Journey to Guatemala in 1838.* New York, Wiley & Putnam, 1839.

Montúfar, Rafaél. *El General Francisco Morazán.* Guatemala, Tipografía Americana, 1896.

Montúfar y Coronado, Manuel. *Memorias para la Historia de la Revolución de Centro-América.* Guatemala, Tipografía Sánchez & de Guise, 1934.

Montúfar y Rivera, Lorenzo. *Reseña histórica de Centro-América,* Guatemala, Tipografía de la Unión, 1887.

Morelet, Arthur. *Travels in Central America.* New York, Leypoldt, Holt, Williams, 1871.

Muriel, Domingo. *Fasti Novi Orbis et Ordinationum apostolicarum,* Venice, Antonio Zatta, 1776.

Pardo, J. Joaquín. *Efemérides* para escribir la historia de la muy noble y muy leal Ciudad de Santiago de los Caballeros del Reino de Guatemala, Guatemala, Tipografía Nacional, 1944.

Pineda de Mont, Manuel. *Recopilación de Leyes de Guatemala.* Guatemala, Imprenta de la Paz, 1872.

Ramírez Colóm, José M. *Reseña biográfica de don Ricardo Casanova y Estrada,* Guatemala, Sánchez & de Guise, 1912.

Real Academia de Historia. *Colección de Documentos inéditos de Ultramar.* Madrid, Rivadeneyra, 1895.

Recopilación de Leyes de los Reynos de las Indias. Mandadas imprimir y publicar por La Magestad Católica del Rey don Carlos II, Madrid, Antonio Balbas, 1756.

Recopilación de Leyes emitidas por el Gobierno Democrático de la República de Guatemala, Guatemala, Tipografía El Progreso, vols. I, II, 1881 ; vol. III, 1883.

Remesal, Antonio de. *Historia general de las Indias Occidentales y particulares de la gobernación de Chiapas y Guatemala,* Guatemala, Tipografía Nacional, 1932, 2nd edition.

Ribadeneyra y Barrientos, Antonio Joaquín de. *Manual Compendio de el Regio Patronato Indiano.* Madrid, Antonio Marin, 1755.

Rodríguez, José Ignacio. *American Constitutions.* Washington, Government Printing Office, 1906.

Salazar, Ramón A. *Historia del Desenvolvimiento Intelectual de Guatemala,* Guatemala, Tipografía Nacional, 1897.

——. *Historia de Veintiún Años: La Independencia de Guatemala,* Guatemala, Tipografía Nacional, 1928.

Solorzano y Pereyra, Juan de. *Política Indiana.* Madrid, 1776.

Squier, Ephraim G. *Nicaragua.* New York, Appleton and Company, 1852.

Stephens, John L. *Incidents of Travel in Central America.* New York, Harper's, 1842.

Stoll, Otto. *Guatemala: Reisen und Schilderungen aus den Jahren 1878-1883*, Leipzig, F. A. Brockhaus, 1866.

Thompson, George Alexander. *Narrative of an Official Visit to Guatemala*, London, J. Murray, 1829.

Tourón, R. P. *Histoire Générale de l'Amérique depuis sa decouverte*, Paris, Hérissant Fils, 1768.

Tumin, Melvin M. *San Luis Jilotepeque: A Study in Social Relations*, Evanston, Northwestern University Press, 1944.

Urruela, don Juan María de. *Defensa de Guatemala y su Política*. Guatemala, Imprenta de la Paz, 1849.

Valladares, Manuel. *Próceres de la Independencia*. Guatemala, Aguïrre Velásquez & Co., 1911.

Vásquez, Francisco. *Crónica de la Provincia del Santísimo Nombre de Jesús de Guatemala*, Guatemala, Tipografía Nacional, 1937.

Vélez Sarsfield, Dalmacio. *Relaciones del Estado con la Iglesia*. Buenos Aires, Librería la Facultad, 1919.

Vilanova Meléndez, Ricardo. *Apuntamientos de Historia Patria Eclesiástica*, San Salvador, Imprenta la Luz, 1911.

Villacorte y Calderón, J. Antonio. *Elementos de Historia Patria*. Guatemala, Tipografía Nacional, 1938.

Ximénez, Francisco. *Historia de la Provincia de San Vicente, de Chiapas y Guatemala*, Guatemala, Tipografía Nacional, 1929-31.

Zeceña, Mariano. *La Revolución de 1871*. Guatemala, Tipografía Sánchez de Guise, 1898.

Zubieta, Pedro A. *Apuntamientos sobre las Primeras Misiones Diplomáticas de Colombia*, Bogotá, Imprenta Nacional, 1924.

1 Only such references are included in the Bibliography as have been used in the text.

COLLECTIONS OF DOCUMENTS MICROFILMED BY AUTHOR

National Archives of Guatemala.
Archives of the Palace of the Archbishop of Guatemala.
Archives of the Sisters of Charity, Guatemala.

ARTICLES

Desdevises du Dézert, Georges. " L'Eglise Espagnole des Indes à la fin du XVIIIe siècle ", *Revue Hispanique*, XXXIX, 1917, pp. 112-293.

Goubaud Carrera, Antonio. " El Guajxaquip Báts, ceremonia calendárica indígena ", *Anales de la Sociedad de Geografía e Historia de Guatemala*, vol. XII, No. 1, 1935, pp. 39-49.

Hopkins, Frederick C., S.J., " The Catholic Church in British Honduras ", *Catholic Historical Review*, vol. IV, pp. 304-314.

Mecham, J. Lloyd. " Latin America's Fight against Clerical Domination ", *Current History*, January, 1929, pp. 567-570.

——. " The Origins of the *Real Patronato de Indias* ", *Catholic Historical Review*, vol. VIII, No. 1, pp. 205-228.

Siegel, Morris. "Religion in Western Guatemala: a Product of Acculturation", *American Anthropologist*, vol. 43, 1941, pp. 62-76.

Statesman's Year-book, vol. LXXX, 1946, p. 985.

Vela, Manuel. "Guatemala, hace ciento catorce años," *Anales de la Sociedad de Geografía e historia de Guatemala*, Guatemala, vol. XII, 1935, pp. 3-22.

Wagley, Charles. "Economics of a Guatemalan Village", *American Anthropologist*, vol. 43, 1941, pp. 19-32.

Williams, Mary Wilhelmine. "The Ecclesiastical Policy of Francisco Morazán and the other Central American Liberals", *Hispanic American Historical Review*, vol. III, No. 2, May, 1920, pp. 119-143.

NEWSPAPERS

La Acción Social Cristiana, Guatemala, 1946.

Boletín Oficial, Guatemala, 1871, 1872, 1873, 1874, 1875.

El Crepúsculo, Guatemala, 1872.

Gaceta de Nicaragua, 1867, 1873.

La Hora, Guatemala, 1946.

El Imparcial, Guatemala, 1946.

Mediodía, Guatemala, 1946.

Nuestro Diario, Guatemala, 1897.

Verbum, Guatemala, 1946.

La República, Guatemala, 1897.

La Verdad, León, Nicaragua, 1871, 1872, 1873, 1874.

INDEX

Academy of the Sisters of Notre Dame, opened, 143; converted into National Institute for Girls, 183

Acción Social Cristiana, Catholic periodical of Guatemala, 214

Act of Independence, religious clauses in, 270-271, 308

Alexander VI, pope, grants to the Kings of Castile, 17, 18, 19; Bulls of, 18, 19

Alcayaga, José Antonio, cleric, delegated Vicar General by Casáus in exile, 104, 114; resigned, 114

Alvarado, don Pedro, *vice patron real*, 321

Alvárez de Toledo, Juan Bautista, bishop, first native raised to See of Guatemala, 61; active in moving of capital, 328

Ángulo, Pedro de, bishop, nominated by Emperor to See of Vera Paz, 26, 320

Antonelli, Jacobo, Cardinal Secretary of State, signed Concordat with Guatemala, 140

Arbizu-Samayoa Treaty, article concerning Jesuits, 152, 294

Arce, don Manuel José, President, took part in revolt in Salvador, 66; elected President of the Confederation, 66

Arellano, Mariano Rossell, Archbishop, consecrated, 210; difficulties of task, 210

Arévalo, Juan José, President, elected, 214; opposition toward Church, 214, 215, 217, 228, 312

Arroyo, Angel María, cleric, protested law requiring civil marriage, 187, 188; negotiated new treaty with Holy See, 200; elected President of National Assembly, 203; resigned office, 205

Augustinians, possessions of, 42; foundation of, 50; status of, 50, 55; moved to new capital, 329

Avila, José Ignacio, cleric, named Vicar of Salvador by archbishop, 113

Aycinena, Col. José de, President, sent by Bustamante y Guerra to put down revolt in Salvador, 66; enforced edicts on forbidden books, 91

Aycinena, marquis Juan José de, cleric, named bishop of Trajanopolis *in partibus*, 36; signed declaration of independence, 68; vice-president of Second Constitutional assembly, 126; rector of University, 131; drew up treaty with Spain, 143

Aycinena, Miguel José, Provincial Prior of Dominicans, 88

Aycinena, Pedro de, foreign minister under Carrera, 144

Bancroft, Hubert, H., cited on character of Carrera, 143; on character of Barrios, 174

Barillas, Manuel Lisandro, President, elected to office, 205; dissolved Assembly, 205; assumed supreme power, 205

Barnoya, Ignacio, Dominican, granted citizenship in Guatemala, 84

Barrios, Justo Rufino, President, seizure of Church property, 59; incited revolution, 147; named Provisional President, 168; elected President, 174; anti-clerical measures, 168-173, 185, 186, 187, 189, 199, 301-304, 306, 311; died in battle, 203; personal attitude toward religion, 204-5

Barrundia, José Francisco, President, assumes office, 92; expels archbishop, 92, 107; expels religious, 107; supported by Federal Congress, 107

Barrutia y Croquer, José María, cleric, named bishop *in partibus*, Camaco, 36; appointed Vicar Capitular and auxiliary of See, 133

Batres, don Diego, cleric, became Vicar General on resignation of Alcayaga, 114; confirmed in faculties by Holy See, 122, 287-288

Batres Jáuregui, Antonio, quoted on possessions of Dominicans, 54; on conditions during Cerna's rule, 144; on religious attitude of Barrios, 205

Batres, don Rafaél, Treasurer of Government Commission for erection of school to be conducted by Jesuits, 133

347

archdiocese during absence of Casáus y Torres, 77

Discalced Carmelites, founded, 50; status in 1818, 50; abolished, 87

Divorce, decreed by Gálvez, 123; decree revoked, 123, 125; laws in favor definitely rescinded by Carrera, 130; decreed by Barrios, 186, 310

Dominicans, sent to Indies with permission of King, 26; possessions of, 42, 47, 48, 49, 54, 55, 58, 59, 60, 128, 129, 169, 179, 182, 300; founded in Guatemala, 49; establishment of Hospital of San Alexis, 51; cession of land to Indians, 55; cooperation with government, 78, 103; opposition to civil authorities, 88; expelled, 105; secularization of lay brothers, 109; influence over Indians in Sacatepéquez, 129; celebration of Feast of Seven Dolors in church of, 225; status, 236; abolished, 284; established Vicariate in Jocotenango, 314; assigned administration of Vera Paz, 317; work in Province of Tzendales, 321; moved to new site of capital, 329; census of, 339

Dunlop, Robert Glasgow, cited on Carrera's attitude to political parties, 128; on restoration of Church property, 128

Dunn, Henry, Anglican clergyman, cited on conditions in Guatemala in 1827 and 1828, 92-99

Durou y Sure, Louis, Archbishop, installed, 209

Economic Society of Friends of Guatemala, reinstalled, 129

Editor Constitucional, El, revolutionary periodical of Guatemala, 62

Education, under Church auspices, 21, 49, 50, 51, 56, 131, 143, 145, 211, 212, 259, 260, 261; present restrictions, 212; of Indians by Church, 259, 260, 261; controlled by *patronato real,* 313, 330

El Salvador, see Salvador

Escobar, José Bernardo, President, resigned after short rule, 137

Espinosa y Palacios, don Francisco Apolinario, Vicar General, protested expulsion of religious and confiscation of their property, 169, 301; summoned before jury, 169;

expelled, 174; protested from exile, 176

Estrada Cabrera, don Manuel, President, took office, 207; continued reforms, 207; forced to resign, 208; relations with Church, 312

Evangelicals, name applied to all Protestants in Guatemala, work of, 245-252; attitude of Church toward, 252; attitude of local government toward, 252

Eximiae devotionis, Bull of Patronage, 18

Expropriation of ecclesiastical property, 57, 58, 60, 100, 101, 120, 128, 129, 167, 169, 170, 172, 173, 178, 179, 181-184, 199, 200, 300, 302, 303-304, 311

Fathers of the Propagation of the Faith, founded *Colegio de Cristo Crucificado,* 50, 315; status in 1818, 50; forced to take oath of allegiance, 83

Ferdinand VII, king, claimed right of *patronato* over Guatemala, 30; addressed decree to archbishop of Guatemala asking loyalty, 32; imprisoned don Antonio Larrazábal, delegate from Guatemala, for defence of rights of Americans, 61; corresponded with Pope Leo XII over *Patronato real,* 265 ff.

Fiebres, los, radicals of Revolution period in Guatemala, 62, 242

Filisola, Vicente, President of Provisional Congress, sent by Iturbide to insure union of Guatemala with Mexico, 69; issued decree for maintenance of *status quo,* 74

Flores, Cirilo, lieutenant-general of Guatemala, attacked and killed by radicals, 89, 90

Franciscans, sent by King to Guatemala in 1801, 26, 318; possessions of, 42, 49, 55, 58; status in 1818, 49, 55; ordered to turn over funds of *Bula de Cruzada* to new government, 52; Provincial signed Declaration of Independence, 68; cooperation with government on oath of allegiance, 79; expelled from Guatemala, 105, secularization, 109; nationalization of the property of, 181, 182, 200, 332, 333; status today, 236; abolished, 284; granted Chair at University,

of property, 132; schools again flourishing, 145; opposition to, 149; abolished, 169; secularized, 169, 170; property nationalized, 173 ff.; suppression, 197; legislation against, 197; some permitted to return, 211; in Guatemala today, 213, 214; under royal control, 260 ff.; decree regulating entrance and profession, 271, 272; ordered removed to motherhouses, 275-276; taking into custody all religious not expelled; decree granting pension in exile, 279-280; inventory ordered of possessions of expelled religious, 281-282; suppression of all monasteries of, 282; decree declaring all nuns free to return to world with dowries, 286-287; decree declaring secularized religious eligible to inherit and enjoy rights of citizenship, 287; decree of expropriation; decree abolishing, 301-303; property seized, 302; legislation against, 302, 303; suppression of all convents of nuns, 304; legislation controlling, 310; decree of expulsion, 310; decree suppressing religious orders of women under Barrios, 311; requested to increase output on their plantations, 327; decree prohibiting professions and solemn vows of women, 340; decree of expropriation, 340

República, La, periodical, 207

Ripalda, Catechism of, 140

Rivera Cabezas, Antonio, president, reforms of, 118; edited El Melitón, 118

Rivera Paz, Mariano, president, established a conciliatory government, 125; revoked all anti-clerical decrees of Gálvez, 125; cooperated with Church authorities, 133; legislation favorable to Church, 133

Riviera y Jacinto, Julian Raymundo, archbishop, consecrated in Rome, 208; removed by Holy See, 208; died in New Orleans, 208

Rodríguez, don Mariano, Treasurer of the Archdiocese of Guatemala, imprisoned and condemned to exile, 104

Rubio y Pilona, Alberto, cleric, intimate friend of Barrios, 204

Ruíz de Bustamante, don Pedro, cleric, named alternative Vicar General by Casáus on exile, 114; election by Chapter cancelled by government, 116

Saénz Manozca y Murillo, Juan, bishop, took possession of see on authority of kings before arrival of Bulls, 25

Salazar, Fr. Manuel, cleric, elected Secretary of the Second Constitutional Assembly, 126

Saldaña y Pineda, Tomás, bishop *in partibus*, Antigona, 36

Salesians, order of, status, 236

Santa Rosa, revolt in, 153, 155

Salvador, El, controversy concerning diocese, 35; erection of see by civil authorities declared null and void by Confederation and Holy See, 65; conflict with archbishop of Guatemala, 73; refused hospitality to Jesuit exiled from Guatemala, 152; ratified agreement with Guatemala outlawing Jesuits, 184; revolt in, 307, 308; separation from see of Guatemala, 330

Secularization of religious orders, of men, 109, 110, 170, 177, 282, 302; of nuns, 122, 177, 304; of lay brothers, 339 ff.; Barrios attempts to justify his secularizing religious, 170

Semana, La, cited on work of university, 145

Seminario Tridentino, assisted financially by King as *patron real*, 322

Separation of Church and State, declared complete, 196, 197

Serviles, conservatives in Central America, 73, 83; ridiculed in *El Melitón*; attempted to discredit Liberals among working classes, 85

Seventh Day Adventists, work in Guatemala, 246

Sinibaldi, don Alejandro Manuel, President, renounced office almost immediately, 205

Sisters of Charity, opened orphan asylum and free school for girls in 1854, 131; signed contract with government to take over hospitals in Guatemala, 142; exempted from all legislation against religious or-

Date Due

JAN 1 7 '58			